THE JUDGE, THE JUDICIARY AND THE COURT

The Judge, the Judiciary and the Court is aimed at anyone interested in the Australian judiciary today. It examines the impact of the individual on the judicial role, while exploring the collegiate environment in which judges must operate. This professional community can provide support but may also present its own challenges within the context of a particular court's relational dynamic and culture. The judge and the judiciary form the 'court', an institution grounded in a set of constitutional values that will influence how judges and the judiciary perform their functions. This collection brings together analysis of the judicial role that highlights these unique aspects, particularly in the Australian setting. Through the lenses of judicial leadership, diversity, collegiality, dissent, style, technology, the media and popular culture, it analyses how judges work individually and as a collective to protect and promote the institutional values of the court.

Gabrielle Appleby is a professor at the Faculty of Law & Justice at UNSW in Sydney, Australia. She is the Director of The Judiciary Project at the Gilbert + Tobin Centre of Public Law and her books include *Judicial Federalism in Australia* (2021), *Australian Public Law* (3rd ed., 2018), *The Role of the Solicitor-General: Negotiating Law, Politics and the Public Interest* (2016); and *The Tim Carmody Affair* (2016).

Andrew Lynch is a professor at the Faculty of Law & Justice at UNSW in Sydney, Australia. He researches constitutional law, judicial dissent and judicial appointments. A Fellow of the Australian Academy of Law, his books include *Blackshield & Williams' Australian Constitutional Law and Theory* (2014, 2018), *Australia's Greatest Judicial Crisis: The Tim Carmody Affair* (2016) and *Great Australian Dissents* (2016).

THE JUDGE, THE JUDICIARY AND THE COURT

Individual, Collegial and Institutional Judicial Dynamics in Australia

Edited by

GABRIELLE APPLEBY
University of New South Wales, Sydney

ANDREW LYNCH
University of New South Wales, Sydney

CAMBRIDGE
UNIVERSITY PRESS

University Printing House, Cambridge CB2 8BS, United Kingdom

One Liberty Plaza, 20th Floor, New York, NY 10006, USA

477 Williamstown Road, Port Melbourne, VIC 3207, Australia

314–321, 3rd Floor, Plot 3, Splendor Forum, Jasola District Centre, New Delhi – 110025, India

79 Anson Road, #06–04/06, Singapore 079906

Cambridge University Press is part of the University of Cambridge.

It furthers the University's mission by disseminating knowledge in the pursuit of education, learning, and research at the highest international levels of excellence.

www.cambridge.org
Information on this title: www.cambridge.org/9781108494618
DOI: 10.1017/9781108859332

© Cambridge University Press 2021

This publication is in copyright. Subject to statutory exception and to the provisions of relevant collective licensing agreements, no reproduction of any part may take place without the written permission of Cambridge University Press.

First published 2021

A catalogue record for this publication is available from the British Library.

Library of Congress Cataloging-in-Publication Data
Names: Appleby, Gabrielle, editor. | Lynch, Andrew, 1973- editor.
Title: The judge, the judiciary, and the court : individual, collegial, and institutional judicial dynamics in Australia / edited by Gabrielle Appleby, University of New South Wales, Sydney; Andrew Lynch, University of New South Wales, Sydney.
Description: Cambridge, United Kingdom ; New York, NY : Cambridge University Press, 2021. | Includes bibliographical references and index.
Identifiers: LCCN 2020042880 (print) | LCCN 2020042881 (ebook) | ISBN 9781108494618 (hardback) | ISBN 9781108796712 (paperback) | ISBN 9781108859332 (epub)
Subjects: LCSH: Justice, Administration of–Australia. | Judges–Australia. | Courts–Australia.
Classification: LCC KU3497 .J828 2021 (print) | LCC KU3497 (ebook) | DDC 347.94/01–dc23
LC record available at https://lccn.loc.gov/2020042880
LC ebook record available at https://lccn.loc.gov/2020042881

ISBN 978-1-108-49461-8 Hardback

Cambridge University Press has no responsibility for the persistence or accuracy of URLs for external or third-party internet websites referred to in this publication and does not guarantee that any content on such websites is, or will remain, accurate or appropriate.

CONTENTS

List of Figures vii
List of Tables viii
List of Contributors ix
Foreword xiv
   Chris Maxwell
Table of Cases xvi

   PART I   The Judge, the Judiciary and the Court   1

1 The Judge, the Judiciary and the Court: the Individual, the Collective and the Institution   3
   GABRIELLE APPLEBY AND ANDREW LYNCH

2 Re-examining the Judicial Function in Australia   22
   JOE MCINTYRE

3 The Chief Justice: Under Relational and Institutional Pressure   50
   GABRIELLE APPLEBY AND HEATHER ROBERTS

   PART II   Debates and Challenges to the Judicial Role   81

4 Dismantling the Diversity Deficit: Towards a More Inclusive Australian Judiciary   83
   BRIAN OPESKIN

5 Technology and the Judicial Role   116
   MONIKA ZALNIERIUTE AND FELICITY BELL

6 Emotion Work as Judicial Work   143
   SHARYN ROACH ANLEU AND KATHY MACK

7 The Persistent Pejorative: Judicial Activism   163
   TANYA JOSEV

PART III   The Judiciary as a Collective   187

8   Judicial Collegiality   189
    SARAH MURRAY

9   Individual Judicial Style and Institutional Norms   208
    ANDREW LYNCH

10 Values and Judicial Difference in the High Court   233
    RACHEL CAHILL-O'CALLAGHAN

PART IV   Perceptions   257

11 Judges and the Media   259
    MATTHEW GROVES

12 The Good Judge in Australian Popular
    Television Culture   283
    PENNY CROFTS

    Index   307

FIGURES

2.1 Species of dispute resolution methods   29
4.1 Median age of judicial officers, by type and sex, Australia, 1996–2016   102
4.2 Religious affiliation of judicial officers, Australia, 1996–2016   104
4.3 Ancestry of judicial officers and Australian population, 2016   106
4.4 Highest educational level of judicial officers, by type, Australia, 1996–2016   108
4.5 Sex ratio of judicial officers by court level, Australia, 2000–2019   110
10.1 Value analysis of *HML v The Queen*   245
10.2 Value analysis of *BBH v The Queen*   247
10.3 Value analysis of *Lee v New South Wales Crime Commission*   250
10.4 Value analysis of *X7 v Australian Crime Commission*   251
10.5 Value analysis of *Rowe v Electoral Commissioner*   253

TABLES

4.1 Composition of the Australian population 96
4.2 Marital status of judicial officers, by sex, Australia, 1996–2016 103

CONTRIBUTORS

PROFESSOR GABRIELLE APPLEBY

Dr. Gabrielle Appleby is a professor at the Faculty of Law & Justice, UNSW Sydney. She researches and teaches in public law, with her areas of expertise including the role, powers and accountability of the executive, the role of government lawyers and the integrity of the judicial branch. She is the Director of The Judiciary Project at the Gilbert + Tobin Centre of Public Law and was the founding editor of Australia's national public law blog, AUSPUBLAW. She is currently the constitutional consultant to the clerk of the Commonwealth House of Representatives. In 2016–2017, she worked as a pro bono constitutional adviser to the Regional Dialogues and the First Nations Constitutional Convention that led to the Uluru Statement from the Heart. Her books include *Judicial Federalism in Australia; History, Theory, Doctrine and Practice* (Federation Press, 2021), *Australian Public Law* (Oxford University Press, 3rd ed, 2018), *The Role of the Solicitor-General: Negotiating Law, Politics and the Public Interest* (Hart Publishing, 2016); and *The Tim Carmody Affair* (NewSouth Publishing, 2016). Gabrielle has also spent time working for the Queensland Crown Solicitor and the Victorian Government Solicitor's Office.

DR. FELICITY BELL

Felicity Bell, PhD, is the research fellow for the Future of Law and Innovation in the Profession (FLIP) research stream at the Faculty of Law & Justice at UNSW Sydney, supported by the Law Society of NSW. As the principal researcher for FLIP, Felicity's current research is focused on change and innovation affecting the legal profession. She is the author (with Professor Michael Legg) of *Artificial Intelligence and the Legal Profession* (Hart, 2020). She has examined new technologies in legal practice, lawyers' identities, professionalism and ethics, and family law and children's law and has published extensively in these areas.

DR. RACHEL CAHILL-O'CALLAGHAN

Rachel Cahill-O'Callaghan, PhD (Law), PhD (Science), is currently a reader at Cardiff School of Law and Politics (Cardiff University, Wales). She moved into the study of law from a successful career in academic science and her research combines both specialities, drawing on theories and techniques from psychology to understand judicial decision-making. This chapter was supported by a research visitor fellowship (UNSW) and research leave fellowship (Cardiff University) and builds on the work developed in her monograph *Values in the Supreme Court: Divisions, Decisions and Diversity* (Hart Publishing, 2020).

PROFESSOR PENNY CROFTS

Dr. Penny Crofts is a professor at the Faculty of Law, University of Technology Sydney. She is an expert on criminal law and models of culpability. Her research is cross-disciplinary, drawing upon a range of historical, philosophical, empirical and literary materials to enrich her analysis of the law. Her research is in the area of socio-legal studies, coalescing around issues of justice in criminal law in practice and theory, and makes a distinctive contribution to critical evaluations of criminal legal models of culpability and enforcement. Penny is currently analysing criminal legal conceptions of organisational culpability through horror film and philosophies of wickedness.

PROFESSOR MATTHEW GROVES

Matthew Groves is the Alfred Deakin Professor of Law and Director of Research in the Law School of Deakin University, Australia. Matthew conducts research in public law, most notably administrative law and human rights. He has published and edited many books including Aronson, Groves and Weeks, *Judicial Review of Administrative Action and Government Liability* (Thomson Reuters, 6th ed, 2017) and Groves, Meagher and Boughey (eds), *The Legal Protection of Rights in Australia* (Hart Publishing, 2019). Matthew is general editor of the *Australian Journal of Administrative Law* and a fellow of the Australian Academy of Law.

DR. TANYA JOSEV

Dr. Tanya Josev is a senior lecturer in the Melbourne Law School. She researches twentieth century Australian and United States legal and political history, with particular interests in judicial biography, the history of legalism and the politics of the culture wars as they relate to the judiciary. Tanya's recent award-winning book, *The Campaign Against the Courts: A History of the Judicial Activism Debate* (Federation Press, 2017), explored the intellectual and political history of the bifurcated understanding of the judicial role as involving activism versus restraint.

PROFESSOR ANDREW LYNCH

Andrew Lynch teaches and conducts research in the field of Australian constitutional law in the Faculty of Law & Justice at UNSW Sydney. His research concentrates on the topics of federalism, judicial dissent, judicial appointments reform and legal responses to terrorism. He is the author of books including *Blackshield & Williams' Australian Constitutional Law and Theory* (Federation Press, 6th ed, 2014; 7th ed, 2018) and *Australia's Greatest Judicial Crisis – The Tim Carmody Affair* (NewSouth Publishing, 2016). Andrew is also an editor of *Tomorrow's Federation: Reforming Australian Government* (Federation Press, 2012) and of *Great Australian Dissents* (Cambridge University Press, 2016).

PROFESSOR KATHY MACK

Kathy Mack (BA magna cum laude, Rice University; JD Stanford Law School; LLM University of Adelaide) is Emerita Professor, Flinders University. She is the author of a monograph, book chapters and articles on alternative dispute resolution (ADR) and articles on legal education and evidence. Since 1994, with Matthew Flinders Distinguished Professor Sharyn Roach Anleu, Kathy has been engaged in socio-legal research into the Australian courts and judiciary, including an investigation of the production of guilty pleas and research into the everyday work of the judiciary. Their latest books are *Performing Judicial Authority in the Lower Courts* (Palgrave, 2017) and *Judging and Emotion: A Socio-Legal Analysis* (Routledge, 2021).

DR. JOE MCINTYRE

Dr. Joe McIntyre is a senior lecturer in law at the University of South Australia, having previously taught in Canada and the UK. He undertook his PhD thesis at the University of Cambridge where he explored the nature and implications of the judicial function. His subsequent research specialises in pure and applied judicial theory. Joe is the author of *The Judicial Function: Fundamental Principles of Contemporary Judging* (Springer, 2019).

DR. SARAH MURRAY

Professor Sarah Murray is a professor at the University of Western Australia Law School and researches in the areas of constitutional law and court innovation. She has published across a range of Australian and international journals and is the author of *The Remaking of the Courts: Less-Adversarial Practice and the Constitutional Role of the Judiciary in Australia* (Federation Press, 2014). Sarah is also a co-author of *The Constitution of the Commonwealth of Australia: History, Principle and Interpretation* (Cambridge University Press, 2015) and *Winterton's Australian Federal Constitutional Law: Commentary & Materials* (Thomson Reuters, 3rd ed, 2014); (Thomson Reuters, 4th ed, 2017).

PROFESSOR BRIAN OPESKIN

Brian Opeskin is a professor of law and former associate dean (research) at the University of Technology Sydney. He previously held positions as professor of legal governance at Macquarie University; head of the law school at the University of the South Pacific in Vanuatu; deputy president of the Australian Law Reform Commission; associate professor at Sydney University; and associate to Justice Mason at the High Court of Australia. He researches in the broad field of public law and has written widely on constitutional law; courts, judges and jurisdiction; and international migration law. Brian is a fellow of the Australian Academy of Law.

PROFESSOR SHARYN ROACH ANLEU

Sharyn Roach Anleu is Matthew Flinders Distinguished Professor of Sociology at Flinders University and Fellow of the Australian Academy of the Social Sciences. She is the author of *Law and Social Change* and four editions of *Deviance, Conformity and Control*. With Emerita Professor Kathy Mack, Sharyn leads the Judicial Research Project, undertaking empirical socio-legal research into the Australian judiciary and its courts. Their latest books are *Performing Judicial Authority in the Lower Courts* (Palgrave, 2017) and *Judging and Emotion: A Socio-Legal Analysis* (Routledge, 2021). In 2018 Sharyn and Jessica Milner Davis co-edited *Judges, Judging and Humour* (Palgrave).

DR. HEATHER ROBERTS

Dr. Heather Roberts is an associate professor at ANU Law. She researches in constitutional law, property law and the history and biography of superior courts and is internationally recognised as a leading expert on court ceremonies. In her current research, funded by a fellowship from the Australian Research Council, she is examining how ceremonies in Australian Supreme Courts portray changing perceptions of the essential attributes of judges and judging. She is the founding convenor of the ANU Law School's Visiting Judges Program, and co-director for the Australian Network of Japanese Law. Prior to entering academia, Heather was a solicitor at one of Australia's largest commercial law firms.

DR. MONIKA ZALNIERUTE

Dr. Monika Zalnieriute is a senior lecturer and Australian Research Council DECRA Fellow (2021–23) at the Faculty of Law & Justice at UNSW Sydney, where she leads a research stream on 'Technologies and Rule of Law' which explores the interplay between law, technology and politics in the digital age. Monika has published in leading law journals, including *Modern Law Review*, *American Journal of International Law*, *Yale Journal of Law & Technology*, *Harvard International Law Journal*, *Berkeley Journal of Gender, Law and Justice*, and the *Stanford Journal of International Law*. She is currently working on a monograph on the geopolitics of data privacy law. These days Monika spends a lot of her time thinking and writing about the rule of law and political economy of technology.

FOREWORD

> Judicial life is perhaps one of the most individual – and lonely – of professional callings.

The opening line of this volume immediately signals its distinctiveness of purpose and perspective. Acknowledging the vital public and governmental functions which courts perform, the authors want to understand – want their readers to understand – the realities of judicial life, the nature of the judicial role and of judicial leadership, and the relationship between the work of the individual judge and the institutional framework of the court.

The questions addressed here are of central importance. Do institutional and personal values influence a judge's decisions? Can a chief justice satisfy the demands of efficiency and accountability while respecting the independence of the individual judge? How do judges on a multi-member bench manage disagreement while preserving collegiality? Why have we been so slow to remedy the 'diversity deficit' in Australian courts?

The assumption on which the collection rests is that, in the often-heated debate about individual court decisions, these critical issues are rarely acknowledged. If judicial work is to be fairly evaluated, the authors would argue, it is necessary to understand the complexity of the 'relational dynamics' between judges, between judges and courtroom participants, between courts and the media, and between courts and the wider community.

The informing notion is that of the court as a human institution, of the judge as an individual called upon to exercise the power of the State, who must learn how to discharge the responsibility of making decisions which affect people's lives. The chapters of this book explore, from a range of different perspectives, how individuals – and courts – respond to the high expectations properly placed on them.

The emotional dimension of judging, for example, is rarely spoken of. Every day, in every court, judges are having to manage their own human responses to the circumstances playing out before them, while at the same time dealing with the emotions of others involved in the proceeding. Conscious of her public duty, the judge strives to be objective and dispassionate, while giving expression to her essential humanity.

This is a very important book precisely because it is not written by judges. The elucidation of the judicial role is at once scrupulously independent – probing, challenging and questioning – and strikingly insightful. Importantly, there is a spirit of generosity in the writing, an implicit acceptance that Australian courts and judges go about their work conscientiously and thoughtfully, with a proper appreciation of both the responsibility and the privilege of judicial office.

The development of legal scholarship in this field is greatly to be welcomed. Its further development will, no doubt, be enhanced by collaborative engagement with judges and retired judges, of the kind which took place so productively at the 2018 UNSW workshop from which this publication originated.

The Honourable Justice Chris Maxwell AC, President of the Court of Appeal, Supreme Court of Victoria
August 2020

CASES

ALA15 v Minister for Immigration and Border Protection [2016] FCAFC   135
Attorney-General (Cth) v The Queen (1957) 95 CLR   23
Attorney-General for South Australia v Raschke [2019] SASCFC   25, 46
Australian Capital Television v Commonwealth (1992) 177 CLR   175
BBH v The Queen (2012) 245 CLR   241, 245, 249, 250
BDS17 v Minister for Immigration and Border Protection [2018] FCA   135
Brandy v Human Rights and Equal Opportunity Commission (1995) 183 CLR   23, 25
Brodie v Singleton Shire Council (2001) 206 CLR   41
Building Construction Employees and Builders Labourers Federation of NSW v Minister for Industrial Relations (1986) 7 NSWLR   24
Burnie Port Authority v General Jones Pty Ltd (1994) 179 CLR   41, 175
Burns v Corbett [2018] HCA   24, 46
Cattanach v Melchior (2003) 215 CLR   41
Chu Kheng Lim v Minister for Immigration, Local Government and Ethnic Affairs (1992) 176 CLR   25
CIT17 v Minister for Immigration and Border Protection (2018) 265 FCR   280
Cole v Whitfield (1988) 165 CLR   41, 175
Commonwealth v Tasmania (1983) 158 CLR   175
Davis v Commonwealth (1988) 166 CLR   175
DPP (Cth) v Besim [No 2] (2017) 52 VR   59, 165, 166
Ebner v Official Trustee in Bankruptcy (2000) 205 CLR   135
Gambaro v Mobycom Mobile Pty Ltd [2019] FCAFC   280
Gaudie v Local Court of New South Wales [2013] NSWSC   273, 274
Gilbertson v State of South Australia [1978] AC   24
Gloucester Resources Ltd v Minister for Planning (Gloucester Resources) [2019] NSWLEC   274, 275
Grollo v Palmer (1995) 184 CLR   24, 89
Hilton v Wells (1985) 157 CLR   24
Hinz v Berry [1970] 2 QB   222
HML v The Queen (2008) 235 CLR   241, 242, 244, 245, 246, 248, 249
Huddart Parker and Co Pty Ltd v Moorehead (1908) 8 CLR   24
In re Judiciary and Navigation Acts (1921) 29 CLR   24, 27

TABLE OF CASES

International Finance Trust Co Ltd v New South Wales Crime Commission (2009) 240 CLR   24
Jacobellis v Ohio, 378 US 184, 197 (1964)   194
Jorgensen v Fair Work Ombudsman (2019) 371 ALR   280
Kable v Director of Public Prosecutions (NSW) (1996) 189 CLR   6, 24, 57, 89
Kirk v Industrial Relations Commission (NSW) (2010) 239 CLR   24
Koowarta v Bjelke-Petersen (1982) 153 CLR   175
Law Offices of Herssein & Herssein, PA v United Services Automobile Association, 271 So 3d 889 (Fla Sup Ct, 2018)   284
Lee v New South Wales Crime Commission (2013) 251 CLR   241, 250, 253
Liversidge v Anderson [1942] AC   201
Mabo v Queensland [No 2] (1992) 175 CLR   165, 174, 175
McFarlane v Tayside Health Board [2000] 2 AC   41
Nationwide News Pty Ltd v Wills (1992) 177 CLR   175
New South Wales v Commonwealth (1915) 20 CLR   23
Nicholas v The Queen (1998) 193 CLR   25
Palmer v Ayers (2017) 259 CLR   25
Pettit v Dunkley [1971] 1 NSWLR   212
Pfennig v The Queen (1995) 182 CLR   245, 246, 249
Pintarich v Federal Commissioner of Taxation (2018) 262 FCR   142
Queensland v Commonwealth (1977) 139 CLR   236, 237
R (on the application of Miller) v Secretary of State for Exiting the European Union [2018] AC   268
R (on the application of UNISON) v Lord Chancellor [2017] UKSC   43
R v Bevan; Ex parte Elias and Gordon (1942) 66 CLR   24
R v Davison (1954) 90 CLR   25
R v Deputy Industrial Injuries Commissioner; Ex parte Moore [1965] 1 QB   33
R v Gray (Howard Alexander) [1900] 2 QB   264
R v Hegarty; Ex parte City of Salisbury (1981) 147 CLR   25
R v Joske; Ex parte Shop Distributive and Allied Employees Association (1976) 135 CLR   24
R v Kirby; Ex parte Boilermakers Society of Australia (1956) 94 CLR   6, 23, 57
R v Mambolo [2001] 3 SA   286
R v Trade Practices Tribunal; Ex parte Tasmanian Breweries Pty Ltd (1970) 123 CLR   25
Radmacher (formerly Granatino) v Granatino [2011] 1 AC   270
Re Dingjan; Ex parte Wagner (1995) 183 CLR   25
Re Wakim; Ex parte McNally (1999) 198 CLR   237, 238
Richmond Newspapers Incorporated v Virginia 448 US 555 (1980)   263
Rowe v Electoral Commissioner (2010) 243 CLR   239, 241, 254
South Australia v Totani (2010) 242 CLR   24
Southern Pacific Co v Jensen, 244 US 205, 221 (1917)   43

State of Wisconsin v Loomis, 881 N.W.2d 749 (Wis. 2016)   125
Thomas v Mowbray (2007) 233 CLR   25
Trident General Insurance Co Ltd v McNiece Bros Pty Ltd (1988) 165 CLR   175
United Public Workers of America v Mitchell, 330 US 75 (1947)   27
Victorian Stevedoring and General Contracting Co Pty Ltd v Dignan (1931) 46 CLR   23
Vietnam Veterans' Association of Australia (New South Wales Branch Inc) v Gallagher (1994) 52 FCR   116, 135, 142
Wainohu v New South Wales (2011) 243 CLR   24, 89, 130, 212
Waterside Workers' Federation of Australia v JW Alexander Ltd (1918) 25 CLR   24, 25
Wik Peoples v Queensland (1996) 187 CLR   60, 175
Wilson v Minister for Aboriginal and Torres Strait Islander Affairs (1996) 189 CLR   23, 24, 25
X7 v Australian Crime Commission (2013) 248 CLR   241, 243, 250, 251, 252, 253, 254

PART I

The Judge, the Judiciary and the Court

1

The Judge, the Judiciary and the Court
The Individual, the Collective and the Institution

GABRIELLE APPLEBY AND ANDREW LYNCH

I The Individual Judge

Judicial life is perhaps one of the most individual – and lonely – of professional callings. On appointment, a judge takes an oath to 'do right to all manner of people according to law without fear or favour, affection or ill-will.'[1] At that moment, she shoulders an individual responsibility to meet the highest expectations of the law.[2] This expectation, and concomitant scrutiny, will continue throughout the judge's career. Legal, political and public commentary may welcome her on appointment, examining the appropriateness of her credentials, experience and political neutrality. There may be ongoing critique of the quality of her judicial conduct in court, her decisions and reasoning, all of which must, subject to few exceptions, be performed in the public eye. Even upon her retirement, her conduct and any transgressions it reveals, may be the subject of critical public comment. In performing her institutional role, the judge is afforded no personal anonymity.

Individual judges and external commentators will bring different ideas and concepts of what 'doing right' with 'independence and impartiality' requires in the judicial role. Across the course of a judge's career, there will be ample opportunities for judicial 'choice': choice as to the legal method she brings to particular issues; choice as to how to undertake case management; choice as to how to exercise the many judicial discretions

---

[1] This form of the oath taken from the *High Court of Australia Act 1979* (Cth) s 11, Schedule.
[2] This chapter, and others in the book, have selected the female pronoun for the individual judge rather than the male pronoun, both pronouns, or the plural pronoun. In this introduction, our decision reflects our desire to emphasise the individual judge, without reinforcing the male gender bias of the judiciary, which continues to be reflected in the composition of judiciaries across the world.

conferred upon her across diverse areas of law; choice as to how to navigate the ethical dilemmas that may arise for her; choice about whether, and how, she engages in extra-curial activities, not just the acceptance of formal *persona designata* public appointments, but also speeches, publications, interviews and even online through social media; choice about whether she undertakes judicial education and well-being programs and, if so, which she prioritises. Legal, political and public scrutiny and criticism of the individual choices of the judge will be performed through innumerable different normative prisms, and undoubtedly one of the challenges for a judge is that there is no set of universally agreed-upon standards which she is expected to meet.

Exacerbating this challenge is the expectation that, when an individual judge is thought to have chosen a course that transgresses these standards, she will not respond publicly in her own defence. However, there is an increasing acceptance that there may be a collective judicial response, particularly if there is a perception that the criticism goes beyond individual judicial choices and threatens the institutional values of the court.

II The Judicial Collective

At the moment of appointment and acceptance of individual responsibility, the judge also joins a collective – 'the judiciary' – comprising other individuals who have taken the same oath, will be facing the same challenges in performing their role, and will be subject to the same targeted scrutiny in doing so. Even within a framework of ultimate individual responsibility, this professional community may bring with it some relational support, but also creates its own challenges.

The relational dynamics and cultures that develop between individual judges within and across courts has the capacity to substantially affect how judicial functions are performed. Judicial relationships encompass the peculiarities of the judicial administrative hierarchy. As explored by Gabrielle Appleby and Heather Roberts in their chapter in this volume, the head of jurisdiction has administrative and institutional responsibilities but relatively limited capacity to defend, support and also discipline individual judges. They consider how individual chief justices can use the status of the office with its constrained power within the judiciary as well as in its extra-judicial relationships to produce a substantive conception of judicial leadership.

Different judges join different institutional collectives. Depending on their court level, for some judges one of the most important aspects of their relationships with other judges will occur through the appellate process, their individual judgments subject to review, affirmation or rejection by another judge or panel of judges, sometimes, although not always, in a different court. As is explored particularly in the chapters by Sarah Murray, Andrew Lynch and Rachel Cahill-O'Callaghan in this volume, within multi-member appellate courts, judges will exercise their constitutional functions alongside other individual judges. Their collective decision will determine the outcome of the cases that come before them. There is real scope for individual judges to approach and perform this relational dimension of their role differently. Doing so may affect not just the outcome of particular cases, but the manner in which the individual judge meets her personal responsibility and how she engages with colleagues to uphold and promote the institutional values of the Court.

The identification of the individual as a member of the judiciary extends beyond a particular court to encompass the judiciary as a whole. While this must always have been true to some degree, nowadays the benefits of cross-jurisdictional judicial engagement are explicitly fostered through the existence of collective institutions. In Australia, this has included the Judicial Conference of Australia (JCA), a representative body established in 1993 and comprising more than 750 serving and retired judicial officers across Australia. The JCA has a role in publicly defending the judiciary (including individual judges) and undertaking community education about the role of courts and judges, as well as working for legal institutional reforms relating to the judicial system. The Australian Institute of Judicial Administration brings together judicial officers with tribunal members, court administrators, legal practitioners, legal academics, librarians and others, for the predominant purpose of undertaking research into judicial administration and conducting judicial education programs. Education and professional development is the mission of the National Judicial Commission of Australia, established in 2002 and funded by Commonwealth, State and Territory governments. New South Wales and Victoria have their own dedicated, judge-led bodies for education, complaints and support. To facilitate communication about mutual interests and concerns among court leadership, there is the Council of Chief Justices of Australia. Internationally, organisations such as the International Association of Judges, the Commonwealth Magistrates' and Judges' Association and the International Association of Women Judges bring a cross-cultural dimension to the judicial collective. The existence of these bodies may be thought to alleviate, at least to some degree, the hallmark of judicial office as individual isolation.

III The Judicial Institution

On appointment, the judge assumes not just an individual role, nor membership of a collective, but acquires an institutional office: as a member of 'the court'. Indeed, this institutional office is the source of the judge's individual responsibilities; and a judge's understanding of her individual judicial role will be heavily influenced by her interpretation of the role of the court.

In Australia, the courts as institutions sit within a constitutionalised separation of powers, incorporating normative institutional requirements, including, for instance, minimum requirements and protections around appointment and removal.[3] At the federal level, there is a relatively formal separation of the judicial branch from those of the executive and legislature,[4] with strict rules maintaining the independence and impartiality of the judiciary and the exercise of judicial power. At the state and territory level, while there is no formal constitutional separation of powers, the role of the courts of those jurisdictions within the federal judicial structure effectively incorporates many of the same requirements established at the federal level.[5] At every level within the Australian judicial hierarchy, courts must be independent and impartial; they must exercise appropriate judicial discretion and cannot act under the dictate of the political branches of government; and they must exercise their power in accordance with fair judicial process. Additionally, the High Court and the State Supreme Courts must be able to exercise their supervisory jurisdictions over government power; this function cannot be denied to them.[6]

These constitutional imperatives give rise to normative frameworks that both protect and directly affect how individual judges perform their role and meet their commitments to independence and impartiality. As former Chief Justice Murray Gleeson said, the capacity of judges to honour their oath 'does not rest only upon their individual consciences.

---

[3] See s 72 of the *Australian Constitution* with respect to federal judges.

[4] The principle established in *R v Kirby; Ex parte Boilermakers' Society of Australia* ('*Boilermakers Case*') (1956) 94 CLR 254.

[5] This originates from the principle established in the case of *Kable v Director of Public Prosecutions (NSW)* (1996) 189 CLR 51.

[6] See discussion of the Chapter III constitutional principles that apply to federal and state courts in, for instance, James Stellios, *The Federal Judicature: Chapter III of the Constitution Commentary and Cases* (Federation Press, 2010); Gabrielle Appleby, Anna Olijnyk, James Stellios and John Williams, *Judicial Federalism in Australia: History, Theory, Doctrine and Practice* (Federation Press, 2021).

It is supported by institutional arrangements.'[7] However, those arrangements and norms rarely provide specific direction as to how an individual judge might best resolve the many choices that they confront in their role.

Nonetheless, the constitutional requirements and institutional context often correlate with a set of judicial 'values' that provide principled guidance to the individual judge. 'Independence and impartiality' are the most recognisable judicial values, and indeed, these are constitutionalised. But the legal, societal and political expectations of the court will give rise to other values that may not be formal, let alone constitutional, that can also influence the performance of the roles of judge and judiciary. But many more are now readily accepted and emerging. In this volume, Appleby and Roberts, Felicity Bell and Monika Zalnieriute, and Murray, for instance, employ in their analysis a normative framework of six judicial values identified by Canadian academics Richard Devlin and Adam Dodek: independence, impartiality, accountability, representativeness, transparency and efficiency.[8] Of course, this list of institutional values is not the only one, and no list will be uncontested nor stagnant. To Dodek and Devlin's catalogue might be added, for instance, values that emerge from contemporary debates around the importance of access to justice, the judicial responsibility to protect individual liberty, the importance of maintaining judicial wellbeing, or, as Murray posits in her chapter, judicial 'collegiality' could be emerging as a value particularly on multi-member courts.

How judicial values are understood and prioritised will, obviously, influence the performance of the judicial role. This can itself occur at an institutional level. For instance, growing societal expectations not only of independence but also accountability has led many jurisdictions to establish new institutional mechanisms for dealing with complaints pertaining to the misconduct of individual judges. Additionally, how judges personally identify and prioritise the values that are attendant on their office can have a profound effect. For instance, an individual judge might adopt a particular approach to case management, conduct of

---

[7] Murray Gleeson, 'The Right to an Independent Judiciary' (Speech delivered at 14th Commonwealth Law Conference, London, September 2005) <www.hcourt.gov.au/assets/publications/speeches/former-justices/gleesoncj/cj_sept05.html>.

[8] Richard Devlin and Adam Dodek, 'Regulating Judges: Challenges, Controversies and Choices' in Richard Devlin and Adam Dodek (eds) *Regulating Judges: Beyond Independence and Accountability* (Edward Elgar, 2016) 1, 9.

the courtroom and delivery of judgments that prioritises efficiency as a judicial value. Depending upon the relational position of the individual judge, particularly if holding a leadership role as head of jurisdiction, it may be that these personal decisions produce changes in the collective practices of a particular section of the judiciary.

IV The Individual, the Collective and the Institution in Judicial Scholarship

The individual, collective and institutional dimensions of the judicial role have emerged clearly in scholarship on the judiciary. In Australia, scholarship has been focussed around a number of key areas, each associated with one of these dimensions and often the dynamics between them.[9] There has been of course, much commentary on the performance of the curial role by individual judges, that is, an analysis of their substantive decisions, which includes doctrinal analysis of the development of the law through these decisions, as well as commentary and critique of the judicial method of the judge in coming to those decisions. In Australia, the latter has been dominated by debates around the appropriateness of the orthodox Australian commitment to a formalistic approach, often referred to as 'legalism', particularly in constitutional interpretation; and the challenges posed to this by other more value-explicit forms of reasoning, pejoratively, and as Tanya Josev argues in her chapter, problematically, referred to by conservative commentators under the label of 'activism',[10] closely associated with the legal realist movement in the United States.

The constitutional status of a strong separation of judicial power at the federal level, and with that having consequences also for the State and Territory courts, has ensured an understandably significant scholarship

---

[9] For those who have looked more broadly and deeply at the judicial role across a number of dimensions, although these are increasingly dated with emerging challenges and trends in the judicial role, including the contemporary debates around collegiality, activism, diversity, transparency, and the relationship with the media, see Tony Blackshield, Michael Coper and George Williams (eds), *The Oxford Companion to the High Court of Australia* (OUP, 2001); Brian Opeskin and Fiona Wheeler (eds), *The Australian Federal Judicial System* (Melbourne University Press, 2003); and Enid Campbell and H P Lee, *The Australian Judiciary* (CUP, 2nd ed, 2013).

[10] And see also Tanya Josev, *The Campaign against the Courts: A History of the Judicial Activism Debate* (Federation Press, 2017).

on the institutional requirements and limitations of the courts in which judges serve.[11] There is also steady interest in the broader institutional frameworks within which individual judges are appointed and perform their role.[12]

There is further scholarship that looks at other aspects of the judicial role: there are also socio-legal studies of the individual experience of performing the judicial role in a contemporary setting;[13] life-writing studies of individual and groups of judges, including histories and biographies;[14] and, although still relatively rare, politico-legal studies of particular 'courts', that is, attempts to understand the political motivations and power of individual and collective members of the judiciary during particular eras.[15]

This edited collection contributes to the existing Australian judicial scholarship in two ways. It does so, first, by engaging more directly with the interrelationship between the three dimensions of the judicial role. This commitment to exploring the dynamic effect that arises at the

---

[11] This includes the extensive scholarship on the constitutional requirements of Chapter III at both federal and state level, and the judicial interpretation and evolution of these requirements. For an introduction to some of this extensive work, see, for instance, Stellios, n 6; Appleby et al., n 6; Rebecca Ananian-Welsh and Jonathan Crowe (eds), *Judicial Independence in Australia: Contemporary Challenges, Future Directions* (Federation Press, 2016).

[12] This includes, for instance, the growing scholarship that looks at judicial appointments, discipline and ethics. For a small selection of more recent work in these particular areas, see, for instance, Elizabeth Handsley and Andrew Lynch, 'Facing up to Diversity? Transparency and the Reform of Commonwealth Judicial Appointments 2008–2013' (2015) 37 *Sydney Law Review* 187; Gabrielle Appleby and Suzanne Le Mire, 'Judicial Conduct: Crafting a System that Enhances Institutional Integrity' (2014) 38 *Melbourne University Law Review* 1; Gabrielle Appleby and Suzanne Le Mire, 'Ethical Infrastructure for a Modern Judiciary' (2019) 47 *Federal Law Review* 335.

[13] See, for instance, the extensive scholarship of Sharyn Roach Anleu and Kathy Mack in this area, for instance, Sharyn Roach Anleu and Kathy Mack, *Performing Judicial Authority in the Lower Courts* (2017, Palgrave).

[14] See further Sarah Burnside, 'Australian Judicial Biography: Past, Present and Future' (2011) 57 *Australian Journal of Politics and History* 221 and Tanya Josev, 'Judicial Biography in Australia: Current Obstacles and Opportunities' (2017) 40 *University of New South Wales Law Journal* 842.

[15] See the major works of Brian Galligan, *Politics of the High Court : A Study of the Judicial Branch of Government in Australia* (1987) (University of Queensland Press); Haig Patapan, *Judging Democracy: The New Politics of the High Court of Australia* (Cambridge University Press, 2000); Jason Pierce, *Inside the Mason Court Revolution The High Court of Australia Transformed* (Carolina Academic Press, 2006); Rosalind Dixon and George Williams (eds), *The High Court, the Constitution and Australian Politics* (Cambridge University Press, 2015).

intersection of the individual, collective and institutional identities of the judge is central to the way in which the chapters have been conceived of and developed by their authors. Second, it undertakes this analysis by reference to recent events and contemporary challenges which provide both an impetus for academic attention and a lens through which to direct that gaze.

V Contemporary Debates and Challenges

In Australia, the need for a moment of critical scholarly engagement with the tripartite dimensions of the judicial role has been made more acute following several recent incidents and events that have sparked considerable and varied debate. The shock of judicial officers taking their own lives and subsequent reporting on the emotional toll of judging on the individual judges themselves has placed the previously under-discussed issue of judicial emotions and well-being on the judicial, government and scholarly agenda.[16] At the same time, continuing revelations of judicial misconduct in jurisdictions that lack an independent system to deal with complaints against judges has extended the conversation to the need to reconsider the desirability of more robust institutional arrangements.[17] And inexorably, the rise of technological innovation in the practice of government and law has placed demands on the courts to embrace its potential with an appropriate degree of caution.[18] In short, the Australian judicial landscape is one in which pressure is acute – whether this is of individual performance and stress, of ensuring there are sufficient means

---

[16] See, for instance, some recent reporting: Peter Wilmoth, 'Loneliness, panic attacks, insomnia: Life for some on the judicial bench' *Good Weekend, Sydney Morning Herald* (4 August 2018) and Alexandria Utting, 'Potts pans the 'bully' bench', *Courier-Mail* (27 December 2019). See Carly Schrever, Carol Hulbert and Tania Sourdin, "The psychological impact of judicial work: Australia's first empirical research measuring judicial stress and wellbeing" (2019) 28 *JJA* 141.

[17] See further on this Hagar Cohen, 'Who watches over our judges', *Background Briefing* (8 September 2019) <www.abc.net.au/radionational/programs/backgroundbriefing/judge-street-under-scrutiny-again-v2/11480818>'; Damian Carrick, 'Who judges the Judges' *The Law Report* (30 July 2019) <www.abc.net.au/radionational/programs/lawreport/who-judges-the-judges/11339280>.

[18] See discussion of the general challenges of the embrace of technology within government and its implications for the rule of law and the courts in Monika Zalnieriute, Lyria Bennett-Moses and George Williams, 'The Rule of Law and Automation of Government Decision-Making' (2019) 82 *Modern Law Review* 425.

of accountability to the community, or of the need to adapt to the practices made possible in a rapidly digitising world.

Many of the contributions to this collection engage with these pressure points, even sometimes with the same incidents and examples. This demonstrates that often events and issues do not pose a singular challenge to the judicial role but, rather, will pose simultaneous institutional, collective and individual challenges to be navigated by judges, governments and other actors.

One remarkable development over the course of the last decade, that had ongoing reverberations on the High Court of Australia and beyond, was sparked by a speech delivered by Justice Dyson Heydon in the year of his retirement from the High Court. In his speech, *Threats to Judicial Independence: The Enemy Within*, Heydon alleged that one of the greatest threats to individual judicial independence came from within the court itself, that is, from the other members of the judiciary.[19] This resulted in a flurry of judicial explanation of the judicial role, the appropriate bounds of the interrelationship between individual judges within a multi-member court, and the judge's responsibility as a member of a collective institution.[20] The disagreement that this episode revealed shows little sign of abating; and the issue might even be said to have been the defining preoccupation of current Chief Justice Susan Kiefel in her public pronouncements since assuming leadership of the Australian judiciary.[21] The explanations of the judicial role elicited by Heydon's provocation drew, with different emphases, on institutional values of the court – including its obligations to the predictability and certainty of the law (rule of law values), the independence and integrity of

---

[19] Published as J D Heydon, 'Threats to Judicial Independence: The Enemy Within' (2013) 129 *Law Quarterly Review* 205.
[20] See, for instance, Stephen Gageler, 'Why Write Judgments?' (2014) 36 *Sydney Law Review* 189; Peter Heerey, 'The Judicial Herd: Seduced by Suave Glittering Phrases?' (2013) 87 *Australian Law Journal* 460; Sir Anthony Mason, 'Reflections on the High Court: Its Judges and Judgments' (2012) 37 *Australian Bar Review* 102; Susan Kiefel, 'The Individual Judge' (2014) 88 *Australian Law Journal* 554; P A Keane, 'The Idea of the Professional Judge: The Challenges of Communication' (Speech delivered at the Judicial Conference of Australia Colloquium, Noosa, 11 October 2014) .
[21] Susan Kiefel, 'Judicial Methods in the 21st Century', Supreme Court Oration (Speech delivered at the Banco Court, Supreme Court of Queensland, 16 March 2017); Susan Kiefel, 'Judicial Courage and Decorum of Dissent' (Selden Society Lecture, Supreme Court of Queensland, 28 November 2017); and noting a yet to be published speech of Kiefel CJ reported in M Pelly, 'Chief Justice Susan Kiefel says High Court has changed the way it works' (*Australian Financial Review*, 16 August 2018).

the judiciary (separation of powers values), and the efficiency of justice – and explained how individual judges and, collectively, the 'judiciary' must act to protect and assert these values. Following Heydon's paper, academics also entered the fray, analysing the position taken by Heydon and others in response, reflecting on the extent to which this revealed disparate conceptions of the role of the judge across the Australian judiciary.[22]

In 2020, an investigation commissioned by the Chief Justice upheld complaints by a number of female associates that they had experienced sexual harassment while working for Heydon during his years at the High Court. This was accompanied by an investigative exposé by a major news outlet, containing the claim that Heydon's conduct was said to be an 'open secret' in the profession,[23] and allegations of further incidents of sexual misconduct.[24] Following the outcome of the investigation, Chief Justice Kiefel expressed an unqualified apology to the complainants whose 'accounts of their experiences at the time have been believed'.[25] Heydon denied the allegations. These subsequent shocking developments have overlaid the earlier debate about individual judicial autonomy and collective responsibilities with a further complexity. It may be possible to divorce the competing perspectives on judicial method from the predatory harassment that Heydon engaged in while serving on the Court. However, both illustrate the challenging intersection of the individual and institutional judicial experience.

In this collection, the debate about individual responsibility and intercurial dynamics arises in a number of contexts. Joe McIntyre argues that his normative conceptualisation of the judicial role and its dual responsibilities to dispute resolution and social governance encourages judges to express their individual reasons for dispute resolution in full and

---

[22] Gabrielle Appleby and Heather Roberts, 'He Who Would Not Be Muzzled: Justice Heydon's Last Dissent in *Monis v The Queen*' in Andrew Lynch (ed) *Great Australian Dissents*, (Cambridge University Press, 2013), 335; Andrew Lynch, 'Keep Your Distance: Independence, Individualism and Decision-Making on Multi-Member Courts' in Ananian-Welsh and Crowe, n 11, 156; Joe McIntyre, 'In defence of judicial dissent' (2016) 37 *Adelaide Law Review* 431.

[23] Kate McClymont and Jacqueline Maley, 'High Court inquiry finds former Justice Dyson Heydon sexually harassed associates', 22 June 2020, *Sydney Morning Herald*.

[24] Natassia Chrysanthos, 'The stakes are so high: Inside the two-year Heydon investigation', 25 June 2020, *Sydney Morning Herald*.

[25] 'Statement by the Hon Susan Kiefel AC, Chief Justice of the High Court of Australia', High Court of Australia, 22 June 2020.

celebrates the need for diversity in decision-making. Murray's chapter on collegiality explores the various different ways that collegiality is understood, in the debate sparked by Heydon and elsewhere by judicial actors, to explain how it can have a substantial positive impact on the deliberative processes of multi-member courts. Lynch approaches the topic of judicial style against the backdrop of the current institutional practice of joint authorship of reasons in the High Court, considering whether this suppression of individuality comes at the cost of benefits long recognised within the common law tradition. Cahill-O'Callaghan explores the value-diversity that can drive judicial dissent on multi-member courts as an important part of creating a democratically legitimate judicial institution, and the dissenting judge as playing an important collective role in 'holding a mirror' to the values adopted and prioritised by the majority. Matthew Groves's chapter on judicial engagement with the media explores a number of interventions by Heydon as a sitting and then former judge, in which he criticised the practices and work ethic of sitting judges, and considers whether judicial engagement with the media in this way presents a danger to judges and the judiciary.

Another event that generated significant debate across Australian judicial commentariat in recent years was the criticism in 2017 by three sitting federal government ministers of the Victorian Supreme Court over the Court's record in sentencing terrorists. The Victorian Court of Appeal, presided over by Chief Justice Marilyn Warren, was at the time sitting on a high-profile terrorist sentencing appeal. In their chapter, Appleby and Roberts consider the response of the Chief Justice in calling a special hearing for the Ministers to show cause why they should not be held in contempt, and the different interpretations of this action as either a swift and appropriate defence of separation of powers and judicial independence, or an overreaction that undermined the judicial values of transparency and accountability. In her chapter, Josev looks at the incident as the most contemporary invocation of the conservative criticism of 'activist judges', and the challenges this label presents to genuine objective discussion about the approach of individual judges.

This volume capitalises on a uniquely Australian moment to consider these issues, and the focus of the analysis in this collection is predominantly Australian. At the same time, however, the issues raised by these events and challenges are not unique to Australia, and many of the chapters explicitly locate the Australian debate within an international comparative frame, and many more, while not explicitly comparative, have resonances with similar debates that are occurring or emerging overseas.

VI Overview of the Collection

The Judge, the Judiciary and the Court commences with this introduction to the themes of the book and contains two substantive chapters. In his chapter 'Revisiting the Judicial Function in Australia', McIntyre looks beyond the constitutional explanation and protection of courts and judges in Australia and presents a normative conceptual understanding of the judicial function: how *should* judges act as part of a judicial institution? He develops an argument that the judicial function extends to two core, albeit closely interwoven, roles. The first is the role of the courts in settling disputes within a society, and so the judge has a role in settling the disputes of others in accordance with established legal method. The second is that which the courts fulfill in facilitating social governance. The individual judge must be aware of the impact of the particular resolution of a case and the development of the law that it involves, on the broader legal, social and political environment in which it is made. In navigating the judicial function, an individual judge must engage with the tension that McIntyre identifies between 'the pursuit of clarity, predictability and order on one hand, and responsive and just flexibility and change on the other.' The institutional judicial function presents the individual judge with inherent choices, to be navigated, and scrutinised. McIntyre proffers this reconceptualisation of the judicial function as a set of tools to invite discussion, and debate, about what this means for preferable and desirable actions of the judge in the context of the collective judiciary and the institution of the court.

In 'The Chief Justice: Under Relational and Institutional Pressure', Appleby and Roberts critically analyse a particular institutional role within the court, the chief justice, by reference to how individual incumbents may navigate the many different relationships maintained by that officeholder both within and external to the Courts. They go beyond the relationships between and within the three constitutional branches of government, and look to a broader set of relationships, with the profession, the public, the media and with the academy. The chief justice performs a unique position within the court, with shared judicial curial responsibilities, but unique administrative and extra-curial obligations and expectations. The normative framework that they develop to evaluate individual chief justices' performance of their role is explicitly founded on Devlin and Dodek's six institutional values. Their analysis of a series of contemporary events in which chief justices have attempted to protect, defend or promote judicial values reveals the need for a more transparent framework to evaluate the work of individual chief justices, but also the inherently subjective nature of any evaluative attempt, as it will still require interpretation of institutional values and navigation between them.

In Part II, *Debates and Challenges to the Judicial Role*, four chapters take a fresh look at a number of pressure points, continuing and emerging, that arise in relation to the contemporary Australian court. In his chapter, 'Dismantling the Diversity Deficit: Towards a More Inclusive Australian Judiciary', Brian Opeskin looks at the much-canvassed, although not yet resolved, issue of judicial diversity. He provides a unique contribution to this debate through a statistical demographic analysis drawing on a customised data set of judicial responses to diversity questions from the national census. Opeskin warns that while the current data provides important information from which to assess the diversity characteristics of Australia's judges and magistrates, it remains insufficient, and more information on judicial characteristics is required to better inform these debates. Opeskin identifies that individual, collective and institutional dimensions of the judicial role are all affected by the diversity deficit. It speaks directly to the characteristics of individual judges and whether they possess the relevant diversity characteristics; and, as Opeskin identifies, it also speaks to the equal opportunities available or denied to individuals seeking the judicial role, and the different perspectives and views as to how to exercise their individual responsibility on the bench, thus potentially improving the individual and collective performance of the judicial role by expanding the experiences through which it is interpreted. But the diversity deficit debate is not generally framed with respect to individual judges; rather, it relates to the diversity that is exhibited (or lacking) across the judicial institution. Institutionally, diversity will ensure that the bench comprises the best judicial minds and is perceived as legitimate in the eyes of the community that it serves. As to what steps might be taken to redress the deficit, Opeskin identifies strategies that target the individual but will also require cultural and institutional change.

Zalnieriute and Bell in their chapter 'Technology and the Judicial Role' provide an important foundational contribution to the contemporary discussions about the impact of technology on the court as an institution and the performance by individual judges of the judicial role. The chapter traverses relatively well-covered ground in relation to the use of technology to improve judicial systems (such as through e-filing and discovery, and the use of technology to facilitate hearings) before engaging with the more complex and contested debates about the extent to which machine learning techniques and other artificial intelligence applications can assist in the exercise of an individual judge's discretion. They canvass the arguments in favour of efficiency and consistency and those that raise concerns as to the introduction of bias and discrimination in the exercise of often opaque machine-learning algorithms. Drawing on Devlin and Dodek's institutional values, they offer a number of warnings about the overly extensive adoption of automated systems in judicial decision-making. They highlight the importance of retaining individualised human oversight and discretion at the judicial level in a system in which the processes, particularly governmental, over which they exercise review are increasingly automated.

Roach Anleu and Mack's chapter, 'Emotion Work as Judicial Work', engages with the growing scholarship on the emotional dimensions of judicial work, looking at how individual judges channel emotion as strategies in their work in and outside the courtroom. The chapter takes a novel methodological approach, analysing in depth two segments from interviews with judicial officers to understand the myriad strategies through which particular experienced emotions are regulated and displayed as a positive resource by individual judges as they interact with litigants, judges and others, to achieve their various objectives, and the different factors that influence that management. The chapter has as its overriding emphasis the experience and agency of individual judges in managing emotion in their work but places that within its institutional and organisational setting that provides norms and boundaries that the individual judge must negotiate in managing and displaying emotion, including the conception of 'appropriate judging' and the dominant expectation within our judicial culture of 'judicial dispassion', through which the law is administered neutrally and objectively.

In 'The Persistent Pejorative: Judicial Activism', Josev looks at the ongoing deployment of the 'judicial activist' insult in commentary on how individual judges, and at times particular collective courts, such as the Mason and Brennan Courts and more recently the Victorian Supreme Court, perform their role. The term, although often deployed in public and political commentary, continues to be opaque as to the particular criticism at which it is actually targeted, and Josev's chapter draws out a number of meanings that are variously ascribed to it, often in a manner that layers a number of meanings, all of which are intended to denounce the individual judicial officers, or the collective benches that they are a part of. Josev then looks at *who* deploys this term, finding it to be one preferred by conservative political commentators and generally shunned by scholars and judicial officers themselves. In its deployment in this climate it is used as a personal insult, often intentionally without precise meaning as to the particular nature of the judicial transgression involved. As such, as a tool of critique of the judicial role, it has 'clouded rather than clarified discussion'. She calls upon academic lawyers to take the debate beyond the obfuscation of 'activism', and rather push towards greater clarity and transparency in the conservative critique of courts, thus allowing for a more informed debate as to the appropriate performance of the judicial role.

Part III of the book is titled *The Judiciary as a Collective* and contains three chapters. In her chapter, 'Judicial Collegiality', Murray directly addresses the collective judicial dynamic in her examination of the increasingly used, but nonetheless opaque, multi-definitional and layered, concept of 'collegiality'. She explores and expands the concept beyond one in which judges choose to write together, or whether they enjoy a personal rapport, or how particular appellate courts are constituted. For Murray, judicial collegiality is ultimately the key force through which multi-member courts collectively deliberate about judicial decisions. The concept has clear individual and institutional dynamics. Collegiality depends on the culture that is created by the particular individual judges involved at any given time: as Justice Albie Sachs of the South African Constitutional Court commented, a 'collegial court ... has its own vitality, its own dynamic, its own culture'. Different courts, led by different chief justices, will also establish different institutional rules that affect the collegiate dynamics, including, for instance, how judgments are allocated and drafted, and the conduct of pre- and post-judicial conferences. Murray posits that the concept has the potential to enhance, positively, the deliberative processes of appellate judicial decision-making and could be considered a judicial institutional 'value', alongside other values such as representativeness, efficiency or transparency. The value of collegiality is thrown into the pot of judicial values that include independence, which some, such as Heydon, have argued can be compromised through inappropriate collegiate pressure, but it can also promote other values, including judicial efficiency, and the judicial obligation to come to the best quality judicial decision-making, and the sharing of diverse judicial experience.

In 'Individual Judicial Style and Institutional Norms', Lynch establishes what is encompassed by the idea of 'style' in judicial reasons and why this may be of value and something worth striving for in judges' performance of their role. Through a synthesis of judicial pronouncements on the topic from judges in common law jurisdictions, he identifies recurring themes and typologies that are used by judges when they reflect upon what is meant by style – and the manifestations of which are to be either applauded and emulated or lamented and avoided. Lynch frames this discussion in the context of the High Court of Australia's contemporary practice of 'joining in' to a draft opinion any justice who agrees with it, so that individual authorship is obscured from plain view. This practice, which has been frequently explained and justified by Chief Justice Kiefel and defended by some other members of the Court, reveals an interesting dynamic between the individual and institutional conceptions of the judicial role. Lynch contrasts the practice, and its consequences for the benefits that are to be obtained by the conscious development of individual judicial style, with the modes of collective expression of agreement in the final courts of the United Kingdom and United States.

In 'Values and Judicial Difference in the High Court', Cahill-O'Callaghan provides us with a new way of understanding collective judicial dynamics through a content analysis of Australian High Court judgments. Selecting a series of 'hard decisions' decided by the Court and comparing majority and dissenting opinions, she conducts a values-based analysis, informed by a well-established values-framework used in psychology studies. This demonstrates that, rather than simple differences over the interpretation of the law, divergences between judges in deciding cases can be located in differences in the values espoused by judges in their reasoning, and how they prioritise and balance competing values in deciding disputes. This highlights the importance of the individual judge behind any decision. She reflects on the significance of values diversity on the bench, arguing that dissenting views on values expression and prioritisation can encourage debate within the collective judiciary and result in decisions that are more transparently aware of their own value decisions. Further, value-diversity on the bench can contribute to greater institutional legitimacy of the court in a value-diverse society. Cahill-O'Callaghan concludes her analysis with an argument for increased judicial diversity so as to reflect greater value diversity and prioritisation across the collective bench.

Part IV concludes the book with *The Perceptions of the Judiciary*. Groves's chapter analyses contemporary judicial engagement with the media. This contemporary engagement occurs at a time when judges are no longer restrained by convention from speaking out to the media; the traditional role of law officers to defend the judges has been openly doubted across common law systems; the media, politicians and others are more inclined to criticise judges; and the jurisdiction of the courts in many countries has extended into more highly politically sensitive matters, particularly in the human rights sphere. Through a series of case studies, including those in which judges have engaged with the media or the media has been independently critical of judges or the judiciary, the chapter makes the argument that while the work of the media is vital to democracy and public accountability for the work of the courts, it can also damage their foundational legitimacy. Poorly informed, critical coverage of individual judges and the broader judiciary can have detrimental consequences for individual judges as well as undermine public confidence in the curial institution. Groves confronts the challenge this posits, with judges constitutionally constrained in their responses to such reportage and responses sometimes exacerbating damage done. Nonetheless, Groves argues that judges must engage, as individuals or as an institutional collective, even if reluctantly and with caution.

Lastly, Penny Crofts explores the popular culture portrayal of judges in her chapter, 'The Good Judge in Australian Popular Television Culture'. She questions why judges often play a secondary role, where popular culture is otherwise highly saturated with legal themes, and considers the extent to which this reflects community assumptions about the role of the judge. Of those portrayals of judges that do exist, she considers what they reveal about public expectations of a 'good judge'. Perhaps unsurprisingly, Crofts concludes that much of the explanation for the secondary role of the judge lies in the focus of the media in more dynamic story lines, or how characters deal with judicial institutional resolutions of conflicts. Crofts also surmises that it reveals a public perception of the judge as replaceable, interchangeable, a 'potted plant', not an individual who has a particular impact on the story line. It is only when the judge bucks this stereotype and provides 'justice' beyond what the law appears to sanction, either as a good or bad judge, grappling with pressures and interests outside of the strict 'legal resolution', that the judge emerges from the shadows of the plotlines. In these portrayals, it is the individuality of the judge that emerges from beyond the expected staid institutional secondary judicial character.

VII Conclusion and Acknowledgments

Through the chapters briefly outlined above, our hope is that this volume provides a timely contribution to current discussions about the state of the Australian judiciary and the challenges it presently faces. It is clear that some of these issues are familiar, indeed perhaps perennial, but here they are considered in a fresh light or with the benefit of contemporary experience. Included in this category are the chapters that examine leadership, diversity, emotion, disagreement and representations of the judicial figure in popular culture. Elsewhere, the focus is on matters that have shifted quickly since the turn of the century – the contestability of the judicial role and the lack of government defence of the judiciary, sometimes open hostility from the executive that may be abetted by media, and of course the looming yet uncertain impact of artificial intelligence upon human justice systems. We do not claim the coverage of these complex issues within this book as exhaustive of all that the Australian judiciary faces – doubtless there are others, and even regarding those discussed here other minds may identify different opportunities and risks or prescribe alternative solutions. But the assembled chapters of this volume do, we believe, capture an array of the essential issues that need attention and debate in thinking about the future of the Australian judiciary.

Our confidence in this respect derives in part from the methodology employed in order to bring this publication into being. In July 2018, we hosted a roundtable at the Gilbert + Tobin Centre of Public Law at the Faculty of Law, University of New South Wales. We thank our colleague Associate Professor Sean Brennan, then Director of the Centre, for his enthusiastic and material support of this workshop.

Most of the contributing authors presented earlier versions of the chapters contained in this publication for extensive discussion by their academic peers, including invited expert discussants and also, crucially, five judicial participants who generously gave of their time as 'critical friends' of the workshop. Those former and serving judicial officers were Anna Katzmann (Federal Court of Australia), François Kunc (New South Wales Supreme Court), Sir Anthony Mason (former Chief Justice of the High Court of Australia), Chris Maxwell (President of the Victorian Court of Appeal) and Keith Mason (former President of the New South Wales Court of Appeal). The views expressed in the chapters of this book are, of course, the responsibility of their respective authors alone and are not to be attributed to any of the judicial participants at the workshop – but we certainly wish to thank the latter for the insights they shared and suggestions they made, all of which undoubtedly helped to guide the subsequent direction of the papers as they were then revised for publication along lines that are relevant and stimulating to a judicial readership. We also wish to give additional thanks to President Maxwell for his generosity in penning such a splendid foreword for the book.

Lastly, we thank our contributors for their commitment to this project, the cooperative and collegial spirit they brought to it and their receptiveness to feedback. We gratefully acknowledge the immense industry of Ki On Alex Wong and thank him for his thoughtful editorial assistance in readying the full manuscript for delivery to the publisher. We also thank Finola O'Sullivan at Cambridge University Press for her enthusiastic response to the book proposal and Marianne Nield and all the team at CUP for their work on this publication.

2

Re-examining the Judicial Function in Australia

JOE MCINTYRE

I Introduction

Australia has a public law fixation with the role of courts. Its peculiar mix of Westminster, US constitutionalism and autochthonous innovations has created a particular focus on judicial power. The limits and protection of Australian courts have taken on an outsized juridical significance in a country without a bill of rights (and with limited constitutionally protected rights). Indeed, the rigorous protection of Australian courts, and the judicial power they exercise, has been one of the distinguishing features of recent Australian constitutional law.

As a result, Australia has a far more extensive judicial and scholarly discourse on the nature and limits of judicial power, and the role of courts, than other comparable jurisdictions. This constitutional context is, however, itself limiting – it creates a tendency to *constitutionalise* issues regarding the role of courts, to think in terms of the contingent and textually dependant question of what the Australian Constitution permits, rather than to directly examine the issue of the judicial role. The question, in Australia, 'What is the judicial role?' too quickly becomes 'What are the constitutional limits of judicial power?' or 'What are the constitutionally mandated essential characteristics of a court?' However, this focus on constitutionality has at times tended to obscure a deeper reflection on the underlying concept of the scope of the judicial role. This approach elevates the permissible over the ideal.

This chapter pushes back against this tendency in setting out a *conceptual*, rather than a *constitutional*, exposition of the judicial function. It is against this context that this chapter presents a systematic and coherent articulation of the judicial function as a conceptual rather than constitutional inquiry. It argues that this function involves a unique institutional blend of dispute resolution and social governance. In the current Australian judicial environment, with its particular focus on efficiency and collegiality,[1] this explicit recognition of the dualist nature of the judicial role is controversial but critical.

This approach challenges us not to think in technical and prescriptive ways about actions of individual judges (or the operation of the broader institution), but rather to consider which actions are preferable and desirable. There is an important difference between focusing on how judges *should* act rather than on how they are *permitted* to act. There is inevitably much greater scope for disagreement in such an approach – particularly between individual judges – yet also greater scope for intellectual honesty and generative reflection. This chapter provides one set of tools to help foster such a discussion and presents one conception of what courts should do.[2] To that extent it aims to support, rather than conclude, a conversation about the role of the judge, the judiciary and the court – and the personal, collegial and institutional dynamics between them.

A   The Constitutional Context

Australia's federal structure demands the oversight of its constitutional limits. In Australia this has translated into judicial oversight[3] and the recognition of an implicit separation of power[4] that operates to principally isolate judicial power.[5]

At the Commonwealth level, the High Court has jealously protected the separation of judicial power, ensuring that only Chapter III courts may exercise that power[6] and that such federal courts may not exercise non-judicial power.[7] Against the potential rigidity of these principles, the Court has allowed a degree of flexibility in the application of the

---

[1] Susan Kiefel, 'The Individual Judge' (2014) 88 *Australian Law Journal* 554.
[2] For a more fulsome and expansive discussion of the role of the court see Joe McIntyre, *The Judicial Function: Fundamental Principles of Contemporary Judging* (Springer, 2019).
[3] *R v Kirby; Ex parte Boilermakers Society of Australia* (1956) 94 CLR 254, 278 ('*Boilermakers' Case*').
[4] For example the discussion by Dixon J in *Victorian Stevedoring and General Contracting Co Pty Ltd v Dignan* (1931) 46 CLR 73.
[5] *Attorney-General (Cth) v The Queen* (1957) 95 CLR 529, 540; *Wilson v Minister for Aboriginal and Torres Strait Islander Affairs* (1996) 189 CLR 1, 10–11.
[6] *New South Wales v Commonwealth* (1915) 20 CLR 54 ('*Wheat Case*'); *Brandy v Human Rights and Equal Opportunity Commission* (1995) 183 CLR 245.
[7] *Boilermakers' Case* (1956) 94 CLR 254; *Re Wakim; Ex parte McNally* (1999) 198 CLR 511.

separation of judicial powers doctrine – for example in the operation of courts-martial,[8] incidental powers[9] and the *persona designata* exception.[10]

At the state level, the separation of judicial powers doctrine is not directly applicable.[11] However, starting with the decision in *Kable v DPP (NSW)*,[12] the High Court has extended certain constitutional protections to the integrity and operation of state courts. The extent and efficacy of that protection have been a matter of ongoing litigation and debate, and while initially tightly constrained, the doctrine appears to have been reinvigorated in recent years.[13] In this environment, the Court has been increasingly willing to infer constraints in the Commonwealth Constitution on the operation of state courts[14] and tribunals.[15]

Taken together, the development and exposition of these doctrines have led to a particular emphasis in Australian jurisprudence, from the earliest days of Federation onwards,[16] on the articulation of the nature and limits of judicial power. Indeed, it is from those earliest cases that the most cited definition of judicial power is found – that of Griffith CJ in *Huddart Parker and Co Pty Ltd v Moorehead*: "'judicial power" ... means the power which every sovereign authority must of necessity have to decide controversies between its subjects, or between itself and its subjects, whether the rights relate to life, liberty or property'.[17]

---

[8] *R v Bevan; Ex parte Elias and Gordon* (1942) 66 CLR 452.
[9] *Boilermakers' Case* (1956) 94 CLR 254, 269–70; *R v Joske; Ex parte Shop Distributive and Allied Employees Association* (1976) 135 CLR 194.
[10] *Hilton v Wells* (1985) 157 CLR 57; *Grollo v Palmer* (1995) 184 CLR 348; *Wilson v Minister for Aboriginal and Torres Strait Islander Affairs* (1996) 189 CLR 1.
[11] For example, *Building Construction Employees and Builders Labourers Federation of NSW v Minister for Industrial Relations* (1986) 7 NSWLR 372; *Gilbertson v State of South Australia* [1978] AC 772;
[12] *Kable v Director of Public Prosecutions (NSW)* (1996) 189 CLR 51.
[13] *International Finance Trust Co Ltd v New South Wales Crime Commission* (2009) 240 CLR 319; *South Australia v Totani* (2010) 242 CLR 1; *Wainohu v NSW* (2011) 243 CLR 181.
[14] *Kirk v Industrial Relations Commission (NSW)* (2010) 239 CLR 531.
[15] *Burns v Corbett* [2018] HCA 15.
[16] For example, *Huddart Parker and Co Pty Ltd v Moorehead* (1908) 8 CLR 330; *Wheat Case* (n 6); *Waterside Workers' Federation of Australia v JW Alexander Ltd* (1918) 25 CLR 434; *In re Judiciary and Navigation Acts* (1921) 29 CLR 257
[17] *Huddart Parker and Co Pty Ltd v Moorehead* (1908) 8 CLR 330, 357.

Since that time, the Court has returned again and again to the definition of the concept[18] and has regularly recognised the difficulty of attempting to formulate a comprehensive definition of judicial power.[19] In the absence of conceptual clarity and precision, the Court has adopted a broad range of factors to assess whether a given action is judicial (or interfering with judicial action), including consideration of historical practices,[20] the character of the tribunal,[21] the processes utilised[22] and the consequences of the decision.[23] Disagreement as to the extent of, and limits on, judicial power continue to occupy the courts.[24]

This constitutional context has created an environment that is particularly fertile for the critical analysis of the role, conduct and limits of courts. Strikingly, this discourse has commonly been led by judges extra-judicially.[25] This has had implications for the nature and form of that discourse (and indeed the broader academic discourse), leading to the eschewing of the jurisprudential or empirical approaches common in other jurisdictions. Rather, there has been a tendency to focus on the discrete and the particular, to 'constitutionalise' the analysis of courts by considering what is *permissible*.

---

[18] For example, *R v Trade Practices Tribunal; Ex parte Tasmanian Breweries Pty Ltd* (1970) 123 CLR 361, 374–75 (Kitto J); and *Wilson v Minister for Aboriginal and Torres Strait Islander Affairs* (1996) 189 CLR 1, 11 (Brennan CJ, Dawson, Toohey, McHugh and Gummow JJ).

[19] *Brandy v Human Rights and Equal Opportunity Commission* (1995) 183 CLR 245, 267; more recently see *Palmer v Ayers* (2017) 259 CLR 478, 496 (Gageler J).

[20] *R v Davison* (1954) 90 CLR 353, 368, 382; *Chu Kheng Lim v Minister for Immigration, Local Government and Ethnic Affairs* (1992) 176 CLR 1, 27; *Thomas v Mowbray* (2007) 233 CLR 307, 328.

[21] *R v Hegarty; Ex parte City of Salisbury* (1981) 147 CLR 617, 628 (Mason J); *Re Dingjan; Ex parte* Wagner (1995) 183 CLR 323, 360.

[22] *Nicholas v The Queen* (1998) 193 CLR 173, 208–9.

[23] Principal among these is the direct enforceability of decisions: See *Waterside Workers' Federation of Australia v JW Alexander Ltd* (1918) 25 CLR 434, 451; *Brandy v Human Rights and Equal Opportunity Commission* (1995) 183 CLR 245, 268. See James Stellios, *The Federal Judicature: Chapter III of the Constitution Commentary and Cases* (LexisNexis, 2010) ch 4, 107–213.

[24] See *Attorney-General for South Australia v Raschke* [2019] SASCFC 83, [89]–[94] (Kourakis CJ).

[25] Perhaps the most influential such contribution was Dixon's doctrine of 'strict and complete legalism': Sir Owen Dixon, 'Address upon Taking the Office as Chief Justice of the High Court' in Susan Crennan and William Gummow (eds), *Jesting Pilate and Other Papers and Addresses by The Rt Hon Sir Owen Dixon* (Federation Press, 3rd ed, 2019) 289. Other notable contributions include: Sir Frank Kitto, 'Why Write Judgments?' (1992) 66 *Australian Law Journal* 787; JD Heydon, 'Threats to Judicial Independence: The Enemy Within' (2013) 129 *Law Quarterly Review* 205; Kiefel, 'The Individual Judge' (n 1).

There is, however, another way to think about the role of courts – one that does not conflate the concept of the judicial *function* with the related, yet distinct, constitutional issue of judicial *power*. Whereas the constitutional approach considers the specific institutional limits imposed by a particular constitution (which may involve some consideration of the intended role of courts), this approach flips the analysis to directly examine the nature of the judicial function (which may say something about constitutional limits). This approach offers an opportunity to examine the operation, limits, and reform of courts in a new light, liberated from the constraints of constitutional history.

To be clear, my focus is not on the judicial decision-making method, nor on the jurisprudential analysis of the nature of law (which may or may not give insights into the nature of judging).[26] This chapter is, instead, an attempt to step back from the analysis of courts in specific jurisdictions, such as Australia, to provide a conceptual overview of the contemporary role or function of courts in modern democratic states.[27] It argues that – at least for such states – there is emergent stability in the concept of the judicial function.[28] It concludes by briefly highlighting how such a conception may help reframe a number of contemporary debates concerning the Australian judiciary.

B   The Basic Parameters of the Judicial Function

What then are the basic parameters of this judicial function? In a sense, they should be relatively apparent to any jurist who pauses to reflect upon them: the judiciary is engaged in some form of both dispute resolution and dispute prevention/governance.[29]

---

[26] Questions of method are clearly related to those of function. For a full discussion of this relationship, and an attempt to articulate a derivative method, see McIntyre, *The Judicial Function* (n 2) pt III.

[27] In this I mirror the approach of Aharon Barak, 'Foreword: A Judge on Judging: The Role of a Supreme Court in a Democracy' (2002) 116 *Harvard Law Review* 19, 24.

[28] As Baar argues, in such systems judiciaries share 'a set of common roles and responsibilities, despite national differences in ideologies and political system': Carl Baar, 'The Emergence of the Judiciary as an Institution' (1999) 8 *Journal of Judicial Administration* 216, 217.

[29] Alan Rose, 'The Model Judiciary: Fitting in with Modern Government' (1999) 4 *Judicial Review* 323, 325. See also Melvin Eisenberg, 'The Principles of Legal Reasoning in the Common Law' in Douglas Edlin (ed), *Common Law Theory* (Cambridge University Press, 2007) 81.

First, the idea of the judge resolving disputes is ancient; references to appointed officers in permanent dispute resolution bodies appear in the *Book of Exodus*[30] and in ancient Egyptian texts.[31] There have been public dispute-resolving bodies, courts, throughout history, from the Provincial Courts of Imperial China[32] to the Seigniorial Courts of Medieval England.[33] The judicial function inarguably involves a particular form or type of dispute resolution,[34] and in the absence of a dispute a court cannot discharge its *judicial* function.[35] Understanding the *judicial* form of dispute resolution requires, therefore, the careful delineation of the judicial from other forms of dispute resolution, including its institutional form and relationship to the state.

Dispute resolution is, though, an insufficient (if necessary) description of the judicial role. A court is not 'simply a publicly funded dispute resolution centre',[36] but a core 'institution of governance'[37] that affects the governance and regulation of society as a whole.[38] Even in the resolution of private disputes, the judiciary serves a range of public purposes including the enforcement of legal rights and obligations, the articulation and development of the law, the public affirmation of right and wrong and the public denunciation and deterrence of culpable conduct.

To understand the nature of the judicial function it is necessary to understand the judicial form of these two related, yet discrete, social roles. The challenge is to move beyond these basic parameters, to

---

[30] See *Exodus* 18:13–24, where Jethro advises Moses on the creation of a court system for the exiled Israelites.
[31] See Lorne Neudorf, 'Judicial Independence: The Judge as a Third Party to the Dispute' [2015] *Oxford University Comparative Law Forum* 2.
[32] Martin Shapiro, *Courts: A Comparative and Political Analysis* (University of Chicago Press, 1981) 174.
[33] See Sir Frederick Pollock and FW Maitland, *The History of English Law: Volume I* (Cambridge University Press, 2nd revised ed, 1968) 530.
[34] Shapiro (n 32) 8, 17.
[35] See, for instance, *In re Judiciary and Navigation Acts* (1921) 29 CLR 257; *United Public Workers of America v Mitchell*, 330 US 75 (1947); AM Gleeson, 'Judging the Judges' (1979) 53(7) *Australian Law Journal* 338.
[36] JJ Spigelman, 'Judicial Accountability and Performance Indicators' (2002) 21 *Civil Justice Quarterly* 18, 26.
[37] PN Bhagwati, 'Role of the Judiciary in Developing Societies: New Challenges' in TMS Abas and DV Sinnadurai (eds.), *Law, Justice and the Judiciary: Transnational Trends* (Professional Law Books Publishers, 1988) 38.
[38] Gerard Brennan, 'Judging the Judges' (1979) 53(11) *Australian Law Journal* 767, 768.

understand concretely and specifically what is involved in both the judicial form of dispute-resolution and the judicial form of social governance.

II The Judicial Form of Dispute Resolution

The starting point in understanding the judicial function must be the basic proposition that the judiciary is involved in resolving disputes. We are intuitively familiar with the idea of an impartial judge who decides disputes 'by finding out the facts of the case and applying the law to those facts'.[39] These process and impartiality requirements are, however, insufficient to describe the judicial role.

To understand the distinguishing features of judicial dispute resolution, it is necessary to contrast it with other forms of dispute resolution. This requires a general taxonomy for the characterisation of dispute-resolution methods.

A A Taxonomy of Dispute-Resolution Methods

While disputes are an inevitable aspect of the human social condition,[40] where they are inadequately or inappropriately resolved they risk becoming socially pathological. Social cohesion demands that every community possess a range of mechanisms for the resolution of disputes.

This necessarily broad range of mechanisms, responding to an infinite variety of disputes, complicates any attempt to develop a taxonomy of dispute-resolution mechanisms.[41] In this chapter, I develop a more comprehensive taxonomy by focusing on two distinct elements: (1) the substantive criteria utilised and (2) the procedure followed. Conceptually, there are three fundamental substantive criteria by which the dispute is resolved:

1. **Resolution by Might** resolves the dispute by reference to a property, characteristic, or ability of the *disputants*. In its most basic form, the dispute is resolved by the strongest simply taking by force that which they desire.

---

[39] Robert French, 'In Praise of Unelected Judges' (2009) 36(9) *Brief* 19, 20.
[40] Jerzy Wroblewski, *The Judicial Application of Law* (Kluwer, 1992) 52–3; Simon Roberts, *Order and Disorder: An Introduction to Legal Anthropology* (Penguin, 1979) 45.
[41] Existing examples include Paul Bohannan (ed), *Law and Warfare: Studies in the Anthropology of Conflict* (University of Texas Press, 1967) 13; Roberts (n 39) 69; Wroblewski (n 41) 52–3.

	'Might'	'Merit'	'Chance'
Inter-Party	(1) Inter-Party Might	(3) Inter-Party Merit	(5) Inter-Party Chance
Third-Party	(2) Third-Party Might	(4) Third-Party Merit	(6) Third-Party Chance

Procedural Criteria / Substantive Criteria

Figure 2.1 Species of dispute resolution methods

2. **Resolution by Merit** resolves the dispute by reference to a property or characteristic of the *dispute* independent of the disputants. It is the strength (merit) of the parties' positions that is determinative.
3. **Resolution by Chance** resolves the dispute without reference to either the strength of the parties or their position. While such resolution is by nature arbitrary (with both might and merit irrelevant), it is nonetheless capable of fairness.

Similarly, there are two foundational procedural approaches by which a dispute resolution method may operate:

1. **Inter-Party Resolution:** First, the disputants may resolve the dispute between themselves. Two-party (dyadic[42]) negotiation is the classic example.
2. **Third-Party Resolution:** Alternatively, the disputants may refer the matter to another party and allow the decision of that party to resolve the dispute. Arbitration is an example of third-party (triadic[43]) dispute resolution.

The combination of these substantive and procedural elements creates six categories for the characterisation of dispute-resolution methods as shown in Figure 2.1.

Resolution by Reference to Might – The Battle

In the first family of resolution methods – might – the dispute is resolved by reference to properties of the disputants; it is the ability or skill of the parties (their strength), not the underlying merit of their position, that determines the dispute; the quality of the underlying claim is irrelevant. There are two subspecies of might-based resolution:

---

[42] Alec Stone-Sweet, *Governing with Judges: Constitutional Politics in Europe* (Oxford University Press, 2000) 11.
[43] Ibid. 15.

1. **Inter-Party Might:** The first of these involves the resolution of the dispute directly by the parties, whether through duel, battle or war. At its simplest, there are no rules, merely the challenge, brutal conflict and victor's triumph. However, there can also be great complexity. Examples include the ritualised process of the ancient 'trial by battle'[44] and other similar, highly regulated forms of battle.[45] This form of resolution is broader than simply fighting: the relevant 'property' may include skills, talents and innate abilities, such as the ability to build alliances or persuade allies to participate.[46]
2. **Third-Party Might:** The second, rarer, subspecies involves reliance upon a third party to resolve the dispute by reference to the might of the disputants. One example is the Eskimo *nith*-song contest, where the disputants improvise songs before the assembled, with the victor acclaimed by the heartiest applause.[47] Another example may involve disputants resolving to settle a matter by means of a boxing match scored by a third-party referee.

Resolution by Reference to Merit – The Claim of Right

In contrast, the merit-based family of resolution methods connects the resolution of the dispute to the underlying properties of the dispute, providing some rational foundation for the outcome by reference to the content and merits of the dispute. Merit-based resolution speaks the language of rights, justice, obligation, lawfulness and equity. Again, there are two subspecies of merit-based resolution:

1. **Inter-Party Merits:** The first of these subspecies represents perhaps the most common and efficient dispute resolution method. At its simplest, the two disputants directly negotiate, attempting to persuade the other of the merits of their position and to reach an agreement (often based on compromise). While the basic bilateral model

---

[44] See George Neilson, *Trial by Combat* (William Hodge, 1890) 6; Sir William Holdsworth, *A History of English Law: Volume II* (Methuen, 3rd ed, 1923) 308; Pollock and Maitland (n 33) 39.

[45] One example is the 'buffeting' combat of certain Eskimo groups: E Adamson Hoebel, 'Song Duels among the Eskimo' in Paul Bohannan (ed), *Law and Warfare: Studies in the Anthropology of Conflict* (University of Texas Press, 1967) 255. See also Roberts (n 39) 58.

[46] A very clear example is the 'Trial by Witnesses' in Norman England: Holdsworth (n 44) 302.

[47] Edward Moffat Weyer, *The Eskimos: Their Environment and Folkways* (Yale University Press, 1932) 226; Hoebel (n 45) 256; Roberts (n 39) 60, 89.

depends upon the disputants alone,[48] the model can be made more complex by the intervention of third parties, ranging from the passive information-conduit of a go-between, to the more active promotion of settlement by a conciliator or mediator. Ultimately, though, all such methods remain inter-parties resolution as settlement depends upon the consent and agreement of the parties.

2. **Third-Party Merits:** In the absence of agreement, one solution is to delegate responsibility for resolution to a third party.[49] This subspecies encapsulates a wide range of discrete mechanisms, depending upon the criterion of merit, the nature of the third party and the forms followed. Merit may be assessed by reference to a range of criteria, from formal legal and religious norms, looser principles such as fairness and justice, or by the vaguer still *ex aequo et bono of* the arbitrator.[50] The relevant considerations may be broadly or narrowly defined and may involve only the interests of the disputants or more general social interests. Secondly, the nature of the third party may vary significantly, whether chosen by the disputants or holding a relevant office (whether judge, priest, king or chief).[51] That decision-maker may be qualified by special training or expert knowledge and may possess permanent institutional character or an *ad hoc* nature. Finally, these mechanisms may employ a range of methods to regulate procedure, forms of participation and reasoning, from the highly formalised proceedings of a Supreme Court to the flexible guidance of a parent among feuding children. Nevertheless, all forms of third-party merit resolution have in common a basic foundation in rationality: the third party must in some way assess merit by applying the relevant criteria to the determined factual circumstances in some reasoned and justifiable manner. Ultimately, for inter-party resolution, consent and agreement is determinative; for third-party resolution, it is the *decision* of the third party that terminates the dispute.

Resolution by Reference to Chance – The Toss of the Coin

The third family of dispute resolution methods ignores both the might of the parties and the merits of their position to resolve the dispute by

---

[48] Roberts (n 39) 69.
[49] Shapiro (n 32) 1; Stone Sweet (n 42) 15.
[50] Baron Patrick Devlin, *The Judge* (Oxford University Press, 1979) 84.
[51] To Roberts this distinction between authority from consent and authority from office is the principal distinction between arbitrator and adjudicator: Roberts (n 39) 70.

reference to a purely external criterion. While this resolution by reference to 'chance' may not provide a *rational* resolution (and in that sense is arbitrary), it does assume the impartiality of blind fate[52] to provide an unbiased and fair way of making difficult decisions. These methods provide a means for decisions to be reached in a regulated, organised and socially legitimate way, without any requirement for a rational or justifiable *reason* for the final decision. There are two forms of chance-based resolution:

1. ***Inter-Party Chance:*** In the first of the subspecies the parties agree to directly settle their dispute by reference to an event over which they have no control and for which the merit of their positions is irrelevant. The paradigm examples include the toss of a coin or the drawing of lots.[53]
2. ***Third-Party Chance:*** In the second subspecies the resolution is delegated to a third party. This involves more than simply a judge tossing the coin[54] and includes any case where there is an *absolutely* unfettered decision-maker. With both might and merit irrelevant, the parties have no control or impact upon the outcome; it becomes purely random and arbitrary. An example is the Anglo-Saxon trial by ordeal which operated as dispute resolution by chance.[55]

The above taxonomy provides a language and conceptual framework for the exposition of dispute-resolution mechanisms generally, helping to identify the defining features of any particular method. Moreover, this approach invites a critical analysis of the comparative advantages and costs of any given method *as a system of dispute resolution*. This involves a critique of both the ability of the mechanism to effectively terminate the dispute and of the operational 'costs' of that mechanism. An ineffective mechanism, one that leaves the disputants feeling unduly aggrieved, ignores the underlying conflict, or operates in an illegitimate manner, may prolong the dispute. An unduly costly mechanism (with operational 'costs' extending beyond the financial to include the broader impact upon

---

[52] Wroblewski (n 40) 53.
[53] This ancient method continues to perform an important role in social practices such as jury selection (see *Juries Act 1974* (UK) s 11(1)) and as a tie-breaking role in elections (See *Election Act 1993* (NZ) s 191(9)).
[54] See David Pannick, *Judges* (Oxford University Press, 1987) 1.
[55] See William J Tewksbury, 'The Ordeal as a Vehicle for Divine Intervention in Medieval Europe' in Paul Bohannan (ed), *Law and Warfare: Studies in the Anthropology of Conflict* (University of Texas Press, 1967) 268.

the disputants, their relationship and the interests of the general community) may be worse than the dispute itself. Thus, the violent extermination of one's opponent *may* be highly effective at terminating a dispute but has significant negative broader impacts. Any analysis of costs should examine the implications of both *utilising* the method and of *failing* to resolve the dispute: it may be that the cost of relinquishing of control to a third party may be outweighed by the benefit of resolution of the dispute – irrespective of outcome – in granting certainty and the opportunity to come to rebuild a valuable relationship.[56]

B   The Judicial Form of Third-Party Merit-Based Dispute Resolution

This taxonomy helps to expose the distinctive characteristics of the judicial form of dispute resolution as one type of third-party merit-based resolution (among many). The archetypal judge is not swayed by the toss of a coin[57] or by who is the strongest/richest/mightiest disputant. Rather the judge is a disinterested third party, finally and authoritatively determining the dispute on its merits without any need for subsequent agreement by the disputants. The judicial form of the third-party merit-based resolution method is distinguished by the following factors:

1. **The Criteria of Merit:** First, judicial resolution assesses the merits of the dispute by reference to a particularly narrow set of criteria: law. For these purposes it is sufficient to put aside 'persistent'[58] jurisprudential questions as to the nature of law and to note that law represents a special type of social norm distinguished by its 'higher degree of clarity, formalisation, and binding authority'.[59] While there may be doubt as to the precise scope and boundary of law, there remains broad agreement as to the general content of legal norms. The judge must decide the dispute by determining which disputant has the best position in law (even if this requires some consideration of non-legal matters).
2. **The Nature of the Third Party:** Second, judicial resolution is distinguished by the nature of the third-party decision-maker: the 'judge'. The judge holds office as an official adjudicator and derives authority

---

[56] Ibid. 15.
[57] *R v Deputy Industrial Injuries Commissioner; Ex parte Moore* [1965] 1 QB 456, 488 (Diplock LJ).
[58] HLA Hart, *The Concept of Law* (Oxford University Press, 2nd ed, 1994) 3.
[59] Stone Sweet (n 42) 11.

from that office.[60] That office is generally part of a permanent institution, the court, which exists independently of the dispute, and the judges may act individually or collectively. The judge is distinguished by a high level of impartiality, with much of the legitimacy and authority of the judicial determination dependent upon this impartiality. As a general rule, judges possess extensive legal education and experience in legal practice.

3. **The Formality, Process and Decision-Making Method:** Third, judicial resolution is distinguished by the high degree of formality: rigid processes and regulated methods. Judicial resolution involves elaborate systems of fact-finding that regulate rules of evidence and procedure – even if the precise content of these rules may legitimately vary between systems. Finally, judicial resolution is distinguished by the highly refined and regulated judicial decision-making method that regulates the identification and application of the governing norms, the exercise of judicial discretion and the scope of legitimate influences and interests. Again, while *between* judicial systems there is some methodological variation,[61] *within* any judicial system there is a broad and deep consensus as to the content of that method.

The 'highly specialised mode of conflict resolution'[62] that is the judicial form of dispute resolution is distinguished by the way these distinctive elements are blended together. The criterion of law means only a small aspect of the broader dispute (and underlying conflict of interests) is considered by the judge, with other considerations relevant to the dispute (whether fairness, morality or the interests of the parties and the community) not directly relevant to the judicial assessment of merit. The efficacy of judicial resolution of the dispute relies upon the parties (and society) being convinced that the clarity, predictability and finality of the narrow legal norms outweigh the sidelining of these broader considerations. The nature of the judge as an institutional, professional, independent and impartial adjudicator is critical in this assessment. Similarly, by having a formal and visible process, conducted in public and governed by a determinate judicial decision-making method, judicial resolution not only avoids charges of arbitrariness but promotes a

---

[60] Roberts (n 39) 70.
[61] Even this is surprisingly superficial: see Mitchell Lasser, *Judicial Deliberations: A Comparative Analysis of Judicial Transparency and Legitimacy* (Oxford University Press, 2004).
[62] Wroblewski (n 40) 54.

reputation for personal judicial and institutional integrity. This in turn promotes the finality of judicial resolutions, as judicial determinations gain a certain moral, as well as legal, imperative. The very narrowness of judicial resolution can create a 'virtuous circle' where the final judicial determination is imbued with a certain moral imperative.

III   The Judicial Form of Social Governance

The judicial function involves, however, more than simply dispute resolution. Courts are 'state actors',[63] performing an indisputable function of government. In this public governance aspect of the judicial function, the judiciary not only determines and develops the law, but helps maintain the system of *governance by law*.

The judicial function form of social governance is best understood by outlining how mechanisms of dispute resolution can operate as instruments of social governance.

A   Dispute Resolution and Social Governance

Those who govern any society must be concerned with the regulation and resolution of disputes. While disputes may be inevitable, left unchecked they cause social disease, disrupting the ordered interactions necessary to the survival of any society.[64] The resolution of disputes is fundamentally entwined with the maintenance of the basic degree of order implied in the idea of 'society'.[65] The resolution of disputes is a necessary aspect of the maintenance of order, promotion of stability, and the enhancement of the general well-being central to good governance of a society.

As societies have become more complex, they have required increasingly elaborate systems of dispute resolution to preserve public order, with emerging institutions of governance inevitably becoming involved in dispute resolution.[66] This has held true from African chiefdoms,[67] to

---

[63] Baar (n 28) 216.
[64] Roberts (n 39) 28.
[65] For example, social life in any community requires sufficient order such that that 'children can be reared and consistent arrangements made for the provision of food, drink and shelter': Roberts (n 39) 30.
[66] See JH Baker, *An Introduction to Legal History* (Butterworths, 3rd ed, 1990) 16.
[67] Roberts (n 39).

Anglo-Saxon[68] and Norman England.[69] Not all forms of dispute resolution are matters of social governance, and they will only take on that form where:

1. there exist formalised institutions of government; and
2. the dispute resolution mechanisms are incorporated into the institutions of power and rules within broader society.

This convergence between the interests of government and dispute resolution represents more than simply having the local government official available as a 'big man' for adjudicating disputes.[70] Most directly, the official may advance the interests and policies of the government through the decision itself. Alternatively, the provision of an effective *service* of dispute resolution may enhance legitimacy and reputation of the government.[71] More diffusely, the very act of application of norms by the official may reinforce social norms to make them more effective.[72] The social impact of dispute resolution extends well beyond the disputants.

To understand this governance role, it is necessary to understand how dispute resolution mechanisms can utilise both 'power' and 'rules' to contribute to governance within a society.

B   *The Judicial Function and Governance through 'Power'*

Governance through 'power' involves the ability to *actively* and *directly* affect the interests, rights and behaviour of another party. The connection between dispute resolution and the active exercise of governmental power is ancient – consider the imperial administrator (British District Officer or Chinese Mandarin) who kept the peace, collected taxes and acted as judge.[73] As the resolution of disputes directly promotes order

---

[68] FW Maitland, *The Constitutional History of England* (Cambridge University Press, 1908) 4.

[69] Thus following the anarchy of Stephen's reign, Henry II revolutionised the procedures of the courts of England: see Pollock and Maitland (n 33) 137; George Burton Adams, *Council and Courts in Anglo-Norman England* (Yale University Press, 1926) 127.

[70] Shapiro (n 32) 21.

[71] Shapiro notes that conquerors have routinely utilised institutions of dispute-settlement to control territories and consolidate legitimacy by providing a better service than their predecessors: Shapiro (n 32) 22–4.

[72] Ibid. 22.

[73] Shapiro (n 32) 20.

within a society, there is a strong incentive for governors to utilise their power to promote effective and efficient dispute-resolution.

The principal use of governmental power to aid dispute resolution is through the regulated use of force. By the term 'force', I refer to the ability to use direct inter-personal violence to promote one's interests. The use of force (violence) is one of the most ancient forms of dispute resolution. However, centralised states have typically claimed a monopoly on violence.[74] This monopolisation has a profound impact on systems of dispute resolution, directly prohibiting some might-based methods of dispute resolution,[75] while indirectly affecting the efficacy of other methods. A resolution method linked to the enforcement methods of the state gains prominence once the ability to personally undertake violent redressive action is removed.[76]

The judicial form of dispute resolution is distinguished by its particularly close relationship to the institutions of 'power' within a society and is regarded as *the principal* dispute resolution system of the modern democratic society, providing a key plank in maintaining social order.[77] As Couture forcefully argued:

> The first impulse of a rudimentary soul is to do justice by his own hand. Only at the cost of mighty historical efforts has it been possible to supplant in the human soul the idea of self-obtained justice by the idea of justice entrusted to authorities. . . . A civil action, in final analysis, then, is civilization's substitute for vengeance.[78]

The performance of this role is powerfully aided by the intimate connection between the judiciary and other institutions of government. Compliance with judicial decisions is not left to diffuse social pressure or the goodwill and integrity of the disputants but is ensured through the enforcement abilities of the state.[79] Indeed, judicial dispute resolution is uniquely able to call directly upon the state to utilise force to enforce its decisions,[80] positioning it as a uniquely effective final resolver of disputes.

---

[74] Ibid. 41. See Hans Kelsen, *General Theory of Law and State* (Russell & Russell, 1945) 21.
[75] For example, by criminalising the gentleman's duel: *R v Rice* (1803) 3 East 581.
[76] Oliver Wendell Holmes, 'The Path of the Law' (1897) 10(8) *Harvard Law Review* 457.
[77] As Devlin notes, in resolving disputes, the judiciary 'secures us from comparable disorders within the nation': Devlin (n 50) 4.
[78] Eduardo J Couture, 'The Nature of the Judicial Process' (1950) 25 *Tulane Law Review* 1, 7.
[79] See Holmes (n 76) 457. See also Ronald Dworkin, *Law's Empire* (Hart Publishing, 1998) 93.
[80] Dworkin (n 79) 93.

In this way, the judicial function involves a direct exercise of social control over the disputants to promote social order. Conceived of in this way, judicial resolution is not a service provided to private individuals but a public act of governance with broad public benefits.

C   The Judicial Function and Governance through 'Rules'

The public benefit of judicial resolution is, of course, far broader than contributing to the maintenance of social order. Judicial decisions help secure 'the effectiveness and integrity of the Law':[81] that is, they help governance through 'rules'.

Governance through rules operates as a more subtle, indirect and generalised form of social control. Rather than relying upon the immediate exercise of power, an effective rule is autonomous and self-policing; the actor alters his/her conduct to conform to that rule *because* it is the rule. As rules are a pervasive and passive influence on behaviour, a governor who controls the content of the rules gains a powerful ability to influence social behaviour.

The use of rules takes on a particular significance in the context of dispute resolution and governance. As rules can demarcate rights and responsibilities, and articulate how resources should be allocated in society, they can guide behaviour in a way that minimises the potential for disputes to arise in the first place. Where disputes do arise, rules can aid settlement both by suggesting solutions to conflicts and by providing standards for evaluating the disputed behaviour.[82] As these norms have an 'autonomous existence ... external to, and pre-dating, the dispute',[83] they can be particularly important in lending legitimacy and authority to a third-party dispute resolver.

However, rules-based resolution can promote good governance by impacting, and indeed altering, the rule itself. The application of rules for dispute resolution can affect those rules in several discrete ways. These different modes of normative governance are particularly significant for the judicial governmental function which, through the special relationship between judicial resolution and the law, profoundly affect the legal normative order in at least four distinct ways:

[81] Couture (n 78).
[82] Stone Sweet (n 42) 11.
[83] Ibid.

1. *Reinforcing Social Rules through Application:* The mere act of applying a rule to resolve a dispute reinforces that rule, affirming its ongoing validity and providing the necessary degree of vitality to avoid ossification. Without sufficiently regular application, rules lack the necessary degree of vitality required to guide behaviour. Where a legal rule is publicly applied by a judge, it is reaffirmed and re-energised:[84] the very act of applying law to resolve a dispute affirms and reinforces that law, helping to maintain its.[85] By applying a law to the resolution of a dispute, the judge affirms its contemporary relevance as a valid guide to future behaviour.[86]

2 *Increasing the Predictability of Rules:* Second, the application of a rule helps make the substantive content of that rule clearer and its operation more predictable, increasing its efficacy as a guide to behaviour and mechanism of governance. Clear and predictable rules allow people to structure their affairs to avoid disputes.[87] This role is particularly significant in the judicial context: each interpretation of a legal rule in one dispute provides some meaningful prediction as to how that rule may be interpreted in similar future disputes. In turn, this allows parties to better order their affairs to avoid conflicts and prevent disputes.[88] The importance of this clarifying interpretive role cannot be overstated: other dispute-resolution methods operate in the court's shadow,[89] while prior judicial decisions help predict what may transpire in future judicial proceedings.[90] Through this process of interpretation (which in all cases involves a foundation of interpretive

---

[84] Shapiro (n 32) 25.
[85] Ibid. 28. Daniel Misteravich, 'The Limits of Alternative Dispute Resolution: Preserving the Judicial Function' (1992) 70 *University of Detroit Mercy Law Review* 35, 40–1.
[86] As Pound notes, 'abstract rules can prevent controversy only because and to the extent that men know they are potentially efficacious in action': Roscoe Pound, 'The Place of Procedure in Modern Law' (1917) 1(2) *Southwestern Law Review* 59; See also Brian Dickson, 'A Life in the Law: The Process of Judging' (2000) 63 *Saskatchewan Law Review* 373, 388; Wroblewski (n 40) 52.
[87] See, for example, Holmes (n 76) 460–61; Lon L Fuller, *The Morality of Law* (Yale University Press, 1969) 55; Hart (n 58) 37–8.
[88] Rose (n 29) 328.
[89] Marc Galanter, 'The Radiating Effects of Courts' in Keith Boyum and Lynn Mather (eds), *Empirical Theories about Courts* (Longman, 1983) 121.
[90] Ibid. As Galanter notes, this clarification includes not only the rules that may govern the dispute but also 'possible remedies and estimates of the difficulty, certainty and costs of securing particular outcomes'.

discretion[91]), judicial decisions clarify the substantive content of legal rules and promote the consistent application and operation of those rules.[92]

3 ***Maintaining Coherence between Rules:*** The application of rules in dispute resolution can clarify the relationships *between* rules (how those rules interact), making the operation of the broader normative regime clearer, more coherent and more predictable. Judicial decisions are particularly significant in this context, as the efficacy of the law depends upon legal norms operating as a part of a broadly unified, coherent and consistent system. Without secondary rules to determine priorities and conflicts between rules, multiple (potentially inconsistent) rules may be applicable to a dispute, resulting in unpredictability and arbitrariness.[93] Judges remain the principal guardians of the systemic coherence of law, guiding the 'development of a uniform and coherent *body of law*'.[94] This role flows from the institutional nature of judicial dispute resolution (which allows these principles to develop over time through the aggregation of discrete choices) and the publicly discursive nature of the judicial decision (which makes this ongoing dialogue publicly accessible).

4 ***Altering the Substantive Rule:*** Finally, dispute resolution mechanisms can provide a quick and flexible means of altering the substantive content of the rules, enabling those rules to evolve and respond to changing social contexts in a quick, flexible but ultimately orderly manner often in response to changing circumstances as highlighted by concrete disputes. In one sense, every public application of a rule alters that rule by confirming that the rule extends to capture the given circumstance. However, that act of interpretation and application can more strongly alter the content of the rule. For example, a prior interpretation may be abandoned as not reflecting the proper purpose of the rule, or because that rule reflects a policy that is no longer

---

[91] As Barak notes: '[i]nterpretation without judicial discretion is a myth': Barak (n 27) 81; See also French (n 39) 4. While that discretion may be very tightly constrained – a cursory confirmation that there is nothing difficult or ambiguous presented by the current fact/law interplay – it retains a necessary and non-zero character. See McIntyre, *The Judicial Function* (n 2) pt III.

[92] As Wroblewski observes, 'some degree of uniformity of judicial application of law appears as one of the conditions of the controlling functions of law': Wroblewski (n 40) 57.

[93] For Dworkin, this drive to systemic integrity and coherence is one of the defining features of a legal normative order: Dworkin (n 79) ch 7.

[94] Dickson (n 86) 378 (emphasis added). Ibid. 217.

appropriate. By helping to ensure that rules mirror desired social purposes (such as justice), such mechanisms can strengthen the entire order of normative governance. Judicial decision-making operates in a dynamic and changing social context where legal rules can become outdated, and even general principles may be required to evolve over time. In addition to the 'trivial'[95] or 'weak' forms of law-making (described above) that inevitably follow every judicial application of law, the judiciary can also engage in a more active or 'strong' type of law-making, radically restating, reinterpreting or indeed abandoning specific legal rules to better maintain the law generally. A particular rule may need reform where it reflects outdated social values,[96] where it has been rendered an outlier[97] by shifting principles, or where the accretion of inconsistent rules has created such a state of confusion and incoherence in the law.[98] Finally, the relevant law may be sparse and inadequate so that the unavoidable choice will inevitably become a precedent and guide for future decisions.[99]

If judicial decisions are to retain their moral imprimatur and legitimacy for both dispute resolution and social governance,[100] legal rules cannot be permitted to depart too far and too systematically from broad social values. By altering substantive rules to better respond to these values, judicial decisions not only help to regulate relationships and patterns of behaviour,[101] but help, in Barak's words, to bridge 'the gap between law and society'.[102] The role of the judge is, in this regard, to maintain the vitality of the law as a dynamic and effective normative system; to 'help the law achieve its purpose'.[103]

---

[95] Ibid.
[96] Consider the rejection of the 'marriage' defence to rape: *R v R* [1992] 1 AC 599.
[97] Consider the approach taken in abandoning the 'highway authority immunity' (*Brodie v Singleton Shire Council* (2001) 206 CLR 512) or the rejection of the 'rule in *Ryland v Fletcher*' (*Burnie Port Authority v General Jones Pty Ltd* (1994) 179 CLR 520).
[98] Consider the approach of the High Court of Australia in attempting to bring clarity to Australian Constitution s 92 jurisprudence: *Cole v Whitfield* (1988) 165 CLR 360.
[99] Consider the approach taken in 'wrongful life' tort cases: *Cattanach v Melchior* (2003) 215 CLR 1; *McFarlane v Tayside Health Board* [2000] 2 AC 59. Bingham describes such cases as occurring in 'an authoritative desert': Lord Tom Bingham, *The Business of Judging: Selected Essays and Speeches 1985–1999* (Oxford University Press, 2000) 39.
[100] In this vein, Rose argues that courts must 'be responsive to the needs of society and aware of its values, expectations and fears': Rose (n 29) 324.
[101] Barak (n 27) 28.
[102] Ibid. 27–8.
[103] Ibid. 28. See also Dickson (n 79) 378.

Every judicial application of legal rules directly impacts that law, strengthening, maintaining and reforming it. This active process of alteration helps to ensure the law is well adapted to its social purposes, and that concrete meaning is given to social values.[104] The publicly declared judicial decision provides a clear articulation of the content of the law, increasing the efficacy of the law as a means of social ordering by diminishing uncertainty and enhancing the possibility of settlement.[105] Moreover, in making the inevitable choices between legally valid alternatives, judicial resolution can affect the development and evolution of the law, altering, over time, the substantive content of the law.

Judges make law. Where the law is uncertain, inconsistent or incoherent, judges are required to make choices that may substantively alter that law. Law-making is an unavoidable aspect of both the dispute-resolution and governance aspects of the judge and is inherent – to a greater or lesser degree – in every judicial decision.[106] This role is an inevitable aspect of the public and authoritative application of law, with each decision – whether very weakly or very strongly – changing the law:

> *The meaning of the law before and after a judicial decision is not the same.* Before the ruling, there were ... several possible solutions. After the ruling, the law is what the ruling says it is. The meaning of the law has changed. New law has been created.[107]

This ability to alter, through application, the very legal rules that are applied is at the very core of the judicial function,[108] and 'fundamentally differentiates the judicial system from other forms of dispute-resolution'.[109]

The normativity of judicial decisions is often misunderstood, attacked as being antidemocratic: 'law-making by unelected judicial officers'.[110] The judicial form of law-making is, however, fundamentally different from the legislative form of law-making.[111] A legislator has a broad power to prospectively change the law in the abstract, without reference

---

[104] Owen Fiss, 'Foreword: The Forms of Justice' (1979) 93 *Harvard Law Review* 1, 2.
[105] Devlin (n 50) 89.
[106] As Dworkin argues, judges 'unquestionably 'make new law' every time they decide [a] ... case': Dworkin (n 79) 6. See also Barak (n 27) 121.
[107] Barak (n 27) 121 (emphasis added).
[108] Misteravich (n 85) 41.
[109] Rose (n 29) 330.
[110] Ibid. 332.
[111] As Jennings notes, the 'court has no purely legislative competence': Sir Robert Jennings, 'The Judicial Function and The Rule of Law in *International Law at the Time of Its Codification: Essays in Honour of Roberto Ago* (Dott A Giuffré Editore, 1987) vol III, 145.

to discrete circumstances, principles or systemic operation. The judicial capacity to alter the law occurs strictly in the context of the particular dispute.[112] Judicial law-making is retrospective in effect for the particular dispute, and defeasible and contingent in the broader consequence. Moreover, it remains tightly constrained by the judicial decision-making method.[113] Even where decisions appear to affect radical change in the law, those changes build upon prior developments, debates and diverse trends in other aspects of the law.[114] The judicial mode of normative development is, by and large, a slow and conservative accretive process.[115] When understood in this way, judicial law-making must be seen as complementing, rather than competing with, legislative law-making.

D Conclusions Regarding 'Judicial' Governance

The governance aspect of the judicial role, in regard to its impact on order and legal rules, is an inherently public role, serving public interests.[116] This conception of judicial resolution as a public good is marginalised by the conception of judicial resolution as a private good.[117] Moreover, such a privatised 'service delivery' conception misunderstands the inherent tension between the general and the particular that is at the heart of the judicial role.

Judicial governance requires that a careful balance be struck between the interests of stability and predictability on one hand and flexibility in

---

[112] Douglas Drummond, 'Towards a More Compliant Judiciary?: Part I' (2001) 75 *Australian Law Journal* 304, 367; Barak (n 27) 32.
[113] As Jennings notes, where a court creates law 'in the sense of developing, adapting, modifying, filling gaps, interpreting, or even branching out in a new direction' that decision must 'be seen to emanate reasonably and logically from existing and previously ascertainable law': Jennings (n 111) 145.
[114] See Robert French, 'Courts under the Constitution' (1998) 8 *Journal of Judicial Administration* 7, 15.
[115] The two classic statements of this 'interstitial' nature of judicial law-making were made by two of the great twentieth century US judges: Justice Holmes in *Southern Pacific Co v Jensen*, 244 US 205, 221 (1917) and Judge Learned Hand in Learned Hand, 'The Nature of the Judicial Process: Book Review' (1922) 35(4) *Harvard Law Review* 479.
[116] See Judith Resnik, 'Migrating, Morphing, and Vanishing: The Empirical and Normative Puzzles of Declining Trial Rates in Courts' (2004) 1 *Journal of Empirical Legal Studies* 783; Hazel Genn, *Judging Civil Justice: The 2008 Hamlyn Lecture* (Cambridge University Press, 2010) 16–20.
[117] See the critique in Resnik (n 116) 813. The contrasting view of judicial resolution as a public good is developed in the decision of the UK Supreme Court in see *R (on the application of UNISON) v Lord Chancellor* [2017] UKSC 51 [66]–[71].

the interests of justice on the other. While at times interests of justice must be sacrificed to maintain normative order and predictability (a 'harsh judgement' is given to maintain 'fidelity to the law'),[118] the social legitimacy and acceptability of the judicial role (and the law itself) are imperilled if substantial injustice dominates (too many cases containing 'too much law and not enough justice'[119]). For Pound, this struggle to reconcile the conflicting demands of the need of stability and of the need of change was at the heart of all thinking about law.[120] Cardozo describes this as the tension between 'the spirit of change, and the spirit of conservation',[121] while Blackshield identified it as the never-resolved antimony 'between readiness and resistance to change'[122] which requires 'giving effect (and meaning) to *both* sets of values'.[123] Only by simultaneously striving for both objectives of responsive change and stability, in messy tension rather than glorious isolation, can the judiciary properly promote the ends of both good governance and effective dispute resolution.

This alertness to the systemic consequences of the decision necessarily flows from the role of the judge as institutional third-party decision-maker. In the narrow sense, this impacts the administration of legal rules: the judge acts within the context of a system, and his or her ruling must integrate into it.[124] More broadly, however, the judge must be conscious of the impact of any decision on the ability of the judiciary to continue to perform its social role. The efficacy of judicial determinations depends upon the broader social legitimacy of the courts, and the individual judge having some responsibility in maintaining the requisite social confidence in the courts.[125]

Ultimately, the consequences of judicial decisions have an impact far beyond direct dispute resolution. The judiciary is more than a mere

---

[118] Devlin (n 50) 85–6.
[119] Ibid.
[120] Roscoe Pound, *Interpretations of Legal History* (Macmillan, 1923) 1.
[121] Benjamin Cardozo, *The Paradoxes of Legal Science* (Columbia University Press, 1928) 7.
[122] Anthony R Blackshield, 'Five Types of Judicial Decision' (1974) 12(3) *Osgood Hall Law Journal* 539, 541. See also Julius Stone, *Legal System and Lawyers' Reasonings* (Stevens & Sons, 1964) 209–12, 229–34; See also Aharon Barak, 'On Society, Law and Judging' (2011) 47(2) *Tulsa Law Review* 297, 299.
[123] Blackshield (n 122) 543.
[124] Barak (n 27) 30. Fuller described this as a 'problem of system': Lon L Fuller, *Anatomy of the Law* (Greenwood Press, 1968) 94.
[125] John Doyle, 'The Judicial Role in a New Millennium' (2001) 10 *Journal of Judicial Administration* 133, 135.

service of government; it is a core *institution* of government.[126] At the simplest level, as the primary dispute settlement mechanism of the State, judicial decisions helps to minimise the social disorder and chaos caused by unresolved conflicts. Moreover, judicial decisions reinforce the law by its visible application, increasing its vitality, clarity, predictability and coherence. By slowly altering the law to ensure it reflects the social values, judicial decisions make the law more dynamic and responsive, and better able to guide social conduct. The judicial function provides the spark of vitality that enlivens law within any society. It does this by blending together two distinct aspects: through dispute resolution it governs, and through governance it resolves disputes.

IV Revisiting the Judicial Function

The unique way in which the two aspects of dispute resolution and social governance are woven together into a coherent single function is the truly distinct nature of the judicial function. On the one hand, the judicial role involves a very particular type of third-party merit-based resolution where the judge (a pre-appointed public officer, distinguished by impartiality, training and professionalism, and operating as part of a permanent judicial institution) decides the case by rationally assessing the dispute's merits by reference to law. On the other hand, each judicial decision is an act of governance, not only backed by the enforcement mechanisms of the state, but impacting the legal norms they apply and administer. The effects of this act of law-making radiates beyond the particular dispute. Critically, though, these two aspects are not separate, but fundamentally entwined.

The judicial function is a true alloy in that it performs a function in a manner unachievable by reference purely to either one of the constituent roles. The essential nature of the judicial function elegantly weaves these two roles together into a single coherent function: each constituent role constrains and limits the other, yet also liberates and empowers it. The judicial development of legal norms operates and arises strictly within the context of dispute resolution.[127] To resolve the dispute, the judge must determine the law according to which the dispute is settled. The inevit-

---

[126] See ibid. 134; Bhagwati (n 37) 38.
[127] Drummond (n 112) 367.

able by-product of this is the creation of law.[128] The public, institutional and formal nature of the judicial decision means that courts, by applying 'the abstract rule of law to concrete cases', in a meaningful sense create 'the legal rule for the case before them'.[129] Of course, the normative impact of a given decision may be minimal or significant, and the extent to which the decision alters the law varies from one legal system to another.[130] Nevertheless, each act of judicial dispute resolution involves an aspect of judicial normative development. Similarly, as each decision promotes social order by providing a peaceful method of settling disputes, the judicial function promotes order by removing the sense of injustice caused by unresolved disputes.[131] To effectively perform these interwoven roles, the judge is required to embrace the virtuous tension between the pursuit of clarity, predictability and order on one hand and responsive and just flexibility and change on the other.

What then, are the possible implications of such an examination of the judicial function in an Australian context?

First, this conceptual approach may help inform specific practical problems encountered in Australian constitutional law arising from its separation of powers jurisprudence. As is well known, the question of whether a power is judicial or non-judicial currently requires 'a notoriously difficult and unpredictable balancing exercise'[132] of a range of characteristics or 'indicia'.[133] The practical implications of the subtleties and sometimes problematic uncertainties of this exercise have most recently arisen in relation to the newly proclaimed constitutional fetters on the operation of state 'super-tribunals', which we now know depends, to some extent, on whether they are 'courts' or otherwise exercising 'judicial power'.[134] With this, and other constitutional applications

---

[128] Barak (n 122) 299: See also William Landes and Richard Posner, 'Adjudication as a Private Good' (1979) 8 *Journal of Legal Studies* 235, 236.
[129] Hersch Lauterpacht, *The Function of Law in the International Community* (Clarendon Press, 1933) 263.
[130] Barak (n 122) 299.
[131] Devlin (n 50) 3.
[132] Rebecca Ananian-Welsh, 'CATS, Courts and The Constitution: The Place of Super-Tribunals in the National Judicial System' (2020) 43 *Melbourne University Law Review* (852).
[133] See (nn 18–24). See Rebecca Welsh, 'A Path to Purposive Formalism: Interpreting Chapter III for Judicial Independence and Impartiality' (2013) 39(1) *Monash Law Review* 66, 74.
[134] See, for instance, *Burns v Corbett* (2018) 92 ALJR 423; *Attorney-General for South Australia v Raschke* (2019) SASCFC 83. See Anna Olijnyk and Stephen McDonald, 'State Tribunals, Judicial Power and the Constitution: Some Practical Responses' (2018) 29 *Public Law Review* 104.

resting on the differentiation between judicial and administrative powers, definitions that are informed by the conceptual framework developed in this chapter may provide a more stable means of analysis. This approach may provide a more holistic touchstone of function that shifts the focus away from the current multifactorial assessment, more directly considering *what* it is courts and tribunals may do, rather than simply *how* they do it.

Second, the approach can provide a normative framework to assess the legitimacy of various curial reforms. One such reform is the development of a doctrine of binding dicta by the Court. In the 2007 decision of *Farah Constructions v Say-Dee Pty Ltd*,[135] the High Court appeared to significantly restrict the legal discretion of lower courts, asserting that lower courts are bound by 'seriously considered dicta' of the High Court.[136] This approach, championed by Heydon J,[137] has been described as effecting a 'profound shift in the rules of judicial engagement',[138] and been criticised for generating ambiguities[139] and stagnating the law.[140] From a judicial function perspective, such a development appears to sanction a form of judicial law-making divorced from dispute resolution – definitionally the new normative statement is unnecessary for the instant dispute. The purported bindingness (as opposed to mere persuasion) formally abandons the functional duality, sundering the exercise of power from the derivative methods and forms of accountability. Another development that this approach could be usefully used to evaluate relates to procedural reforms to judicial practices.[141] For example, the emergence of neo-proceduralism in civil litigation,[142]

---

[135] (2007) 230 CLR 89.
[136] Ibid. 150 [134], 159 [158].
[137] JD Heydon, 'How Far Can Trial Courts and Intermediate Appellate Courts Develop the Law?' (2009) 9 *Oxford University Commonwealth Law Journal* 1.
[138] Keith Mason, 'President Mason's Farewell Speech' (2008) 82 *Australian Law Journal* 768, 769.
[139] Matthew Harding and Ian Malkin, 'The High Court of Australia's Obiter Dicta and Decision-Making in Lower Courts,' (2012) 34 *Sydney Law Review* 239, 252–5.
[140] James Lee, 'Precedent on High: The High Court of Australia and "Seriously Considered Dicta"', *Opinions on High* (Blog Post, 21 August 2013) <http://blogs.unimelb.edu.au/opinionsonhigh/2013/08/21/lee-precedent-on-high>.
[141] See Joe McIntyre, 'A Framework for Civil Justice Reform Pt I: Theory,' (2013) 35(8) *The Law Society Bulletin* 12; Joe McIntyre, 'A Framework for Civil Justice Reform Pt II: Politics and Practice' (2013) 35(9) *The Law Society Bulletin* 18.
[142] See Joe McIntyre and Lorne Neudorf, 'Judicial review reform: avoiding effective review through procedural means?' (2016) 16 *Oxford University Commonwealth Law Journal* 65, 92–5.

exemplified by the High Court's decision in *Aon Risk Services*,[143] tolerates (and even promotes) a determination of disputes on grounds other than their underlying substantive legal merits of the core dispute. The imposition of strict case management principles in the name of systemic efficiency has had the effect of increasing interlocutory proceeding, allowing the summary resolution of disputes on technical grounds in a way that avoids the substantive merits. While efficiency is no doubt a worthy goal, such developments move the judicial resolution away from the third-party merit resolution by reference to law that founds its social legitimacy.

Third, the approach, with its embrace of tensions, uncertainty and evaluative discretion, can inform the ongoing discussion of intra-curial dynamics in the Australian Court. The issue of judicial collegiality was flung to the forefront of juridical conversation in Australia by an explosive campaign waged by Heydon J, as he approached retirement, in a series of speeches provocatively entitled '*Threats to Judicial Independence: The Enemy Within*'.[144] Unsurprisingly, the campaign provoked an immediate string of responses including from sitting and former High Court justices.[145] In the subsequent years, Kiefel CJ has waged a counter-campaign promoting 'collegiality' and collective decision-making;[146] and it has been observed that the Court has increasingly favoured a 'minimalist, largely propositional style of reasons'.[147] The theory of judicial function developed in this chapter speaks to each of these issues: the recognition of the normative governance of role of courts challenges this observed trend, while the evaluation-rich nature of the function recognises (and indeed celebrates) a degree of diversity in decision-making.

While these are, of necessity, but the briefest illustration, and each of these examples would justify substantial analysis, for the purposes of this

---

[143] *Aon Risk Services Ltd v Australian National University* (2009) 239 CLR 175.

[144] Heydon, 'Threats to Judicial Independence: The Enemy Within' (n 24).

[145] These responses are collated and discussed in Joe McIntyre, 'In Defence of Judicial Dissent' (2016) 37 *Adelaide Law Review* 431, 434–7; and Andrew Lynch, 'Collective Decision-Making: The Current Australian Debate' (2015) 21(1) *European Journal of Current Legal Issues* (available online at: http://webjcli.org/index.php/webjcli/article/view/407/518).

[146] Susan Kiefel, 'Judicial Methods in the 21st Century' (Speech, Banco Court, 16 March 2017). See also Sarah Murray's chapter, 'Judicial Collegiality' in this collection.

[147] Margaret J Beazley, 'Judgment Writing in Final and Intermediate Courts of Appeal: "A Dalliance on a Curiosity"' (2015) 27(9) *Judicial Officers Bulletin* 1.

chapter, it is enough to show that we can approach each of these issues from a different direction, one that is founded upon a conceptual understanding of the role of the court. This chapter briefly sets out *one* such conception and invites a broader conversation about the role of the judge, the judiciary and the courts in contemporary Australia.

3

The Chief Justice

Under Relational and Institutional Pressure

GABRIELLE APPLEBY* AND HEATHER ROBERTS**

I Introduction

Commenting on judicial leadership in 2016, then Australian High Court Chief Justice Robert French asked:

> Does [judicial leadership] have some useful meaning which can be applied in some way to how we choose and how we weigh up the work of the persons appointed to head our courts? Or is it really a conceptual desert populated by many single instances of leadership – each a product of the personality of the officeholder, the composition of the court during the term of office and the other contingencies of history including the personal relationships between the Chief Justice and the Attorney-General, the profile of the cases that come before the court and their impact on civil society?[1]

Chief Justice French was undoubtedly correct when he emphasised both the importance of an individual's stamp on the performance of the

---

* The authors would like to thank Trent Ford and Matthew Faltas for their excellent research assistance during the development of this chapter. We would also like to thank Rowena Maguire, James Duffy, Peta Stephenson, Lorne Neudorf, Keith Mason, Andrew Lynch, Chris Maxwell, Sir Anthony Mason, François Kunc, Anna Katzmann, Rosalind Dixon, Joe McIntyre, Rachel Cahill O'Callaghan, Heather Elliott, Tania Sourdin, John Lowndes, Helen Murrell and Michael Coper for comments provided on earlier versions of this chapter.
** Dr Roberts gratefully acknowledges the funding of the Australian Research Council in developing this chapter (DECRA DE180101594).
[1] Robert French, 'The Changing Face of Judicial Leadership: A Western Australian Perspective' (2017) 91 *Australian Law Journal* 322, 322. This speech reflected on the tenure of Chief Justice David Malcolm, for Malcolm's own reflections on the role, see David K Malcolm, 'The Role of the Chief Justice', (2008) 12 *Southern Cross University Law Review* 149.

chief justice's functions[2] and the impact of surrounding circumstances. Further, consistent and recurring pressures on the chief justice flow from the court's relationship with other institutional and non-institutional actors – pressures that can challenge the underlying values of the judicial institution. Only by recognising the importance of the individual response in the context of these relational aspects can we begin to identify the necessary and desirable attributes of chief justices and create a framework through which to evaluate their performance of the role.

Discussion of the relational aspects of the role will tend naturally to be dominated by separation of powers concerns; that is, the judiciary's relationship with the legislative and the executive branches. It is in these relationships, and within the judiciary itself, that many of the most dramatic tensions and pressures have historically arisen. The importance of these particular relationships is seen, for instance, in the *Guidelines for Communications and Relationships between the Judicial Branch of Government and the Legislative and Executive Branches*, adopted by the Council of Chief Justices of Australia and New Zealand, and which emphasises the responsibility of the head of jurisdiction in such exchanges.[3] However, other tensions and pressures arise across a broader set of relationships: with the profession, with the public and media, and with the academy.

We argue that the chief justice's management of these relationships must cohere with the values that underpin the judiciary as an institution. It is the mark of a successful chief justice to protect and promote these values in the face of relational pressures exerted by other actors in all aspects of performance: curial, administrative and extra-curial.

We have adopted a values framework that draws on the work of Richard Devlin and Adam Dodek, who develop a list of six values to

---

[2] In this chapter, the concept of 'chief justice' refers to heads of jurisdiction, that is, the chief justice of the High Court of Australia, the chief justices of the Federal Court and Family Court; the chief judge of Federal Circuit Court; the chief justices of the State and Territory Supreme Courts, chief judges of district/county courts; and chief magistrates. We do not include presidents of courts of appeal, although necessarily involving leadership responsibilities. We focus on the similarities in the chief justice's role across these diverse jurisdictions, rather than detailing the jurisdiction-specific legal frameworks.

[3] 'Guidelines for Communications and Relationships between the Judicial Branch of Government and the Legislative and Executive Branches Adopted by the Council of Chief Justices of Australia and New Zealand on 23 April 2014', *Council of Chief Justices Australia and New Zealand* (PDF, 23 April 2014) <www.ccjanz.gov.au/images/publicfiles/guidelines-judicial-legislative-and-executive-government.pdf>.

'guide and govern a judiciary'.[4] Their list is informed by regulatory theory and is subjected to testing through a comparative analysis of the manifestation and defence of these values in modern judiciaries. Devlin and Dodek's list includes traditional and well-accepted judicial legitimacy values – independence, impartiality, and accountability – and extends to values that are increasingly significant for a modern judiciary – representativeness, transparency and efficiency. Of course, any list of values will be contested, and there may be other values that might be usefully added in the future, for instance, access to justice.

Section II of the chapter lays the foundation for our analysis through an overview of the existing academic and judicial commentary of the role of chief justice. Section III is structured around Devlin and Dodek's six judicial legitimacy values. Drawing on a number of modern examples from across Australia, we examine the pressures brought to bear on these values across the various relational aspects of the chief justice's role and evaluate the effectiveness of responses in protecting and promoting judicial legitimacy values.[5] What we see repeatedly through these examples is that there are often disagreements that arise in relation to whether a particular institutional value has come under threat, as well as whether the chief justice's response, or lack of response, was apt to promote or protect the value in the particular circumstance. We do not shy away from divergent interpretations that are possible in our examples; rather we posit that, given these differences, it is important to create a normative framework through which to analyse and evaluate these disagreements, and thus gain a richer and more nuanced understanding of the conduct of the chief justice's role and those points of disagreement.

II Judicial Leadership and Reflections on the Office of Chief Justice

Leadership of the judicial branch has long been a fascination of scholars, legal professionals and judges themselves. This section provides an outline

---

[4] Richard Devlin and Adam Dodek, 'Regulating Judges: Challenges, Controversies and Choices' in Richard Devlin and Adam Dodek (eds), *Regulating Judges: Beyond Independence and Accountability* (Edward Elgar, 2016) 1, 9.

[5] Our account is limited temporarily to examples drawn from post-WWII on the basis that before this period different norms and expectations governed the performance of the role: Fiona Wheeler, '"Anomalous Occurrences in Unusual Circumstances"? Extra-Judicial Activity by High Court Justices: 1903 to 1945' (2013) 24 *Public Law Review* 125.

of key contributions across three broad fields of scholarship – psychological leadership, narrative-based and self-reflective literature – and places our relational analysis and its values framework within it.

First, within the wealth of multidisciplinary literature on leadership, with its focus on psychology of leadership and an individual's leadership attributes and performance, exists the scholarship on judicial leadership.[6] Many of the leadership typologies developed in this setting focus on the *intellectual* leadership of chief justices and judges within a court, that is, how individuals influence the doctrinal direction of the court.[7] The contribution of these works lies in providing heuristic devices to examine the power exercised by individual judges, particularly in collective decision-making environments. A highly influential work in this field is that of David Danelski, whose analysis of the different types of leadership exercised by chief justices in the United States theorised a dichotomy between task and social leadership.[8] The typology framing of this scholarship directs its attention to an assessment of a judge's performance against the created framework rather than providing a framework through which to examine the chief justice's responsibilities in the promotion and protection of underlying judicial values, which is the focus of this chapter.

Narrative-based literature provides the second category of works examining the role of Australian Chief justices. One subset of this

---

[6] In the Australian context, see Katherine Lindsay and David Tomkins, 'Hail to the Chief! The Roles and Leadership of Australian Chief Justices as Evidenced in Extra-Curial activity 1964–2017' (2017) 40(2) *University of New South Wales Law Journal* 712.

[7] Although some of the more recent scholarship has extended these typologies to the chief justice's leadership beyond the judicial decision-making realm.

[8] David Danelski, 'The Influence of the Chief Justice in the Decisional Process' in Walter F Murphy and C Herman Pritchett (eds), *Courts, Judges and Politics: An Introduction to the Judicial Process* (1961, Random House) 497. This typology has been adopted in a number of other analyses, including, see, e.g., Alan Paterson, *Final Judgment: The Last Law Lords and the Supreme Court* (Hart Publishing, 2013); CL Ostberg, Matthew E Wetstein and Craig R Ducat, 'Leaders, Followers and Outsiders: Task and Social Leadership on the Canadian Supreme Court in the Early 'Nineties' (2004) 36(3) *Polity* 505. New frameworks have also been developed, for instance, Rosemary Hunter and Erika Rackley, 'Judicial Leadership on the UK Supreme Court' (2018) *Legal Studies* 1; Richard Cornes, 'A Point of Stability in the Life of the Nation: The Office of Chief Justice of New Zealand – Supreme Court Judge, Judicial Branch Leader, and Constitutional Guardian and Statesperson' [2013] (4) *New Zealand Law Review* 54; Lindsay and Tomkins (n 6); Patrick McCormick, 'Assessing Leadership on the Supreme Court of Canada: towards a typology of Chief Justice performance' (1993) 4 *Supreme Court Law Review* 409.

category is life-writing about judges: for example, brief vignettes,[9] entries in scholarly encyclopedia[10] intellectual biography,[11] Festschrift and other collections reflecting on the contributions and legacy of retired chief justices,[12] collective biographies of courts or subsets of justices,[13] and monograph-length studies of individual justices.[14] With their differences in length, purpose and audience, such narratives also differ in the extent to which they provide an account of the relational tensions inherent in the chief justices' role and an evaluation of the individual's performance of the role.[15] There are volumes that provide comparative biographical assessments of tenures of chief justices, for instance, John Emerson's *First Among Equals: Chief Justices of South Australia since Federation*,[16] and,

---

[9] See, for instance, Susan Purdon and Aladin Rahemtula (eds), *A Woman's Place: 100 years of Queensland Women Lawyers* (Supreme Court of Queensland Library, 2005).

[10] See, for instance, the entries in the *Australian Dictionary of Biography* (Web Page) <http://adb.anu.edu.au/> and Michael Coper, Tony Blackshield and George Williams (eds), *Oxford Companion to the High Court of Australia* (Oxford University Press, 2011).

[11] See, for instance, Harry Hobbs, Andrew Lynch and George Williams, 'The High Court under Chief Justice Robert French' (2017) 91 *Australian Law Journal* 53 and John Gava 'When Dixon Nodded: Further Studies of Sir Owen Dixon's Contracts Jurisprudence' (2011) 33(2) *Sydney Law Review* 157.

[12] These can vary in their emphasis on biographical, intellectual and institutional contributions of these justices. Contrast, for example, Ian Freckelton and Hugh Selby (eds) *Appealing to the Future: Michael Kirby and His Legacy* (Thomson Reuters, 2009); Cheryl Saunders (ed), *Courts of Final Jurisdiction: The Mason Court in Australia* (Federation Press, 1996); Robin Creyke and Patrick Keyzer (eds), *The Brennan Legacy: Blowing the Winds of Legal Orthodoxy* (Federation Press, 2002). A differing approach is provided in Rosalind Dixon and George Williams (eds), *The High Court, the Constitution and Australian Politics* (Cambridge University Press, 2015), which uses the eras of chief justices to undertake a particular assessment of the court's influence.

[13] See, for example, Graham Fricke, *Judges of the High Court of Australia* (Hutchinson Australia, 1986); Michael White and Aladin Rahemtula, *Queensland Justices on the High Court* (Supreme Court of Queensland Library, 2003).

[14] See, for example, Roger B Joyce, *Samuel Walker Griffith* (University of Queensland Press, 1984); Joan Priest, *Sir Harry Gibbs: Without Fear or Favour* (Scribblers Publishing, 1995); Michael Pelly, *Murray Gleeson: The Smiler* (Federation Press, 2014). There are, of course, other forms of literature dedicated to the lives of individual chief justices. See, for instance, Zelman Cowen, *Sir John Latham and Other Papers* (Oxford University Press, 1965).

[15] A comparison of the biographies of Dixon CJ and Barwick CJ provides an example of these differences. In both biographies the role of the chief justice - beyond crafting judgments - clearly emerges, as does the range of competing personal, relational and institutional forces that influence the performance in, and legacy of, each man's tenure as chief justice. See Philip Ayres, *Owen Dixon* (Melbourne University Press, 2007) and David Marr, *Barwick* (Allen & Unwin, 2nd ed, 2005).

[16] John Emerson, *First Among Equals: Chief Justices of South Australia since Federation* (Federation Press, 2006).

when read collectively, the magisterial *Lives of the Chief Justices*, written by JM Bennett.[17] The narrative work that comes closest to providing a systematic values-based framework for assessing the role of chief justice is the account of Chief Justice Tim Carmody's short tenure in the Queensland Supreme Court.[18] Nonetheless, a critical examination of leadership performance through a values-based institutional framework in works such as these occurs only as a coincident, and not as a systematic articulation and assessment of the role against the values emergent in their studies.

The final set of works relevant to our own is the reflections from serving or retired chief justices themselves.[19] Of particular note for our project is the speech delivered by former South Australian Chief Justice John Doyle, who offers a description and analysis of the role through the lens of internal leadership and provides a set of qualities of leadership that start to draw upon institutional judicial values as they manifest relationally.[20] He lists eight leadership qualities, which include developing a sense of the institution, a collective commitment to justice, and communicating this throughout the court and to the public.[21]

Drawing on the wealth of this foundational work, the balance of this chapter takes an explicitly values-based framework to assess how chief justices across Australia over the last 60 years have used the various dimensions of the office to protect and promote, and sometimes undermine, judicial values.

III Judicial Legitimacy Values and Relational Pressures

This section explores how the office of the chief justice responds to relational pressures that threaten the values that underpin judicial legitimacy. We intentionally eschew management and organisational behavioural

---

[17] See, for instance, the discussion of industry and interpersonal dynamics in JM Bennett, *Sir James Dowling: Second Chief Justice of New South Wales, 1837–1844* (Federation Press, 2001).

[18] Rebecca Ananian-Welsh, Gabrielle Appleby and Andrew Lynch, *The Tim Carmody Affair: Australia's Greatest Judicial Crisis* (NewSouth Publishing, 2016).

[19] Not included in this review are the 'State of the Judicature' speeches delivered by a number of chief justices, as well as chief justice's swearing-in and (where available) retirement speeches. We draw on these as primary sources in the balance of the analysis.

[20] John Doyle, *Learning Leadership Qualities* (Conference Paper, International Organisation for Judicial Training, 27 October 2009).

[21] See also the list of leadership qualities expounded in Marilyn Warren, 'How We Lead' (Speech, 2011 Leadership Victoria Oration, 31 August 2011).

leadership 'values' on the basis that the leadership of a court is distinct, founded on the institutional differences and commitments of the judicial branch. Leadership of a court, we argue, should not be evaluated on its own terms, but rather against a standard derived from that institution's status and role.

We extend our framework of judicial legitimacy values beyond the traditional dichotomy between independence and accountability, accepting that such a dichotomy underestimates the normative complexity of the judicial role and the judicial institution and sets up a false zero-sum trade-off between the two values. Most importantly for our project, the traditional dichotomy provides insufficient analytical tools through which to analyse and understand the judiciary.[22] Devlin and Dodek proffer a set of six values that, we argue, captures the complexity of the institutional values the chief justice is responsible for protecting and promoting: independence, impartiality, accountability, representativeness, transparency and efficiency. In identifying their six values, Devlin and Dodek accept that 'values are contested, deeply contextual, in need of considered calibration, and in a continuous state of flux'.[23] The framework might extend in future, for instance, to include as separate values matters we have currently considered as part of other values, such as access to justice (which we consider in relation to efficiency). A number of contemporary issues that have emerged for the judiciary, such as challenges around maintaining judicial well-being, are not neatly divisible into the judicial value framework we have adopted, but arise for consideration with respect to multiple values.[24]

Devlin and Dodek contend in their work that no one value 'trumps' another.[25] In Australia, however, the values of independence and impartiality in particular have been doctrinally constitutionalised.[26] This, we accept, necessarily imports a degree of hierarchy. Further, individual judges will also prioritise different values, influenced by her own views of the role of the Court in society as well as the broader social, economic and political pressures of their tenure and the position and legitimacy of the court at that particular time. Despite the prioritisation that these

---

[22] Devlin and Dodek (n 4) 1–3.
[23] Ibid. 12.
[24] See further Carly Schrever, Carol Hubert and Tania Sourdin, 'The Psychological Impact of Judicial Work: Australia's First Empirical Research Measuring Judicial Stress and Wellbeing' (2019) 28 *Journal of Judicial Administration* 141.
[25] Devlin and Dodek (n 4) 12.
[26] *R v Kirby; Ex parte Boilermakers' Society of Australia* (1956) 94 CLR 254 and *Kable v Director of Public Prosecutions (NSW)* (1996) 189 CLR 51.

realities bring, in many instances debates about conflict of values can equally be reframed by placing the values not in tension or conflict with each other, but rather as operating concurrently or even in a reinforcing manner.

In the remainder of this part, we explain the nature of each of the values in our framework, before examining the relational dimensions of the chief justice's role that can and does place pressure on each value. Through a necessarily limited number of discrete examples drawn from a range of Australian jurisdictions and periods, we then consider how different chief justices have responded to pressures, and whether such responses could be considered 'successful' protective defences or promotions of the value. We see promotion as distinct from defending existing processes and institutions that protect judicial values, and, rather, active promotion of change to *better* protect those judicial values, whether that change be necessary because of the emergence of a new judicial value (such as transparency or representativeness), or because of changing social and political circumstances (such as the attorney-general's move away from the role of public defender of the courts).

A   Independence

Judicial independence is perhaps the most well known and most frequently claimed institutional judicial value,[27] and so whether a chief justice is able to promote and defend this value could be viewed as a minimum indicator of success within the office. It is often broken down into the idea of personal independence and institutional independence, or decisional and institutional independence, as well as manifesting in the idea of administrative or fiscal independence. Its aim is to ensure objective judgment unimpeded by pressures from state and nonstate actors. In this sense, the value of independence is closely associated and has many resonances with the value of judicial *impartiality*. Impartiality, as Devlin and Dodek explain, refers to 'decision making that is free from personal, social, cultural, economic or institutional bias, and which fairly

---

[27] There are too many references to this value to include in this footnote. For a recent articulation of the value, see Catherine Holmes, 'Preserving the Independence of the Judiciary' (University of Southern Queensland Public Lecture, University of Southern Queensland, 26 May 2016) <https://archive.sclqld.org.au/judgepub/2016/holmes260516.pdf>.

assesses the rights and interests of the parties involved'.[28] In this chapter we consider the two together, as judicial impartiality is a necessary dimension of independent judicial decision-making.

There are many possible transgressions into independence and impartiality, and the history of the Australian judiciary offers illustrations of chief justices acting in ways to protect and promote the value of independence and impartiality, as well as instances in which chief justices have failed, or perceived to have failed, to do so.[29] A prominent example of the latter has been the continuing practice of many chief justices of the State Supreme Courts to accept the office of Lieutenant-Governor. By accepting this role these chief justices have not simply been accepting a position *within* the executive branch, but serving as titular *head* of that branch, which has been increasingly identified as the source of potential bias, real and perceived.[30]

In this section we consider how two different chief justices have responded to government criticism of the judiciary and use those different responses to illustrate the complexity of navigating values in response to independence pressures, particularly when they emerge publicly from government quarters. While in these examples we have focused on the response by the chief justice, we also acknowledge the development of a wider capacity for institutional response developed in Australia particularly through the Judicial Conference of Australia (JCA). The JCA may itself respond when such incidents arise and has also published a set of policies that can guide the conduct of heads of jurisdictions.[31]

In 2017, Chief Justice Marilyn Warren of the Victorian Supreme Court called a special hearing of the court in which three Ministers were required to show cause why they should not be held in contempt over statements made about the Victorian Court's record of sentencing in terrorism trials, including that it was constituted by 'hard-left activist

---

[28] Devlin and Dodek (n 4) 9.

[29] See, for instance, Chief Justice Carmody's purported attempt to protect independence that was viewed by many others as an affront to it: Ananian-Welsh, Appleby and Lynch (n 18).

[30] See also Damien J Cremean, 'State Chief Justices as Lieutenant Governors: Federal Jurisdiction' (2010) 18 *Australian Journal of Administrative Law* 3; Matthew Stubbs, 'The Constitutional Validity of State Chief Justices acting as Governor' (2014) 25 *Public Law Review* 197; Rebecca Ananian-Welsh and George Williams, 'Judges in Vice-Regal Roles' (2015) 43(1) *Federal Law Review* 119.

[31] See further John Lowndes, 'Becoming Stronger and Moving Forward Together: The Role of Judicial Associations in the Modern Era' (2019) 24(1) *Commonwealth Judicial Journal* 6.

judges' (Assistant Minister to the Treasurer Michael Sukkar), that the Court was becoming a forum for 'ideological experiments' (Health Minister Greg Hunt) and that the judges were 'divorced from reality' (Minister for Human Services Alan Tudge).[32] Her Honour explained that such statements breached the principle of separation of powers and reflected a lack of understanding of the importance of the independence of the judiciary, particularly from the political arms of government.[33]

In taking her action, Warren CJ was widely lauded as protecting judicial independence against an unwarranted and dangerous attack. However, retired High Court justice Dyson Heydon argued that the actions represented an overreaction by the Court, one which did more to damage the reputation of the Court because of its failures to respect judicial process values than to promote them.[34] Further, Heydon took aim at what he perceived to be the chief justice's attempt to stymie the ministers' public discussion of the Victorian Court, arguing that suffocation of public criticism of the judiciary undermines other judicial values, those associated with transparency and accountability.[35] The different interpretations of Warren's actions on the institutional values of the Court demonstrates the different weight that individuals, even those steeped in the traditions of the law, will give to institutional values. This in turn underscores the challenges of leadership in this space, particularly as chief justices will often be required to respond in time-pressured scenarios. For some, a swift and decisive public intervention might be seen as the only acceptable response in the circumstances, but these quick responses also bring a danger of unintended institutional consequences.

This complexity might encourage chief justices to be more circumspect about a public response and, instead, favour a private dialogue with the executive branch to try to remedy the public position. Such an approach was taken by Chief Justice Sir Gerard Brennan, two decades earlier, when

---

[32] The incident is chronicled further in Emilios Kyrou, 'The Independent, Low Profile Third Arm of Government' (1 December 2017) *Law Institute Journal* available online at <https://www.liv.asn.au/Staying-Informed/LIJ/LIJ/December-2017/The-independent-low-profile-third-arm-of-governme>.

[33] See further reference to the statements of the Court in *DPP (Cth) v Besim [No 2]* (2017) 52 VR 296, 298 [6] (the Court).

[34] See JD Heydon, 'Does Political Criticism of Judges Damage Judicial Independence?: Judicial Power Project Policy Exchange' (2018) 37(2) *University of Queensland Law Journal* 9.

[35] Ibid. 16–17.

then acting Prime Minister Tim Fischer famously accused the High Court of undue delay in issuing judgment in the *Wik Peoples v Queensland*[36] (*Wik*) decision. In that instance, Brennan CJ wrote privately to Fischer:

> You will appreciate that public confidence in the constitutional institutions of Government is critical to the stability of our society. By a convention which is based in sound practice, judges do not (and certainly should not) publicly attack the members of the political branches of government, and the members of the political branches of government do not (and certainly should not) attack the judges except on substantive motion in the Parliament. This convention does not restrict criticism of Court judgments, but it does restrict criticism of judicial integrity or devotion to judicial duty.[37]

Choosing first to write privately in this way may reflect the observation of Chief Justice French that the leadership responsibility of the Chief is to 'maintain functional communications with the government and to ensure that division and conflict does not grow and become entrenched'.[38] But Chief Justice Brennan's letter did not reduce executive critique of the Court post-*Wik*; Fischer ultimately levelling his infamous comment that 'Capital C' conservatives[39] were needed on the High Court bench. It was in this climate that Brennan CJ, rather than addressing the government's challenges directly in the public arena, pursued a broader and longer-term course of public education. This included a decision to 'make [the High Court's] procedures more understandable and its decisions more easily available',[40] and to allow unprecedented access to filmmaker Darryl Dellora to display the justices 'at work' – in conference, in chambers, and informally discussing their role.[41] Another strategy included proposing the creation of a Public Information Officer role, for the purpose of '[responding] appropriately from time to time to comment and criticism of the Court'.[42] In these ways, Brennan CJ chose

---

[36] (1996) 187 CLR 1.
[37] Letter from Sir Gerard Brennan to Tim Fischer, 3 January 1997, quoted in Enid Campbell and HP Lee, *The Australian Judiciary* (Cambridge University Press, 2001) 57.
[38] French (n 1) 325.
[39] Niki Savva, 'Fischer Seeks a More Conservative Court', *The Age* (Late Edition, Melbourne, 5 March 1997).
[40] *High Court of Australia: Annual Report 1997-98* (Report, 13 November 1998) 6.
[41] *The Highest Court* (Film Art Doco, 1998).
[42] *High Court of Australia: Annual Report 1999-2000* (Report, 12 September 2000) 5.

to promote judicial independence by opening up the court, rather than responding directly to public criticism.

The different approaches evident in the actions of Chief Justices Warren and Brennan – a direct and public response as against a more measured, longer term and less direct response – both have their critics and their defenders. Depending on the larger political context in which the issues arise, one response might be seen as more appropriate, or likely to be effective, than the other. And, of course, one approach does not have to be pursued at the expense of another: Warren CJ was also innovative throughout her tenure in opening up the Victorian Court, particularly with the advent and public-engagement opportunities afforded by technology.

B Accountability

Accountability is now a well-accepted judicial value and can be seen, for instance, as manifesting in long-established rights: the right to appeal, the open court principle, and the judicial obligation to furnish reasons for decisions. One more contemporary form in which the value has arisen is the now well-established system of judicial education,[43] and chief justices across Australia have taken leadership roles in the promotion and support of continuing judicial education programs in areas of substantive law, judge craft, and broader social and cultural context.[44] More recently, the growing imperative for programs and support to ensure judicial well-being intersects with accountability as a value, most controversially where complaints against individual judicial officers have sometimes arisen when health issues have caused failures in the delivery of justice.

Accountability as a judicial value is sometimes, incorrectly, pitted against the value of independence. Devlin and Dodek describe accountability in a way that is complementary to, and supportive of, the coextension of the two values.[45] We would go even further and argue that the accountability of the judiciary has an *independent* virtue in promoting

---

[43] See also Gabrielle Appleby, Suzanne Le Mire, Andrew Lynch and Brian Opeskin, 'Contemporary Challenges Facing the Australian Judiciary: An Empirical Interruption' (2019) 42(2) *Melbourne University Law Review* 299, 333–6.

[44] Reflecting the responsibility of the chief justice in judicial education, in 2006, the National Standard for Professional Development of Australian Judicial Officers was endorsed by the Council of Chief Justices, the Council of Chief Judges and the Council of Chief Magistrates.

[45] Devlin and Dodek (n 4) 9.

confidence in the judiciary amongst a public increasingly expectant of transparency and oversight, particularly in the face of judicial indiscretions.[46] In this section, we explore different levels of chief justices' proactivity in promoting the institutional value of accountability, by reference to their responses to the often publicly controversial issue of complaints against the judiciary and judicial discipline.

The Chief Justice and Judicial Discipline

Judges are expected to comply with high ethical standards, which promote confidence in their independence and impartiality. Robust procedures and institutions to deal with complaints about judicial conduct and determine appropriate disciplinary responses (short of conduct that warrants removal) are associated both with the value of accountability as well as promoting transparency in the judicial branch. There have been concerns expressed that the introduction of more formalised accountability processes, such as independent complaints and disciplinary models, if not carefully designed, could undermine judicial independence. Equally, however, carefully crafted accountability systems could support public regard for the judiciary, and its independence and impartiality. They provide a forum for complaints and alleged transgressions to be dealt with in a transparent and rigorous way.[47]

Under the traditional system of judicial ethics and discipline, the Chief Justice performs a central role. In 1996, the Council of Chief Justices of Australia and New Zealand commissioned the first edition of the Guide to Judicial Conduct, a nonbinding practical guide to navigating ethical dilemmas for the judiciary.[48] Procedures for dealing with alleged judicial misconduct are, generally, that complaints can be made to the head of jurisdiction, who can then investigate and respond, including by speaking to the judge involved and, if necessary, deploy their administrative powers to resolve the issue. In recognition of the shortcomings of the informal system, some jurisdictions have introduced a more formalised commission-led process.[49]

---

[46] See also Gabrielle Appleby and Suzanne Le Mire, 'Judicial Conduct: Crafting a System that Enhances Institutional Integrity' (2014) 38(1) *Melbourne University Law Review* 1.
[47] See further discussion of these debates in Appleby and Le Mire (n 46).
[48] This is now in its third edition (2017): The Council of Chief Justices of Australia and New Zealand, *Guide to Judicial Conduct* (Australasian Institute of Judicial Administration, 3rd ed, 2017).
[49] New South Wales (which established its Judicial Commission of NSW in 1986: *Judicial Officers Act 1986* (NSW)), South Australia (the Judicial Conduct Commissioner

The informality of the traditional process, the limited powers of the chief justice to remedy transgressions, as well as her or his other responsibilities to the court as an institution, have created great difficulties for chief justices wishing to promote accountability of the judicial institution.

The challenge of competing pressures was evident in the unenviable position the status quo created for former Chief Justice Murray Gleeson during and after the attack made by Senator Bill Heffernan under cover of parliamentary privilege on High Court Justice Michael Kirby in 2002.[50] Senator Heffernan wanted an inquiry into Kirby J's alleged misuse of a Commonwealth car to pick up male prostitutes. The allegations sat in the public arena for six days until they were proven to be false. A number of prominent legal associations and individuals publicly defended Kirby J; the High Court, and Gleeson CJ, were silent.

For some, the chief justice was the logical public defender of the judiciary in these circumstances. But this belies the complexity of the institutional and relational pressures that were being brought to bear on Gleeson CJ at that time. He had to contemplate what his role was as chief justice, given the unwillingness of the attorney general to defend against a cross-institutional attack on one of his court's judges. He may have suspected that the allegations were spurious, and they were later proven to be such. He may also have deplored the Senator's misuse of parliamentary process, and the lack of due process afforded to Kirby J. However, at the time, he would also have been aware of the need to maintain public confidence in the reputation of the judiciary, and ensure that Australia's highest court was not seen to be above the law or him to be seen as trying to cover up improper conduct. Indeed, what the entire incident reveals is the complexity of the tensions imposed on a chief justice, and that sometimes it may *not* be appropriate for the chief justice to respond publicly to complaints and criticisms about individual judges, and that doing so can actively undermine key judicial values. The incident also underscores the need for a robust mechanism for receiving,

---

established in 2015: *Judicial Conduct Commissioner Act 2015* (SA)), Victoria (the Judicial Commission of Victoria in 2016: *Judicial Commission of Victoria Act 2016* (Vic)) and the ACT (ACT Judicial Council in 2017 via amendments to the *Judicial Commissions Act 1994* (ACT)). In 2020, the Northern Territory became the most recent jurisdiction to introduce a commission: *Judicial Commission Act 2020* (NT).

[50] For a more detailed explanation, see Campbell and Lee (n 37) and Pelly (n 14).

investigating and resolving complaints against judges, and an independent public spokesperson to defend judges, and the judiciary.

In the area of judicial discipline, individual chief justices have responded differently to their responsibilities under the traditional disciplinary system. In each response we see, however, an overarching expression of concern for how her actions and responsibilities might promote the value of accountability while also addressing any concerns around incursions into judicial independence.

Some chief justices have been more proactive even under the traditional scheme, highlighting what the office *can* do to promote accountability. For instance, former South Australian Chief Justice Len King took a proactive role in assuring practitioners that complaints received against judges 'would be received sympathetically and treated seriously'.[51] He explained this allowed him to promote accountability directly, in relation to individual complaints, but also to keep his 'finger on the pulse' so as to head off more serious problems on the Court.[52]

Others, however, have appeared somewhat reluctant to claim too proactive a role under the system, lest the public be misled as to the extent to which a chief justice can promote accountability under the current framework.[53] In 2014, South Australian Chief Justice Chris Kourakis was confronted with this dilemma. A district court judge had pleaded guilty to driving with excessive blood alcohol just when it had been announced she would be elevated to the Supreme Court.[54] In the face of intense media attention,[55] the chief justice made an unusual move, issuing a public media release the day following the incident. He explained to the public his limited authority as chief justice, that the office 'has no authority to suspend the constitutional operation of

---

[51] John Emerson 'The Office of Chief Justice of South Australia under Len King' (2011) 32 *Adelaide Law Review* 177, 182.

[52] Ibid.

[53] See also Senate Legal and Constitutional Affairs References Committee, Parliament of Australia, *Australia's Judicial System and the Role of Judges* (Report, December 2009) 69 [6.33], quoting letter from Chief Justice Wayne Martin to Jim McGinty, Attorney-General (WA), 10 November 2006, 2.

[54] Sean Fewster, 'Drink-Driving Supreme Court Judge Anne Bampton Apologises, Fined $1300 and Disqualified from Driving for Eight Months', *The Advertiser* (online, 15 January 2014) <www.adelaidenow.com.au/news/south-australia/drinkdriving-supreme-court-judgeannebampton-apologisesfined-1300-and-disqualified-from-driving-for-eight-months/story-fni6uo1m-1226801748176>.

[55] See, for instance, '20 People to Watch', *The Advertiser* (Adelaide, 4 January 2014) 36.

a judicial appointment'.[56] Responding to what he described as 'the reasonable concerns of the public arising out of offending of this kind by a serving judicial officer', the chief justice placed the judge on restricted duties in relation to driving and alcohol-related offences.[57] Chief Justice Kourakis clearly accepted the responsibilities of, and expectations on, the chief justice to promote accountability within the judiciary, but was also at pains to explain to the public the limited powers available to him to do so.

In contrast to this example, in 2018, Chief Justice of the Northern Territory Michael Grant opened the legal year by announcing that it was time to revisit the question of reform of judicial discipline in the Territory. His speech was given following a long-running public controversy over the conduct of a Magistrate in Alice Springs. He announced his support for the creation of a new, independent disciplinary system in the Northern Territory.[58] In this announcement, we see a chief justice actively promoting the value of judicial accountability by proposing reform, at a point in time in which public and media pressure on the judiciary was particularly high. The cross-institutional dynamics of this reform should also be considered: governments have traditionally been wary of the dangers of pursuing judicial reform for fear of being seen as encroaching on judicial independence. By actively calling on the government to act, the chief justice gave 'permission' to the Executive branch to enter the highly contested space of judicial regulation.

C Transparency

Closely associated with the value of accountability is that of transparency, or as Devlin and Dodek explain, 'the commitment to openness and candour'.[59] Annual reporting, and public statements and reporting in other forms, is one way that chief justices have more recently expanded their responsibility to promote transparency. Such reports have frequently been employed as a vehicle through which chief justices express

---

[56] See full press release: Chris Kourakis, (Media Release, Court Administration Authority of South Australia, 15 January 2014) <www.courts.sa.gov.au/ForMedia/Pages/General-Media-Releases.aspx?IsDlg=1&Filter=41>.
[57] Ibid.
[58] See Michael Grant, 'Opening of the Legal Year' (Speech, Parliament House, 1 February 2018) <https://supremecourt.nt.gov.au/__data/assets/pdf_file/0009/727029/address-at-the-opening-of-the-legal-year-function-2018.pdf>.
[59] Devlin and Dodek (n 4) 9.

frustration at their court's inability to control resourcing and funding as well as explain the workload of the court.[60] Reports also outline new initiatives, such as the courts' embrace of technological innovation. chief justices must also respond to the value of transparency when asked by academic researchers whether they may engage in empirical study of the inner workings and attitudes of the judiciary within their court.

The Chief Justice and Technology

The degree to which new technologies should be implemented, or responded to by the courts, has been a recurring question facing the legal profession and the judiciary. [61] Many values may be promoted by technological change, including transparency and efficiency (in which we have included access to justice). Technological developments pose a particular challenge for chief justices for a number of reasons. Unlike developments in judicial education, which would be familiar to judges having come from the well-established requirements of continuing professional development in the law, chief justices may not necessarily understand the opportunities and threats that technology poses for traditional judicial processes, or the possibility of new critique based on big data becoming available about the Court's work. This will mean that chief justices need external experts to assist them, and also may need significant funding to achieve desired reform outcomes.

There are also different views as to how judges should respond to technological developments. While some areas might be relatively uncontroversial, for instance the use of electronic filing and discovery; other areas might prove more controversial, such as the extent to which televising proceedings and use of social media relay commentary to the public. Tempering the use of technology to promote these values are concerns that use of mass media and social media may trivialise court

---

[60] See, for instance, *Supreme Court of Queensland: Annual Report 2016–17* (Report, 31 October 2017) 8 and *High Court of Australia: Annual Report 2014–15* (Report, 12 November 2015) 16.

[61] Courts throughout Australia and the world have adopted a variety of technological approaches to respond to the challenges imposed by COVID-19. At the time of writing it is still too early in the pandemic to assess whether these emergency responses will affect long-term change in court's technology practices. Some of these issues are explored in Joe McIntyre, Anna Olijnyk and Kieran Pender, 'Courts and COVID-19: Challenges and Opportunities in Australia' on AUSPUBLAW (04 May 2020) <https://auspublaw.org/2020/05/courts-and-covid-19-challenges-and-opportunities-in-australia>

proceedings, thereby undermining perceptions of the dignity, status and impartiality of the judiciary.

In Australia, we have seen other responses. For example, rather than presenting the risk of oversimplification as a reason for limiting social media access, in Victoria Warren CJ explained that the risks of social media in 'skewing of information'[62] about court proceedings and judicial procedures informed her decision to change her Court's policies to actively embrace institutional use of social media (as distinct from an individual judge's decision to use social media).[63] This was particularly acute in relation to sentencing matters – a topic over which courts are continually criticised in the media and by politicians. The Court's response was to allow itself, and media organisations, to tweet from court, but interestingly, the public were not. Chief Justice Catherine Holmes of the Queensland Supreme Court has explained that while her Court would engage on social media, she would not be the one doing the tweeting.[64] This is in contrast to the more traditional use of the media: through press releases or conducting interviews, where, at least in more recent times, the chief justice would be the expected voice of the Court.

In the United States, concerns around trivialisation, misinformation through misuse of footage, as well as around disruption to the collegiality of the courtroom dynamic have been so strong as to prevent, to date, the Supreme Court from embracing technology in televising proceedings at all.[65] In Australia there has been significant expansion in the televising of court proceedings; although chief justices have addressed some of the

---

[62] 'Courts Must Use Facebook, Twitter to Counter "Skewing Of information": Chief Justice', The Sydney Morning Herald (online, 1 September 2011) <www.smh.com.au/technology/courts-must-use-facebook-twitter-to-counter-skewing-of-information-chief-justice-20110901-1jmr1.html>.
[63] Which has been addressed, for instance, in the most recent edition of *Guide to Judicial Conduct* (n 48).
[64] Catherine Holmes, 'Presentation of Queen's Counsel; Recognition of Newly-Admitted Barristers and Traditional Exchange of Christmas Greetings' (Speech, Banco Court, 14 December 2016) <https://archive.sclqld.org.au/judgepub/2016/holmes14122016.pdf>. Chief Justice Catherine Holmes of Queensland explained at a ceremonial sitting of her Court that the filming and broadcasting of sentencing remarks in Queensland was similarly motivated by a desire to ensure that more information was available to the public about how sentencing was determined.
[65] For the Supreme Court's most recent explanation of the reasons for the refusal, see Robert Barnes, 'Supreme Court Justices Tell Congress They Are Not Considering Televising Hearings', *Washington Post* (online, 8 March 2019) <www.washingtonpost.com/politics/courts_law/supreme-court-justices-tell-congress-they-are-not-considering-televising-hearings/2019/03/07/5fb28684-4116-11e9-9361-301ffb5bd5e6_story.html?noredirect=on>.

concerns that this raises in myriad ways. In Victoria, the Supreme Court now broadcasts 'Sentencing Webcasts' on its website, providing the courts with a proactive channel to the public for one of its most controversial areas of decision-making. The chief justice's ultimate responsibility for the fraught decision of whether to televise proceedings is reinforced by the fact that the chief justice of the Supreme Court requires her officer to be consulted before a presiding judge permits the filming or released of video footage in her courtroom. Other chief justices have pursued different responses to the challenges that irresponsible media coverage can create. The chief justice of the County Court of Victoria, Peter Kidd, was even more proactive than the Supreme Court, working with Channel Nine's A Current Affair' in 2018 'to produce a feature that demystifies the work of the Court, with interviews by the chief justice and senior puisne justice and dispels some common misconceptions about sentencing and judges'.[66] In addition to the national television broadcast of the feature program, the Court website also hosts a video of the program.[67]

In each of these examples, we see chief justices alive to the challenges of a world in which media is more diverse and accessible through online fora, and commentary on the work of the judiciary may thus be less informed unless the Court is more actively engaged across these same platforms. These responses have often themselves required the judiciary to harness new technology and resulted in a judiciary driven move towards greater transparency and not less. This has not been without its own challenges to other institutional judicial values and requires chief justices to navigate innovative paths within their jurisdiction. No doubt, as the judiciary becomes more familiar with the new technology and media, the judicial responses will start to coalesce, just as we have seen in other now more established areas of reform.

D Efficiency

Devlin and Dodek define this value as 'the aspiration that social and personal investments in the judiciary and the judicial process are cost-effective'.[68] Efficiency promotes public confidence, in the expectation

---

[66] 'A Current Affairs Goes Inside the County Court', *County Court Victoria* (Web Page, 3 October 2018) <www.countycourt.vic.gov.au/news-and-media/news-listing/2018-10-03-current-affair-goes-inside-county-court>.
[67] Ibid.
[68] Devlin and Dodek (n 4) 9.

that public moneys will be managed in a way that ensures greatest utilisation of a scarce resource. In this regard, this value is tied to accountability, for a significant aspect of Court reporting an explanation and defence of how the Court manages its allocated funding. Beyond efficient money-management, however, chief justices manage efficiency pressures in a number of ways. This might be, for instance, in the initiation of procedural changes and reforms to the Court to improve the efficiencies of trial. It has also formed part of the contemporary debate occurring in the High Court of Australia around the institutional benefits of joint judgment writing.[69] In this part, we explore the chief justice's responsibility for her court's timely delivery of judgments.

The Chief Justice and the Delivery of Judgments

The timely delivery of judgments has been identified as a key dimension of access to justice. This is now recognised, for instance, by the Productivity Commission's annual reporting on government service delivery, which includes various statistics on the finalisation and disposal of cases.[70] Individual courts have published standards against which they tell litigants they can expect judgments to be delivered.[71]

Delay in delivery of judgments has been the cause of complaints against judges and excoriating media reporting. Generally, chief justices have responded by removing judges from sitting duties to permit them time to complete outstanding judgments. This response has received mixed reactions, with the media unsympathetic to giving 'time off' to judges and with other judges, including at times the appointment of temporary judges, having to step in to shoulder a proportionally increased caseload.[72]

---

[69] See particularly the invocation of efficiency by Kiefel CJ in, for instance, Susan Kiefel, 'Judicial Methods in the 21st Century' (Speech, Banco Court, 16 March 2017) 8.

[70] See, for instance, *Report on Government Services 2018: Justice* (Report, 2018) pt C, ch 7 <www.pc.gov.au/research/ongoing/report-on-government-services/2018/justice/courts/rogs-2018-partc-chapter7.pdf>.

[71] Many courts have established these standards, for example, in the Western Australian Supreme Court it is 6 months: 'Court of Appeal Hearings', *Supreme Court of Western Australia: Court of Appeal* (PDF, 19 October 2017) <www.supremecourt.wa.gov.au/_files/Court%20of%20Appeal%20Hearings.pdf>.

[72] See, for instance, reporting on a judge's delays, and the judge's removal from court work, in: Jenna Clarke, 'Refshauge Gets Break to Clear Case Backlog', *The Canberra Times* (online, 04 February 2013) <www.canberratimes.com.au/national/act/refshauge-gets-break-to-clear-case-backlog-20130203-2dsxm.html>.

Other chief justices have implemented more innovative and tailored responses, actively promoting the value of efficiency through a range of avenues, as well as emphasising the connection between efficiency and supporting judicial wellbeing. Such responses also demonstrate the connection of the responsibilities of chief justice with those faced by others with administrative leadership responsibilities in a variety of workplaces.[73] For instance, when he was the chief justice of New South Wales, Murray Gleeson tried a variety of measures to support Justice Vince Bruce, against whom a number of complaints had been made pertaining to his delayed judgment delivery. In 1997, Gleeson CJ had indicated publicly that judgments in his court should be delivered within six months, while, at the same time, Bruce had delays extending across years. As chief justice, Gleeson deployed a number of soft tactics to support the judge: talking and supporting him in relation to his depression, offering research assistance and even personal support to talk over problems, and providing him with guidance as to how to best use counsel to assist in final judgment writing.[74] Together, they prepared a timetable for the delivery of the judgments, with Gleeson CJ providing Bruce with a reduced case load during this period to assist him achieve it.

In addition to providing individual support to judges, a chief justice may also see her role as defending judges against unfair media criticism and public expectations around delivery of judgments. While efficiency might be a modern judicial value, it is tempered against other values, including judicial independence and the quality of justice. In September 2018, *The Australian* reported delays in the Family and Federal Circuit Courts,[75] and then published a speech by retired High Court of Australia judge, Dyson Heydon, in which he referred to the damage caused by delay, and that timely delivery of judgments was a judicial duty.[76] Later, in October, the *Australian Financial Review* published its own ranking of individual judicial productivity in the Federal Court of Australia by

---

[73] Andrew Lynch and Alysia Blackham, 'Reforming Responses to the Challenges of Judicial Incapacity' (2020) 48 *Federal Law Review* (214).
[74] Pelly (n 14) 182.
[75] Nicola Berkovic, 'Family Court Delay Puts New Life on Hold', *The Weekend Australian* (online, 8 September 2018) <www.theaustralian.com.au/business/legal-affairs/family-court-delay-puts-new-life-on-hold/news-story/690f5473ece80f99d9ff0b639de61d8b>.
[76] Dyson Heydon, 'Judgment Times: Courts in the Crosshairs', *The Australian* (online, 29 September 2018) <www.theaustralian.com.au/news/inquirer/judgment-times-courts-in-the-crosshairs/news-story/b46a19cc3941f5c004afe619772c1cbf>.

reference to how quickly they have delivered judgment.[77] Chief Justice of the Federal Court James Allsop formally responded to the article, referring to the data relied upon as flawed, and the analysis as 'simplistic' and 'unfair' to the Court and the individual judges: 'They are of no utility in providing an insight into the institution's work or services provided by a group of judges whom I know to be dedicated and extremely hard working'.[78] He lashed back at the press, defending judicial independence and specious attempts at transparency, saying the list 'appears calculated simply to embarrass individual judges'.[79]

In a later speech, Allsop CJ went further, continuing to defend the judicial institution he leads against the criticisms. He explained that such figures, if they were to be accepted, rather than give rise to criticism should rather give rise to a series of questions targeted at understanding why it happened. He went on: 'It may have been for reasons of work allocation and workload, time allocation, illness or the pressure of other work. ... The cause may be seen as my fault as head of jurisdiction'.[80] So we see revealed in his response an explanation of a dual responsibility for a chief justice in relation to efficiency: the responsibility to support individual judges to ensure the efficient achievement of justice, while simultaneously defending them against unfair criticism.

As part of this wider defence, Allsop CJ problematises a focus on 'efficiency', particularly if it is measured only through quantitative production-based metrics. Rather, Allsop CJ seeks what he prefers to refer to as 'accountability' (a more traditional judicial value).[81] He offers an explanation of the commitments and responsibilities of a judge, to allow for a more-informed, human-focused evaluation of the executive of the judicial role, and accountability for the public spending by Parliament and the effective and efficient operation of the courts. A similar response is seen in the 2019 Opening Law Term Address of Chief Justice of the New South Wales Supreme Court TF Bathurst, who argues that while quantitative analysis may have a place, in relation to the

---

[77] Aaron Patrick, 'In the Federal Court, Speed of Justice Depends on the Judge', *The Australian Financial Review* (online, 26 October 2018) <www.afr.com/business/legal/in-the-federal-court-speed-of-justice-depends-on-the-judge-20181014-h16mk9>.

[78] 'Statement by Chief Justice Allsop', *Federal Court of Australia* (Web Page, 29 October 2018) <www.fedcourt.gov.au/news-and-events/29-october-2018>.

[79] Ibid.

[80] James Allsop, 'Courts as (Living) Institutions and Workplaces' (2019) 93 *Australian Law Journal* 375, 376.

[81] Ibid.

judiciary, 'what accountability, or a deficit of accountability requires is a far more nuanced approach'.[82] He highlights that quantitative measures of efficiency not only miss many important qualitative explanatory factors, but they provide too great a focus on one value, overlooking the other important values that the judge and court must protect and promote, including independent, fair and impartial judicial process.[83]

These examples demonstrate that a chief justice's responsibility for delivering an efficient judicial institution has a number of facets: as the head of jurisdiction, they must be alive to the need (and expectation) for the courts to deliver justice efficiently for those involved; they must do so in a way that is perceived as fair, while also supporting individual judges within that system to manage with the complexity and demands of judicial office; finally, they have a responsibility to explain these many dimensions, complexities and intersections of these facets of responsibility to the public. All this must be done while also ensuring that the public are aware of the other values at stake including general judicial accountability and judicial independence, and prevent misinformed, one-eyed focus on a single, deceptively simple-to-measure, metric.

E   Representativeness

Devlin and Dodek's framework recognises that within the six core institutional values of the judiciary, representativeness is the most recent addition.[84] They define representativeness as the principle that 'the composition of the judiciary is broadly inclusive of the diversity of the larger population, particularly on the variables of gender, race, class and disability'.[85] In part the contested nature of this value lies in the fact that sharp differences of opinion exist regarding what constitutes a judiciary that is 'broadly inclusive' of a diverse population. The extent to which the judicial appointment process can, or should, be modified to achieve that objective is also fiercely contested.[86] These differences are in turn

---

[82] TF Bathurst, 'Who Judges the Judges, and How Should They be Judged?' (Speech, 2019 Opening of Law Term Address, 30 January 2019) 3 <www.supremecourt.justice.nsw.gov.au/Documents/Publications/Speeches/2019%20Speeches/Chief%20Justice/Bathurst_20190130.pdf>.
[83] Ibid 17–18, 21.
[84] Devlin and Dodek (n 4) 15.
[85] Ibid.
[86] See Graham Gee and Erika Rackley (eds), *Debating Judicial Appointments in an Age of Diversity* (Routledge, 2017).

influenced by varied perspectives regarding *why* representativeness matters.[87] This may include different assessments of whether, and to what extent, diversity enriches decision-making by ensuring that the backgrounds, experiences and values of those exercising judicial power are diversified; or as playing a more amorphous role in maintaining public confidence in the judiciary; and/or as demonstrating equality of access to positions of public power.[88]

In light of these complexities, evaluating a chief justice's success in explaining, promoting and defending the representativeness of the judiciary during her tenure will also, inevitably, be highly contested. This is so because each chief justice will place different weight on the value; there will be a variety of interpretations as to how representativeness intersects with other institutional values (in particular independence and the concept of "merit"); and there will be disagreement as to how best to promote representativeness. Finally, it must be recognised that an individual chief justice operates within a broader environment and must be sensitive to how the political actors of the time are framing representativeness, in the judiciary and wider social contexts. We explore these tensions in this section through the chief justice's role in advising on judicial appointments.

The Chief Justice and Judicial Appointments

Appointments to the bench in Australia remain within the 'gift of the Executive'. At various stages a number of jurisdictions have experimented with judicial appointment committees, which usually include a current or former head of jurisdiction, while some jurisdictions have had formal requirements that attorneys general consult with key stakeholders about future appointments, which may include chief justices.[89] However, the content of such discussions generally remains a closely guarded secret. Glimpses of the process, and chief justices' attitudes and advice, may at times be gleaned from narrative accounts of a chief justice's tenure, but these remain fragmentary at best.

---

[87] Rosemary Hunter, 'More than Just a Different Face? Judicial Diversity and Decision-Making' (2015) 68 *Current Legal Problems* 119, 123.
[88] See Brian Opeskin's chapter, 'Dismantling the Diversity Deficit: Towards a More Inclusive Australian Judiciary', in this collection.
[89] See Marilyn Warren, "'Appointment Process of a New Judge'" (VSC) [2010] VicJSchol 53.

In these circumstances, extra-judicial speeches provide a more readily available source of insight into chief justices' attitudes towards the value of representativeness. Within the vast literature produced by chief justices extra-judicially, beyond *what* is said by a chief justice, the timing, the intended audience, the choice of venue, as well as the repetition of the theme across multiple speeches are significant indicators of the chief justices' attitudes towards the value.

The 'State of the Judicature' addresses presented by Brennan CJ in 1997 and those of Gleeson CJ between 1999 and 2007 provide illustrative, contrasting examples. The 'State of the Judicature' address was inaugurated by Barwick CJ in 1977 and has a long and prominent history.[90] During his tenure as chief justice, Gleeson delivered five 'State of the Judicature' addresses. At none of these occasions did he speak to gender or cultural representativeness, although he did note in his final speech the value of career diversity on the bench.[91] His Honour offered current statistics on the size of the judiciary, but none on its diversity, despite such statistics being readily available and present in earlier State of the Judicature addresses.

Through this silence, representativeness was neither identified nor defended by Gleeson CJ as an institutional value, let alone couched as one that senior judges might have a responsibility to promote. Through silence Gleeson CJ also ignored, at least explicitly, the perception of a tension between representativeness and more traditional values. But silence is not neutral. Through silence we can draw an inference of a prioritisation of values. Gleeson was a strong advocate for a more traditional conception of the judicial role: the judge as a defender of the rule of law through legalistic application of the law.[92] The performance of the judge's role in this way has been identified by feminist scholars as presenting merit and technical legal competency as mitigating against the need for representativeness.[93] Chief Justice Gleeson's position was consistent with the political zeitgeist: John Howard as then Prime Minister had repeatedly rejected the need for proactive measures to increase representation in the political realm, repeatedly emphasised the need to prioritise merit in appointments,

[90] See reflections on the nature of the speech in Brian Opeskin, 'The State of the Judicature: A Statistical Profile of Australian Courts and Judges' (2013) 35 *Sydney Law Review* 489.
[91] In particular his emphasis was on the appointment of judges from the ranks of solicitors as well as the traditional pool of the Bar.
[92] Murray Gleeson, 'The Rule of Law and the Constitution', *The Boyer Lectures* (ABC Radio National, 19 November 2000).
[93] Erika Rackley, *Judging and the Judiciary: From Difference to Diversity* (Routledge, 2013).

and returned the High Court to an all-male bench upon the retirement of Justice Mary Gaudron in 2003. In the absence of leadership by either the political branch or the chief justice of Australia at that time, it is noteworthy that a puisne judge of the High Court, Michael McHugh, stepped in to defend the value of representativeness and impress upon senior legal professionals their obligation to promote it.[94]

In contrast, a decade earlier in 1997, Brennan CJ delivered a State of the Judicature highlighting and defending representativeness as a legitimate institutional value. On that occasion he went further and identified as the salient issue how to correct under representation of minority groups in the legal profession. Brennan's remarks were made at a particularly acute moment in executive-judicial relations, with various threats to judicial independence emerging. Despite this, and the need for the chief justice to respond to protect the institutional reputation of the judiciary, Brennan CJ still spoke on representativeness. We can take from this that he did not see representativeness as necessarily existing in tension with independence. Included in his remarks was the following:

> Suggestions are sometimes made that the judiciary is not properly representative. In some respects, that is true. There are too few women judges and too few from what might be termed an 'ethnic' background. That under-representation reflects the under-representation of women and minorities among our leading advocates. The real question is how to remove the obstacles and attitudes that restrain the under-represented groups from advancing to the ranks of the leading advocates and thence to judicial appointment. Particular and valuable insights are contributed by competent judges drawn from groups that are now under-represented.[95]

While identifying the need for active steps, these remarks stop short of those made by other chief justices, such as Warren, who have framed the remedying of gender inequity in the profession as a positive obligation on the part of its senior members, whether through 'cross-generational promotion' of women, or as a 'duty to gender' that women lawyers owe when considering whether to accept judicial appointment.[96]

---

[94] Michael McHugh, 'Women Justices for the High Court' (Speech, Western Australian Law Society, 27 October 2004).
[95] Gerard Brennan 'State of the Judicature' (1998) 72 *Australian Law Journal* 33, 39.
[96] Pamela Tate, 'Speech for the Honourable Justice Marilyn Warren AC Chief Justice of Victoria' (Speech, Farewell Breakfast hosted by the Women Barristers' Association and Victorian Women Lawyers, 14 September 2017) 1.

In his remarks, Brennan CJ also drew out more explicitly the intersection between a value of representativeness and the idea that legal excellence or merit is the essential touchstone of judicial appointment. He observed:

> Other things being equal, it would strengthen the judiciary to have an increase in the proportion of women judges and judges drawn from minority groups. Yet it would be an erroneous policy, demeaning of an appointee's dignity, to appoint a judge on grounds other than merit. The judiciary cannot be appointed to represent a class or interest; it is appointed to find the facts accurately, to apply the law impartially and to exercise judicial discretions reasonably, irrespective of the class or interest to which any litigant belongs.[97]

Given feminist scholars have long questioned the portrayal of merit as a neutral identifier of judicial appointability,[98] the inclusion of this statement might appear to detract from the enthusiasm of Brennan CJ's promotion of representativeness. However, it is unsurprising that he addresses this relationship directly, given the wider political context in which the remarks are made. When read in their entirety, his Honour's remarks are better understood as suggesting that proactive steps must be taken to redress the long-term disadvantage presented by systemic discrimination to ensure merit appointments are properly representative, and that a more complex relationship exists between the values.

IV Conclusion

The importance and peculiarities of the role of the chief justice demands a study and critique beyond isolated historical instances of individual's performance as Chief, or an analysis of the functions and duties of the role. Based on the institutional values proposed by Devlin and Dodek, our chapter has presented a normative framework as an evaluative tool of individual's performance of the role of chief justice, in her curial and extra-curial activities and obligations. The examples we have drawn upon through the chapter demonstrate a range of responses by chief justices to relational pressures, and how these have been navigated in ways which, with varying success, have promoted, protected and defended judicial institutional values. Although many of these values have been envisaged as

---

[97] Brennan (n 95) 39.
[98] See Rackley (n 93).

diametrically opposed, these examples also demonstrate that interpretative choices are available to chief justices in how they conceptualise, articulate and promote the relationship between the values: as either in tension, complementary, or reinforcing. An individual's capacity to successfully engage with all six institutional values, the traditional and the contemporary, might also usefully guide selection and appointment of future chief justices.

Our analysis might give rise to contemplation of the utility of appointing an independent officer to engage in at least some of the chief justice's responsibilities in defending and promoting judicial institutional values, particularly with respect to the interface with the government, the public and in new forms of media. But, while to some extent an independent officer might be able to provide a source of defence and promotion of institutional values that is separate from the judiciary so that concerns around incursions, or perceived incursions, into judicial independence and impartiality do not emerge, we believe that it risks institutional ineffectiveness. Even in those jurisdictions where press and public engagement officers have been appointed, it is the intervention by the chief justice that will often shift, and even end, uninformed public or political debate. The chief justice, by virtue of the reputation and status of the office and her positioning in relationships with government and with the public by virtue of the office, is uniquely placed to protect and promote judicial institutional values in a way that we do not believe can be replicated in an independent officer.

Postscript

In 2019, six former associates approached the chief justice of the High Court of Australia, Susan Kiefel, with complaints of sexual harassment against former High Court judge Dyson Heydon. How Chief Justice Kiefel responded to these complaints provides us with an opportunity to review the utility of our normative framework.

Taking seriously her responsibilities for accountability within the Court, Chief Justice Kiefel worked with the Court's Principal Registrar, Philippa Lynch, to establish an independent inquiry to investigate the complaints. That inquiry found the complaints to be established, and the chief justice then issued a public statement which gave a rare insight into curial investigations and response. The chief justice's statement explained that the Court's response had been both to the individuals involved, to whom she as chief justice had spoken individually and apologised, and to implement wider institutional responses directed at creating better workplace protections and support for associates during their time of employment on the Court.[99]

Chief Justice Kiefel later further explained that she was continuing to work on improving the Court's processes. This response came following a letter written to her by more than 500 women working in the law in July 2020 commending her response, and informing her of a request made to the Attorney-General to review the frameworks for disciplining and appointing judges.[100] In addition, she stated that she would lead a conversation with the Council of Chief Justices of Australia and New Zealand regarding further actions that might be taken by courts across these jurisdictions. Her continued work to address sexual harassment in the courts is an important dimension of making the legal profession a safer and more supportive workplace for women. Sexual harassment remains a challenge that confronts women across all stages of their career, and can often cause talented, committed women to leave the law, undermining the representativeness of the profession.

Insight into how Chief Justice Kiefel prioritised and navigated judicial institutional values in her response is best revealed by contrasting her actions with those of other chief justices.

For example, one of the associates involved alleged that a former justice had approached then Chief Justice Murray Gleeson regarding at least one instance of harassment by Mr Heydon. It is unknown whether Gleeson took any steps in relation to the complaints during his time as chief justice.[101] If this allegation is true, it reveals a lack of transparency in the court's accountability processes, and may also suggest major inadequacies in the nature of the response by the former chief justice given the conduct alleged.

---

[99] Statement of the Honourable Chief Justice Kiefel AC, 22 June 2020, available at <https://cdn.hcourt.gov.au/assets/news/Statement%20by%20Chief%20Justice%20Susan%20Kiefel%20AC.pdf>.

[100] Letter available at 'Deep cultural shifts required: open letter from 500 legal women calls for reform of way judges are appointed and disciplined' *The Conversation*, 6 July 2020 <https://theconversation.com/deep-cultural-shifts-required-open-letter-from-500-legal-women-calls-for-reform-of-way-judges-are-appointed-and-disciplined-142042> and the authors are both signatories to that letter.

[101] Kate McClymont and Jacqueline Maley, 'Two High Court Justices "knew of complaints against Dyson Heydon"' *Sydney Morning Herald*, 25 June 2020, <www.smh.com.au/national/two-high-court-judges-knew-of-complaints-against-dyson-heydon-20200624-p555pd.html>.

Chief Justice Kiefel's response has been commended for the personalised understanding she has shown to the complainants, as well as for her transparent response that addresses concerns about a judicial workplace culture that is unsafe for women. While these issues were acutely revealed by the conduct in question, the chief justice has not transposed them a broader call for institutional reform directed at misconduct by judges. This can be contrasted with the example we have already canvassed in the chapter: the response of the Northern Territory Chief Justice Michael Grant, in 2018, to repeated racist behaviour in one of the Territory's lower courts. As Chief Justice Grant's actions in the Northern Territory reveal, there is also an opportunity for Chief Justice Kiefel to work with the Attorney-General to further promote the values of transparency and accountability beyond the specific sphere of sexual harassment in the judicial workplace.

PART II

Debates and Challenges to the Judicial Role

4

Dismantling the Diversity Deficit

Towards a More Inclusive Australian Judiciary

BRIAN OPESKIN*

I Introduction

For much of its history, the Australian judiciary has been highly homogenous – comprising largely white, middle-aged, Christian males from privileged socio-economic backgrounds, following similar career trajectories. This is not what contemporary Australia looks like. As the beneficiary of 70 years of post-war immigration, Australia has received more than 7.5 million migrants,[1] making society increasingly diverse in ethnicity, language, and religion. Nor is the population largely male, as it was in the early years of European settlement: in 2018 there were 200,000 more females than males across the nation.[2]

The gap between the composition of the judiciary and that of the general population has been called the 'diversity deficit',[3] and there have been mounting calls to redress it. Some inroads have been made, especially in relation to gender, and yet overall the diversity deficit appears resistant to swift dismantling. For example, a study of the Australian legal profession has suggested that, while the number of Asian Australians coming through law schools has been increasing for some time, this has not been reflected in the senior echelons of the legal profession and the

---

* I wish to thank Ellen O'Brien for research assistance and Thalia Anthony, Beth Goldblatt, Rosemary Hunter, Rebecca Kippen, Helen Menard, Heather Roberts, Cheryl Saunders and the present editors for their insightful comments on a draft.
[1] Janet Phillips and Joanne Simon Davies, 'Migration to Australia: A Quick Guide to the Statistics' (Research Paper Series 2016–17, Parliament of Australia Library, 18 January 2017) 1.
[2] Australian Bureau of Statistics, *Australian Demographic Statistics, Dec 2018* (Catalogue No 3101.0, 20 June 2019).
[3] See, for instance, JUSTICE, *Increasing Judicial Diversity* (Report, April 2017).

judiciary.[4] In a 2015 snapshot, it found that Asian Australians account for 9.6% of the population but only 3.1% of law firm partners, 1.6% of barristers, and 0.8% of the judiciary. This raises the question of whether the profession has a 'bamboo ceiling'.[5]

Unlike some liberal democracies, Australia makes no constitutional or legislative provision for judicial diversity in any form.[6] Apart from minimal statutory qualifications for office, the time-honoured traditions of English constitutional practice continue to apply to judicial appointments, despite their abandonment in that country. This leaves 'virtually unfettered executive discretion' to the government of the day as to who is chosen and what characteristics they possess.[7] This discretion can be – and has been – both a blessing and a curse for diversity.[8] An emboldened government might take inclusion to heart in making appointments that stray from the homochromatic practices of the past; or, in the absence of appetite or pressure for reform, atavistic habits might hold sway. Current legal structures therefore embody a latent capacity for change, even if it is imperfectly realised.

This chapter contributes to the social project of promoting a more inclusive Australian judiciary by asking four questions about the diversity of judicial officers:

1. *Why does judicial diversity matter?* Section II examines the four most persuasive justifications for diversity, and two common critiques.
2. *What characteristics are important for a diverse judiciary?* Given the array of characteristics that distinguish one individual from another, section III investigates which we should focus on for the purpose of programmatic action.
3. *How do we measure the diversity deficit?* This requires data on two matters, which are addressed in section IV: the composition of the population and the composition of the judiciary. The former is readily

---

[4] Asian Australian Lawyers Association, *The Australian Legal Profession: A Snapshot of Asian Australian Diversity in 2015* (Report, 2015).
[5] Ibid. 4.
[6] Compare Canada: *Supreme Court Act*, RSC 1985, c S-26 s 6; South Africa: *Constitution of the Republic of South Africa Act 1996* (South Africa) s 174(2); and the United Kingdom: *Constitutional Reform Act 2005* (UK) s 27(8).
[7] Ronald Sackville, 'The Judicial Appointments Process in Australia: Towards Independence and Accountability' (2007) 16 *Journal of Judicial Administration* 125, 137.
[8] Andrew Lynch, 'Diversity without a Judicial Appointments Commission' in Graham Gee and Erika Rackley (eds), *Debating Judicial Appointments in an Age of Diversity* (Routledge, 2018) 101, 104.

available from data collected in the national census, but the latter faces a substantial hurdle because there are no comprehensive public statistics on judicial diversity in Australia, other than for gender. Section V informs this question by reporting on a new dataset, namely, customised data summarising the responses of judges and magistrates to the diversity questions in Australia's periodic national census.

4. *What action is needed to redress the diversity deficit?* This is taken up in section VI. One step is to improve the career pipeline so that underrepresented groups are present in greater numbers in the talent pools from which judicial officers are selected. Another step is to improve selection processes so that historically disadvantaged groups are encouraged to consider a judicial career, and more likely to achieve one if they do. But diversity gains made through a benign appointments process can be quickly lost through later attrition, and hence a strategy is needed to create a judicial environment in which a newly diverse judicial population is willing to render substantial service. Additionally, judicial education should be utilised to give *all* judges a more sensitive understanding of diversity issues affecting matters they adjudicate, thus making them better judges regardless of their own diversity characteristics.[9]

The issues canvassed here have exercised the minds of thoughtful writers over many years, especially in relation to race and gender. This chapter synthesises key questions in those debates, but its special contribution is to add insights from demography to inform appropriate reforms. Demography can assist in identifying key diversity characteristics, and in quantifying diversity deficits by providing reliable data sources and the tools for analysing them.

II Justifying Judicial Diversity

This section considers the main justifications for judicial diversity, drawing on arguments from equality, quality, utility, and legitimacy. The conceptual bases of the justifications differ, and this has implications for reform, but in combination they provide compelling grounds for action to remedy diversity deficits in the judiciary.

---

[9] Erika Rackley, *Women, Judging and the Judiciary: From Difference to Diversity* (Routledge, 2013) 185–87.

The first rationale for judicial diversity – *the argument from equality* – is a rights-based argument which posits that persons eligible for appointment as judicial officers are entitled to equal opportunity, or at least freedom from discrimination, regardless of attributes such as race, sex, or creed. These rights extend not only to appointment (a frequently discussed equality domain) but also to working conditions, promotion, training, education, discipline, and removal. Through this lens, judicial diversity is not a characteristic of individuals, nor an objective of the judicial system, but an outcome that flows from adherence to the principle of equality, applied one appointment at a time.[10]

The argument from equality is a moral argument, not a legal one. The suite of anti-discrimination laws that have been enacted in Australia since the mid-1970s prohibits discrimination in 'employment',[11] but despite the breadth of this term and the fact that anti-discrimination laws bind the Crown,[12] judicial appointments lie outside their purview. Judges and magistrates are not employees; they are holders of statutory office, and the executive is not legally restrained by anti-discrimination laws in appointing them. Moreover, in some respects, statutes expressly differentiate judicial officers from other workers by imposing mandatory retirement ages that do not apply in any other industry sector bar one.[13] Despite these legislative circumstances, the moral argument for equality in the treatment of judicial officers is compelling in light of the body of international law that promotes 'respect for human rights and for fundamental freedoms for all without distinction as to race, sex, language, or religion'.[14]

A second rationale for judicial diversity – *the argument from quality* – is that it will improve judicial decision-making by avoiding the narrowness of experience and knowledge implicit in a collection of homogeneous, even if excellent, judges.[15] Summed up by High Court Justice

---

[10] Noah Feldman, 'Justifying Diversity', *New York Review of Books* (2018) 65(19) 27, 27–28.
[11] For a history, see Beth Gaze and Belinda Smith, *Equality and Discrimination Law in Australia: An Introduction* (Cambridge University Press, 2017) 29–46.
[12] *Anti-Discrimination Act 1977* (NSW) ss 4, 5 and cognate provisions in other jurisdictions.
[13] Australian Law Reform Commission, 'Access All Ages: Older Workers and Commonwealth Laws (Report No 120)' (ALRC, 2013) 98–103. The other exception is the Australian Defence Force.
[14] *Charter of the United Nations* art 1(3).
[15] JUSTICE (n 3) [2.6].

Michael Kirby with respect to gender on the Bench, 'women are not just men who wear skirts', they have different life experience and sometimes a different way of looking at problems.[16]

In the voluminous, and often controversial, literature on this question, many conceptual explanations have been proffered for the transformative potential of having women on the Bench.[17] As Boyd explains it,[18] 'informational theory' suggests that women have a different experience of the world to men, and this can play a role in countering the 'gender-based myths, biases, and stereotypes [that] are deeply embedded in the attitudes of many male judges, as well as in the law itself.'[19] The 'different voice' theory posits that women are differently constituted to men, and judge matters relationally through an ethic of care.[20] 'Representational theory' suggests that women serve as representatives of their gender and work to advance their group's substantive interests through their decisions.[21] By contrast, 'organisational theory' suggests that the professionalisation and training of all judges, including women, acts as a powerful constraint on judicial action, countering the effect of their diverse characteristics.[22] Many of these explanations of the impact of gender diversity on judicial decision-making can be applied to other characteristics, such as Indigeneity.[23] They can also be applied to the issue of intersectionality,

---

[16] Michael Kirby, 'Women in the Law: What Next?' (2002) 16 *Australian Feminist Journal* 148, 154–55. See also the controversial 'wise Latina woman' comment by Sonia Sotomayor, 'A Latina Judge's Voice' (2002) 13 *Berkeley Law Raza Journal* 87, 92.

[17] For books alone, see Sally Kenney, *Gender and Justice: Why Women in the Judiciary Really Matter* (Routledge 2013); Rackley (n 9); Ulrike Schultz and Gisela Shaw (eds), *Gender and Judging* (Hart Publishing, 2013); Graham Gee and Erika Rackley (eds), *Debating Judicial Appointments in an Age of Diversity* (Routledge, 2018).

[18] Christina Boyd, 'Representation on the Courts? The Effects of Trial Judges' Sex and Race' (2016) 69 *Political Research Quarterly* 788.

[19] Bertha Wilson, 'Will Women Judges Really Make a Difference?' (1990) 28 *Osgoode Hall Law Journal* 507, 512.

[20] Carol Gilligan, *In a Different Voice: Psychological Theory and Women's Development* (Harvard University Press, 1982).

[21] For an equivalent argument in relation to race, see Jonathan Kastellec, 'Racial Diversity and Judicial Influence on Appellate Courts' (2013) 57 *American Journal of Political Science* 167.

[22] Herbert Kritzer and Thomas Uhlman, 'Sisterhood in the Courtroom: Sex of Judge and Defendant in Criminal Case Disposition' (1977) 14 *Social Science Journal* 77.

[23] Martin Nakata, *Disciplining the Savages, Savaging the Disciplines* (Aboriginal Studies Press, 2007) 213–17.

which arises when individuals experience disadvantage as a result of interconnected social categorisations, such as race *and* gender.[24]

A third rationale for judicial diversity – *the argument from utility* – was described by Chief Justice Beverley McLachlin (Canada's first female Chief justice) when discussing justifications for increasing the number of women on the Bench: 'It seems to me that modern societies cannot afford to lose the intellectual power and energy of half the population. ... We need the wisdom, not only of wise men, but of our wise women.'[25] The argument is based on the premise that some groups have been excluded historically from participating in the judiciary, and that promoting their career progression will expand the pool of candidates available for selection. The corollary is that, with a larger pool of candidates, there will be a better chance of a good judicial appointment.[26] This justification thus serves as an antidote to the claim that greater diversity will dilute the importance of 'merit' in judicial selection, and hence impair the quality of the judiciary.[27]

A fourth rationale for judicial diversity – *the argument from legitimacy* – is that there is inherent value in having courts that 'look like Australia'[28] because fair representation legitimates the courts in the eyes of the community they serve. High Court Justice Michael McHugh made this point forcefully in relation to gender when remarking that nothing breeds social unrest as quickly as a sense of injustice: 'The need to maintain public confidence in the legitimacy and impartiality of the justice system is to me an unanswerable argument for having a judiciary in which men and women are equally represented'.[29]

The judiciary needs the trust of the public because 'courts cannot act with effective authority (as opposed to brute force) if those with whom

---

[24] Kimberle Crenshaw, 'Demarginalizing the Intersection of Race and Sex: A Black Feminist Critique of Antidiscrimination Doctrine, Feminist Theory and Antiracist Politics' [1989] *University of Chicago Legal Forum* 139.

[25] Quoted in Lady Hale, 'Making a Difference: Why We Need a More Diverse Judiciary' (2005) 56 *Northern Ireland Legal Quarterly* 281, 286.

[26] JUSTICE, *The Judiciary* (Report, 1972) 10, referring not to the appointment of women but of solicitors.

[27] Harry Gibbs, 'The State of the Australian Judicature' (1985) 59 *Australian Law Journal* 522, 527.

[28] To paraphrase Feldman (n 10) 6.

[29] Michael McHugh, 'Women Justices for the High Court' (Speech, Western Australia Law Society, 27 October 2004) 6.

they deal do not take them seriously.'[30] This helps to explain the High Court's resurgent interest, since the mid-1990s, in maintaining public confidence in the judiciary in constitutional jurisprudence.[31]

The preceding justifications for judicial diversity have been challenged by two common critiques. One critique is that diversity is unnecessary because the obligation of impartiality embodied in the oath of office requires judicial officers to 'do right to all manner of people according to law without fear or favour, affection or ill-will'.[32] But even if one assumes that judges sincerely attempt to dispense justice according to this tenet, the critique ignores the compelling literature on unconscious bias in decision-making.[33] This bias refers to the stereotypes that affect our understanding, actions, and decisions in an unconscious manner, whether positively or negatively.[34] The point is not that judges may be intentionally unfaithful to their duty but that judges of a particular race, sex, class, or creed may do so unconsciously. The argument for greater judicial diversity does not claim to eliminate these unconscious biases, since everyone is susceptible to them, but to replace one dominant norm with a plurality of cross-cutting affiliations so that courts are less systemically biased. This signals that increasing judicial diversity may bring about a number of changes, including different substantive results; different modes of reasoning leading to the same result; and different user experience in the court room.

A further critique is that the judiciary has historically performed its functions with substantial success, and it should be conserved in its present form because its composition has been no barrier to serving societal needs. It does appear to be broadly accepted that the Australian judiciary has discharged its functions well over the long arc of history.[35]

---

[30] Susan Kenny, 'Maintaining Public Confidence in the Judiciary: A Precarious Equilibrium' (1999) 25 *Monash University Law Review* 209, 210.

[31] See, for instance, *Grollo v Palmer* (1995) 184 CLR 348; *Kable v Director of Public Prosecutions (NSW)* (1996) 189 CLR 51; *Wainohu v New South Wales* (2011) 243 CLR 181.

[32] See, for instance, *High Court of Australia Act 1979* (Cth) sch. On impartiality, see The Council of Chief Justices of Australia and New Zealand, *Guide to Judicial Conduct* (Australasian Institute of Judicial Administration, 3rd ed, 2017) 5, 11–18.

[33] The critique is also flawed because it addresses only one justification for diversity (quality), and leaves unanswered the arguments from equality, utility and legitimacy.

[34] Cheryl Staats et al., *State of the Science: Implicit Bias Review* (Report, Kirwan Institute, Ohio State University, 2017) 10.

[35] Murray Gleeson, 'The State of the Judicature' (Speech, Australian Legal Convention, 10 October 1999) 1.

And yet, when one examines judicial performance through the prism of specific groups – particularly those historically excluded from the ranks of the judiciary – the record is less adulatory. Judicial treatment of women and Aboriginal and Torres Strait Islander people are cases in point. Much has been written on concealed gender biases in the law – many of which are the product of judge-made common law or unfavourable judicial interpretation of broad statutory discretions.[36] Additionally, the failure of the legal system to deal even-handedly with Aboriginal and Torres Strait Islander people is well chronicled, especially in the area of criminal justice.[37] Thus, even if one accepts the assessment that the judiciary has *generally* served the community well, some marginalised sections of society have not shared that experience, and it is reasonable for them to have an expectation of change.

III   Identifying Diversity Characteristics

If diversity does matter, the next question is: 'What characteristics are important for a diverse judiciary?' Self-evidently, not every characteristic provides a point of interest: there is 'no argument for the [judicial] appointment of Leos or those born on Sunday.'[38] Public discourse in Australia has focussed largely on gender; in the United States, on gender and race; and in Canada, on gender and geography. But there are many other attributes of potential interest. This section argues that the choice of diversity characteristics should be guided by the two considerations discussed in the following sections.

---

[36] Regina Graycar and Jenny Morgan, *The Hidden Gender of Law* (Federation Press, 1990). The Australian Feminist Judgments Project has made similar observations: Heather Douglas et al. (eds), *Australian Feminist Judgments: Righting and Rewriting Law* (Hart, 2014).

[37] Heather McRae and Garth Nettheim (eds), *Indigenous Legal Issues: Commentary and Materials* (Thomson Reuters, 4th ed, 2009); Thalia Anthony, *Indigenous People, Crime and Punishment* (Routledge, 2013) 13–20. For a contemporary complaint, see Emilia Terzon and Jacqueline Breen, 'Complaint Lodged against Judge Who Made "Offensive", "Discriminatory" Comments to Aboriginal Defendants', *ABC News* (online, 26 July 2019) <www.abc.net.au/news/2019-07-26/complaint-lodged-nt-judge-discriminatory-offensive-aboriginal/11349360>.

[38] Erika Rackley and Charlie Webb, 'Three Models of Diversity' in Graham Gee and Erika Rackley (eds), *Debating Judicial Appointments in an Age of Diversity* (Routledge, 2018) 283, 297.

A   Implications from the Justifications for Diversity

As a matter of principle, the identification of relevant diversity characteristics should be informed by the rationales for promoting judicial diversity. Regrettably, different rationales do not produce congruent results.

The clearest implications emerge from the *argument from utility*, which claims that removing barriers to the career progression of historically excluded groups will increase the likelihood of good appointments. The logic of this argument suggests that the larger the excluded group as a proportion of the general population, the greater the benefit of including them. As a basis for action, we should identify the characteristics with the largest diversity deficits and systematically eliminate the gaps. This reasoning is salient for women, who comprise more than half the adult population and have thus been the most sizeable excluded group.

The broadest list of diversity characteristics emerges from the *argument from legitimacy*, namely, the claim that there is inherent value in having courts that 'look like Australia'. On this rationale, the ideal judicial composition is driven by community perceptions and the need to ensure public trust in the integrity of the courts. The more the Bench reflects the diverse and overlapping attributes of the general population, the more likely the public is to accept its capacity to 'do right to all manner of people'. The Bench should thus be as varied as the population itself.

The *argument from equality* is the most problematic because equality law provides no sure guidance; and coherent principles that identify which attributes are important to diversity have proved elusive.[39] The immutability of a characteristic has been a touchstone in international jurisprudence, but there is uncertainty about whether an immutable trait is 'a trait that has not been chosen, a trait that cannot be changed, or a trait that an individual should not be forced to change'.[40] Others have suggested 'visibility' or 'irrelevance' as criteria for inclusion among the protected grounds.[41] It is not intended to resolve these differences here,

---

[39] See the debates in Deborah Hellman and Sophia Moreau (eds), *Philosophical Foundations of Discrimination Law* (Oxford University Press, 2014).
[40] Michael Helfand, 'The Usual Suspect Classifications: Criminals, Aliens and the Future of Same-Sex Marriage' (2009) 12 *University of Pennsylvania Journal of Constitutional Law* 1, 6.
[41] Gaze and Smith (n 11) 73–5.

but to point to the indeterminacy of the justifications for diversity in identifying judicial diversity characteristics.

B Implications from the National Census

A supplementary means of gaining insight into the diversity characteristics that should command our attention is to reflect on Australia's national census, which has a bearing on at least three justifications for diversity, especially the argument from legitimacy. A census is a complete enumeration of a population at a point in time, but it is far more than a head count. From its earliest days, the census was seen 'as crucial not only to democracy but also to good government'.[42] The census has been described as 'the most important source of statistical information in the country', and its data assists in 'identifying, and in providing remedies for, numerous social problems'.[43] In Australia, this is underpinned by its mandatory nature (only the religion question is optional),[44] and by the fact that it is conducted every 5 years rather than every 10 (which is the international norm).[45]

The information collected through successive censuses has not been static. The first national census in 1911 asked only 14 personal questions. With later enumerations, the information collected expanded because of increasing social complexity, changing attitudes towards the responsibilities of government, and the growing capacity of technology to produce useful information from raw data.[46] Since 1977, the Australian Bureau of Statistics ('ABS') has conducted public consultations in the intercensal period; on each occasion receiving hundreds of submissions on the topics flagged for review.[47] The purpose of the periodic reviews is to ensure that the census questions remain relevant to contemporary public policy and accord with international best

---

[42] Australian Bureau of Statistics, *Informing a Nation: The Evolution of the Australian Bureau of Statistics 1905–2005*, ABS Cat. No. 1382.0 (ABS, 2005) 74.
[43] Australian Law Reform Commission, *Privacy and the Census* (Report No 12, November 1979) 3–4.
[44] *Census and Statistics Act 1905* (Cth) ss 10, 11, 14.
[45] United Nations Department of Economic and Social Affairs, 'Principles and Recommendations for Population and Housing Censuses: Revision 3' (Report, ST/ESA/STAT/SER.M/67/Rev.3, 2017) 4.
[46] Australian Law Reform Commission, *Privacy and the Census* (n 43) 4.
[47] JK Cornish and J Paice, 'Topic Selection for the Australian Census of Population and Housing' (1986) 2 *Journal of Official Statistics* 457.

practice, while preserving the benefits of long data series that permit temporal comparisons.

Space does not permit an exposition of the history of every census question, but several points would emerge from such an account.[48] First, there is a vibrant national conversation about these issues, which has been informed by thousands of submissions from the public and stakeholders for over 40 years. Second, the catalogue of characteristics is far more substantial than may be thought relevant from the literature on judicial diversity. That literature has focused on race, gender, geography and professional background, whereas Australia's census history suggests a range of other variables in evaluating the diversity of public institutions. Third, this is a dynamic inquiry in which the characteristics of interest today are not necessarily congruent with those of interest yesterday.

Today, statute authorises the Australian Statistician to collect information via a census on 'matters' prescribed by regulation; and the regulations specify a broad range of topics in relation to persons, households, and dwellings.[49] For *persons*, the current list of prescribed matters covers 22 enumerated items with numerous subcategories, which were the subject of over 50 questions in the 2016 census. Relevant to this study, the prescribed matters include 11 characteristics of potential interest to judicial diversity:

- sex
- age
- marital status
- religion
- citizenship
- Aboriginal or Torres Strait Islander origin
- ancestry
- country of birth
- languages spoken
- disability, and
- educational status.

---

[48] For a list of census topics from 1911–2016, see Australian Bureau of Statistics, 'Census of Population and Housing: Nature and Content, Australia, 2016, Cat. No. 2008.0' (ABS, 2015).
[49] *Census and Statistics Act 1905* (Cth) ss 8, 27; *Census and Statistics Regulation 2016* (Cth) rr 10–12.

This study does not claim that inclusion of a topic in the national census should be the sole criterion for identifying the characteristics of importance to judicial diversity, because census topics may be both over-inclusive and under-inclusive. Over-inclusiveness may arise because some census topics may have no great significance for judicial diversity. Under-inclusiveness may arise because some relevant statistics are collected by methods other than a census or are not systematically collected at all (for instance, data on judges' professional backgrounds). Nevertheless, the census carries a certain gravitas in identifying characteristics of national interest. In this sense, it is a valuable touchstone for assessing which diversity characteristics matter now and in the future. To this end, the 11 points listed above are used as a working list of relevant judicial diversity characteristics.

IV Measuring the Diversity Deficit

The question of how to measure the diversity deficit is a critical inquiry because it is otherwise impossible to know whether there is a diversity deficit, to understand its nature or extent, or to track whether remedies meet with success or failure. Measuring the diversity deficit requires data on the diversity characteristics of (a) the general population and (b) the judiciary so a comparison can be made between them. This exercise needs to be undertaken separately for each diversity characteristic because, although it is convenient to refer to *the* diversity deficit, there are as many potential deficits as there are variables being tracked.

Discussing diversity deficits in these terms appears to suggest a purely quantitative approach to the topic, and to a degree this is unavoidable. However, no-one seriously suggests that a more inclusive judiciary mandates a strict arithmetic accounting for all historically disadvantaged groups.[50] For one thing, mathematical congruence does not speak to some of the accepted justifications for diversity; for another, there are problems of indivisibility for small courts –the impossibility of 3.5 female justices on the High Court, for instance.[51] Yet, one cannot say that the

---

[50] Shimon Shetreet, 'The Normative Cycle of Shaping Judicial Independence in Domestic and International Law: The Mutual Impact of National and International Jurisprudence and Contemporary Practical and Conceptual Challenges' (2009) 10 *Chicago Journal of International Law* 275, 313.

[51] The High Court currently comprises seven judicial officers: *High Court of Australia Act 1979* (Cth) s 5.

judiciary is a fair reflection of society if one pays no regard at all to the composition of that society. Diversity deficits are thus a relational concept between the two components examined in the next two sections.

A   Composition of the Australian Population

Australia is well served by data collected from the periodic national census; as well as by registration systems for births, deaths and marriages; administrative collections; and surveys on specialised topics. As a result, there is a rich account of the composition of the population. Table 4.1 presents select data on the 11 key compositional variables identified in section III(B), taken predominantly from the 2016 census.

Although the values of these variables are shown at a point in time, there can be significant *temporal* variations in some variables.[52] This is vital to the debate about judicial diversity because the quest for greater inclusion is a moving target – diversity is not something that is achieved and can then be forgotten. Australia's ethnic composition provides an illustration. The proportion of the population born overseas increased from 18% in 1966 to 28% in 2016,[53] and this has been matched by growing plurality in ancestry, religion and languages spoken at home. If, hypothetically, there was a judiciary that could have been fairly described as ethnically diverse in 1966, a similarly composed Bench would not deserve that appellation today.

Moreover, the table shows the values of variables in the national population, but there can be major *geographic* differences. For instance, in the 2016 census the proportion of people who identified as Aboriginal or Torres Strait Islander ranged from 25.5% in the Northern Territory to 0.8% in Victoria, with a national average of 2.8%.[54] Such geographic variability has implications for the ideal composition of the judiciary in

---

[52] Other variables, such as sex and age, do change over time at a population level, but only slowly: see Brian Opeskin and Rebecca Kippen, 'The Balance of the Sexes: The Feminisation of Australia's Population, 1901–2008' (2012) 18 *Population, Space and Place* 517.
[53] Australian Bureau of Statistics, 'Census of Population and Housing: Reflecting Australia – Stories from the Census, 2016, Cultural Diversity in Australia, Cat. No. 2071.0' (ABS, 2017).
[54] Australian Bureau of Statistics, 'Census of Population and Housing: Reflecting Australia – Stories from the Census, 2016 – Aboriginal and Torres Strait Islander Population, Cat. No. 2071.0' (ABS, 2017) Table 1.

Table 4.1 *Composition of the Australian population*

Variable	Measure	Value	Age Group	Year	Source
Sex	Sex ratio (males per 100 females)	98.4	All	2018	a
	Sex ratio (males per 100 females)	96.4	40–69	2018	a
Age	Median age (males)	36.4 years	All	2016	a
	Median age (females)	38.1 years	All	2016	a
	Median age (persons)	37.3 years	All	2016	a
Marital status	Married	62.9%	40–69	2016	b
	Never married	15.2%	40–69	2016	b
	Divorced	14.2%	40–69	2016	b
	Widowed	2.9%	40–69	2016	b
	Separated	4.8%	40–69	2016	b
Religion	Christianity	52.1%	All	2016	b
	No religion, secular	30.1%	All	2016	b
	Islam	2.6%	All	2016	b
	Buddhism	2.4%	All	2016	b
	Hinduism	1.9%	All	2016	b
Citizenship	Australian	82.4%	All	2016	b
	Not Australian	10.7%	All	2016	b
Indigeneity	Aboriginal or Torres Strait Islander	2.8%	All	2016	b
Ancestry	English	36.1%	All	2016	b
	Australian	33.5%	All	2016	b
	Irish	11.0%	All	2016	b
	Scottish	9.3%	All	2016	b
	Chinese	5.6%	All	2016	b
Country of birth	Born overseas	28.4%	All	2016	c
	Born overseas or with one parent born	49.3%	All	2016	c
Language	Speaks a language besides English at home	21.0%	All	2016	b
	Speaks a language besides English at home	25.1%	40–69	2016	b

Table 4.1 (cont.)

Variable	Measure	Value	Age Group	Year	Source
Disability	Has need for assistance with core activities	5.1%	All	2016	b
	Has need for assistance with core activities	4.6%	40–69	2016	b
Education	Postgraduate Degree	5.2%	40–69	2016	b
	Graduate Diploma and Graduate Certificate	2.7%	40–69	2016	b
	Bachelor Degree	14.7%	40–69	2016	b
	Below Bachelor Degree	28.0%	40–69	2016	b
	No non-school qualification	35.8%	40–69	2016	b

Sources: (a) ABS, *Australian Demographic Statistics, Sep 2018*, (Catalogue No 3101.0, 2019); (b) ABS, *Census Table Builder* (Report, 2016); (c) ABS, *Census of Population and Housing: Reflecting Australia, Stories from the Census, 2016* (Catalogue No 2071.0, 2017)

each state and territory, as well as for the composition of resident judges in federal courts.

These population data, like all social science data, have limitations arising from the methods of collection and analysis. An ongoing issue in census data quality is the level of nonresponse to specific questions or to the entire survey. The ABS has developed sophisticated methods for correcting for these known sources of error. These include a post-enumeration survey of 50,000 households, which is used to measure undercount or overcount, and to re-base the enumerated population accordingly.[55] In 2017, an Independent Assurance Panel concluded that the 2016 census data was fit-for-purpose and could be used with confidence; the data being of comparable quality to other censuses in Australia and abroad, and in line with independent data sources.[56]

---

[55] Australian Bureau of Statistics, 'Census of Population and Housing: Understanding the Census and Census Data, Australia, 2016, Cat. No. 2900.0' (ABS, 2017).
[56] Sandra Harding et al., 'Report on the Quality of 2016 Census Data' (Report, June 2017) iii.

B Composition of the Australian Judiciary

Compositional data for the population provides a starting point for comparing the diversity of the Australian judiciary. In 2017–18, there were 1,117 full-time-equivalent judicial officers in Australia.[57] Using population data as a benchmark for diversity, we may ask whether there are 569 female judicial officers (i.e., 96.4 males per 100 females); 51 judicial officers with a disability (4.6%); 31 who identify as Aboriginal or Torres Strait Islander (2.8%); 317 who are foreign-born (28.4%); and 280 who speak a language other than English at home (25.1%).

Anyone with a passing familiarity with the Australian judiciary would answer no on every count. Yet a reliable assessment of these diversity deficits is hampered by a significant 'data deficit': executive governments in Australia publish no statistics on the diversity of the judges and magistrates they appoint; nor do courts report on these matters in their annual reports. What we know about the Australian judiciary can be gleaned only from scholarly research, which is generally limited in scope because the data must be compiled meticulously from biographical information about individual judicial officers, uneven public records, or expensive social science surveys. The result is a fragmented understanding of the attributes of the judiciary and their evolution over time. What is missing, but sorely needed, is a comprehensive database that is overseen by government or an independent body with the imprimatur to collect, analyse and publish data about the judiciary for the benefit of the public.

In the absence of such a database, five scholarly studies give a flavour of what is presently known about the composition of the Australian judiciary. The studies vary in their methodologies, chosen courts, sample size, temporal frame and attributes studied; yet despite these differences they reach substantially similar conclusions about the Bench.

An important early study by Neumann examined the social backgrounds of the seven chief justices and 24 justices who served on the High Court from 1903 to 1973.[58] The collective portrait presented a picture not of diversity but of grave homogeneity:

---

[57] Productivity Commission, 'Report on Government Services 2019' (Report, 2019) Table 7A.24.
[58] Eddy Neumann, *The High Court of Australia: A Collective Portrait, 1903–1973*, Occasional Monograph 6 (University of Sydney, Dept. of Government and Public Administration, 2nd ed, 1973).

the typical High Court justice is a male white Protestant raised in Sydney or Melbourne ... and of British ethnic origins. He is from upper middle rather than upper class background ... he usually goes to a high status high school (usually private) and then to Sydney or Melbourne university where he has a brilliant academic record.[59]

This study was complemented in 2000 by Goldsmith's empirical profile of three federal courts (High Court, Federal Court, and Family Court) at two points in time (1978 and 1998).[60] He concluded that, as Australia has become home to people from a greater variety of social backgrounds, there have been changes in the kind of people appointed to federal courts, but these changes were subtle: 'the Australian federal judiciary continues *not* to be representative of the population at large', and in 1998 judges were still likely to be male, middle-aged, white, Christian, privately educated, and former barristers.[61]

Lee and Campbell added to this picture in their 2011 study of the same federal courts as Goldsmith's study, plus eight state and territory Supreme Courts, encompassing 272 judges, acting judges, and associate judges.[62] Focusing on the antecedents to judicial appointment, they found that 26% of judges had completed a higher degree in law (master's or doctorate); 71% were barristers who had taken silk; only 17% had been practising as a solicitor at the time of appointment; and 27% had prior judicial experience as a magistrate, master or judge.

More recently, a study by Bartlett and Douglas reflected on the backgrounds and career trajectories of judges of the Federal Court and the state and territory Supreme Courts.[63] Again, a picture emerges of a judiciary of relatively uniform educational and career background, with judges predominantly recruited from a long career at the private Bar. The authors concluded that the senior judiciary today is a 'relatively educationally and ethnically homogeneous group'.[64]

---

[59] Ibid. 105–6.
[60] Andrew Goldsmith, 'A Profile of the Federal Judiciary' in Brian Opeskin and Fiona Wheeler (eds), *The Australian Federal Judicial System* (Melbourne University Press, 2000) 365.
[61] Ibid. 397 (emphasis added).
[62] HP Lee and Enid Campbell, *The Australian Judiciary* (Cambridge University Press, 2nd ed, 2013) 35–40, 317–19.
[63] Francesca Bartlett and Heather Douglas, 'Benchmarking a Supreme Court and Federal Court Judge in Australia' (2018) 8 *Oñati Socio-Legal Series* 1355.
[64] Ibid. 1358.

Contrasting with the above research, in methodology but not results, are the studies by Mack and Roach Anleu based on national surveys of magistrates and judges.[65] Their work has some advantages over the other studies, including direct survey rather than piecemeal documentary research; broader coverage of jurisdictions and court levels (theirs is the only study to include the lower courts); and a larger sample size.[66] Comparing the judges' survey results with population data, the authors reported that: 'larger proportions of judges, compared with Australians generally, are male, older, have grown up in a large city, identify as Australian, have no religious affiliation, attended a private or Catholic school and are married/partnered.'[67]

V Judges and Magistrates in the National Census: A New Dataset

Existing scholarship on the characteristics of the Australian judiciary appears to have overlooked a rich seam of data on judges and magistrates, namely, the national census. Every person who is present in Australia on census night is required to complete the census and, because that requires respondents to state their occupation, the ABS has a complete record of the answers of judicial officers to the census questions. These data are not publicly available but were supplied to the author by the ABS on a commercial basis.[68] The data covers three censuses (1996, 2006, 2016), and nine variables (age, marital status, religion, Indigenous status, ancestry, country of birth, languages spoken at home, disability, educational status) cross-tabulated by sex (male, female) and type of judicial officer (judge, magistrate).

This new dataset has major advantages over the information sources used in prior studies. It is based on an enumeration of the entire corpus of judicial officers rather than a sample, so no question arises as to

---

[65] Kathy Mack and Sharyn Roach Anleu, 'Who Are the Magistrates? Demographic and Social Characteristics' (Report No 3/06, 2006); Kathy Mack and Sharyn Roach Anleu, 'The National Survey of Australian Judges: An Overview of Findings' (2008) 18 *Journal of Judicial Administration* 5.

[66] The respondents comprised 210 magistrates in 2002, 242 magistrates in 2007, and 309 judges in 2007.

[67] Mack and Roach Anleu, 'The National Survey of Australian Judges: An Overview of Findings' (n 65) 12.

[68] Australian Bureau of Statistics, 'Customised Report' (ABS, 2019). Purchase of the data was supported by the Melbourne Law School Research Support Funds Scheme.

representativeness. It provides slices of cross-sectional data at intervals, thus allowing diversity characteristics to be tracked over time. And the cross-tabulation by sex and type of judicial officer permits an exploration of the correlations between gender, court hierarchy and diversity variables.

The dataset also has limitations. It was not possible to examine census data prior to 1996 because the data were not coded for occupational classification at a sufficiently granular level; not all questions were asked in all three censuses; and the ABS has a policy of randomising the counts in cells with small values to prevent identification of particular individuals. This 'introduced random error'[69] had an unfortunate impact on the question about Aboriginal or Torres Strait Islander status, which could not be analysed further. The main findings that can be drawn from the dataset are reported in the following discussion.

A Age

Across the 20-year period 1996–2016, there has been substantial aging of the judiciary. This is apparent in median ages, which have increased by 5.7% for judges (57.3 to 60.5 years) and by 16.4% for magistrates (50.2 to 58.4 years) (Figure 4.1). This may be contrasted with the increase in the median age of the general population by 9.4% (34.0 to 37.2 years). The median age of judges and magistrates is necessarily higher than the general population because it reflects subpopulations defined by the senior career status of its members. Throughout the period, the median age of judges was higher than that of magistrates, but the gap is narrowing. Similarly, there is a gender gap in age structure: the median age of male judicial officers is higher than that of females, but that gap is also narrowing. This convergence is bringing about increasing homogeneity *within* the judiciary with respect to age. At the same time, there has been increasing divergence from the general population. Although the Australian population is also aging, the judiciary has been ageing at a faster rate: for example, the proportion of officers aged 60 and over has more than doubled (23% in 1996, 49% in 2016), probably reflecting the slow growth in the size of the judiciary and the reduced opportunity to appoint younger members to the Bench.

---

[69] Australian Bureau of Statistics, 'Census of Population and Housing: Census Dictionary, 2016, Cat. No. 2901.0' (ABS, 2016).

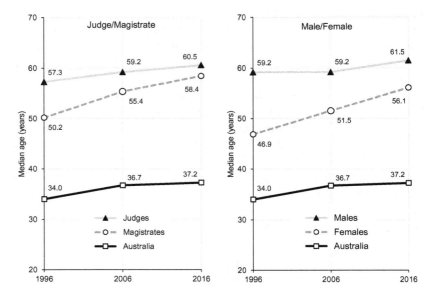

Figure 4.1 Median age of judicial officers, by type and sex, Australia, 1996–2016.
Sources: ABS, *Customised Report* (Report, 2019); ABS, *Australian Historical Population Statistics 2019*, (Catalogue No 3105.0.65.001, 2019)

B Marital Status

The data recorded the registered marital status of judicial officers across five categories: never married, married, widowed, divorced and separated but not divorced. There were only minor differences in marital status between judges and magistrates, and Table 4.2 thus reports on both groups combined. The most prominent differences are by gender: female judicial officers were less likely to be married than males (in 2016, 56% versus 79%), and this corresponded with a higher proportion of females than males who were separated, divorced or never married. In 2016, female judicial officers were nearly three times more likely than males to be never married (22% versus 8%). When judicial officers are compared with the general population aged 40–69 years (Table 4.1), they are more likely to be married (in 2016, 71% versus 63%). The judiciary (which remains male-dominated) thus appears to have bucked the

Table 4.2 *Marital status of judicial officers, by sex, Australia, 1996–2016*

	Males				Females				Persons			
	1996	2006	2016	Change	1996	2006	2016	Change	1996	2006	2016	Change
	%	%	%		%	%	%		%	%	%	
Never married	3.7	5.2	8.3	4.6	22.1	18.9	22.1	0.0	5.9	9.1	13.0	7.1
Married	89.3	87.3	78.8	-10.6	55.8	59.6	56.1	0.3	85.4	79.5	71.0	-14.4
Widowed	1.2	1.7	1.0	-0.2	0.0	2.5	32	32	1.0	1.9	1.3	0.7
Divorced	3.3	5.5	8.4	5.1	16.3	16.4	132	-3.1	4.9	8.6	10.1	5.2
Separated	2.4	3.1	2.2	-0.2	5.3	2.9	5.1	-0.6	2.3	3.0	3.2	0.4
Total	100	103	99		100	100	100		100	102	99	

Source: ABS, *Customised Report* (Report, 2019).

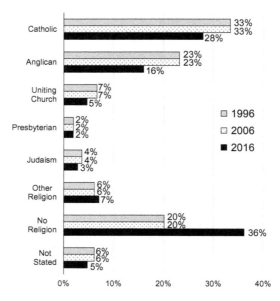

Figure 4.2 Religious affiliation of judicial officers, Australia, 1996–2016.
Sources: ABS, *Customised Report* (Report, 2019).

Western trend towards declining marriage rates and rising rates of nonmarital cohabitation,[70] although this is less so for female judicial officers.

C Religion

Figure 4.2 shows the religious affiliation of judicial officers over the three censuses. In 2016, Christian religions predominate, with 50% of judicial officers claiming affiliation with one of four Christian groups (Catholic, Anglican, Uniting or Presbyterian). The next largest religion in 2016 was Judaism (3%), with all other religions combined amounting to 7%. Some

---

[70] Kathleen Kiernan, 'Cohabitation and Divorce across Nations and Generations' in Lindsay Chase-Lansdale, Kathleen Kiernan and Ruth Friedman (eds), *Human Development across Lives and Generations: The Potential for Change* (Cambridge University Press, 2004) 139.

36% of judicial officers claimed no religion. Religious affiliation shows interesting dynamic trends. From 1996–2016, Christian groups experienced a declining share among the judiciary, with secularism absorbing the difference ('no religion' rose from 20% in 1996 to 36% in 2016 for males and females combined). Compared with the general population data, it appears that major religious beliefs, or nonbeliefs, are distributed similarly in the judiciary and the Australian population, and both are consistent with the trend towards secularisation in Western societies.[71] It is possible that some smaller religious groups (Islam, Buddhism, Hinduism) are less represented in the judiciary than in the general population, but the aggregation of these groups into 'other' in the customised data makes it impossible to tell.

D Ancestry

The ancestry question was not asked in the 1996 census, and hence the data only permit comparison between 2006 and 2016. The census question allowed two ancestries to be specified, with 992 judicial officers giving 1,423 responses in 2006 and 1,075 judicial officers giving 1,605 responses in 2016. Because of this, percentages cited here sum to more than 100%. There were very few differences in ancestry by gender or by type of judicial officer. In 2016, 29% of judicial officers gave their ancestry as Australian (Figure 4.3). Of the foreign ancestries, the large majority (94%) were Anglo-Celtic (English, Irish, Scottish), which significantly exceeded the prevalence of these groups in the general population (56%). The next largest ancestries among judicial officers were German and Italian. A comparison with the top ancestries in the general population is stark. The relative proportion of Australian, English, German, and Italian ancestry in the two groups is reasonably similar, but there is a near threefold over-representation of Irish ancestry, and a near twofold over-representation of Scottish ancestry, in the judiciary. Some other ancestries (Chinese, for example) are significantly under-represented in the judiciary.

---

[71] Peter Nynäs, Mika Lassander and Terhi Utriainen (eds), *Post-Secular Society* (Transaction Publishers, 2012).

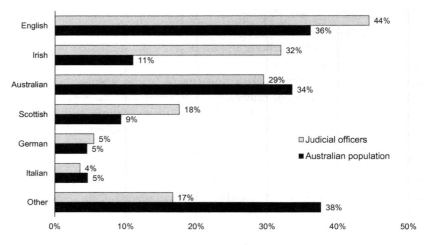

Figure 4.3 Ancestry of judicial officers and Australian population, 2016.
Sources: ABS, *Customised Report* (Report, 2019); ABS, *Census Table Builder* (Report, 2016)

E   Country of Birth

A substantial majority of judicial officers were born in Australia, and this was true regardless of gender, type of officer or census year. In 2016, 86% were Australian-born and 14% foreign-born. For those judicial officers who were foreign-born, the top countries of birth in 2016 were England (5.3%), New Zealand (1.7%), Scotland (1.4%) and South Africa (0.9%). By contrast, in the general population 28% were foreign-born, with the top foreign countries of birth being England (3.9%), New Zealand (2.2%), China (2.2%) and India (1.9%).[72] It is apparent that the judiciary has less cultural diversity than the population at large in terms of country of birth, with 14% of the former but 28% of the latter being foreign-born. There is also significantly less cultural and geo-political diversity among those judicial officers who are foreign-born compared with the general population.

---

[72] Australian Bureau of Statistics, 'Census of Population and Housing: Reflecting Australia - Stories from the Census, 2016, Cultural Diversity in Australia, Cat. No. 2071.0' (n 53)

F Languages Spoken at Home

Overwhelmingly, judicial officers speak English at home. In 2016, only 4.2% spoke a language other than English at home, up from 2.9% in 1996. The difference between judges and magistrates was generally not marked, but there were differences by gender. For example, in 2016, female magistrates were nearly twice as likely as male magistrates to be non-English speakers at home (7.4% versus 3.8%) – a pattern that is apparent in all three censuses but does not extend to judges. By contrast, 25.1% of the Australian population aged 40–69 years at the last census spoke a language other than English at home (Table 4.1). This is six-times the percentage for judicial officers, indicating that the judiciary is much less linguistically diverse than the general population.

G Disability

The data show very low levels of disability among the judiciary. In 2006 and 2016, the census asked whether the respondent ever needed someone to help with self-care, body movement, or communication activities. It also asked the reason for any such need, including a health condition, disability, young or old age or difficulty with the English language. In 2006, no judicial officers had need for assistance, and in 2016 only 0.7% had such a need, all of them judges rather than magistrates. This compares with the population average of 4.6% of those aged 40–69 years who had a need for assistance. Judicial officers in 2016 were thus six times less likely to experience one of the stated types of impairment than others of their age. However, these figures need to be interpreted with care because the collection of census data on disability has a long history of difficulties of definition and reporting.[73] For example, while mental disability is not excluded from the ambit of the census questions, nor does it appear to be their main focus. It is possible that mental impairments are under-reported, even in the context of an anonymised census, as there is growing empirical evidence of high levels of mental stress among the Australian judiciary.[74]

---

[73] Australian Bureau of Statistics, *Informing a Nation: The Evolution of the Australian Bureau of Statistics 1905–2005*, ABS Cat. No. 1382.0, above (n 42) 104. See also United States Census Bureau, 'Measuring Disability in a Census' (Working Paper, Select Topics in International Censuses, June 2017).

[74] Carly Schrever, Carol Hulbert and Tania Sourdin, 'The Psychological Impact of Judicial Work: Australia's First Empirical Research Measuring Judicial Stress and Wellbeing' (2019) 28 *Journal of Judicial Administration* 141.

H Educational Status

One would expect judicial officers to have a higher level of education than the general population and this is borne out by the data. In 2016, across all judicial officers, 66% had a bachelor's degree, 6% a graduate diploma/certificate and 22% a postgraduate degree, as their *highest* qualification completed. Comparing this with the Australian population aged 40–69 years (Table 4.1), judicial officers are more than four times as likely to have a bachelor's degree or postgraduate degree as their highest qualification. This makes judicial officers educationally distinct from the general population, but not in an adverse way. There was little variation in educational levels by gender, but there were differences by type of officer and over time. Figure 4.4 shows that judges and magistrates have become more highly educated over the 20-year period, with increasing proportions having postgraduate degrees – for judges, 16% in 1996 to 25% in 2016; for magistrates, 6% in 1996 to 17% in 2016. Judges have higher educational levels than magistrates, with a differential of about

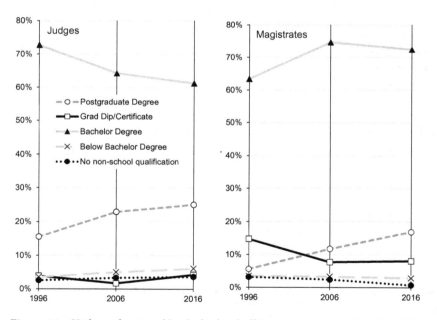

Figure 4.4   Highest educational level of judicial officers, by type, Australia, 1996–2016. Sources: ABS, *Customised Report* (Report, 2019)

8–12 percentage points in the proportion with postgraduate degrees. Among those with postgraduate qualifications, there is a small but growing proportion with doctorates rather than masters. In the decade from 2006 to 2016, the percentage of judicial officers with doctorates doubled from 1.3% to 2.7%.

I Gender

The gender gap on the Bench has, historically, been the most egregious of diversity deficits because it has excluded half the adult population. In practice, gender has been in the vanguard of the diversity movement, but it is dealt with last in this chapter because the most useful data come from a source other than the national census. Since 2000, the Australasian Institute of Judicial Administration (AIJA) has collected statistics on the gender of Australian judicial officers, arranged by jurisdiction and court level.[75] These data reveal that a fundamental transformation has begun in the gender composition of the judiciary, but it is not yet complete. This is shown in Figure 4.5, using the 'sex ratio' – the standard demographic measure of gender composition – defined as the number of males per 100 females. For all courts combined, there has been a persistent year-on-year improvement in the sex ratio. In 2000 there were 481 male judicial officers for every 100 female judicial officers, but by 2019 there were 168 males for every 100 females – a near threefold improvement. Alternatively stated, women now comprise 37% of the Australian judiciary. Yet despite these developments, there are sizable differences by court level. Male dominance increases with the status of the court, and thus the greatest gender imbalances are generally found in the higher courts. In 2019, the sex ratio was 253 for the Supreme Courts (including High Court, Federal Court, and Family Court), and 194 for District/County Courts, but 131 for Magistrates Courts. The improvement over time in the sex ratio for all courts combined has been driven largely by improvements in the Magistrates Courts, which account for more than half the judiciary.

---

[75] 'AIJA Judicial Gender Statistics', *The Australasian Institute of Judicial Administration* (Web Page, 6 March 2019) <https://aija.org.au/research/judicial-gender-statistics/>. No data were collected for 2003.

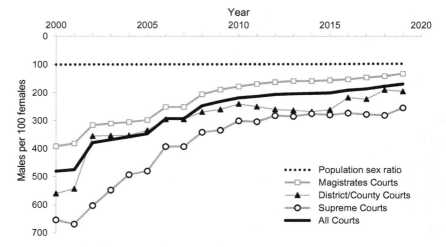

Figure 4.5 Sex ratio of judicial officers by court level, Australia, 2000–2019.
Notes: As no AIJA judicial gender data were collected in 2003, the sex ratios for that year are shown as the average of the adjacent years.
Sources: AIJA, *Judicial Gender Statistics* (various years); ABS, *Australian Demographic Statistics*, (Catalogue No 3101.0, various years); ABS, *Australian Historical Population Statistics 2019* (Catalogue No 3105.0.65.001, 2019)

J Summary

The conclusions to be drawn from sections IV and V can be summarised in three propositions. First, there is a detailed account of the attributes of the Australian population, which has been collected over many decades by the ABS. That account reveals a society that has evolved in richness and complexity. Second, existing scholarship on the attributes of Australia's judges and magistrates presents piecemeal portraits, which point to a Bench that is far from a fair reflection of the diverse society it serves. Third, the census data analysed here offers fresh insights into judicial diversity. It corroborates many of the findings of earlier studies but broadens the range of characteristics examined. Relative to the general population, judicial officers are aging faster and are more likely to be married, to have Anglo-Celtic ancestry and to have attained higher levels of education. They are less likely to have been born overseas, to speak a foreign language at home or to be living with a disability.

But their religious affiliations appear to be similar to those of other Australians.

VI Redressing the Diversity Deficit

Turning to the final question of what programmatic steps are needed to redress the diversity deficit, this section identifies four strategies relating to the judicial pipeline, judicial selection, judicial conditions and judicial education.

A *Judicial Pipeline*

Most judicial officers in Australia are appointed from the practising Bar, and therefore one cannot expect a diverse Bench without a diverse Bar. Similarly, the Bar is fed by law schools, and therefore one cannot expect a diverse Bar without a diverse body of law graduates. In consequence, it is critical to view judicial diversity not as an endpoint, but as the outcome of a dynamic process that involves a career pipeline stretching back to secondary school. Priming the pipeline with diverse students in law schools is a necessary step, but this alone will not guarantee a diverse judiciary by means of a 'trickle up' effect because barriers to career progression cause attrition from the pipeline at many points along the way.[76] Understanding the location, size and causes of that attrition is important to crafting potential remedies.

Addressing one piece of this puzzle, in 2012 the Law Council of Australia commissioned a national empirical study to investigate the drivers for attrition of women from the legal profession, including solicitors in private firms, in-house lawyers, barristers, lawyers in community legal centres and other legal roles.[77] It found that the key 'push factors' for female practitioners were workplace culture; long hours and high pressure (which made it difficult to balance professional and personal life); and lack of promotional opportunities. The report also identified key differences in the experience of female barristers and female solicitors in private practice, which are important given historical

---

[76] Rackley (n 9) 31–6.
[77] Law Council of Australia, 'National Attrition and Re-engagement Study (NARS) Report' (Report, 2013).

reliance on the Bar as the primary pool of potential judicial appointees: compared with female solicitors, female barristers reported heavier workloads, longer hours, greater difficulty in managing work-life balance and greater isolation.[78] Several strategies were proposed to address the problem of attrition, focusing around the themes of workplace culture and flexible work practices; mentoring and sponsorship; transparency and accountability; and leadership and role modelling. Not all these remedies can be directly translated from gender diversity to other diversity characteristics, but they do reveal the complexity of the changes that will be needed if diversity deficits are to be dismantled.

B Judicial Selection

Another mechanism for alleviating a diversity deficit is to remove barriers to the appointment of people with the diversity characteristics that are in short supply. Legal arrangements in Australia already permit this, but because current arrangements neither encourage nor require such action, attention has been drawn to ways in which selection processes might be altered to facilitate greater diversity.

There has been one noteworthy attempt to reform judicial selection procedures in Australia in this regard.[79] Between 2008 and 2013, the Federal Labor Government introduced a new process for the selection of judges to three federal courts, inspired by reforms in the United Kingdom, and explicitly motivated by a concern to improve diversity.[80] However, the experiment was dissolved by the incoming Coalition Government in 2013, and no official data has ever been published on the number or diversity characteristics of appointments made under the trialed arrangements.[81]

The adoption of new methods of judicial selection is not a quick fix for a large diversity deficit. The strategy requires perseverance because changes in the attributes of new appointees (a *flow* variable) will affect

---

[78] Ibid. 6.
[79] On diversity in state and territory appointments, see Judicial Conference of Australia, *Judicial Appointments: A Comparative Study* (Report, December 2015).
[80] Attorney-General's Department, Australian Government *Judicial Appointments: Ensuring a Strong, Independent and Diverse Judiciary through a Transparent Process* (Report, April 2010).
[81] The media reported that the Coalition's judicial appointments were less favourable to women than under the preceding Labor Government: Nicola Berkovic, 'Female Judges at Low under Coalition', *The Australian* (Canberra, 18 December 2015) 8.

the prevalence of that attribute in the population of judicial officers (a *stock* variable) incrementally over time. Long periods of judicial service, underpinned by tenure of office, thus act as a brake on judicial turnover and ensure that diversity will arrive unhurriedly, if at all. Or, to misappropriate the aphorism of the German Nobel Laureate, Max Planck, equality on the Bench advances one funeral (or retirement) at a time.

C Judicial Conditions

Diversity gains made through the appointments process can also be quickly lost through later attrition. This can be seen in the AIJA data on gender diversity: over the decade 2010–2019, half of the Australian Supreme Courts have either made no gains or have gone backwards in their sex ratios, while the District Courts, on an aggregate basis, have experienced three periods of reversal. Tracking the composition of departures from the Bench can therefore be as important as tracking the composition of appointments. An important third strategy is thus to create a judicial environment that is attractive to diverse appointees – one in which a newly diverse judicial population is willing to render substantial service.

Some adverse environmental factors may be hard to eradicate. In the 1980s, a literature emerged on the 'chilly climate' faced by many women in educational settings.[82] The phenomenon described the 'overall effect of subtle differential treatment, sometimes minor in any particular instance, that creates an uncomfortable atmosphere for women, undermines morale, and lessens productivity.'[83] In 2003, Backhouse adapted the chilly climate literature to examine the barriers faced by women judges in Canada, and she identified the behavioural patterns of male peers who sought to marginalise their female colleagues. These behaviours posed a risk to women already on the Bench (a chilling effect on decision-making) as well to women not yet on the Bench (a chilling effect on the willingness of women to accept appointment if offered).[84] She concluded, in terms also relevant to Australia, that successful diversification of the judiciary requires

---

[82] Roberta Hall and Bernice Sandler, 'The Classroom Climate: A Chilly One for Women?' (Association of American Colleges, 1982).
[83] Joan Krauskopf, 'Touching the Elephant: Perceptions of Gender Issues in Nine Law Schools' (1994) 44 *Journal of Legal Education* 311, 315.
[84] Constance Backhouse, 'The Chilly Climate for Women Judges: Reflections on the Backlash from the Ewanchuk Case' (2003) 15 *Canadian Journal of Women and the Law* 167, 181–83.

a working environment in which diversity is seen as having institutional value; not as something to be jettisoned by a nontraditional judge in service to the appearance of judicial impartiality.[85]

D   Judicial Education

A final strategy is to use judicial education to give *all* judges a more sensitive understanding of 'the diverse human experiences which are presented to courts on a daily basis'.[86] Unlike the preceding strategies, judicial education does not encourage the judiciary to become more diverse or to stay that way, but it does make judicial officers more aware of the relevance of diversity to the performance of their functions – described by one Canadian Supreme Court judge as a needed 'change in attitudes, not simply a change chromosomes'.[87] Because judicial education speaks only to one justification for diversity – the goal of improving judicial decision-making – it is a strategy that must be paired with others if the full benefits of diversity are to be realised.

The value of judicial education lies in the fact that, even if a specific diversity deficit is eliminated, there will still be many judges who do not possess that attribute. Consider the example of Indigeneity. If 2.8% of the Australian judiciary were Indigenous, there would be no Indigenous diversity deficit (if assessed on a national basis), since that is also the proportion of Indigenous people in the national population. Yet that would still leave 97.2% of the judiciary as non-Indigenous, many of whom will hear and determine matters affecting Indigenous people. Moreover, no judicial appointee (even a 'diversity appointment') can embody all diversity attributes. An Indigenous judge may have a special affinity for legal issues affecting the Indigenous community, but if that judge is a heterosexual male in good mental health, he may be none the wiser about disadvantage arising from sexuality, nonbinary gender, or mental illness. Because judicial officers will encounter individuals of diverse backgrounds in the course of their work, preparedness for that inevitability, through judicial education, is highly desirable.

---

[85] See also Erika Rackley, 'Rethinking Judicial Diversity' in Ulrike Schultz and Gisela Shaw (eds), *Gender and Judging* (Hart Publishing, 2013) 501, 504, 511–14.

[86] Claire L'Heureux-Dubé, 'Making a Difference: The Pursuit of a Compassionate Justice' (1997) 31 *University of British Columbia Law Review* 1, 9.

[87] Claire L'Heureux-Dubé, 'Outsiders on the Bench: The Continuing Struggle for Equality' (2001) 16 *Wisconsin Women's Law Journal* 15, 30.

VII Conclusion

This chapter has examined the composition of the Australian judiciary and the way in which it reflects (or does not reflect) the diversity of the population. The examination of gender diversity in section V is an example of a positive transformation by which the composition of the Bench increasingly looks more like the population at large. If the justifications for judicial diversity are accepted, this is to be applauded. It will have provided greater equality of opportunity for women aspiring to the senior ranks of the legal profession; improved judicial decision-making; expanded the talent pool, thus allowing for better appointments; and given members of the public greater trust in the courts as an institution. Yet it is important to resist a Panglossian assessment of progress. This change is still a considerable distance from the goal of parity with the proportion of women in the general population; it has taken a generation to achieve; it has been marked by the slowest improvements in the highest courts (other than the High Court itself); and it has not been inexorable. This fitful progress is no surprise. The appointment of judicial officers is a matter of executive discretion, creating the potential for variable approaches across space, time and politics. The observed advances in gender diversity have thus been won (and sometimes lost) in an environment that lacks both planning and coordination.

Despite these challenges, gender is an easy case because it is the one diversity variable for which there is accessible public data. The chapter has argued that there are many other diversity characteristics relevant to assessing the appropriate composition of the judiciary, and the national census is an invaluable tool for identifying the characteristics germane to understanding the social fabric of the nation's institutions.

One stumbling block to further progress is the absence of transparent and accessible data on the diversity characteristics of Australia's judges and magistrates. Too often, what is not measured is not seen or valued. If Australia is to make genuine inroads into closing judicial diversity deficits in all their dimensions, the time has arrived for governments to address the data deficit that feeds it. Australia has already taken tentative steps towards greater judicial diversity in some areas. Armed with better knowledge, more can be done to fill the judicial pipeline with diverse candidates; employ better procedures for selecting them; value their diversity once on the Bench; and educate the entire corpus of judges and magistrates about diversity issues affecting participants in the judicial system.

5

Technology and the Judicial Role

MONIKA ZALNIERIUTE AND FELICITY BELL[*]

'The advent of machine learning tools and their integration with legal data offers a mechanism to detect in real time, and thereby remedy judicial behaviour that undermines the rule of law'.[1]

–Daniel L Chen, 2019.

'The law is not so ignorant or disdainful of human nature as to assume that judges or quasi-judicial decision-makers are automatons'.[2]

–Justice Heerey, 1994.

I Introduction

Technology is often seen as having transformational capacity to make societal institutions not only more efficient but also more democratic, accessible, accurate and fair. Ranging from welfare and criminal justice, to healthcare, national security and beyond, technology today is deployed not only to improve the efficiency of public services, but increasingly, to automate elements of, or even entirely replace, humans in decision-making processes.[3] The courts have not been an exception to this trend and have for a number of years invested in digital uplift projects. Beyond the routine use of technology, such as digital filing and discovery which is widely accepted and largely self-explanatory, many jurisdictions are

---

[*] We acknowledge we contributed equally to this chapter, we rotate authorship order in our joint publications.

[1] Daniel L Chen, 'Machine Learning and the Rule of Law' in M Livermore and D Rockmore (eds), *Computational Analysis of Law* (Santa Fe Institute Press, forthcoming).

[2] *Vietnam Veterans' Association of Australia (New South Wales Branch Inc) v Gallagher* (1994) 52 FCR 34 ('*Vietnam Veterans*').

[3] This is not new: some of the earliest AI systems designed for law were as decision-support systems for government administrators: see, for instance, Peter Hammond, 'Representation of DHSS Regulations as a Logic Program' (Conference Presentation, Expert Systems'83, 14-16 December 1983).

considering the introduction of more sophisticated applications. Many are asking whether machine learning ('ML') techniques and other artificial intelligence applications should play a role in assisting tribunals and judiciary in decision-making, and how that might correspondingly transform the role of judges.[4] In this chapter, we ask how these new uses of technology might, in turn, impact judicial values and judges' own sense of themselves and even transform the judicial role in contemporary societies.

The use of sophisticated technological tools by the judiciary is still in its 'infancy'[5] – and has often been met with resistance[6] – but there are indications that such tools will be increasingly deployed. Attempts to 'support' judicial decision-making through the use of structural aids have a long history; arguably, the increasing use of algorithmic risk assessments in the United States (US) criminal justice system[7] marks the latest such attempt. Algorithmic methods are also infusing private dispute resolution, notably for minor online transactions. Unsurprisingly, there are suggestions that similar methods could be deployed in public settings.[8] A proposal for an 'automatic online conviction' process has been stalled in the United Kingdom (UK) Parliament since 2017.[9] Steps toward circumscribing the judicial role have also been taken, by removing judges from the determination of some disputes altogether: Estonia recently announced plans to create a 'robot judge' for small claims.[10] Thus far, these steps toward automation have focused on offences or private disputes where judges need not, in routine cases, exercise judicial

---

[4] See, for instance, Tania Sourdin, 'Judge v. Robot: Artificial Intelligence and Judicial Decision-Making' (2018) 41(4) *University of New South Wales Law Journal* 1114; Jesse Beatson, 'AI-Supported Adjudicators: Should Artificial Intelligence Have a Role in Tribunal Adjudication?' (2018) 31(3) *Canadian Journal of Administrative Law and Practice* 307.

[5] Sourdin (n 4) 1115.

[6] Danielle Kehl, Priscilla Guo and Samuel Kessler, 'Algorithms in the Criminal Justice System: Assessing the Use of Risk Assessments in Sentencing. Responsive Communities Initiative' (Research Paper, Berkman Klein Center for Internet & Society, 2017).

[7] Ibid.

[8] Dave Orr and Colin Rule, 'Artificial Intelligence and the Future of Online Dispute Resolution' (Discussion Paper, New Handshake, undated).

[9] UK Ministry of Justice, *Transforming Our Justice System: Assisted Digital Strategy, Automatic Online Conviction and Statutory Standard Penalty, and Panel Composition in Tribunals* (Government Response Cm 9391, February 2017).

[10] This is not a new idea: Anthony D'Amato, 'Can/Should Computers Replace Judges?' (1977) 11 *Georgia Law Review* 1277.

discretion. That is, the UK proposal is focused on strict liability, summary offences which are not punishable by imprisonment, such as fare evasion and possession of unlicensed fishing equipment.[11] Estonia's plans form a part of its larger project of civic digitisation and the creation of dispute resolution mechanisms online.[12] Nevertheless, substantial claims are made about the capacity of artificially intelligent systems to mimic more complex human decision-making; or even to perform to a more accurate standard.

The increasing experimentation and proposals to automate judicial decision-making, or elements of it, with ML tools attract conflicting narratives. On the one hand, some see the technologisation of the judicial role as inevitable and call for a speedy embrace of automation by the courts to better perform their public role.[13] On the other hand, concerns are raised that automation tools when used in *any* decision-making process may introduce bias and discrimination, thereby giving rise to individual and collective harms. Often such technological tools – which may be created by private companies and shielded behind trade secrets[14] – are not subject to the same accountability or oversight mechanisms as other public actors in our legal systems, including, notably, judges. This raises questions about their compatibility with fundamental principles of justice. Scholars have focused on these harms in the context of administrative decision-making, which has been automated to a larger extent than other areas.[15] Different areas of decision-making, however, entail different effects. In terms of judicial decision-making, judges themselves must make both procedural and substantive decisions; decisions as to facts, and decisions as to law which may require different levels of discretion; decisions as to both past events and what might occur in the future. The automation of procedural steps, while it may still be significant, is quite different to automating a substantive decision, for

---

[11] UK Ministry of Justice (n 9) 8 [16]; see also Jane Donoghue, 'Reforming the Role of Magistrates: Implications for Summary Justice in England and Wales' (2014) 77 *Modern Law Review* 92.

[12] Nathan Heller, 'Estonia: The Digital Republic', *The New Yorker*, (online, 11 December 2017) <www.newyorker.com/magazine/2017/12/18/estonia-the-digital-republic>.

[13] See especially Eugene Volokh, 'Chief Justice Robots' (2019) 68(6) *Duke Law Journal* 1135.

[14] Rebecca Wexler, 'Life, Liberty, and Trade Secrets: Intellectual Property in the Criminal Justice System' (2018) 70(5) *Stanford Law Review* 1343.

[15] Cary Coglianese and David Lehr, 'Regulating by Robot: Administrative Decision Making in the Machine-Learning Era' (2017) 105(5) *Georgetown Law Journal* 1147.

instance. This demands a nuanced approach to the use of technology in judicial decision-making.[16]

This chapter does not provide an exhaustive analysis of the judicial role and technology. Rather, we sketch how technology is – or may soon be – used by the judiciary: from digitisation of court filing and administrative systems, to automation of decision-making in small claims litigation, to ML software in criminal sentencing. We then examine the judicial values affected by, in particular, the use of automated systems in judicial decision-making. This synthesis lays an analytical foundation for understanding where the technology might go in the future and the dangers it could bring for the judicial role, thereby informing the future use and regulation of such systems.

The remainder of this chapter is divided into two main sections. Section II begins with a discussion of the spectrum of technology used by Australian courts, before explaining the ways in which technologies could be used in the particular context of judicial decision-making. We argue that the context even of seemingly straightforward digital uplift is important, as the reification of technology as efficient, value-neutral and beneficial carries over into more value-laden applications such as those mentioned above. Accordingly, in section III we consider the implications of such automation on foundational judicial values of transparency and accountability, judicial independence, impartiality, diversity and efficiency. Finally, in section IV, we conclude that the role of courts as institutions run by humans – not machines – is especially important now, as lower-level (yet significant) administrative decisions are increasingly automated with little (if any) human oversight. More than ever, a human judiciary is needed to safeguard individual rights and entitlements from the effects of automated decision-making by government and in the private sphere.

II From Digitisation to Automation: The Spectrum of Technologies Used by Courts

Technological tools used by the courts vary from simple digitisation of court registries to deployment of more complex technological systems designed to assist or even replace judicial officers in the decision-making

---

[16] Monika Zalnieriute, Lyria Bennett Moses and George Williams, 'The Rule of Law and Automation of Government Decision-Making' (2019) 82(3) *The Modern Law Review* 425.

process. Digitisation processes are critical for courts' efficient operation in the twenty-first century. While basic technological uplift may seem self-explanatory, these straightforward steps are a necessary precursor to more sophisticated uses. For example, the electronic data available to courts which implement e-filing could be used to train an ML program.[17] Moreover, even what might appear to outsiders to be simple digital uplift, may be challenging for courts to implement, given issues of scale, the bureaucratic nature of large and complex organisations and the hierarchical nature of courts. Courts have finite resources and must choose how best to deploy technology as one of many competing priorities along with personnel and physical environs. Here, we briefly introduce judicial use of technology with several examples before turning to discuss the legal implications of deploying such systems in section III.

A Digitisation

Traditionally, law and the legal system are associated with paper documents. The growth of corporate prosecutions and large-scale inquiries (such as Royal Commissions) in the 1980s and '90s are thought to have prompted the use of computers in managing the volume of documents through cataloguing.[18] Now, it is possible for trials to take place within courtrooms which are entirely digital, with documents electronically filed,[19] as well as other features such as 'digital court reporting, telephone conferencing, hearing loops, real time transcripts, desktop mirroring, multimedia evidence playback and video conferencing'.[20] The use of video-link can obviate the need for judges, lawyers or parties to be physically present in courtrooms. This is of especial benefit to children and other vulnerable witnesses in giving evidence while physically

---

[17] James Allsop, 'Technology and the Future of the Courts' (Speech, TC Beirne School of Law, University of Queensland, 26 March 2019) 5.

[18] Ros Macdonald and Anne Wallace, 'Review of the Extent of Courtroom Technology in Australia' (2004) 12(3) *Willian and Mary Bill of Rights Journal* 649; Peter Vickery, 'Managing the Paper: Taming the Leviathan' (2012) 22(2) *Journal of Judicial Administration* 51.

[19] Allsop (n 17) 5–6; and see 'e-lodgement', *Federal Court of Australia* (Web Page) <www.fedcourt.gov.au/online-services/elodgment>; Marilyn Warren, 'Embracing Technology: The Way Forward for the Courts' (2015) 24(4) *Journal of Judicial Administration* 227.

[20] Robert McDougall, 'The Uses and Abuses of Technology in the Courtroom' (Keynote Address, Society of Construction Law, Australia Conference of 2013, 2 August 2013) 4, [7].

removed from the courtroom environs.[21] However, studies have also found the use of video-link problematic for its unreliable functionality (poor sound and image quality and transmission), communication (for instance, those appearing by video unable to effectively communicate with their lawyer or exchange documents) and difficulty in time-management (people on remand waiting hours in holding cells for their 'appearance').[22] Perhaps the most concerning implications of video-link are for procedural justice in the criminal courts: as McKay concludes, '[t]he administration of justice is not necessarily well-served by substituting a screen for a living human presence'.[23]

In a 2019 speech titled 'Technology and the Future of the Courts', Chief Justice Allsop of the Federal Court of Australia referred to 'internal' and 'external' (or client-facing) digitisation processes.[24] The former describes standard developments, such as e-filing of documents, online databases or digital stamping. This is illustrated well by the Australian National Court Framework, implemented by the Federal Court in 2014.[25] The framework streamlined, synchronised and harmonised the operation of State registries and the functioning and use of individual judges' dockets and involved a move to e-filing, which is offered in some form by most Australian courts.[26]

The Supreme Court of Queensland's efforts to enact a digital trial process are informative. Moving away from reams of paper, an electronic trial involves all documentary evidence being filed as searchable text.[27] This is sometimes referred to as an electronic courtbook.[28] The documents are viewed online, by parties, judge and jury, during the trial. Hyperlinks are used within the courtbook to link between referenced material, which increases the efficiency of searching, and documents may also be annotated electronically. Every document is labelled with a

---

[21] McDougall (n 20).
[22] Carolyn McKay, *The Pixelated Prisoner: Prison Video Links, Court 'Appearance' and the Justice Matrix* (Routledge, 2018) 156–71; Warren (n 19) 231–2.
[23] Ibid. 175.
[24] Allsop (n 17).
[25] 'Australian National Court Framework', *Federal Court of Australia* (Web Page) <https://www.fedcourt.gov.au/about/national-court-framework>.
[26] This is variable – for example, in Tasmania, e-filing is achieved by sending an email attachment: Allsop (n 17) 6.
[27] Sheryl Jackson, 'Court-provided Trial Technology: Efficiency and Fairness for Criminal Trials' (2010) 39(3) *Common Law World Review* 219, 223–4.
[28] McDougall (n 20).

distinct identifier, which makes it easier to reference documents and to deliberate upon any objections to their filing.[29]

Many courts around the world are investigating, if not implementing, even more ambitious external and large-scale digital modernisation projects.[30] In the Canadian province of British Colombia, people with a wide range of small claims disputes are directed first to an online portal.[31] If the parties cannot resolve the proceedings, they may be determined online by a Tribunal Member in lieu of a face-to-face hearing. Similarly, in 2018, the Victorian Civil and Administrative Tribunal (VCAT) implemented an online dispute resolution pilot. Through the pilot, VCAT 'heard 65 cases using the technology, with 71 parties participating in online hearings and 21 cases settled beforehand', and according to VCAT, 'shows exciting potential benefits for the Victorian community'.[32] However, the pursuit of digitisation of the courts for cost-saving and efficiency may sometimes conflict with, rather than promote, access to justice – as noted with the use of video-link. We discuss this tension and its implications for judges and the judicial role in parts III and IV.

B Decision-Support and Automation of Decision-Making

As Allsop CJ noted, without internal digitisation, external digitisation is not feasible.[33] Likewise, general digital uplift supports more sophisticated technologies, focused on the use of artificial intelligence in judicial decision-making. The degree of automation employed may vary along a trajectory starting with what is known as 'decision-support' to 'human-in-the-loop', to the total disappearance of humans from the decision-making process.[34] 'Decision-support' is an information system which supports organisational decision-making, and has a relatively long

---

[29] McDougall (n 20) [13].
[30] Donoghue (n 11) 1000–1; UK Ministry of Justice, *Transforming Our Justice System* (2016).
[31] 'Welcome to the Civil Resolution Tribunal', *Civil Resolution Tribunal* (Web Page) <https://civilresolutionbc.ca/>.
[32] 'Sharing VCAT's Online Dispute Resolution Experience', *VCAT* (Web Page, 21 November 2018) <www.vcat.vic.gov.au/news/sharing-vcats-online-dispute-resolution-experience>; Vivi Tan, 'Online Dispute Resolution for Small Civil Claims in Victoria: A New Paradigm in Civil Justice' (2019) 24(1) *Deakin Law Review* 101.
[33] Allsop (n 17).
[34] See Iyad Rahwan, 'Society-in-the-Loop: Programming the Algorithmic Social Contract' (2018) 20(1) *Ethics and Information Technology* 5; Sailik Sengupta et al., 'RADAR: A Proactive Decision Support System for Human-in-the-Loop Planning' (Conference Paper, AAAI Fall Symposium Series, 9–11 November 2017).

history.[35] Meanwhile, human-in-the-loop is a system with more automation but which still requires human interaction.[36] These different systems are not separate categories but exist on a spectrum moving from fully human decision-making to systems that, while designed by humans, operate largely independent of them.

Decision-support and automation with a human-in-the-loop may involve different techniques, and sometimes combinations of them. We focus on two classic types. The first, sometimes described as the first wave of artificial intelligence (AI) or expert systems, is a process that follows a series of pre-programmed rules to mirror responses of a human expert in a particular domain.[37] A number of early forays in the research field of AI and Law were designed as decision-support systems, such as that developed in the 80s by Sergot and Kowalski at Imperial College London to support decisions made by immigration officials.[38] A current example, EXPERTIUS, is a decision-support system used in Mexico to advise judges and clerks as to whether a plaintiff is eligible for a pension.[39] Generally, these systems function to guide decision-making in situations where rules (such as legislative rules) lend themselves to step-by-step programming and do not have indeterminate concepts, and where facts are uncontroversial or agreed.

As well as preprogrammed systems like these, statistical analyses in judicial decision-making also has some history in, for example, the use of sentencing databases, such as the one created in the NSW Sentencing Information System (later the Judicial Information Research System, JIRS),[40] to support judges in criminal sentencing. While not involving ML, the purpose was to support judges by collating information about

---

[35] Giovanni Sartor and Karl Branting (eds) *Judicial Applications of Artificial Intelligence* (Kluwer Academic, 1998).
[36] Lorrie F Cranor, 'A Framework for Reasoning about the Human in the Loop' (Conference Paper, Usability, Psychology, and Security, 14 April 2008).
[37] Richard E Susskind, *Expert Systems in Law: A Jurisprudential Inquiry* (Clarendon Press, 1987) 114–15.
[38] Marek Sergot et al., 'The British Nationality Act as a Logic Program' (1988) 29(5) *Communications of the Association for Computing Machinery* 370; c.f. P Leith, 'The Rise and Fall of the Legal Expert System' (2010) 1(1) *European Journal of Law and Technology* <https://ejlt.org/index.php/ejlt/article/view/14/1>.
[39] Davide Carneiro et al., 'Online Dispute Resolution: An Artificial Intelligence Perspective' (2014) 41 *Artificial Intelligence Review* 227–28.
[40] 'Judicial Information Research System (JIRS)', *Judicial Commission of New South Wales*, (Web Page) <www.judcom.nsw.gov.au/research-and-sentencing/judicial-information-research-system-jirs>; Janet BL Chan, 'A Computerised Sentencing Information System for NSW Courts' (1991) 7(3) *Computer Law and Practice* 137, 147.

past sentences, enabling judges to discover the range of penalties imposed in the past for similar convictions. JIRS, which is accessible to lawyers as well as judges, thus represents a form of decision-support system, aimed at harmonising sentencing in pursuit of greater consistency.

The second category – or 'second wave' of AI – includes techniques such as supervised machine learning and deep learning.[41] These are systems that 'learn' from data (either collected or constructed) so as to draw inferences about new situations. These decisions may be classification (for instance, that a document is relevant in discovery[42]) or predictive (for instance, that an individual is likely to commit a crime in the future). A variety of data-driven techniques can be used so that a system will 'learn' patterns and correlations to generate predictions or reveal insights. Unlike standard statistical methods, ML is generally iterative (able to continually learn from new information) and capable of identifying more complex patterns in data.

One area of judicial decision-making where second-wave automation tools have already been deployed in practice is the prediction of the likelihood of reoffending in the context of criminal sentencing decisions. For example, in some US jurisdictions, judges can (or may even be required to) use risk-assessment tools such as COMPAS (Correctional Offender Management Profiling for Alternative Sanctions) that draw on historic data and use ML to infer which convicted defendants pose the highest risk of re-offending, particularly where there is a risk of violence, to make decisions about bail or sentence. Many scholars have expressed concerns that judicial use of such tools has been approved by the Conference of US Chief Justices[43] and by the Supreme Court of Wisconsin, as well as in various state statutes.[44] In a test case, *State of*

---

[41] Michael Haenlein and Andreas Kaplan, 'A Brief History of Artificial Intelligence: On the Past, Present, and Future of Artificial Intelligence' (2019) 61(4) *California Management Review* 5–14; J Launchbury, 'A DARPA Perspective on Artificial Intelligence' (YouTube, 15 February 2017) <www.youtube.com/watch?v=-O01G3tSYpU>.

[42] See, for instance, Maura R Grossman and Gordon V Cormack, 'Technology-Assisted Review in E-Discovery Can Be More Effective and More Efficient than Exhaustive Manual Review' (2011) 17(3) *Richmond Journal of Law and Technology* 1.

[43] Conference of Chief Justices/State Court Administrators Criminal Justice Committee, 'In Support of the Guiding Principles on Using Risk and Needs Assessment Information in the Sentencing Process' (Resolution 7, 3 August 2011).

[44] See *State of Wisconsin v Loomis*, 881 N.W.2d 749 (Wis. 2016) ('*Loomis*'). The United States Supreme Court denied certiorari on 26 June 2017: Kelly Hannah-Moffat, 'Algorithmic Risk Governance: Big Data Analytics, Race and Information Activism in Criminal Justice Debates' (2018) 23(4) *Theoretical Criminology* 453; Sharad Goel et al.,

Wisconsin v Loomis ('Loomis'), use of the COMPAS system was held to be permissible on the condition that the decision was not fully delegated to ML software and that the judge was notified of the tool's limitations.[45] Thus, a judge must still consider a defendant's arguments as to why other factors might impact the risk that he or she poses.[46] As judicial sentencing decisions affect the freedom and lives of individuals, the use of algorithms to automate elements of them is particularly controversial.

Finally, in contrast to the use of a tool to supplement decision-making, the Estonian Ministry of Justice automation project seeks to completely adjudicate (albeit with rights of appeal) small contract disputes.[47] The goal is primarily efficiency: both to clear a backlog and to leave judges with more time to determine complex disputes. Reportedly, the project will 'adjudicate small claims disputes under €7,000 ... In concept, the two parties will upload documents and other relevant information, and the AI will issue a decision that can be appealed to a human judge'.[48] European scholars have already noted, though, that subjecting people to automated decisions in this manner may breach the European Union's General Data Protection Regulation,[49] entitling individuals to not be subjected to entirely automated decisions.[50]

III Foundational Judicial Values and Technology

There has been much scholarly analysis of judicial values, sometimes classified as core or traditional (for instance, independence; impartiality)

'The Accuracy, Equity, and Jurisprudence of Criminal Risk Assessment' (Research Paper, Risk-Resilience Research, University of California, Berkeley December 26, 2018).
[45] 881 N.W.2d 749 (Wis. 2016).
[46] Ibid. [56].
[47] 'Justice: Estonian Ministry of Justice wants AI-powered Robot Judge to Clear Backlog of Small Court Disputes' *Ai Everything* (online, 1 April 2019) <https://ai-everything.com/government-estonian-ministry-of-justice-wants-ai-powered-robot-judge-to-clear-backlog-of-small-court-disputes/>.
[48] David Cowan, 'Estonia: A Robotically Transformative Nation', *Robotics Law Journal* (online 26 July 2019) <www.roboticslawjournal.com/global/estonia-a-robotically-transformative-nation-28728942>.
[49] *Regulation (EU) 2016/679 of the European Parliament and of the Council of 27 April 2016 on the Protection of Aatural Persons with Regard to the Processing of Personal Data and on the Free Movement of Such Data, and Repealing Directive 95/46/EC (General Data Protection Regulation)* [2016] OJ L119/1.
[50] Sandra Watcher, Brent Mittelstadt and Chris Russell 'Counterfactual Explanations without Opening the Black Box: Automated Decisions and the GPDR'(2017) 31(2) *Harvard Journal of Law and Technology* 841.

and emerging (for instance, diversity;[51] efficiency[52]). Without ourselves engaging in such an in-depth analysis, in this section we consider how technology, especially automated systems, might either support or undermine key judicial values. We note, too, the broader import of the judicial function, discussed by Joe McIntyre in this collection – the judiciary are not only dispute resolvers (framed in a particular, unique and historically dependent way) but also constitute a form of social governance.[53] Technology's impact on judicial values and on courts as institutions thus shapes not only the resolution of disputes, but also society more generally. While it may be possible to automate judging on a technical level, we doubt the capacity of technological systems to realise these broader goals.

In analysing technology's impact on the judicial role, we identify core judicial values which we consider are most impacted by technology: transparency and accountability; independence; impartiality (equal treatment or absence of bias in decision-making); diversity; and efficiency. This partially borrows from Richard Devlin and Adam Dodek's typology,[54] also applied by Appleby and Roberts in their chapter in this collection.[55] These values often overlap and interconnect in complex ways and we have grouped some in our analysis.

A Open Justice: Transparency and Accountability

Considered to be 'the commitment to openness and candour', judicial transparency, often cited in conjunction with the principle of 'open justice', is one of the most widely accepted judicial values. It requires openness about the working and operations of the court.[56] Transparency is closely related to accountability of the courts by providing a form of

---

[51] See Brian Opeskin's chapter, 'Dismantling the Diversity Deficit: Towards a More Inclusive Australian Judiciary', in this collection.
[52] See Gabrielle Appleby and Heather Roberts' chapter, 'The Chief Justice: Under Relational and Institutional pressure' in this collection.
[53] See Joe McIntyre's chapter, 'Re-examining the Judicial Function in Australia' in this collection.
[54] Richard Devlin and Adam Dodek, 'Regulating Judges: Challenges, Controversies and Choices' in Richard Devlin and Adam Dodek (eds), *Regulating Judges: Beyond Independence and Accountability* (Edward Elgar, 2016) 1.
[55] Appleby and Roberts (n 52).
[56] Devlin and Dodek, 'Regulating Judges' (n 54) 9.

oversight,[57] as beautifully encapsulated in Justice Louis Brandeis's famous quote, '[s]unlight is said to be the best of disinfectants'.[58] In the judicial context, accountability in often understood as 'the commitment to ensure that the values of independence and impartiality are appropriately deployed in the public interest, rather than the interest of the judges themselves'.[59] Both transparency and accountability are necessary for individuals to understand the reasons for decisions affecting them and learn how future decisions might affect them, as well as for trust the courts more generally.

In line with these ideals of open justice, technology has provided the opportunity for the 'world to come into the courtroom'.[60] For example, as early as the 1990s, in a climate of intense critique of the High Court of Australia from Australian political leaders,[61] Brennan CJ pursued a broad course of opening up the Court to enhance public confidence, including making 'its procedures more understandable and its decisions more easily available'[62] and allowing video recording to document the justices at work.[63]

Today, courts are, in many ways, more transparent and accountable due to technology. Most Australian courts now publish decisions online – either on their own websites or on public databases.[64] The High Court now publishes audio-visual recordings of its hearings on its website.[65] Criminal courts have featured 'Sentencing Webcasts' on their websites, as sentencing is the area in which the courts have historically received the most public criticism.[66] The Supreme Court of Victoria regularly posts on Facebook and tweets about recent decisions and developments in the

---

[57] Richard Devlin and Adam Dodek, 'Fighting Words': Regulating Judges in Canada' in Richard Devlin and Adam Dodek (eds), *Regulating Judges: Beyond Independence and Accountability* (Edward Elgar, 2016) 79.
[58] Louis Brandeis, *Other People's Money and How the Bankers Use It* (National Home Library, 1933) 62.
[59] Devlin and Dodek, 'Regulating Judges' (n 54) 9.
[60] Warren (n 19) 235.
[61] The Coalition Government (1996 – 2007) under Prime Minister John Howard.
[62] *High Court of Australia: Annual Report 1997–1998* (Report, 13 November 1998) 6.
[63] *The Highest Court* (Film Art Doco, 1998). The Court also created the role of Public Information Officer: *High Court of Australia: Annual Report 1999-2000* (Report, 12 September 2000) 5.
[64] See, for instance, *Australian Legal Information Institute* (Web Page) <austlii.edu.au>.
[65] 'Recent AV Recordings', *High Court of Australia* (Web Page) <www.hcourt.gov.au/cases/recent-av-recordings>.
[66] Appleby and Roberts (n 52) 17. The authors note that the ultimate decision to release footage lies with the Chief Justice.

law.[67] It also allows the media – but not the public – to post and tweet about ongoing matters, arguably limiting the principle of 'open justice'.[68] Of course, limits on open justice, including suppression orders applying to the media, might be needed to preserve the principle of the fair trial, as was recently illustrated with the criminal trial of Cardinal George Pell.[69]

Therefore, different values of justice might sometimes be in tension with each other, and technology might fortify that tension further by facilitating communications online. Former Chief Justice of the Supreme Court of Victoria Marilyn Warren argues that technology provides the advantage of allowing courts to control the message conveyed to the community.[70] While this may ensure more accurate public understanding of the work of the courts, and temper unfair or factually incorrect media coverage, it may also diminish transparency and consequently accountability of the courts. On the other hand, as we discuss in the following section, technology also enables greater scrutiny of both courts and individual judges, including detailed or large-scale analysis of patterns of decision-making.

Moving from digitisation to technology decision-support and decision-making systems, in theory automated systems offer the potential to make transparent most, or all aspects of the judicial decision-making process, an impossibility in a human judge. For example, Susskind suggested that automated decision-making systems – if designed correctly – could render transparent every step of the decision-making process.[71] However, we are not yet convinced that such tools are very easy to design correctly, and the struggles over early expert systems illustrate the seemingly insurmountable difficulties involved in programming a system to mimic (and explain) legal reasoning. In terms of ML systems, there are even more challenges when it comes to including explainability mechanisms. Wisser suggests that if algorithms usurp judges' decision-making power, then the developers or creators of automated systems should be responsible, similarly to a judge, for explaining their decisions 'in written, protracted, published opinions'.[72] Yet, sometimes

---

[67] Warren (n 19) 227.
[68] Warren (n 19).
[69] See also Kirrily Schwarz, 'Secret's Out: The Storm Around Suppression Orders' (2019) 55 *Law Society Journal* 30.
[70] Warren (n 19) 234.
[71] Susskind (n 37) 114–15.
[72] Leah Wisser, 'Pandora's Algorithmic Black Box: The Challenges of Using Algorithmic Risk Assessments in Sentencing' (2019) 56(4) *American Criminal Law Review* 1811.

those who create algorithmic or ML systems themselves struggle to understand and explain why their programs make a single, discrete decision.[73]

This connects to a much wider challenge that automation poses to transparency, convincingly summarised as three 'forms of opacity' of automation tools.[74] The first form – intentional secrecy – may prevent judicial transparency when automation tools are protected as trade or state secrets under intellectual property (IP) laws. For example, the owners of the COMPAS tool (used in risk assessments for sentencing and bail decisions) have not publicly disclosed the methods or datasets used in its training and development. COMPAS's lack of transparency was the focus of one of the concurring judgments in *Loomis*, where Abrahamson J described the 'court's lack of understanding' of the tool as a 'significant problem'.[75] Her Honour observed that

> making a record, including a record explaining consideration of the evidence-based tools and the limitations and strengths thereof, is part of the long-standing, basic requirement that a circuit court explain its exercise of discretion at sentencing.[76]

Such transparency and analysis of the tool itself would also provide 'the public with a transparent and comprehensible explanation for the sentencing court's decision'.[77] However, the Wisconsin court held that there was no requirement that defense counsel be able to challenge the accuracy of the COMPAS algorithms which remain a trade secret.[78] Arguably, lack of transparency due to intentional secrecy seriously undermines judicial transparency and accountability.[79]

Additional forms of opacity of both expert systems and ML may pose further challenges to judicial transparency, because even if operational information is disclosed, that does not mean that a majority of the public

---

[73] Ibid. 1815.
[74] Jenna Burrell, 'How the Machine 'Thinks': Understanding Opacity in Machine Learning Algorithms' (2016) 3(1) *Big Data and Society* 1.
[75] *Loomis* (n 44) 774.
[76] Ibid. [133], [141].
[77] Ibid. [142].
[78] Ibid. [51]. See also Stanford Pretrial Risk Assessment Tools Factsheet Project, *Stanford Law School* (Web Page) <https://law.stanford.edu/pretrial-risk-assessment-tools-factsheet-project/>.
[79] Katherine Freeman, 'Algorithmic Injustice: How the Wisconsin Supreme Court Failed to Protect Due Process Rights in *State v. Loomis*' (2016) 18 *North Carolina Journal of Law and Technology Online* 75.

will be able to extract useful knowledge from that information.[80] In this context, the significance of judicial reasoning is unparalleled, as it enables the judiciary 'to communicate evidence that their decision making is neutral'.[81] Automated systems generally do not (and possibly cannot) provide reasons for the decision they deliver, but reasons are crucial (and thus imperative[82]) for ensuring that the parties and the public understand the logic behind judicial decision-making. Language is a constitutive element of legal judgments, leading some to proclaim that it 'does not merely represent one of many forms the law can take but is the *only* form capable of realizing foundational rule of law principles'.[83] To illustrate this tension between language and technology, imagine that the technical code of COMPAS was made public. The code would not provide the reasons for the conclusions it reached – and how many of us would be able to read and understand it in the first place? Finally, Burrell has suggested that because humans reason differently than do machines, they cannot always interpret the interactions among data and algorithms, even if suitably trained.[84] Thus, even if we could read the code, we might not be able to understand how the ML system generated its results, as it has gone through a recursive process of refining its results and adjusting the 'weight' accorded to a multitude of different variables. This suggests that transparency, which is crucial for other judicial values and overall accountability of the courts, may erode over time as ML systems become more complex.

B Judicial Independence

Judicial independence is widely recognised as a fundamental judicial value,[85] having 'multiple dimensions' that cover the independence of the individual judge or decisional independence (the 'core' dimension), independence of the judiciary as an institution from interference or usurpation by the other branches of government under the theory of the

---

[80] Burrell (n 74).
[81] Tom R Tyler, 'Procedural Justice, Legitimacy, and the Effective Rule of Law' (2003) 30 *Crime and Justice* 283, 298.
[82] *Wainohu v New South Wales* (2011) 243 CLR 181.
[83] Frank Pasquale, 'A Rule of Persons, Not Machines: The Limits of Legal Automation' (2019) 87(1) *George Washington Law Review* 1.
[84] Burrell (n 74).
[85] Appleby and Roberts (n 52) 7.

separation of powers, as well as independence afforded by administrative and fiscal self-management.[86] The interplay between these three conceptions of independence, as Devlin and Dodek note, varies and manifests differently across different jurisdictions, but judicial independence factors highly, not only in constitutional theory but also in practice.[87]

Some have, however, regarded independence not as a value in itself but as the *institutional* safeguard of impartiality.[88] Irrespective of whether one agrees, independence of the individual judge, or 'decision independence' in Devlin and Dodek's typology, significantly overlaps with the value of *impartiality*, referring to 'decision making that is 'free from personal, social, cultural, economic or institutional bias, and which fairly assesses the rights and interests of the parties involved'.[89]

As Brennan CJ noted, '[t]he principle of judicial independence ... is proclaimed in order to guarantee a fair and impartial hearing and an unswerving obedience to the rule of law'.[90] We discuss impartiality in the following section, focusing here on the institutional, administrative, and fiscal independence of the courts. These are widely identified as key to ensuring the institutional independence of the judiciary. Interestingly, the judiciary has employed technology, especially communication through digital media, to bring wider public awareness about underfunding of courts and fiscal challenges more generally. For example, ahead of an appearance before a budgetary hearing, in an attempt to defend the fiscal independence of the judiciary, Chief Justice Kourakis of the South Australian Supreme Court, released a media statement to ensure public awareness.[91]

Moreover, digital technologies, enabling widespread sharing of information, are an important tool in fighting against judicial corruption, which arguably undermines institutional independence as well as impartiality of the judiciary. Technologies such as electronic case allocation,

---

[86] Devlin and Dodek, 'Regulating Judges' (n 54) 1, 13; Appleby and Roberts (n 52) 7–8.
[87] Devlin and Dodek, 'Regulating Judges' (n 54) 13.
[88] Abeline Dorothea Reiling, *Technology for Justice How Information Technology Can Support Judicial Reform* (Thesis, Leiden University, 2009) 61.
[89] Devlin and Dodek, 'Regulating Judges' (n 54) 9; Devlin and Dodek, 'Fighting Words' (n 57) 78; McIntyre (n 53) 19–21.
[90] Sir Gerald Brennan, 'The State of the Judicature' (1998) 72(1) *Australian Law Journal* 33, 34.
[91] Chris Kourakis, 'Budget Announcement' (Media Release, Court Administration Authority of South Australia, 18 June 2019).

which randomly assigns cases to ensure that judges are not 'cherry-picked' to hear particular cases, and electronic case management systems can provide further oversight by identifying irregularities.[92] Therefore, digital technologies have the capacity to support judicial independence by helping to reduce corruption and increasing 'public trust by providing an effective means of communication between courts and their users and the general public'.[93]

However, moving from simple communication via digital technologies to the deployment of automation tools in the judicial decision-making process itself, the independence of the judiciary could be undermined. This could happen, for instance, because (as explained in the preceding sections) the tool that is relied on to assist judges may use proprietary software, developed by a private company operating for profit. Where such systems are not open source and are protected by IP laws, it is impossible to understand precisely how their outputs have been generated.[94] This impacts both institutional independence and judicial impartiality. For instance, COMPAS employs such proprietary software, so judges do not know how it operates. Yet there are known examples where sentencing judges have overturned plea deals and imposed longer sentences on the convicted person because COMPAS produced very high potential recidivism scores.[95] Judges may be *required* to consider machine-generated risk scores in decision-making.[96] Whether or not the tool itself is accurate, judges must take its projections on face value and cannot interrogate its processes or question its methods. Reliance on – or even a delegation of a decision to – a secretive tool is in tension with the value of judicial independence, which requires that judges are able to independently verify and understand an expert's evidence. The fact that judges do not have (and are unable to acquire) knowledge about the operation of an automated tool arguably has a significant impact on judges themselves and their understanding of the judicial role.

---

[92] Victoria Jennett, *Fighting Judicial Corruption: Topic Guide* (Report, 31 October 2014).
[93] Reiling (n 88) 254.
[94] Melissa Perry, 'iDecide: Administrative Decision-Making in the Digital World' (2017) 91(1) *Australian Law Journal* 29.
[95] Alyssa M Carlson, 'The Need for Transparency in the Age of Predictive Sentencing Algorithms' (2017) 103 *Iowa Law Review* 303.
[96] Partnership on AI, *Report on Algorithmic Risk Assessment Tools in the US Criminal Justice System* (Report, 26 April 2019).

C Impartiality/Equality Before the Law

Impartiality, meaning the quality of not favouring one side or party more than another, is the hallmark of the judge in an adversarial system. It encapsulates an absence of bias or prejudice on the part of the decision-maker. This is important both for individual determinations and in order to retain public confidence in the system of justice. In this sense impartiality it is also a facet of equality or the dispensing of equitable justice, in that like cases are treated alike.[97] This concept of equal treatment is key to a consideration of the impact of technology on the judicial role.

In relation to absence of bias, new forms of communication technology – notably the rise of social networking and social media platforms – have challenged conceptions of how judges ought permissibly to interact with lawyers and others. For example, with increasing Facebook use came questions about whether it was appropriate for judges to be 'Facebook friends' with lawyers or even parties appearing before them.[98] In the US, judges have been 'reprimanded' for their use of social media (including for posting comments about, and 'researching' those appearing before them).[99] It is now common for courts to have guidelines on how judges are to use social media, which generally require judges to consider how their use of social media affects their actual or perceived impartiality.[100]

A more substantive role for technology in buttressing impartiality is in support of judges. For example, decision-support systems might be designed to ensure that decision-makers consider relevant considerations and disregard irrelevant considerations; and that criteria are applied in standardised ways, improving consistency of decision-making. For instance, the earlier mentioned NSW sentencing database was created to reduce inconsistency in sentences, as 'it was felt that if judges had

---

[97] See Zalnieriute et al. (n 16).
[98] Samuel Vincent Jones, 'Judges, Friends, and Facebook: The Ethics of Prohibition' (2011) 24(2) *Georgetown Journal of Legal Ethics* 281; Benjamin P Cooper, 'USA: Saving Face – Ethical Considerations for American Judges Using Facebook' (2014) 17(1) *Legal Ethics* 148–52; Steven Rares, 'Social Media - Challenges for Lawyers and the Courts' (Speech, Australian Young Lawyers' Conference, 20 October 2017) [30].
[99] Cooper (n 98).
[100] Rares (n 98); see, for instance, The Council of Chief Justices of Australia and New Zealand, *Guide to Judicial Conduct* (Australasian Institute of Judicial Administration, 3rd ed, 2017) 43–5.

easier access to historical sentencing patterns, inconsistency in sentencing outcomes might be reduced'.[101] Some claim that properly designed and tested automated systems allow for human biases to be controlled for or removed from the decision-making process.[102] In most instances, however, such systems are designed for use in administrative or government, rather than judicial, decision-making. Justice Perry of the Federal Court has noted that automated systems are not useful in discretionary decision-making.[103] It is also arguably not permissible to direct a judge as to how he or she ought make a decision, which may compromise judicial independence, as noted in the previous section.

Another way that technology – specifically statistical or ML analysis of judicial decision-making – might be used is to illustrate or bring to light the existence of anomalous decisions or patterns of decision-making among the judiciary. An example is the work of researchers at Macquarie University who have built an ML program to analyse patterns of judicial decision-making in migration cases heard in the Federal Circuit Court.[104] As well as highlighting patterns, there are ML systems which can, with sufficient data, predict with good accuracy how judges will determine cases. Thus in certain areas of law automated systems are able to predict the likely outcome of decisions.[105]

These different uses – highlighting possible patterns of differential treatment, perhaps ensuring consistent treatment, and the use of predictive analytics – have ramifications for judicial impartiality. Impartiality mandates that judges operate both without actual bias – essentially, pre-judgment of the case at hand – and apprehended bias, where 'a fair minded lay observer' could reasonably consider that a judge

---

[101] Lyria Bennett Moses and Janet Chan, 'Using Big Data for Legal and Law Enforcement Decisions: Testing the New Tools' (2014) 37(2) *University of New South Wales Law Journal* 643, 660.

[102] Jay Thornton, 'Cost, Accuracy, and Subjective Fairness in Legal Information Technology: A Response to Technological Due Process Critics' (2016) 91(6) *New York University Law Review* 1821, 1840, 1849; Nigel Stobbs, Dan Hunter and Mirko Bagaric, 'Can Sentencing Be Enhanced by the Use of Artificial Intelligence' (2017) 41 *Criminal Law Journal* 261.

[103] Perry (n 94).

[104] 'Who Watches Over Our Judges?', *Background Briefing* (ABC Radio National, 8 September 2019).

[105] See, for instance, Daniel Martin Katz, Michael J Bommarito II and Josh Blackman, 'A General Approach for Predicting the Behavior of the Supreme Court of the United States' (2017) 12(4) *PLoS ONE* e0174698; Mihai Surdeanu et al., 'Risk Analysis for Intellectual Property Litigation' (Conference Paper, International Conference on Artificial Intelligence and Law, 6–10 June 2011).

might not bring an impartial mind to the decision to be made.[106] Generally speaking, attempts to show that an individual judge has acted in a biased manner in a particular case, based solely on statistical analysis of decisions, have not succeeded in Australia, though statistics have been used to publicly critique judges.[107] In the case law, such evidence has been rejected as lacking probative value and held not to demonstrate apprehended or actual bias (which is a stringent test).[108] In a 1994 decision, Heerey J decoupled a pattern of past decision-making from the making of future decisions, saying that a past record of decisions could only suggest a likelihood that future decisions would be decided similarly, which is insufficient to demonstrate bias.[109] In another case, the Full Court of the Federal Court emphasised the importance of context:

> for such raw statistical material to be attributed to the hypothetical observer, it normally would need to be accompanied by a relevant analysis of the individual immigration judgments determined by the primary judge in order that the statistics were placed in a proper context. Absent such analysis, the hypothetical observer would not be able to make an informed assessment of the significance of the raw statistics.[110]

While they may not meet the legal test for apprehended bias, such analyses may still undermine broader concepts of judicial impartiality by appearing to demonstrate tendencies among judges to rule in particular ways. Presentation of such information may fuel public criticism of judges and lead to distrust or disrespect. It may also, especially in commercial contexts, shape the nature of cases which proceed to judicial determination or, if lawyers use data to 'craft' arguments for certain judges, become something of an echo chamber, as each successful application of the data generates confirmatory data.[111] As with any application

---

[106] Margaret Beazley and Chris Frommer, 'The Distinctive Role of the Judge: "The Least Dangerous Branch of Government"' in Michael Legg (ed), *Resolving Civil Disputes* (LexisNexis Butterworths, 2016) 3, 10–11, quoting *Ebner v Official Trustee in Bankruptcy* (2000) 205 CLR 337, 344–5 [6] (Gleeson CJ, McHugh, Gummow and Hayne JJ).

[107] *Vietnam Veterans* (n 2) [26], [33]; *ALA15 v Minister for Immigration and Border Protection* [2016] FCAFC 30 ('*ALA15*'); *BDS17 v Minister for Immigration and Border Protection* [2018] FCA 1683 ('*BDS17*').

[108] *BDS17* [2018] FCA 1683.

[109] *Vietnam Veterans* (1994) 52 FCR 34.

[110] *ALA15* [2016] FCFCA 30 [38].

[111] Frank Pasquale and Glyn Cashwell, 'Prediction, Persuasion, and the Jurisprudence of Behaviourism' (2018) 68(Supplement 1) *University of Toronto Law Journal* 63.

of big data analyses to individuals, there is the risk that individual differences or nuances of a case are overlooked in pursuit of machine-generated patterns.

D   Diversity/Representation

The concept of diversity is a more recent addition to the compendium of judicial values. It is itself a broad notion encompassing differences in geographic location, race, ethnicity, gender, culture, age, education, disability, faith and sexuality.[112] In the judicial context, diversity might include professional background and education. Of course, personal traits, especially those which are immutable, are only aspects of individuals. People may identify with multiple groups, and particular views or attitudes based on identity should not be assumed.[113] Brian Opeskin summarises why a diverse judiciary is beneficial and valuable: it will increase equality of opportunity; quality (diversity will improve decision-making); utility (more meritorious appointments); and legitimacy (public perceptions of representativeness).[114]

The Australian judiciary is not at all diverse in terms of the population it serves, especially with regards to characteristics such as country of birth, gender and disability.[115] The use of automated systems in the employment context has, in some circumstances, increased diversity in private organisations. For example, multinational company Unilever found that using an ML system to evaluate candidates' applications and video interviews significantly increased diversity in hiring.[116] Hiring of nonwhite applicants increased by 10%, and the number of different universities represented among those hired tripled.[117] A number of more basic steps, such as reintroducing merit-based selection procedures,

---

[112] Leslie J Moran, 'Judicial Diversity and the Challenge of Sexuality. Some Preliminary Findings' (2006) 28 *Sydney Law Review* 565, 566. Note also that diversity is distinct from 'inclusiveness'.

[113] Melissa L Breger, 'Making the Invisible Visible: Exploring Implicit Bias, Judicial Diversity, and the Bench Trial' (2019) 53(4) *University of Richmond Law Review* 1039, 1077–8.

[114] Opeskin (n 51).

[115] Ibid.

[116] Bernard Marr, 'The Amazing Ways How Unilever Uses Artificial Intelligence to Recruit & Train Thousands of Employees', *Forbes* (online, 14 December 2018) <www.forbes.com/sites/bernardmarr/2018/12/14/the-amazing-ways-how-unilever-uses-artificial-intelligence-to-recruit-train-thousands-of-employees/#1c938da96274>.

[117] Ibid.

could be taken to address the 'diversity deficit' in the Australian judiciary,[118] however, before invoking a system as sophisticated as that of Unilever.

The possible effect of the judges' own personal qualities on decision-making is called up by the use of ML analytics discussed in the previous section in relation to impartiality.[119] Some work in empirical legal studies has, for example, attempted to connect the personal attributes of judges, such as race or gender, to tendencies to rule in certain ways.[120] Such usage has been recently prohibited in France, preventing the use of ML analytics in relation to individual judges – a change which appears to be primarily protective of the judiciary.[121] On a wider scale, the use of analytics may or may not be useful to the diversity project – it may illustrate patterns but ultimately cannot inform on the quality of judging.

E Efficiency

Finally, efficiency is also a newer addition to the stable of judicial values, though highly relevant to technology. The most common use of the term 'efficiency' is to denote both efficacy and timeliness. This contrasts with how the term is used in economics, which traditionally invokes the concept of maximizing society's well-being,[122] although clearly similar considerations are also relevant for the purposes of efficiency in the judicial setting.

As discussed in section II, most technology projects within courts are aimed at increasing efficiency – usually by saving costs and time. However, the judiciary have a complex relationship with notions of efficiency – obligations to enhance the speed and reduce the cost of

---

[118] Ibid.; Elizabeth Handsley and Andrew Lynch, 'Facing up to Diversity? Transparency and the Reform of Commonwealth Judicial Appointments 2008-13' (2015) 37 *Sydney Law Review* 187, 195-99.

[119] Rosemary Hunter, 'More than Just a Different Face? Judicial Diversity and Decision-Making' (2015) 68 *Current Legal Problems* 119, 124.

[120] See, for instance, the summary of Allison P Harris and Maya Sen 'Bias and Judging' (2019) 22 *Annual Review of Political Science* 241.

[121] LOI n° 2019-222 du 23 mars 2019 de programmation 2018-2022 et de réforme pour la justice (1) (France) JO, 24 March 2019, art 33; 'France Bans Judge Analytics, 5 Years in Prison for Rule Breakers', *Artifical Lawyer* (online, 4 June 2019) <www.artificiallawyer.com/2019/06/04/france-bans-judge-analytics-5-years-in-prison-for-rule-breakers/>.

[122] Jeff Borland, *Microeconomics: Case Studies and Applications* (Cengage Learning, 3rd ed, 2016) 96.

proceedings must not come at the expense of justice.[123] At the same time, efficiency is seen to form part of individual justice ('justice delayed is justice denied'), so the discretion of judges should be exercised with these requirements in mind.[124] This is especially so given that delay may also increase the damage allegedly caused. Yet procedural fairness, an element of justice, necessarily entails cost and delay – hence, the tension between justice and efficiency has traditionally been a difficult one.[125] For example, the use of video-links can reduce costs and time associated with bringing persons to court. It may also enable a person 'to adduce evidence that might not otherwise have been available'[126] and protect vulnerable witnesses. On the other hand, use of video-link is a distinct change to the historical importance accorded to parties and witnesses in court proceedings, and judiciary, 'seeing' one another in person, and may negatively impact a person's ability to be heard.[127]

Communication technologies are among the most important for judicial work, and – with the exception of video-link – largely uncontroversial. Improving document retrieval,[128] minimising paper usage, and having access to real time transcripts of proceedings,[129] all carry efficiency benefits. The goal of efficiency is, however, also the primary argument made for the use of a number of more controversially applied technologies: automation of small claims or minor offences; and use of risk assessments and predictive analytics to 'prioritise' or triage certain cases, or as a means to compel settlement and avoid the use of judicial resources altogether.[130]

One limitation of automated tools applied in the legal domain is their current inability to determine factual disputes. Automation of small claims or family disputes, for example, relies on facts being agreed or

---

[123] See, for instance, *Civil Procedure Act 2005* (NSW) ss 56–60; Michael Legg, 'Reconciling the Goals of Minimising Cost and Delay with the Principle of a Fair Trial in the Australian Civil Justice System' (2014) 33(2) *Civil Justice Quarterly* 157, 170.
[124] *Aon Risk Services Australia Ltd v Australian National University* (2009) 239 CLR 157.
[125] Legg (n 123) 170.
[126] McDougall (n 20).
[127] McKay (n 22).
[128] Jackson (n 27) 236–7.
[129] McDougall (n 20).
[130] Nikolaos Aletras et al., 'Predicting Judicial Decisions of the European Court of Human Rights: A Natural Language Processing Perspective' (2016) 2 *PeerJournal of Computer Science* 93; Felicity Bell, 'Family Law, Access to Justice, and Automation' (2019) 19 *Macquarie Law Journal* 103.

admitted.[131] In an area such as sentencing, by contrast, the facts have already been determined – leading some commentators to argue that this is an ideal area for the application of automated systems.[132] However, the irony of the use of algorithmic risk assessments as only one factor in judicial decision-making is that this is not an especially efficient development, at least as far as judges are concerned. It cannot be saving of judicial time, as the judge must still consider all the other factors and arguments raised. Indeed, adding another factor into the mix (especially given the issues of opacity and bias discussed above) may only increase the complexity of decision-making. Such tools might, of course, increase efficiency if used in plea-bargaining. In other words, the efficiency dividends of most predictive tools lie in preventing matters from coming to court in the first place, rather than in making the process of judging itself more efficient. In turn, this will only be effective and appropriate if, first, they actually do prevent matters from coming to court, rather than just becoming a first step in the process; and second, if other important elements around accountability, transparency and impartiality are not compromised.[133]

IV Conclusion: Role of the Courts as Human Institutions

In this chapter, we have examined the interaction and underlying normative tension between judicial values and increasing reliance on technological tools by the courts. Many applications of technology are beneficial and indeed may enhance judicial values of openness, efficiency and diversity. As we discussed, digital uplift projects, including digital filing and discovery, have increased not only the efficiency of everyday operations of the courts, but also judicial transparency and accountability by opening them up to the world in different ways. We also noted that technology, and especially ML analytics, can be used to promote the diversity of the judiciary.

Yet other uses of technology demand far more circumspection, especially where their deployment imposes constraints on how judging is accessed or conducted. The judicial value of transparency is undermined whenever the courts are relying on tools that themselves lack transparency. The use of privately developed software in criminal sentencing is

---

[131] Bell (n 130).
[132] Stobbs, Hunter and Bagaric (n 102).
[133] Bell (n 130).

perhaps the greatest cause for concern. As Bradley Wendel has argued, it is the moral requirement of accountability which is imperative in legal decision-making.[134] Judges – however full of human biases or inclinations for corruption they may be – gain the accountability for their judicial role via the mechanisms of a public legal system. In contrast, those designing technological systems, who may be private companies, are not bound by accountability to the public. Nor are technological systems themselves able to accommodate the need for accountability, including the giving of reasons.

Our analysis further demonstrates that technology, especially software employing automation or ML, presents challenges for judicial independence and impartiality. Lack of transparency in how such tools operate, often cemented through trade secrecy doctrines, is not compatible with judicial independence. If technology is to assist judges, open source software should be used. Judges would not accept or tolerate relying on expert evidence where the expert need provide no qualifications or demonstrable expertise, no explanation of reasoning or methodology and no assurance of the reliability of their evidence. Lack of transparency also undermines judicial impartiality, and if software is trained on data which itself reflects bias and discrimination against certain groups, programs may continue to replicate those biases, as will judges when using it.

More fundamentally, our analysis has questioned the capacity of technology to uniformly enhance judicial values past simple digitisation, such as court filing and discovery. Even relatively simple tools such as videolink may detract from some aspects of judicial and procedural justice, and more empirical social and psychological research is needed to understand how it transforms the interactions between the parties and the judiciary.

Similarly, we found that the use of automated systems to increase judicial diversity is of limited value – it may illustrate patterns, but ultimately cannot inform on the quality of judging. Likewise, on a decision-making level, we are not convinced that automated systems can enhance judicial efficiency – the value seen as most enhanced by technology – let alone operate in compliance with or promote the other judicial values we have discussed in this chapter. We have several reasons for this position. First, the use of automated systems should be limited to decisions of the lowest level and impact, such as impositions of fines for traffic violations. Second, as discussed in section III, automated systems

---

[134] Wendel (n 137) 42.

are unable determine disputed facts, which are key to many legal disputes. Therefore, it is hard to see how technology can improve judicial decision-making in cases where establishing the facts is of fundamental importance in resolving a dispute. Finally, while facts have already been established in some areas of judicial decision-making, such as criminal sentencing, we consider that automation is nevertheless not suitable in the context of criminal law where decision-making involves (inter alia) constraints on individual liberty.[135] Such judicial decision-making, we believe, should remain with humans.

The spread of automation tools to judicial decision-making is part of the broader political economy of technology – a process by which the law is broken down into quantifiable metrics, which are measured by the tools developed by private actors. Such an approach is dangerous for promoting the ideas that societal problems should be increasingly solved not via human institutions but via technological tools. Allsop CJ has recently described the problems inherent in characterising 'the exercise of judicial power ... in terms of quantitative production'.[136] Fundamentally, we echo the view that judging is a uniquely human process which ought to be retained by humans.[137] For an increasing judicial reliance on information technologies to truly respect and promote judicial values, we agree with Frank Pasquale that a commitment to a "rule of persons, not machines" is needed.[138] A real-world reluctance to accord the status of decision-maker to a nonhuman is illustrated in a recent decision of the Federal Court, which held that an automatically generated letter from the Australian Taxation Office advising an individual about his tax debt did not constitute a 'decision' under the tax legislation.[139] The court held that to be a legally effective decision, a 'mental process' must have been involved – implying the input of a person.[140] Arguably the same logic should apply to judicial decision-making to make it compatible with the judicial values of transparency, accountability, independence, impartiality, diversity and efficiency.

---

[135] See Zalnieriute et al. (n 16).
[136] James Allsop, 'Courts as (Living) Institutions and Workplaces' (Presentation, Joint Federal and Supreme Court Conference, 23 January 2019) 5.
[137] See, for instance, W Bradley Wendel, 'The Promise and Limitations of Artificial Intelligence in the Practice of Law' (2019) 72(1) *Oklahoma Law Review* 21.
[138] Pasquale (n 83).
[139] *Pintarich v Federal Commissioner of Taxation* (2018) 262 FCR 41.
[140] Ibid., note the dissent of Kerr J.

Future research on technology and courts should examine the impact various technologies have on the judges' own sense of self, keeping these judicial values in mind. Recasting Heerey J's remark, 'law is not so ignorant or disdainful of human nature as to assume that judges or quasi-judicial decision-makers [*should be*] automatons,'[141] – which should guide this agenda. Heerey J's remark is particularly relevant now, as we embark on the journey where lower-level (yet significant) administrative decisions are automated with little (if any) human oversight. The rise of automated decision-making in many areas of life means that a human judiciary is particularly needed now to protect individual rights and entitlements, as it has done for centuries.

[141] *Vietnam Veterans* (1994) 52 FCR 34.

6

Emotion Work as Judicial Work

SHARYN ROACH ANLEU AND KATHY MACK[*]

I Introduction

The conventional image of the judge requires impersonal detachment, 'disinterestedness',[1] 'affective neutrality'[2] and suppression of emotion and personal feelings. These attributes are shared with other professions emphasising 'knowledge-based work'.[3] The individual judge in the adversarial legal system is often framed as a mechanism through which impersonal, rational law is applied.[4] This image characterises judicial

---

[*] We appreciate funding, financial and other support from the Australian Research Council (LP0210306, LP0669168, DP0665198, DP1096888, DP150103663), Flinders University, as well as the Australasian Institute of Judicial Administration, the Association of Australian Magistrates and many courts and their judicial officers. We are grateful to several research and administrative assistants over the course of the Judicial Research Project, Flinders University especially to Colleen deLaine, Rhiannon Davies, Jordan Tutton and Rae Wood. All phases of this research involving human subjects have been approved by the Flinders University Social and Behavioural Research Ethics Committee. Earlier versions of this chapter were presented at the workshop: *Judging, Emotion and Emotion Work*, International Institute for the Sociology of Law, Oñati, Spain, 2–4 May 2018; the workshop on *Uncloaking the Judiciary: The judicial role, style and image*, The Judiciary Project, Gilbert + Tobin Centre of Public Law, UNSW Law 9 July 2018; and the Griffith Law School Futures Centre Roundtable, 6 August 2019. We appreciate all the comments, questions and discussion from participants at these events.

[1] Talcott Parsons, *Essays in Sociological Theory* (Free Press, 1954) 35.

[2] Talcott Parsons, *The Social System* (Free Press, 1951) 454.

[3] See Elizabeth Gorman and Rebecca L Sandefur, '"Golden Age," Quiescence, and Revival: How the Sociology of Professions Became the Study of Knowledge-Based Work' (2011) 38(3) *Work and Occupations* 275.

[4] See Sharyn Roach Anleu, Russell Brewer and Kathy Mack 'Locating the Judge within Sentencing Research' (2017) 6(2) *International Journal for Crime, Justice and Social Democracy* 46; Susan A Bandes (ed), *The Passions of Law* (New York University Press, 2001); Susan A Bandes, 'Empathetic Judging and the Rule of Law' [2009] *Cardozo Law Review De Novo* 133; Susan A Bandes and Jeremy A Blumenthal, 'Emotion and the Law' (2012) 8 *Annual Review of Law and Social Science* 161; Margaret Davies, *Asking the Law Question* (Lawbook, 4th ed, 2017); Max Weber, *Economy and Society: An Outline of Interpretive Sociology* (University of California Press, 1978).

work of deliberation and reasoning as cognitive processes unaffected by and distinct from emotion. Terry Maroney suggests this '[i]nsistence on emotionless judging – that is, on judicial dispassion – is a cultural script of unusual longevity and potency'.[5] The cultural script of dispassion requires judicial work to be undertaken with an appropriate judicial demeanour: emotionless, dispassionate, impersonal, detached, and affectively neutral.[6]

In contrast, a growing body of empirical scholarship points to the ways in which emotion necessarily and positively features in judicial work.[7] Judicial officers may experience anger or frustration dealing with other participants, including lawyers,[8] and pride or satisfaction in undertaking their judicial tasks.[9] They may feel sadness, distress, or disgust seeing exhibits, listening to cross-examination, hearing victim impact statements or while reflecting on their decisions.[10] Judicial officers must interpret emotion and its display in others, for example when assessing remorse,[11] and they need to manage others' displays of emotion in the courtroom.[12]

---

[5] Terry A Maroney, 'The Persistent Cultural Script of Judicial Dispassion' (2011) 99(2) *California Law Review* 629, 630.

[6] See Bandes (n 4); Bandes and Blumenthal (n 4); Terry A Maroney, 'Emotional Regulation and Judicial Behavior' (2011) 99(6) *California Law Review* 1485; ibid.

[7] See Stina Bergman Blix and Åsa Wettergren, 'A Sociological Perspective on Emotions in the Judiciary' (2016) 8(1) *Emotion Review* 32; Stina Bergman Blix and Åsa Wettergren, *Professional Emotions in Court: A Sociological Perspective* (Routledge, 2018); Jennifer K Elek, 'Judicial Perspectives on Emotion, Emotion Management, and Judicial Excellence in the USA' (2019) 9(5) *Oñati Socio-Legal Series* 865; Sharyn Roach Anleu and Kathy Mack, 'Magistrates' Everyday Work and Emotional Labour' (2005) 32(4) *Journal of Law and Society* 590; Sharyn Roach Anleu and Kathy Mack, 'Judicial Authority and Emotion Work' (2013) 11(3) *The Judicial Review* 329; Sharyn Roach Anleu and Kathy Mack, 'A Sociological Perspective on Emotion Work and Judging' (2019) 9(5) *Oñati Socio-Legal Series* 831.

[8] Terry A Maroney, 'Angry Judges' (2012) 65(5) *Vanderbilt Law Review* 1207; see, for instance, Jordan Tutton, Kathy Mack and Sharyn Roach Anleu, 'Judicial Demeanor: Oral Argument in the High Court of Australia' (2018) 39(3) *Justice System Journal* 273, 286-88.

[9] Bergman Blix and Wettergren, *Professional Emotions in Court* (n 7).

[10] Tracey Booth, '"Cooling out" Victims of Crime: Managing Victim Participation in the Sentencing Process in a Superior Sentencing Court' (2012) 45(2) *Australian and New Zealand Journal of Criminology* 214; Heather Conway and John Stannard, 'Deconstructing Judicial Disgust' (2019) 9(5) *Oñati Socio-Legal Series* 636.

[11] Kate Rossmanith, Steven Tudor and Michael Proeve, 'Courtroom Contrition: How Do Judges Know?' (2018) 27(3) *Griffith Law Review* 366; Kate Rossmanith, 'Affect and the Judicial Assessment of Offenders: Feeling and Judging Remorse' (2015) 21(2) *Body & Society* 167.

[12] Bergman Blix and Wettergren, *Professional Emotions in Court* (n 7); Sharyn Roach Anleu, Kathy Mack and Jordan Tutton, 'Judicial Humour in the Australian Courtroom' (2014) 38(2) *Melbourne University Law Review* 621, 642-44.

To investigate the place of emotion and emotion management in judicial work, this chapter juxtaposes segments from interviews with two judges as a vehicle first, to unpack the complexity of emotion in judicial work; and second, to examine the practices or strategies judicial officers use to manage emotions – their own and those of others – within the legal institutional context. The chapter first considers concepts of emotion and emotion work, describes the research from which the two interview segments are drawn, and reflects on interviews as data. It then provides the two interview excerpts which are the primary data for this chapter.

II   Emotion and Emotion Work

Socio-legal researchers interested in emotion will be struck by the difficulty of providing a generally accepted definition of emotion. Each discipline, even sub-discipline, offers different starting points, assumptions, understandings, definitions and frameworks for investigating emotion and its properties, often enumerating the deficiencies of other approaches.[13]

Two important points that emerge across much research on emotion are that emotion entails effort and is regulated by social norms.[14] Different concepts, sometimes used interchangeably, signal the kind and level of effort: emotional labour;[15] emotion work;[16] emotion management;[17]

---

[13] See Peggy A Thoits, 'The Sociology of Emotions' (1989) 15 *Annual Review of Sociology* 317, 319–37.
[14] William M Reddy, 'Historical Research on the Self and Emotions' (2009) 1(4) *Emotion Review* 302, 311.
[15] Arlie Russell Hochschild, *The Managed Heart: Commercialization of Human Feeling* (University of California Press, 1983); Amy S Wharton, 'The Psychosocial Consequences of Emotional Labor' (1999) 561 *Annals of the American Academy of Political and Social Science* 158; Amy S Wharton, 'The Sociology of Emotional Labor' (2009) 35 *Annual Review of Sociology* 147; Amy S Wharton, 'The Affective Consequences of Service Work: Managing Emotions on the Job' (1993) 20(2) *Work and Occupations* 205.
[16] Arlie Russell Hochschild, 'Emotion Work, Feeling Rules and Social Structure' (1979) 85(3) *American Journal of Sociology* 551.
[17] Kathryn J Lively and Emi A Weed, 'Emotion Management: Sociological Insight into What, How, Why, and to What End?' (2014) 6(3) *Emotion Review* 202; Sharon C Bolton and Carol Boyd, 'Trolley Dolly or Skilled Emotion Manager? Moving on from Hochschild's Managed Heart' (2003) 17(2) *Work, Employment and Society* 289.

emotion regulation;[18] affective practices;[19] and interpersonal affective work.[20] All imply interaction, interdependence, social relations and anticipate hierarchy. Alternatively, concepts such as background emotions;[21] emotional granularity[22] and service emotions[23] suggest that emotion may be experienced as natural, automatic, or even intuitive, rather than conscious or deliberate. Understanding emotion as something that someone does implies agency or capacity to control, even use, one's own emotional experience and display and to manage the emotions of others. This departs from the classical conceptualisation of emotion as something that emerges in response to an event or situation, perhaps involuntarily.[24] The inter-dependence and interaction that occurs within organisations or in social settings constrains the amount and type of emotion permitted and generates situational expectations or social norms regarding who should or is expected to engage in emotion work, when, how and in what situations.

Judicial work takes place in a social, institutional and legal context in and out of court, constituted by relationships and associated formal and informal interactions with lawyers, court staff, prosecutors, litigants, defendants, and others. In these interactions, emotion is generated, experienced, displayed, interpreted and managed, and shapes the performance of the judicial role and legal authority. Understanding 'emotions as

---

[18] James J Gross, 'Emotion Regulation: Current Status and Future Prospects' (2015) 26(1) *Psychological Inquiry* 1; Terry A Maroney and James J Gross, 'The Ideal of the Dispassionate Judge: An Emotion Regulation Perspective' (2014) 6(2) *Emotion Review* 142.

[19] Margaret Wetherell, 'Trends in the Turn to Affect: A Social Psychological Critique' (2015) 21(2) *Body and Society* 139.

[20] Mariana Craciun, 'The Cultural Work of Office Charisma: Maintaining Professional Power in Psychotherapy' (2016) 45(4) *Theory and Society* 361.

[21] Jack Barbalet, 'Emotions beyond Regulation: Backgrounded Emotions in Science and Trust' (2011) 3(1) *Emotion Review* 36.

[22] Lisa Feldman Barrett, 'Are Emotions Natural Kinds?' (2006) 1(1) *Perspectives on Psychological Science* 28; Lisa Feldman Barrett, 'Solving the Emotion Paradox: Categorization and the Experience of Emotion' (2006) 10(1) *Personality and Social Psychology Review* 20; Maria Gendron and Lisa Feldman Barrett, 'A Role for Emotional Granularity in Judging' (2019) 9(5) *Oñati Socio-Legal Series* 557.

[23] Emily Kidd White, 'Till Human Voices Wake Us: The Role of Emotion in the Adjudication of Dignity Claims' (2014) 3(3) *Journal of Law, Religion and State* 201; Emily Kidd White, 'Efforts of Attention: Judges, Emotions, and Evaluative Legal Concepts' (2019) 9(5) *Oñati Socio-Legal Series* 577.

[24] Lisa Feldman Barrett, *How Emotions Are Made: The Secret Life of the Brain* (Houghton Mifflin Harcourt, 2017).

practices or acts' rather than primarily involuntary responses[25] suggests that emotions can be strategies or resources to enable judicial officers to do their work.

III A Note on Research Design and Method

A perennial question in empirical sociological research on emotion is how to identify and collect reliable, valid data on emotion and emotion work.[26] Interview methodology enables a far-reaching flow of consciousness, though some interviewees are more forthcoming or reflexive than others. Conducting interviews in a conversational style, using open-ended questions, can generate considerable information and insight about emotion in judicial work, which may not have been captured by specific questions as in a survey questionnaire or by asking about particular identified emotions.

Like all data collection techniques, interviews have strengths and limitations. The interview is a co-production between interviewee and interviewer.[27] An interview enables each interviewee to present their (judicial) identity and account for their approaches. The researcher may not be able to gauge the alignment between what an interviewee says and what he or she felt (or did not) or how she or he would behave in the future. As a major aim of the interviews discussed in this chapter is to gain insight into the ways the interviewees themselves interpret and understand their emotions and emotion work, the question of any disjuncture between what the interviewees say and how they may behave is less relevant.[28] This chapter relies on interview excerpts from two different judicial officers as a vehicle to decipher emotion in judicial work. It does not claim representativeness across the population of judicial officers; rather it aims to identify the range of emotion and emotion work in this profession.

---

[25] Monique Scheer, 'Are Emotions a Kind of Practice (and Is That What Makes Them Have a History)? A Bourdieuan Approach to Understanding Emotion' (2012) 51(2) *History and Theory* 193, 206.
[26] See H Flam and J Kleres (eds), *Methods of Exploring Emotions* (Routledge, 2015); Mary Holmes, 'Researching Emotional Reflexivity' (2015) 9(1) *Emotion Review* 61.
[27] Lois Presser, 'Violent Offenders, Moral Selves: Constructing Identities and Accounts in the Research Interview' (2004) 51(1) *Social Problems* 82, 97–9.
[28] Mariana Craciun, 'Emotions and Knowledge in Expert Work: A Comparison of Two Psychotherapies' (2018) 123(4) *American Journal of Sociology* 959.

IV The Interview Segments

The two interviews were conducted as part of a study into judicial officers' experience and perception of changes in the judiciary and the courts as a professional workplace. Two excerpts, each from a different judge from different jurisdictions and court levels, provide especially rich information and reflexivity about emotion.

One segment is from a female interviewee[29] (Judge 37)[30] and the other is from a male interviewee (Judge 6). Relying only on an interview from a female judge could lead to an inappropriate, stereotypical inference that female judges are more attuned to emotion, engage in more emotion work or feel more comfortable discussing their emotions during an interview compared with their male counterparts. While there is an extensive literature on gender and judging generally,[31] there is little empirical consideration of gender, judging and emotion.[32] Australian national survey data identifies some differences between men and women judges in terms of emotion and emotion work.[33] For example, women in the judiciary value emotional capacities such as empathy, compassion and patience, more intensely than their male counterparts, though this may be confounded by court level as the need for emotion work may be greater in lower courts where women judicial officers are disproportionately located.[34] Considerably larger proportions of women, compared with men, assess managing the emotions of court users and a sense of humour as more important in their everyday work, compared with their male counterparts.[35]

---

[29] In 2019, 37% of all judicial officers in Australia are women, though percentages vary by court type and level: 'AIJA Judicial Gender Statistics', *The Australasian Institute of Judicial Administration* (Web Page, 6 March 2019) <https://aija.org.au/research/judicial-gender-statistics/>.

[30] Each interviewee was assigned a number from 1–38, as part of the anonymisation process.

[31] See, for instance, Ulrike Schultz and Gisela Shaw (eds), *Gender and Judging* (Hart Publishing, 2013).

[32] See Heather Douglas et al., 'Introduction: Righting Australian Law' in Heather Douglas et al. (eds), *Australian Feminist Judgments: Righting and Rewriting Law* (Hart Publishing, 2014).

[33] Sharyn Roach Anleu and Kathy Mack, *Performing Judicial Authority in the Lower Courts* (Palgrave Macmillan, 2017) 67-70.

[34] Roach Anleu and Mack, 'Magistrates' Everyday Work and Emotional Labour' (n 7); see also Roach Anleu and Mack, 'A Sociological Perspective on Emotion Work and Judging' (n 7).

[35] Roach Anleu and Mack, *Performing Judicial Authority in the Lower Courts* (n 33) 68-9.

Judge 37 sits on an intermediate court, had been on the bench for about a decade and was aged in her 50s at the time of the interview in 2013. She comments:

37: Some cases are more challenging than others, umm. Some things excite the emotions more than others or sometimes I'll find in a civil case that there'll be a person who just umm, they, they'll be a reminder of some wrong that I think has been done to me in the past, you know, it's just, I don't know that it's, once you identify it I don't think it's hard. I think the hard part's actually identifying it, identifying that you are, umm, responding umm, because of something about you rather than a more objective assessment of what's before you. I do find going back to the transcript of evidence and documents terribly helpful sometimes. I'll come out of court and think I really think I'm going to find for the plaintiff in this case and then because I've moved on to other cases and I haven't been able to get to the decision. So it's a few weeks later, sitting down, I necessarily I have to go back and I read the transcript and stripped of the interpersonal communication where I might have been drawn in by a person and just looking at what they've actually said and then checking that against documentary evidence, I have been surprised on occasions and thought oh I'm glad I had the time to reflect and actually go back and check because I've come to a different view than I might have if I'd given a hasty decision. Umm, that was influenced by how I responded to that particular witness when they were in the witness box. You know sometimes I'll write down I believe this person and then I'll, when I go and do the check I find oh actually – this is a very substantial conflict here, umm, I have to reassess my approach.

SRA: Mmm, and what about the display of emotion? How do you manage the, kind of, external display of emotion and maintain a judicial demeanour?

37: By me?

SRA: Mmm.

37: Well if I feel that I'm in a position where I'm not handling things well, umm, I will, whether it's because I'm upset or frustrated or angry or whether I feel a bit overborne, umm, then I will usually adjourn – and I mean the wonderful thing is you're in control of the court. Poor counsel and parties and witnesses don't have that, umm, the luxury that judges do so, again, self-awareness, if you think gee I'm beginning to speak really harshly or inappropriately or gee wish I hadn't said that thing I just said, I will, I will say look I think now might be a good time for us to have a morning tea break so I'll adjourn for 15 or 20 minutes and then I'll come out and rant and rave and have my cup of tea and go back in calm. Umm, I had umm, I had one case where a victim wanted to read out a Victim Impact Statement and I allowed her to do it, that was before, we recently had a law change that requires the court to do that, umm, if a victim wants to. It was at a time when it wasn't, most people didn't do it, umm, and she was one of nine nieces that a man had serially offended against, maintained sexual relationships with. Horrible, horrible case. The courtroom was packed full of other victims and family members. This man's behaviour had wrenched this family apart because parents didn't believe children, 'Uncle Charlie wouldn't do that', you know, that kind of thing, umm, anyway. As she was speaking I was really quite affected by it and, but there was no way I could stop her in her flow and this was so important that people were weeping in the courtroom and it was, you know, just did the put my hands flat on the bench and just maintained, it was just as still and calm as I could be and umm when she finished I then adjourned. I said I think we need a break before we go on. It was very powerful, thank you, but I think we need a break now. And then everyone was able to go 'Oh God'. So they're just strategies I suppose, different people will do different things.

At the time of the interview, Judge 6 was a relatively recent appointee to a supreme court and was in his 50s when interviewed. He reflects on his approach:

6: I say it to a jury, you know, try and put aside, you know we all have sympathies, prejudices, biases, put them to one side because they're a really bad guide to judgment and that's true. I mean you do see things, I mean you do feel, I mean I do see, I see people who I feel sorry for, I occasionally see people who I think you know are really not very deserving, you know you do feel some antagonism towards them either because of what they've done or sometimes how they conduct themselves but I think, you know, I know for myself that if ever I begin to sort of feel that way I consciously say look just, forget it, put it out of your mind because if, you know I'm mindful that it's just folly, just gets you into so much trouble. So yeh, I don't, yeh so that's how I think I approach it.

SRA: So is there any role for things like compassion or empathy?

6: Well I think, I mean there is, I mean you've got to always, I mean you're dealing with human beings, you know you're dealing with people's lives and you know you can't just be a machine, you know you've got to – you've got to have some understanding of human nature and how people behave and if you don't know those things then sometimes it's going to be very hard to perform judgment. You know how do people behave in certain situations and look there is – sometimes I see people and you know you are sympathetic and you're empathetic with what's happened. What's an example? I mean, you know, you will see offenders who really have never had a chance in life, you know from the day they were born, you know it's just no wonder they are in the situation that they're in and you know I have a lot of sympathy for people in that sort of position, it's not their fault but you know the fact is that you will often see people like that and they nevertheless represent – they've done bad things, they represent a danger to the community, there's not much really that you can do. I mean the way I think you express that is in the way that you try and speak to people in those sorts of situations. I mean I feel often a lot of empathy and sympathy to victims of crime. You know, you see them and you read the victim impact statements and that's just terrible but you can't let that dominate your considerations so look I think we're all you know – judges around here will always, you know, be talking and you'll often say to them you know wasn't that sad, you know, isn't that a sad situation or something like that but you can't decide a case based on that.

SRA: And what about the outward expression of emotions, you know, courts can be very emotional places and a variety of emotions. What's the role of the judge in managing others' emotions?

6: Well I think you've got to keep your shirt on, you know, look I think, you know you're right, you can see some very emotional things and I think that one of the roles of a judge is to just make sure that where emotions are running high, to keep a control on the proceedings.

SRA: How do you do that?

6: Well I mean, look if people are emotional, let's say somebody's in the witness box and crying, well you can't say 'stop crying' because it is emotional for them, you have to just accommodate them as best you can. You know sometimes it's pretty pathetic, you know, here's a glass of water, have a break, something like that, but other times you'll see people who are extremely angry and disruptive and you know sometimes you have to be quite firm with people who are angry and/or deliberately disruptive. I mean I try and keep a reasonably even tone. I try and keep a fairly good humoured tone but sometimes that's impossible. I mean if a witness – I had this happen – although I've been doing appeal work I also made sure that I do some trial work just so that I keep my hand in and I had a trial a couple of weeks ago where a witness was being deliberately difficult and very hard for counsel to control and you know you start off by being polite, even and if that doesn't work well then the tone has to sometimes become firmer and sterner. So you know those sorts of things, but you know, a court where people are very emotional, well you know, sometimes some homicides, some sex cases are like that and you just have to manage them as best you can.

V Emotion in Judicial Work

These interview segments reveal multiple overlapping themes including reflexivity, emotion management practices, background emotions, the limits of judicial emotion work, feeling and display rules. They demonstrate that emotion can be a positive resource or strategy for accomplishing everyday work and goals among judicial officers.

A Reflexivity

The two judges show varying levels of reflexivity about their own emotions and those of others. Mary Holmes explains that '[e]motional reflexivity refers to the intersubjective interpretation of one's own and others' emotions and how they are enacted'.[36] Judge 37 describes her emotions as being excited or triggered by 'a person' who becomes 'a reminder of some wrong . . . done to me in the past'. She acknowledges that such emotions may not easily be identifiable drawing a hard distinction between 'something about you rather than a more objective assessment of what's before you'. While she does not use specific emotion words, she describes the emotion she experienced in court as resulting from her memories of a past event or experience. She strives to erase things about her personal biography from the decision-making process and seeks 'objective assessment'.[37] She distinguishes between emotion in the moment – listening to the plaintiff in court – and 'a few weeks, later' out of court when the emotion has faded when she reads 'the transcript stripped of the interpersonal communication', and the associated feelings. This affirms the authoritative power of printed text over the spoken word and verbal presentation of information.[38] The facts are more important when contained in 'the transcript of evidence and documents'. It devalues the importance of the immediate felt response for legal judgment, precisely because it elicited emotion, thus departing from the expectations of the judicial role.

Elsewhere Judge 37 shows reflexivity when she relies on emotion as a gauge of judicial performance and conformity with professional goals. She states: 'if I feel that I'm in a position where I'm not handling things well, umm, I will, whether it's because I'm upset or frustrated or angry or whether I feel a bit overborne, umm, then I will usually adjourn'. In addition to implying or naming specific emotions – frustration, anger – she describes a general feeling of 'being upset', 'not handling things well'

---

[36] Holmes (n 26) 61; see also Mary Holmes, 'The Emotionalization of Reflexivity' (2010) 44(1) *Sociology* 139; Ian Burkitt, 'Emotional Reflexivity: Feeling, Emotion and Imagination in Reflexive Dialogues' (2012) 48(3) *Sociology* 458.

[37] See also Renata Grossi, 'Law, Emotion and the Objectivity Debate' (2019) 28(1) *Griffith Law Review* 23.

[38] See Kathryn Temple, *Loving Justice: Legal Emotions in William Blackstone's England* (New York University Press, 2019); Linda Mulcahy, 'Eyes of the Law: A Visual Turn in Socio-Legal Studies?' (2017) 44(S1) *Journal of Law and Society* S111.

and 'a bit overborne' as indicators that she might deviate from appropriate judicial conduct and demeanour.

Judge 6 discusses the role of empathy in judging and distinguishes between mechanical and human judging:

> You're dealing with human beings, you know you're dealing with people's lives and you know you can't just be a machine, you know you've got to – you've got to have some understanding of human nature and how people behave and if you don't know those things then sometimes it's going to be very hard to perform judgment.

This statement implies that effective judging is neither mechanical nor devoid of humanity; empathy may be key to performing judgment. Empathy, the capacity to perceive another person's situation, perspective, thoughts and feelings from that other's perspective,[39] is not conventionally thought of as part of the skills or qualities required for judicial office.[40]

Judge 6 also reflects on the role of emotion in court work: 'I say it to a jury, you know, try and put aside, you know we all have sympathies, prejudices, biases, put them to one side'. Nonetheless, he does not reflect on the ease or difficulty in perceiving, identifying, labelling and putting aside emotion. He vividly emphasises a conception of emotion as dangerous, risky, and antithetical to legal rationality: 'they're a really bad guide to judgment.' He then names several emotions: feeling sorry, antagonism, and suggests sympathy and feelings of injustice: 'I see people who I feel sorry for, I occasionally see people who I think you know are really not very deserving, you know you do feel some antagonism towards them either because of what they've done or sometimes how they conduct themselves.' He then reiterates the perception of emotion as risky and what he does in response to recognising those feelings: 'if ever I begin to sort of feel that way I consciously say look just, forget it, put it out of your mind because if, you know I'm mindful that it's just folly, just gets you into so much trouble'. This passage suggests the judge's awareness that he must undertake conscious reflexive monitoring,

---

[39] Susan Bandes, 'Empathy, Narrative, and Victim Impact Statements' (1996) 63(2) *University of Chicago Law Review* 361; Bandes (n 4).

[40] See, for instance, personal qualities contemplated by the Australasian Institute of Judicial Administration: The Australasian Institute of Judicial Administration, *Suggested Criteria for Judicial Appointments* (AIJA, 2015) 4.

especially in the courtroom when emotions 'are generated, interpreted and regulated'.[41]

These interview segments demonstrate how judicial officers must routinely manage their own feelings and emotion display and that of others in their everyday work. Both judges seem to use their emotion as a marker of their judicial performance, which they assess in terms of interconnections with others in court. These judges also display considerable reflexivity about the place of their own and other's emotion in their everyday work.

B Emotion Management Strategies

Several strategies for managing emotions emerge from these interview segments: adjournment, delegation or displacement of emotion work onto other court participants, maintaining an outwardly calm display, and self-talk.

Judge 37 states that, if she feels 'upset or frustrated or angry ... I will usually adjourn.' Later, she elaborates: If 'I'm beginning to speak really harshly or inappropriately or gee wish I hadn't said that thing I just said, I will, I will say look I think now might be a good time for us to have a morning tea break so I'll adjourn for 15 or 20 minutes.' By using an adjournment, she is removing herself from the emotion-inducing situation and 'shield[s] [herself] ... against the kind of exposure that would [might] call into question' her judicial authority and legitimacy.[42]

She articulates a sense of the normative environment by assessing things she has said against norms of judicial conduct: patience, courtesy, dignity. This suggests self-monitoring of behaviour and perhaps awareness that her conduct may cause emotional responses in others who might become annoyed, frustrated or anxious. The adjournment time is embedded in a morning tea break, camouflaging its emotion management function so that it may not be perceived as an inappropriate delay. She is aware of the hierarchy of the court, and the unequal availability of certain emotion management strategies: 'I mean the wonderful thing is you're in control of the court. Poor counsel and parties

---

[41] Ian Burkitt, 'Decentring Emotion Regulation: From Emotion Regulation to Relational Emotion' (2018) 10(2) *Emotion Review* 167, 170.

[42] Craciun, (n 20) 375; see also Maroney and Gross (n 18) 144–8 (considering the emotion-regulation strategies that a judicial officer may employ).

and witnesses don't have that, umm, the luxury that judges do'. Other courtroom participants will have to adopt other emotion strategies.

Judge 37 and Judge 6 indicate ways that managing their own emotions relies on emotion work on the part of others – associates, judicial officers, court staff – but off-stage, beyond the courtroom, in chambers.[43] After adjourning, Judge 37 adds: 'I'll come out [of court] and rant and rave and have my cup of tea and go back in calm.' This anticipates a new audience that will observe her display of emotion and perhaps share her emotions or can be relied on to perform emotion work to enable her to return to court 'calm'. Judge 6 acknowledges: 'we're all you know – judges around here will always, you know, be talking and you'll often say to them, you know, wasn't that sad, you know, isn't that a sad situation or something like that but you can't decide a case based on that'. Not surprisingly, this judge does not characterise these conversations as being emotion management. He mentions the situation as sad, but immediately invokes the judicial role: 'you can't decide a case based on that'. In a study of the Swedish judiciary, such collegial conversations entailed 'talking about emotions without talking about them ... as a way to avoid breaching the feeling rules while still dealing with difficult emotions together'.[44] The transition to a different setting is a move to a place where a judicial officer might expect to receive emotion work from others neither available nor appropriate in the courtroom.

However, Judge 37 points out that an adjournment may sometimes not be available as an emotion management strategy when she describes a woman reading out a victim impact statement. Despite feeling 'quite affected', this judicial officer determined she could not 'stop her in her flow'. Not interrupting may have conveyed empathy and compassion, indicating that this was an appropriate rather than an inappropriate emotion display. This aligns with Mary Lay Schuster and Amy Propen's findings regarding emotional standards and hierarchies in the courtroom.[45] Their US study of victim impact statements finds that judges appreciate expressions of compassion, tolerate expressions of grief but are uncomfortable with displays of anger.

---

[43] See Kathryn J Lively, 'Reciprocal Emotion Management: Working Together to Maintain Stratification in Private Law Firms' (2000) 27(1) *Work and Occupations* 32; Kathryn J Lively, 'Client Contact and Emotional Labor: Upsetting the Balance and Evening the Field' (2002) 29(2) *Work and Occupations* 198.
[44] Bergman Blix and Wettergren, *Professional Emotions in Court* (n 7) 83.
[45] Mary Lay Schuster and Amy Propen, 'Degrees of Emotion: Judicial Responses to Victim Impact Statements' (2010) 6(1) *Law, Culture and the Humanities* 75.

Judge 37 describes putting her 'hands flat on the bench' and remaining 'as still and calm as I could' in front of people who were 'weeping'. In this moment, the bench becomes a 'workaday prop', a resource that enhances emotion management and display for a short period of time.[46] She suggests effort in managing her own emotion to display a calm, non-emotional demeanour to facilitate and perhaps to contain the expression of emotion in the courtroom. Her display of calm is a conscious tool, strategy or resource that can convey empathy and allow intense emotion expression without jeopardising judicial legitimacy. Management of one's own emotions becomes a resource to manage those of others.

This judge is aware of feelings, her own and others, and makes (conscious) choices about her feelings and display, using them as emotion management strategies. She recognises that some visible emotion – being and appearing angry, frustrated, or impatient – may be construed as loss of control, detracting from impartiality and undermining legitimacy and judicial authority. She displays apparent patience but recognises the limited effectiveness of staying calm as a strategy.

She implies that people weeping, and her own experience of being affected, are normal, not out of place during the reading of a victim impact statement in a 'horrible, horrible case'.[47] This emotion work – which also entailed listening, being patient, waiting, not interrupting – was central to the maintenance of professional authority. Similarly Judge 6 comments: 'I mean I feel often a lot of empathy and sympathy to victims of crime. You know, you see them and you read the victim impact statements and that's just terrible but you can't let that dominate your considerations'. Judge 6 is focusing on judicial authority and decision-making which means he 'can't let' emotion 'dominate'. The idea of 'can't let' suggests agency and effort in resisting the pull of emotion. Judge 6 also emphasises the importance of judicial demeanour in emotion management, though he does not use the term calm, either in this excerpt or anywhere in the interview: 'Well I think you've got to keep your shirt on . . . one of the roles of a judge is to just make sure that where emotions are running high, to keep a control on the proceedings'.

These judicial comments highlight the boundaries between the judicial officer and other courtroom participants who may experience and

---

[46] Hochschild (n 15) 42.
[47] See Booth (n 10); Mary Lay Schuster and Amy D Propen, *Victim Advocacy in the Courtroom: Persuasive Practices in Domestic Violence and Child Protection Cases* (Northeastern University Press, 2011).

display emotion. Though others may not experience the same obligations to remain calm or to manage the emotions of others as do judicial officers, they must comply with the emotional regime of the courtroom while perhaps having fewer available strategies, as suggested by Judge 37.[48] Leaving the bench can be a strategy to allow others to manage their emotions as well as for the judicial officer to manage her own feelings.

Judge 6 suggests the idea of self-talk as a judicial emotion management strategy.[49] Ian Burkitt calls this dialogical reflexivity, or "internal conversation".[50] Judge 6's self-talk involves 'consciously [saying] look just, forget it,' to himself, internally – a kind of auto-correction – as part of emotion work, to address both the experience of emotion and the outward display. This internal self-talk can be understood as a conversation between the judge as ordinary person experiencing emotions such as antagonism or sympathy and the judge *qua* judge for whom such feelings are 'just folly' or will get him 'into trouble'.

Judge 37 and Judge 6 each rely on adjournment to manage their own emotion as well as the feelings of others, demonstrating the multifunction nature of this strategy. They suggest that relying on their own self-talk sometimes assists them to display a calm demeanour in the courtroom. Outside the courtroom, they may derive emotion support from others.

C Background Emotions

Not all emotions or emotion work are explicitly expressed, visible to others, immediately obvious or consciously experienced, yet they are embedded in everyday professional work. Jack Barbalet terms these feelings 'backgrounded emotions' and may include feelings of pride, pleasure, loyalty and satisfaction.[51] They 'form the emotional backdrop needed to perform rational and instrumental action',[52] and may be emotions at work in the management of other emotions. For example:

---

[48] See also Bridgette Toy-Cronin, 'Leaving Emotion Out: Litigants' in Person and Judges' Understanding and Responding to the Role of Emotion in New Zealand Civil Courts' (2019) 9(5) *Oñati Socio-Legal Series* 684.
[49] Erving Goffman, *Forms of Talk* (University of Philadelphia Press, 1981).
[50] Burkitt (n 36) 462.
[51] Barbalet (n 21).
[52] Bergman Blix and Wettergren, *Professional Emotions in Court* (n 7) 3.

in managing anger a person may experience pride in their having done so, or a feeling of foolishness for having bothered, or smugness in presenting a self-image that they may feel is inauthentic, and so on. Also, it is likely that the regulation of a person's anger draws on other emotions, such as guilt for getting angry or giving into it, or pity for the person on the receiving end.[53]

Judge 6 names foreground emotions and implies background emotion: 'I mean I feel often a lot of empathy and sympathy to victims of crime. ... but you can't let that dominate your considerations'. He implies that allowing these conscious feelings to dominate would depart from the requirements of judicial office. In the background are emotions generated by his commitment to impartiality, central to judicial identity or self-definition.[54]

Similarly Judge 37's comments suggest background emotions at work. She confesses: 'I have been surprised on occasions ... that [I] was influenced by how I responded to that particular witness when they were in the witness box'. This suggests awareness that departing from the persistent script of judicial dispassion may risk impartiality. She indicates surprise that her self-perception or self-identity as a judge making reasoned, impartial decisions was out of alignment with being emotionally influenced by a witness. She expresses commitment to the process of reflection, relying on and checking the written record of evidence, and appreciates the passage of time between the in-court assessment and coming to a different view later beyond the courtroom. She intimates feelings of relief that this avoided 'a hasty decision' which might be incorrect and result in an appeal potentially causing her feelings of embarrassment or disappointment.

D   Limits of Judicial Emotion Work

Both judges describe their perceptions of the limits of the judicial role in emotion work. Judge 6 acknowledges the lack of resources or strategies a judicial officer can access to facilitate emotion management, even expressing some frustration. After describing a physical manifestation of emotion – crying – he suggests that the offer of water or a break may be 'pretty pathetic' as emotion management strategies. Judge 6 also

---

[53] Barbalet (n 21) 37.
[54] Charles Gardner Geyh, 'The Dimensions of Judicial Impartiality' (2013) 65(2) *Florida Law Review* 493, 498–9; Joe McIntyre, *The Judicial Function* (Springer, 2019) ch 10.

suggests using an 'even tone' or a 'good humoured tone' to manage other kinds of emotions – such as anger – but recognises 'sometimes that's impossible'. The implication is that these strategies may not be available in some contexts or may not be successful, and display of another's anger may not dissipate. He reports having 'a lot of sympathy for people' for 'offenders who really have never had a chance in life'. Yet his sympathy is minimised by the fact that 'they've done bad things, they represent a danger to the community', and those things (criminal offending), and their punishment and community safety are goals of the criminal justice system, of which the courts are a central part. Given such institutional constraints: 'there's not much really you [the judge] can do'. He does identify communication and interaction with defendants as a way of expressing empathy, within constraints: 'the way you try to speak to people in those sorts of situations'.

Judge 37 describes how she maintains or constitutes the parameters of the judicial role. Her use of an adjournment following the reading of a victim impact statement means that any residual emotion among courtroom participants, especially the victims, will need to be managed by others – the prosecutor, family members, friends – outside the courtroom and beyond the trial or sentencing hearing. By displacing and delegating emotion work, she actively and clearly identifies the limits of judicial emotion work, a form of boundary work.[55] It is an example of a moment where the judicial officer places limits on her capacity to share in the participants' emotion, limits which are greater than the boundaries faced by other criminal justice workers[56] or the emotion sharing that can occur in international tribunals.[57]

E Feeling and Display Rules

Feeling rules are norms that 'inform the sense of what is 'proper' feeling in the performance and reading of emotional expression'.[58] Hochschild describes feeling rules as 'guidelines for the assessment of fits and misfits

---

[55] Michèle Lamont and Virág Molnár, 'The Study of Boundaries in the Social Sciences' (2002) 28 *Annual Review of Sociology* 167.
[56] Sarah Goodrum, 'Bridging the Gap between Prosecutors' Cases and Victims' Biographies in the Criminal Justice System through Shared Emotions' (2013) 38(2) *Law and Social Inquiry* 257.
[57] Susanne Karstedt, 'The Emotion Dynamics of Transitional Justice: An Emotion Sharing Perspective' (2016) 8(1) *Emotion Review* 50.
[58] Scheer (n 25) 216.

between feeling and situation'.[59] Different emotional norms or feeling rules apply in different settings,[60] and legal processes have particular emotion regimes. Understanding judging and emotion requires identifying the feeling rules – explicit/formal and implicit/informal – governing judicial work. One source of such feeling rules may be written statements of judicial ethics or conduct guides such as those produced by the Australasian Institute of Judicial Administration, the American Bar Association or the *Bangalore Principles of Judicial Conduct* adopted in many Commonwealth countries.[61] In many jurisdictions, the judicial oath implies feeling rules, by requiring judges to 'do right to all manner of people according to law without fear or favour, affection or ill-will.[62]

Judge 37 and Judge 6 are very aware of the normative environment in which they work, though neither expressly refers to formal rules. For example, Judge 37's comment that 'I have to reassess my approach', comes after her recognition that a witness's performance affected her emotionally and her immediate assessment which she later identified as incompatible with the transcript evidence, raising questions about her impartiality. In addition, her comment 'there was no way I could stop her in her flow' suggests the force of implicit feeling rules that the expression of emotion at that moment was appropriate and to question it would be inappropriate and perhaps escalate anger and distress which would become directed toward the judicial officer. This framing – 'there was no way' – suggests an external, constraint on her actions and emotion display. Her choice to be 'just as still and calm as I could be' may demonstrate empathy in the moment, through her awareness of the

---

[59] Hochschild (n 16) 566.
[60] Lively (n 43); Kathryn J Lively and David R Heise, 'Emotions in Affect Control Theory' in Jan E Stets and Jonathan H Turner (eds), *Handbook of the Sociology of Emotions: Volume II* (Springer, 2014) 51.
[61] The Council of Chief Justices of Australia and New Zealand, *Guide to Judicial Conduct* (Australasian Institute of Judicial Administration, 3rd ed, 2017); 'Model Code of Judicial Conduct', *American Bar Association* (Web Page, 2019) <www.americanbar.org/groups/professional_responsibility/publications/model_code_of_judicial_conduct.html>; Courts and Tribunal Judiciary, *Guide to Judicial Conduct* (Guide, March 2019); *Strengthening Basic Principles of Judicial Conduct*, ESC Res 2006/23, UN ESCOR, 41st plen mtg, Agenda Item 14(c), UN Doc E/RES/2006/23 (27 July 2006) annex. For review, analysis and comment on these materials on judicial conduct see Sharyn Roach Anleu, Jennifer Elek and Kathy Mack, 'Judicial Conduct Guidance and Emotion' (2019) 28(4) *Journal of Judicial Administration* 226; McIntyre (n 54) part IV; Gabrielle Appleby and Suzanne Le Mire, 'Ethical Infrastructure for a Modern Judiciary' (2019) 47(3) *Federal Law Review* 335, 336, 338–40.
[62] *High Court of Australia Act 1979* (Cth) s 11, sch 1.

feelings of the court participants. Her emotion work produces a display which supports judicial authority.

Judicial officers may need to communicate and enforce feeling rules, as well as being subject to them. They must interpret emotionally laden conduct, then decide whether that conduct breaches general norms of civility or specific courtroom norms. Judge 6 describes a situation where: 'a witness was being deliberately difficult and very hard for counsel to control and you know you start off by being polite, even and if that doesn't work well then the tone has to sometimes become firmer and sterner'. He assesses the witness's conduct against courtroom norms and calibrates his judicial response to conform with norms of 'being polite'. If this strategy fails, then his tone may become 'firmer' or 'sterner', indicating a hierarchy of emotion management strategies.

Maintaining order and decorum in court is an expectation of judicial practice.[63] In-court conduct described as 'extremely angry and disruptive', 'deliberately difficult', and 'hard ... to control' are markers of disorder against which order can be generated.[64] By identifying and naming examples of disorder, the judicial officer constitutes (makes and maintains) order. This connects to wider concerns about danger and security in the courtroom, especially where the defendant is not legally represented, or where the legal counsel is not able to control the defendant, so the connection between the person and the judge may be more direct without buffer.[65]

VI Conclusion

Emotion and emotion work are often associated with burnout, stress or unwelcome demands, perhaps especially for professions where detachment is seen as an essential, even defining characteristic.[66] This analysis

---

[63] The Council of Chief Justices of Australia and New Zealand (n 61) 19 [4.1]; Roach Anleu, Mack and Tutton (n 12) 628–9.

[64] We are grateful to Professor Leslie Moran (Birkbeck, University of London), for observations regarding disorder and order which were made at the workshop on *Judging, Emotion and Emotion Work* held at the International Institute for the Sociology of Law, Oñati, Spain, 2–4 May 2018 <www.iisj.net/en/workshops/judging-emotion-and-emotion-work>.

[65] See also Mary Douglas, *Purity and Danger: An Analysis of Concepts of Pollution and Taboo* (Penguin, 1970); Leslie J Moran and Beverley Skeggs, *Sexuality and the Politics of Violence and Safety* (Routledge, 2004).

[66] For results of Australian empirical research on judicial stress and wellbeing, see Carly Schrever, Carol Hulbert and Tania Sourdin, 'The Psychological Impact of Judicial Work:

demonstrates how emotion can be a resource for judicial officers to understand others, to manage their own behaviour, and to achieve essential practical, normative and ethical goals. Identifying the effort, relationality, and facilitative dimensions of judicial emotion and emotion work repositions emotion work as central to judicial performance and enables emotion to be recognised as a positive judicial resource.

Both judges mention the actions, behaviour and feelings of others when they experience, manage and display emotion. This confirms that emotion in judicial work is produced in interaction, shaped by the institutional requirements of impartiality and constrained by legal norms about proper judicial conduct. Interaction between judicial officers and other participants provides the framework through which emotion management strategies are deployed and enables norms about appropriate behaviour and emotion display to become apparent.[67]

Strategies such as adjournment, 'staying as still and calm as I could be', not 'speaking really harshly or inappropriately' or self-talk by 'consciously [saying] look just, forget it,' imply a conception of appropriate judicial practice. This entails implementing feeling rules which prescribe or prohibit certain emotions and emotion displays by the judiciary as well as by others in court. The two judges interviewed appear committed to compliance with and enforcement of feeling rules, but neither specifically articulated them or associated them expressly with any external judicial conduct guidance. Judicial reflexivity about emotion, and emotion work, does not, in itself, erase the dominant cultural script of judicial detachment. The strategies described in the interviews, and the implicit feeling rules in operation, may, in part, incorporate the dominant cultural script of judicial dispassion, which can, itself, be an emotion management resource or a kind of feeling rule or a crucial background emotion.

Australia's First Empirical Research Measuring Judicial Stress and Wellbeing' (2019) 28 *Journal of Judicial Administration* 141.

[67] Michèle Lamont and Ann Swidler, 'Methodological Pluralism and the Possibilities and Limits of Interviewing' (2014) 37(2) *Qualitative Sociology* 153, 156.

7

The Persistent Pejorative

Judicial Activism

TANYA JOSEV*

> It's the attitude of judges like these which has eroded any trust that remained in our legal system ... [the] continued appointment of hard-left activist judges has come back to bite Victorians.[1]

One could be forgiven for thinking that the comment above might have emerged from a 'shock jock' or self-proclaimed culture warrior at the height of the Australian judicial activism debate in the 1990s. During that time, a group of prominent Australian non-lawyers, from newspaper columnists to mining executives, were content to use such language to describe the actions of particular judges in the superior courts of Australia.[2] For many, the appellation of 'activism' has become synonymous with the Mason and Brennan Court eras and the native title and implied rights decisions handed down by the High Court during this period. Some even assume that the term subsided from popular use as

---

* I am grateful to Professors Andrew Lynch and Gabrielle Appleby for their constructive comments on an earlier version of this chapter. All errors remain my own.
[1] Michael Sukkar quoted in Simon Benson, 'Judiciary "Light on Terrorism"', *The Australian* (Sydney, 13 June 2017) 6.
[2] Early examples include journalist Gerard Henderson (the Court has 'convert[ed] to judicial activism': Gerard Henderson, 'March of the High Court Murphyites', *The Sydney Morning Herald* (Sydney, 1 December 1992) 17); Senator Peter Durack, 'Brennan has become pretty activist, and even Mason!', quoted in Margo Kingston, 'Just Who Is Judging Australia', *The Age* (Melbourne, 14 October 1992) 11; and broader critiques, including those of mining executive Hugh Morgan (the High Court has 'given substance to the ambitions of Australian communists and the Bolshevik left': quoted in Gordon Brysland, 'Legal Fundamentalism and Mabo' (1993) 18(5) *Alternative Law Journal* 212, 213); and the historian Geoffrey Blainey (see, for instance, his comments reported in Richard Evans, 'The Blainey View: Geoffrey Blainey Ponders Mabo, the High Court and Democracy' (1995) 96 *Law Institute Journal* 203).

prominent members of the High Court from those years gradually retired from the bench.³

The comment above, however, was *not* made last century: it was made in 2017, by a Federal government minister in the Liberal-National Coalition who had formerly practised as a corporate lawyer and who was expressing concern about the Victorian Court of Appeal's recent track record in sentencing for serious criminal offences.⁴ It was the latest ventilation of a term that has enjoyed regular deployment in public discourse since its emergence almost 30 years ago, in the aftermath of the handing down of the High Court's decision in *Mabo*.⁵ The minister's statement was made in knowledge of the fact that the Victorian Court of Appeal had reserved its judgment in a contentious sentencing decision in relation to terrorism offences.⁶ The comment was made alongside critical remarks by two other Coalition ministers in an article published in *The Australian* newspaper on the Victorian courts' sentencing practices. Collectively, the ministers' comments adverted to the judges *en masse* having an ideological bent; arguably, this implied judicial bias. The term 'activism', in this context, was used as a denunciation of the members of the Court of Appeal. Much has been written in recent times about the events that followed the publication of the article in *The Australian*: the ministers being required to appear before the Court of Appeal to explain why they should not be referred for prosecution for contempt; the initial refusal of the ministers to express contrition for their remarks; the appropriateness of engaging the Commonwealth Solicitor-General to act on their behalf; whether reform proposals on *sub judice* contempt and scandalising the court might be explored in light of these events; and

---

³ This view aligns with the more general appraisal that the Gleeson Court 'retreated' from the 'transformative' agenda set largely by Chief Justice Mason, in favour of a return to legalism – thus inviting less public scrutiny: see generally Jason Pierce, *Inside the Mason Court Revolution: The High Court of Australia Transformed* (Carolina Academic Press, 2006) 248–57. For further discussion of the public reactions to the Mason and Gleeson courts, see Paul Kildea and George Williams, 'The Mason Court' in Rosalind Dixon and George Williams (eds), *The High Court, The Constitution and Australian Politics* (Cambridge University Press, 2015) 244; Rosalind Dixon and Sean Lau, 'The Gleeson Court and the Howard Era: A Tale of Two Conservatives (and Isms)' in Rosalind Dixon and George Williams (eds), *The High Court, The Constitution and Australian Politics* (Cambridge University Press, 2015) 285; Haig Patapan, *Judging Democracy: The New Politics of the High Court of Australia* (Cambridge University Press, 2000) ch 2.
⁴ Michael Sukkar MP.
⁵ *Mabo v Queensland [No 2]* (1992) 175 CLR 1. See also n 2.
⁶ *DPP (Cth) v Besim* (2017) 52 VR 296.

finally, whether this type of political criticism of the courts might or might not erode judicial independence.[7] The response of the Court of Appeal has also received much attention, at least insofar as the court condemned the ministerial comments as 'appalling'.[8] Much less has been said, however, about the persistent use of the activist appellation by politicians and the media; the effect these critiques might have on the public perception of judicial method; and whether this recent episode acts as a portent for the way public scrutiny of the Australian judiciary might be carried out in the future.

What is judicial activism? Why does activism (or an accusation of activism) provoke serious concern amongst politicians, commentators and even judges? Further, if activism is regarded by Federal ministers and others as some sort of aberration from a perceived judicial 'orthodoxy', how might that orthodoxy be construed? This chapter aims to explore the various meanings given to the term in Australia and its current invocation as a professional insult. In examining the meanings given to the term, it should be noted at the outset that it is not an onerous task to conduct a review of the academic literature on point – in contrast to reviewing the proliferation of media reportage and commentary containing the terminology. This is because activism is rarely a topic of scholarly study in its own right in Australia.[9] Only a small number of local scholars, and an even smaller number of Australian judges, have attempted to engage in the taxonomical exercise of defining and making a case for or against activism. As discussed below, there are compelling reasons for this reticence to engage with the terminology. This chapter, similarly, does not present a formal taxonomy for activism; it makes no

---

[7] See, for instance, the analysis in Gabrielle Appleby and Heather Roberts' chapter, 'The Chief Justice: Under Relational and Institutional Pressure' in this collection. See also Victorian Law Reform Commission, *Contempt of Court* (Consultation Paper, May 2019) pt 3; and the views of jurists JD Heydon, 'Does Political Criticism of Judges Damage Judicial Independence?' (Project Paper, Policy Exchange, February 2018) and Catherine Holmes, 'Declaration of Independence', *The Australian* (Sydney, 14 June 2019) 4.

[8] *DPP (Cth) v Besim* (2017) 52 VR 296. See also Emilios Kyrou, 'The Independent, Low Profile Third Arm of Government' (2017) *Law Institute Journal* and Heydon, 'Does Political Criticism of Judges Damage Judicial Independence?' (n 7).

[9] There are only three scholars who have been prepared to employ the term in any regular fashion (albeit self-consciously) in their research over the past 30 years: John Gava, James Allan, and Greg Craven. Others, such as Leslie Zines, Michael Coper, Tony Blackshield and Cheryl Saunders have explicitly distanced themselves from the terminology in their writing. My own recent work focuses on the history of the usage of the term, in distinction from the normative usage employed by Gava, Allan and Craven.

such case for activism to be rehabilitated from its current use as a pejorative and legitimised as a useful descriptor of judicial method. There is no intention here to 'shoehorn' contemporary debates in public and private law spheres into a normative framework. Interestingly, such an exercise *has* been undertaken at length by various scholars overseas.[10] That exercise arguably proceeds on the often unarticulated presumption that a bifurcated understanding of judicial methodology – activism *versus* a particular counterpoint (self-restraint, for instance) – has some utility to both a lay and scholarly readership. This chapter makes no such claim. Instead, this chapter is concerned with understanding the development of activism as a critique in Australia and the fluctuating meanings given to activism over time. It identifies and separates the political sources of the activism critique from the relatively sparse academic and judicial work on the topic. It contends that the language of activism has, in the three decades since its inception in Australia, clouded rather than clarified discussion on judicial decision-making and methodology, and makes some modest proposals as to how to move beyond the activist terminology in public discourse.

I Meanings of Activism

The accusations made against the Victorian Court of Appeal under the rubric of activism in 2017 can only be fully contextualised if a brief survey is undertaken of the various meanings that have been given to the term since its introduction to Australian audiences in the early 1990s. Activism is a term capable of attracting a multiplicity of meanings – meanings which just as often overlap as they do contradict each other. The fact that there is no consensus in any forum as to what constitutes activism renders the term of questionable utility to most academics and lawyers in the context of dialogues about doctrinal and methodological developments. (As observed earlier, it comes as no surprise that there are

---

[10] See, for instance, Ronald Dworkin, 'A Special Supplement: The Jurisprudence of Richard Nixon' (1972) 18(8) *The New York Review of Books* 27; Stephanie A Lindquist and Frank B Cross, *Measuring Judicial Activism* (Oxford University Press, 2009); Thomas M Keck, *The Most Activist Supreme Court in History* (University of Chicago Press, 2004); and the essays in Brice Dickson (ed), *Judicial Activism in Common Law Supreme Courts* (Oxford University Press, 2007). These can be contrasted against descriptive efforts such as Keenan Kmiec, 'The Origin and Current Meanings of "Judicial Activism"' (2004) 92 *California Law Review* 1441 and Craig Green, 'An Intellectual History of Judicial Activism' (2009) 58 *Emory Law Journal* 1195.

no scholars of judicial activism as a *methodological* practice in Australia.) To examine the various meanings given to activism, therefore, one needs to look further afield: to those people that employ the term as a serious descriptor of judicial practice. Almost uniformly, these commentators write for audiences outside the legal arena, although there are some notable exceptions.[11] These commentators predominantly identify with the political right, although again, there are some significant exceptions.[12]

It is not possible here to set out an extended catalogue of usages of the term 'activism' in the Australian popular media and in the literary and current affairs journals of the political left and right.[13] However it is hoped that the following summary of these meanings may suffice to illustrate both how broadly and narrowly activism might be construed in Australia. There are several overlapping themes or meanings associated with activism. The word 'meanings' is used loosely in this chapter: the characterisations of activism are malleable and the protagonists in the activism debate usually apply the term without providing an explicit definition for it. That said, the two most popular meanings given to activism are the most slippery.

The primary meaning given to activism is unadulterated, results-oriented decision-making, devoid of discernible legal method. Despite this definition seemingly being able to accommodate activists with varying political, social or economic world views, the term is used almost uniformly in Australia to describe those judges who hand down what are perceived of as 'leftist' judgments – that is, results that favour particular minorities, stymie the legislative programme of an incumbent

---

[11] The prominent examples are Janet Albrechtsen, a columnist for *The Australian*, Gerard Henderson, a columnist formerly for *The Sydney Morning Herald* and now for *The Weekend Australian*; and Dyson Heydon, formerly a Justice of the High Court of Australia. Andrew Bolt, a commentator with *The Herald Sun* and the *Daily Telegraph* often adopts others' assessments of activism approvingly. Coalition parliamentarians, such as the late Tim Fischer and Rob Borbidge (and more recently, Michael Sukkar) also assailed the High Court on these terms. Activism was a particular preoccupation in the papers of the Samuel Griffith Society, a legal interest group, in the 1990s.

[12] See above n 11. A rare example from the political left is former New South Wales Premier Bob Carr, who opposed a federal statutory Bill of Rights, arguing it would promote activism, 'judicial creep' and zealotry from judges: Bob Carr, 'Bill of Wrongs', *The Australian* (Sydney, 26 April 2008) 19.

[13] But see generally Tanya Josev, *The Campaign against the Courts: A History of the Judicial Activism Debate* (Federation Press, 2017) for a narrative history of the usage of the terminology in Australia. An extensive consideration of the various Australian usages of the term over time can be found in the aforementioned volume in chs 4, 5 and the epilogue.

conservative government, or otherwise further a perceived progressive cause (which usually appears to relate to the protection of civil or human rights). This is largely attributable to the manner in which the term was adopted in Australia, as shall be discussed below. A charge of results-oriented decision-making is, of course, not illegitimate in itself. But a charge of results-oriented decision-making in circumstances where the commentator has not identified the lack of methodological rigour in the decision (indeed, where the commentator has not adverted to any familiarity with the written reasons at all) renders this type of usage deeply flawed. It is a matter of alarm that this type of usage, in this (lack of) context, is commonplace. Most often it is employed in the assessment of a new appointee to the High Court: in recent years, Justices Gageler, Keane and Edelman have all been assessed on these terms in media reportage of their elevation to the Court without any specific reference to their previous work.[14] *The Australian*, for instance, noted with approval in 2015 that the incoming Chief Justice of Queensland, Catherine Holmes, had already declared she was not 'an adventurous judge [nor an] activist judge'; Justice Keane was similarly lauded by the then Federal Opposition for his apparent stance against activism, without any further elaboration.[15]

The results-oriented characterisation is closely associated with the second meaning associated with activism, which relates to judicial disposition. In this usage, judicial activism is a synonym for judicial hubris; it often appears alongside charges that the judiciary is composed of 'philosopher kings', 'unelected judges' or 'elites'.[16] Here, the suggestion is not, at first glance, one of ideological zealotry, but instead a comment on judicial temperament. The judges, in this characterisation, are perceived to consider themselves expertly attuned to the needs and values of contemporary society, even if lacking a mandate to act as expositors of

[14] See, for instance, Editorial, 'An Appointment Made on Merit', *The Australian* (Sydney, 22 August 2012) 13; Joe Kelly, 'Speedy Keane Joins the High Court Club', *The Australian* (Sydney, 21 December 2012) 6; Denis Shanahan, 'Conservative Drive: Courting a Backbone to Resist Judicial Activism' *The Australian* (online, 30 November 2016) <www.theaustralian.com.au/opinion/columnists/dennis-shanahan/conservative-drive-courting-a-backbone-to-resist-judicial-activism/news-story/efcf2b3c8f0d795a7b22a3cef4e7ca9c>; Miranda Devine, 'High Court Choice Shows Libs Just Sit on the Fence', *The Daily Telegraph* (Sydney, 30 November 2016) 13.

[15] Sarah Elks, 'Chief Justice Promises to Make Court "Boring"', *The Australian* (Sydney, 9 September 2015) 7; Kelly (n 14s).

[16] As an example, see John Gava, 'The Rise of the Hero Judge' (2001) 24(3) *University of New South Wales Law Journal* 747.

those values. This lack of mandate would not concern activist judges: in their supposed arrogance, they are convinced that written judgments are the appropriate vehicle for pronouncements on contemporary values. In this critique, it is acknowledged that, however undesirable, such judges are acting within the bounds of acceptable practice in making statements to this effect in developing the law. Thus, the critique proceeds on a personal basis to challenge the judge's particular pretensions. Again, this characterisation of activism is not without problems. It may be specious to suggest hubris alone begets activism; if this were the case, there are various colourful judicial identities from years past that have curiously escaped the designation. Again, while not articulated explicitly in this usage, the targets of this critique appear to be hubristic judges who articulate societal values that are under challenge from the political right.[17]

The third common usage is to define activism by what it is not. This is the classic, bifurcated understanding of activism versus 'orthodox' judicial practices. This is the rubric established in the United States, where the term was coined in the 1940s. However, the Australian variant exhibits some significant differences from the earlier model. In the United States, activism has been pitted against three 'orthodoxies': first and most commonly, self-restraint; less commonly, originalism; and perhaps least compellingly, 'strict constructionism'.[18] The usual American counterpoint to activism, self-restraint, is an equally troubled term, with its own definitional disputes.[19] In the context of the bifurcated analysis, however, self-restraint appears to suggest that a judge would be

---

[17] See, for instance, 'Like [Chief Justice] Mason, [Justice] Kirby was frequently seduced by the hero judge role, making conscience-driven decisions, using his own values as a measuring stick for "community values", ignoring the rule of law, and searching for some international pronouncement to bolster his decision': Janet Albrechtsen, 'The Essence of Good Judgement', *The Australian* (Sydney, 18 June 2014) 14.

[18] For the initial formulation of activism as a counterpoint to self-restraint, see Arthur Schlesinger, Jr., 'The Supreme Court: 1947', *Fortune* (January 1947) 202. Strict constructionism, on the other hand, has never found favour (even in conservative academic circles) as describing any particular interpretive method: see, for instance, Antonin Scalia with Amy Gutmann (ed), *A Matter of Interpretation: Federal Courts and the Law* (Princeton University Press, 1997) 23–4. Republicans, from Presidents Nixon, Reagan and Bush, to Vice President Pence, continue to adopt the term: see, for instance, Josev (n 13) 63–6, 70, 72.

[19] See Richard Posner, 'The Meaning of Judicial Self-Restraint' (1983) 59 *Indiana Law Journal* 1; Richard Posner, 'The Rise and Fall of Self-Restraint' (2012) 100 *California Law Review* 519; Aziz Huq, 'When Was Self Restraint?' (2012) 100 *California Law Review* 579.

hesitant to conduct judicial review in a manner which points towards the invalidation of legislation. Activists have no such hesitancy. In Australia, on the other hand, activism has been construed more broadly as a challenge to Dixonian legalism rather than as mere self-restraint. This usage therefore extends beyond cases involving judicial review. Legalism is presented as a long-standing orthodoxy; it embodies high technique in logic and reasoning, close adherence to precedent, and an unyielding, positivistic belief in 'the law' as an external standard. Activism is defined in the negative in this analysis: it encompasses a disregard of high technique, an ignorance of precedent and a celebration of the indeterminacy of law.[20]

There are some concerns about activism that are squarely focussed on methodological issues. These concerns are most likely to arise (however infrequently) in the course of academic discussion. There are several thematic strands to this type of critique. The first of these is to situate activism as a practice relating to the development of the common law. The term is not usually employed as a personal critique of a judge, but instead as an appraisal of a discrete piece of judicial reasoning. It is also the most anodyne of the usages, and most likely to be employed in critiques of private law decisions. If the development of the common law is seen to progress on a linear, incremental basis, then an act of activism is a significant jump in that progression, made within a single judgment.[21] Opinions will vary as to just how far the steps taken in the judgment have gone beyond mere incrementalism; upon occasion, a critique may be made that a jump has gone as far as to represent a break in common law principle. 'A touch of activism' may or may not be praised in this context. Another methodological usage is to interpret activism in a relatively limited fashion, relating entirely to public law: in this usage, activism denotes the process of implying certain rights or freedoms into the *Australian Constitution*.[22] A third methodological usage is to critique activism as the embracing of certain types of subjective tests of reasonableness or proportionality into public law decisions

---

[20] For a prominent example, see Dyson Heydon, 'Judicial Activism and the Death of the Rule of Law' (2003) 47(1) *Quadrant* 9.
[21] For a prominent example from private law, see Ian Callinan, 'Judicial Activism' (Speech, Bar Association of Queensland Conference, 2–4 May 1997).
[22] As an example, see Greg Craven, 'Judicial Activism: The Beginning of the End of the Beginning' (Speech, Samuel Griffith Society Conference, 12–14 March 2004).

that invite judges to make 'political' appraisals of government actions.[23] A fourth is for a judge to engage with, and rely on, extrinsic materials – for instance, international materials, including treaties and foreign jurisprudence, or contested historical evidence – at the expense of relevant materials intrinsic to the operation of Australian law (namely domestic precedent).[24]

The inconsistencies and overlaps between these competing usages and themes outlined above are not difficult to appreciate – rather, they are readily apparent. Judicial hubris, for instance, is often paired with other meanings of the term, thus conflating doubts about judicial technique with any perceived personal failings of the judge. The most common use of activism (to connote decision-making *devoid* of reasoning) can be contrasted against the handful of usages which suggest methodological practices *are* at the heart of activism. Activism as a code word for 'idol judges' contrasts against the characterisation of activism as anti-legalism (legalism is practised by arguably the most idolised of Australian judges, Sir Owen Dixon) and the usage in which the focus is not on the judge, but on the development of principles. Thematically, many usages of activism appear to reveal a hostility towards rights in general, but there are often conflicting arguments about whether judges interpreting a codified bill of rights or implying (uncodified) rights is of greater concern. Meanwhile, activism can be used to describe a number of discrete methodological concerns at once.

It is easy to see why commentators using the terminology might belatedly discover that they are debating at cross-purposes with their interlocutors. But there is also a remarkable consistency across the various meanings ascribed to the term. Not one of these usages of activism is intended as a compliment. To be accused of activism is to be condemned either as a poor judge or, in extreme cases, as unfit to hold judicial office. This goes some way to explaining why the minister's 2017 statement in relation to the Victorian Court of Appeal aroused so much interest. The minister's reported statement, when read as a whole, might well have suggested to a reader of the *Australian* article that the

---

[23] See, for instance, James Allan, 'Queensland's Alice in Wonderland Bill of Rights a Senseless Transfer of Power', *The Australian* (Sydney, 16 November 2018) 26.

[24] See, for instance, Janet Albrechtsen, 'Activist Judiciary A Looming Menace', *The Australian* (Sydney, 31 October 2007) 16; Peter Connolly and SEK Hulme, *The High Court of Australia in Mabo* (Association of Mining and Exploration Companies, 1993); Blainey (n 2).

relevant judges were results-oriented, with partisan ideological predispositions, and errant in their departure from time-honoured judicial practices (in other words, an amalgam of various meanings described above) and whose behaviour was likely to cause damage to the reputation of the judiciary and compromise the safety of the Victorian public. Activism may not be consistently used to describe a particular practice, but it is consistently used as a condemnation.

II Reasons for the Terminology's Enduring Appeal in Popular Discourse

The popularity of the activism terminology can be attributed to a number of factors. The foremost of these is that activism is attractive as a *broad* (albeit simplistic) descriptor of judicial behaviour: under the more common usages detailed above, one need only know the result of a decision to come to a conclusion about whether any perceived activism has been deployed. The commentator is not required to have detailed legal knowledge – nor, indeed, to make any attempt at reading the impugned judgment – to make the claim of activism. To paraphrase an American constitutional scholar writing on clichéd court reporting, the lure of appellations such as activism is that commentators can criticise judges without having to know much about the case law itself.[25] The following paragraphs examine the continuing appeal of the activism appellation along these lines in the political arena, yet it is also acknowledged that the term has persisted with the unwitting encouragement of some in the wider legal community too.

A Activism's Continuing Appeal in Political Discourse

The terminology is a favourite in the politicians' lexicon, and the circumstances of the term's adoption in Australia help to explain activism's continuing appeal to the political class. The term had been in existence for nearly 50 years in the United States before its migration to Australia. In the United States, in the early years, activism was loosely associated with the counter-majoritarian difficulty, overturning legislation on civil rights grounds, discrete voting blocs on the Supreme Court, and a judicial turn to Realism. I have argued elsewhere that the primary reason for the

---

[25] Randy Barnett, 'Constitutional Clichés' (2007) 36 *Capital University Law Journal* 493.

delay in the language reaching Australia was that Australian academics who were aware of the term's uniquely American connotations deemed it inapplicable in the Australian jurisdiction.[26] In Australia, there was no great reason to adopt the terminology in scholarly writing or in media reportage on the Australian High Court at mid-century: the idea that the High Court could conduct judicial review was not couched in controversy. The due process clause in the *United States Constitution* (the main focus of early analysis under the activism rubric) had no equivalent in the *Australian Constitution*, and although personal relations on the High Court were poor at mid-century, there was no great voting schism that paralleled the blocs of the Supreme Court. Finally, although local interpretations of legal realism were beginning to flower in Australian academia, the justices of the High Court remained committed to legalism, and the international reputation of the supreme legalist, Chief Justice Dixon, only added to the legitimacy of the approach.

It is only the much later American variant of activism – that is, a political slogan adopted by the Nixon and Reagan presidential campaigns – that piqued the interest of an Australian audience, comprising local social conservatives and the political right. Reagan and Nixon both campaigned on the basis that their Republican administrations would temper the aggressive permissiveness of certain public institutions in America; this would be effected by, amongst other policies, appointing staunch anti-activists to the federal bench in order to stymy an existing caucus of 'liberal judges'. In this usage, activism had no fixed definition; the focus was on avoiding perceived progressive judicial outcomes. Similarly, in Australia, the activism appellation was brought to prominence in Australia as part of a concerted charge against 'elites' in what became known as the culture wars in the national politics of the late 1980s and early 1990s. Again, the predominant usage of the term was to describe judges who delivered progressive *results* – not even necessarily engaging in results-oriented decision-making. The first accusations of activism emerged after the *Mabo* judgment on native title was handed down in 1992.

Much is often made of the High Court's self-conscious turn away from legalism in the 1990s, as if the attendant rancour surrounding its decisions can be explained by this departure from 'orthodoxy' alone. Of course, the Court's newfound willingness to articulate policy choices in

---

[26] See generally Josev (n 13) ch 3.

judgments must be recognised as arousing the interest of a much broader audience than before. So must the Court's innovations across a number of public and private law areas, not least in the areas of native title (*Mabo, Wik*) and implied rights (*Australian Capital Television, Nationwide*), but also tort law (*Burnie Port Authority*) and contract law (*Trident*), amongst others.[27] But given that some of the subsequent criticisms of activism suggested a hostility to rights-based jurisprudence and certain types of interpretive practices, then one might have expected that earlier cases such as *Koowarta* in 1982 and *Tasmanian Dams* in 1983 (reliance on 'international materials' via the external affairs power), *Davis v Commonwealth* (freedom of expression) or even *Cole v Whitfield* in 1988 (use of extrinsic historical materials in interpretation) would have attracted the appellation first. What was different about *Mabo* that first drew the activist designation?[28] By the early 1990s, the culture wars (and the associated language adopted from Reagan-era politics) had become entrenched in Australian political discourse. The Court's work now intersected with those 'wars' – and in particular the subset of them relating to the interpretation of Australia's frontier history.

In the aftermath of Australia's Bicentenary celebrations, social conservatives argued that a 'guilt industry' had emerged that emphasised the accounts of Aboriginal dispossession in Australian history, rather than the achievements of British settlement. The High Court judges in *Mabo*, perhaps unwittingly, played in to these concerns, primarily by ruling in favour of the indigenous plaintiffs but also, according to more sophisticated commentators, by explicitly making reference to the work of 'black armband' historian Henry Reynolds in their judgments.[29] Thus the first charges under the rubric of 'unelected judges', judges masquerading as progressive politicians, or activists, were made by not by lawyers at all, but by social conservatives such as the historian Geoffrey Blainey, the mining executive Hugh Morgan, and others. These early critiques were subsumed into wider Coalition campaign strategy in the 1996 Federal

---

[27] *Mabo v Queensland [No 2]* (1992) 175 CLR 1; *Wik Peoples v Queensland* (1996) 187 CLR 1; *Australian Capital Television v Commonwealth* (1992) 177 CLR 106; *Nationwide News Pty Ltd v Wills* (1992) 177 CLR 1; *Burnie Port Authority v General Jones Pty Ltd* (1994) 179 CLR 520; *Trident General Insurance Co Ltd v McNiece Bros Pty Ltd* (1988) 165 CLR 107.

[28] *Koowarta v Bjelke-Petersen* (1982) 153 CLR 168; *Commonwealth v Tasmania* (1983) 158 CLR 1; *Cole v Whitfield* (1988) 165 CLR 360; *Davis v Commonwealth* (1988) 166 CLR 79.

[29] See Blainey (n 2) and Morgan (n 2).

election, and in the years of the Howard Government that followed. In 1996, political strategists for the Coalition and commentators alike suggested that the incumbent Keating Labor government had removed itself from the concerns of 'battlers' and was in the thrall of a new class of progressives with boutique policy concerns. That new class encompassed multiculturalists, indigenous lobbyists, public servants, black armband historians and social-warrior type lawyers.[30] Judicial activists became more explicitly characterised as a subset of the latter after a second major native title decision, *Wik*, was handed down later that year.

After *Wik*, Federal Coalition Ministers and State Premiers alike attacked the Court *en masse* on the basis of the Court's supposed activism in failing to support the notion that the granting of pastoral leases extinguished native title in full: again, activism was alleged not on the basis of the judges' methods, but because of their preference to support 'minority' interests. The language of activism was now in wide usage, thus the implied-rights jurisprudence of earlier years was reevaluated on these terms– although in relation to this topic, activism was occasionally associated with more substantive meanings than mere progressivism.[31] The maliciousness associated with the term nevertheless grew. A sample of the invective published at this time suffices to illustrate that activism had become primarily associated with judicial hubris or progressive outcomes, at least in the popular media. The High Court was, according to commentators and other public figures:

> 'bogus', 'pusillanimous and evasive', guilty of 'plunging Australia into the abyss', a 'pathetic ... self-appointed [group of] Kings and Queens', a group of 'basket-weavers', 'gripped ... in a mania for progressivism', purveyors of 'intellectual dishonesty', unaware of 'its place', 'adventurous', needing a 'good behaviour bond', needing, on the contrary, a sentence to 'life on the streets', an 'unfaithful servant of the Constitution', 'undermining democracy', a body 'packed with feral judges', 'a professional labor cartel'.[32]

---

[30] See generally Pamela Williams, *The Victory* (Allen and Unwin, 1997) 50–2; Carol Johnson, 'Anti-Elitist Discourse in Australia: International Influences and Comparisons' in Marian Sawer and Barry Hindess (eds), *Us and Them: Anti-Elitism in Australia* (Australian Public Intellectual Network, 2004) 117; Sean Scalmer and Murray Goot, 'Elites Constructing Elites: News Limited's Newspapers 1996–2002' in Marian Sawer and Barry Hindess (eds), *Us and Them: Anti-Elitism in Australia* (Australian Public Intellectual Network, 2004) 137.
[31] Josev (n 13) 148–50.
[32] Michael Kirby, 'Attacks on Judges: A Universal Phenomenon' (1998) 72 *Australian Law Journal* 599, 601 (citations omitted).

It is for this reason that the term activism has since become associated solely with judges or judgments perceived to be socially progressive; activism was taken up almost exclusively as a denigratory label by the political right from the outset.

The charge against the elites appears to have contributed to an effective overall political strategy: the Coalition secured repeated election victories in 1996, 1998, 2001 and 2004. The fact that senior members of the Coalition employed the judicial activism terminology repeatedly in reportage about the courts in this period lent activism a certain legitimacy as a descriptor of discernible judicial practice.[33] The grim spectre of ever expanding 'activism' emanating from the courts conjured up an evocative political image far more effective than anything that might be generated in an esoteric discussion of discrete issues in judicial decision-making.

In recent decades, there has been generational change amongst the commentators and politicians, as well as two lengthy periods of Coalition government, yet the activist critiques persist. If, for instance, the Gleeson Court of the early 2000s could be viewed as largely upholding the Coalition's legislative programme, then it might be thought that the force of the political right's campaign against judicial activism should have waned correspondingly. However, in the early 2000s, new targets emerged for critique: charges of judicial activism spread to other jurisdictions, including the Federal Court (particularly in relation to refugee matters); the Family Court; and, in the following decade, the state courts of criminal appeal.[34] The activism denunciation was also sometimes ventilated outside the discussion of discrete cases as a *potential* threat to democracy should parliamentary action be taken to encourage it via the statutory codification of human rights.[35] These arguments were often couched as a sinister warning against the American experience and the partisanship exhibited by the Supreme Court justices in rights cases. This

---

[33] See generally Josev (n 13) 131, 155–60.

[34] See, for instance, John McMillan, 'Federal Court v Minister for Immigration' (1999) 22 *Journal of Administrative Law Forum* 1; Bill Muehlenberg, 'The Threat of Judicial Activism', *Quadrant Online*, (online, 2 November 2008) <https://quadrant.org.au/opinion/bill-muehlenberg/2008/11/the-threat-of-judicial-activism/>.

[35] See Carr (n 12). Journalist Paul Kelly, and the now contentious cleric George Pell also adopted these terms: 'Catholic Archbishop Wary of Bill of Rights' (ABC Local Radio, 30 April 2008): Kelly cited in Andrew Bolt, 'More Rights for Unelected Judges', *Herald Sun Blog* (Blog Post, 13 December 2008) <http://blogs.news.com.au/heraldsun/andrewbolt/index.php/heraldsun/comments/more_rights_for_unelected_judges/P40/>.

theme reached a high point in public dialogue in 2007 to 2009, when the Australia 2020 summit considered bill of rights proposals, as did the National Human Rights Consultation Committee.[36] Activism, when used in popular discourse, is now no longer solely synonymous with any perceived excesses in native title, nor implied rights jurisprudence: most recently it has been employed to describe potential responsibilities given to the Supreme Court of Queensland in that state's statutory bill of rights;[37] in the Victorian courts' alleged propensity to give 'light' sentences to offenders convicted of terrorism offences; and to deprecate the High Court's jurisprudence on section 44 of the *Australian Constitution*.[38]

Interestingly, however, the political strategy involved in employing the activist critique has changed since the Coalition's return to power in 2013 after six years of Labor government. Unsurprisingly, conservative commentators see no benefit in attributing new instances of judicial activism to the permissiveness of the Federal Government when that government consists of a Coalition majority. Therefore any perceived activism is taken as evidence that electoral *stability* is needed to silence a reportedly growing number of agenda-pushing radicals who are funded by the public purse, judges included. This stability, according to the commentators, will ensure that judicial appointments are made to temper any existing activism on the bench. Appointments, therefore, are to be made on the basis of a candidate's anti-activist credentials.[39]

---

[36] Frank Brennan et al., *National Human Rights Consultation* (Report, September 2009). Opponents of a bill of rights published their own volume in the same year: Julian Leeser and Ryan Haddrick (eds), *Don't Leave Us with the Bill: The Case against an Australian Bill of Rights* (Menzies Research Centre, 2009).
[37] James Allan, 'Queensland's Alice in Wonderland Bill of Rights a Senseless Transfer of Power', *The Australian* (Sydney, 16 November 2018) 26, writing in relation to the *Human Rights Act 2019* (Qld); Morgan Begg, 'Fellow Citizens', *Institute of Public Affairs*, (Blog Post, 11 November 2017) <https://ipa.org.au/publications-ipa/in-the-news/fellow-citizens>.
[38] See, for instance, Begg, ibid., discussing *Re Canavan* (2017) 263 CLR 284.
[39] See Shanahan (n 14):

> The Liberal government's appointment [of James Edelman] is ... a conservative political decision... .[Edelman] has the potential for a 28-year career on the High Court ... .This is the true political influence of a conservative government – to have a High Court with a backbone that resists judicial activism.

B The Use of the Activist Language in the Legal Community

Having made the observation earlier that the large majority of the academic community have assiduously avoided the terminology – probably in more recent times because of a recognition of its predominant usage as a derogatory political label – it must also be conceded that the terminology has also persisted in public discourse partly because discrete elements of the wider legal community, either deliberately or unwittingly, have encouraged it since its introduction. The Samuel Griffith Society, a legal interest group founded in 1992 and primarily concerned with preserving federalism, spent several of its early years conducting annual conferences in which activism was a topic of discussion.[40] Some judges, such as Chief Justices Robert French, Murray Gleeson and Sir Anthony Mason and Justices Michael Kirby, Ray Finkelstein and Ronald Sackville, gave public lectures and wrote articles imploring public criticism of the courts to be conducted using more detailed terms[41] But there is a judge who took a different view.

Former Justice of the High Court, Dyson Heydon, a strident critic of activism, added credibility to the term by repeatedly employing it in orations and papers in both public and scholarly contexts. He might even be considered an architect of the term, given that his 2003 oration on the topic (published in four separate journals) promoted several definitions of the term.[42] He described activism variously as the 'illegitimate ... furthering of some political, moral or social program';[43] as a deviation from strict and complete legalism; as a break in common

---

[40] The Samuel Griffith Society's conference proceedings from this period are no longer available online and are not yet available for purchase in hard copy; however, see Josev (n 13) 134–35, 148–50.

[41] Chief Justice Robert French, 'Judicial Activists: Mythical Monsters?' (2008) *12 Southern Cross University Law Review* 59; 'Retiring Chief Justice Murray Gleeson' *The Law Report*, (ABC Radio National, 19 August 2008); 'What is Judicial Activism Anyway?' *The Law Report*, (ABC Radio National, 11 March 1997); Justice Michael Kirby, *Judicial Activism: Authority, Principle and Policy in Judicial Method* (Sweet and Maxwell, 2004); Justice Raymond Finkelstein, 'The Role of the Judge: Judicial Activism and the Rule of Law' (2006) 9 *Flinders Journal of Law Reform* 17; Justice Ronald Sackville, 'Courts and Social Change' (2005) 33 *Federal Law Review* 373. See also Josev (n 13) 166–72, 177–79, 199.

[42] Heydon (n 20). More recent developments in relation to allegations of Justice Heydon's misconduct while on the bench are outside the scope of this chapter but are discussed by Appleby and Lynch in Chapter 1.

[43] Ibid. 9.

law reasoning and a tendency to cite international legal materials; and finally – in echoes of the anti-elitist discourse so favoured in the political arena – he suggested that the activists were part of a 'new class' of lawyers who liked to think like an editorial in *The Guardian*.[44] In this context, activism seemed to be a euphemism for an accusation of judicial illegitimacy – a usage not far removed from the minister's variant in describing the Victorian Court of Appeal some 14 years later. In 2018, however, Heydon's views on the efficacy of the term seemed to have changed – he now saw it as a cliché. Writing in qualified support of the federal ministers who had criticised the Victorian Court of Appeal, and discussing judicial criticism more generally, he observed that:

> what the Ministers said did not rise to the heights of Gladstonian gravitas. But can one say worse of it than that for the most part it was a collection of clichés—tired and demotic? ... Indeed, it is truthful to call some judges that, though people do not normally think in this way of the Victorian Court of Appeal, for more reasons than one.[45]

One wonders whether to interpret this statement as an expression of muted contrition in relation to his own involvement in the activism discourse of 2003, or as a reflection that what was once valuable to him as a descriptor is, through the effluxion of time, now no longer.

Finally, there is one further group that has encouraged the use of the terminology within the legal community. This is a small subset of legal educationalists who teach 'legalism versus activism' as a bona fide jurisprudential dispute to school-aged children and to incoming law students.[46] A question arises as to what secondary materials and references are referred to in these curricula, given the scant academic support for this bifurcated analysis.

C The Echo Chamber of the Judicial Activism 'Debate'

One final observation should be made about the persistence of the term in Australian discourse. It relates to the strategies employed by the

---

[44] Ibid.15.
[45] Heydon, 'Does Political Criticism of Judges Damage Judicial Independence?' (n 7) 9.
[46] Until recently, the Western Australian Constitutional Centre provided a guide that contained these terms: see Western Australian Constitutional Centre, 'Australian Constitutional Issues: Teachers' Pack' (Resource Pack, 2000) 3 (copy on file with author); Victorian Curriculum and Assessment Authority, *Victorian Certificate of Education: Legal Studies Study Design* (Report, 2017) 22. At Melbourne Law School, first year law students are sometimes asked to consider judicial activism as part of their introductory legal reasoning subject (undertaken prior to foundational doctrinal subjects).

'anti-activist' commentariat to perpetuate the use of the activism critique in further argument. Any interlocutor that challenges the activism appellation, or seeks fixed definition before moving to the assessment of specific cases, is often criticised by the commentariat as obfuscating the issues. Members of the anti-activist commentariat see these 'challengers', that is, mainly academics and vocal judges, as surreptitious apologists for judicial activism, or as a cabal determined to thwart wider critiques of the Australian judiciary.[47] The result is that the activism 'debate' is something of an echo chamber: it is perpetuated only by those who have no misgivings about the ambiguities of the terminology.

III Repercussions for the Courts

It can be seen from the foregoing that the development of the judicial activism 'debate' in Australia has been curious: the lack of definitional consensus remains unresolved, while the language of activism has become deeply entrenched in the Australian vernacular and in political debate as a legitimate descriptor of judicial behaviour. Activism has become one of the more popular prisms through which to assess judicial methodology in media reportage and commentary.[48] It is reasonable to ask whether this state of affairs warrants genuine concern. Does a lack of consensus on meaning detract from the usefulness of the term in media reportage on the courts? The media has always dealt in shorthand; politicians deal in pithy sound bites. Why should court decisions or judges be treated any differently in these idioms? Here, I argue that the articulation of meaning matters, even if the protagonists in the activism debate may regard this as an exercise in pedantry.

If debate occurs without any qualification of the *type* of activism supposedly being practised, then the less politically charged forms of 'activism' can be conflated with the primary, political definitions (those associated with judicial illegitimacy: results-oriented decision-making and political hubris). The idea of activism then transforms into a kind of malignancy with no bounds – a one-size-fits-all term to denounce judges or outcomes that have been met with disapproval from commentators. When applied indiscriminately, the entire judiciary

---

[47] See Janet Albrechtsen, 'Judicial Activism: A Question of Power and Politics, Not Law' (Speech, University of New South Wales Constitutional Law Conference, 8 February 2008).

[48] Josev (n 13) 3.

becomes tarred: judges do not generally censure their own (other than through the usual channels of appeal judgments), so their silence is construed by some commentators as tacitly supporting 'activism' amongst their ranks. If it is held to be essential to the rule of law and to judicial independence that the judiciary be held in high public esteem, then one of the simplest ways to erode public confidence in the judiciary would be to accuse its members of an amorphous, creeping activism.

Notwithstanding the term's political allure, no suggestion is made here that all politicians or commentators who adopt the activism appellation *intend* to diminish the judiciary's standing in the Australian community, even if this may be a consequence of their doing so. Nor is it suggested that commentators intend to compel offending judges to modify their judicial behaviour. In fact, the language of activism, at least in the political sphere, is probably not intended to have any effect on judges at all. The critiques, *especially* when made by politicians or newspaper columnists, are primarily directed at a particular constituency and for a particular purpose: to attempt to effect electoral change and/or stability (depending on the party of government). The common usage of activism, relating to results-oriented decision-making and judicial hubris, can be considered as a linguistic 'dog-whistle' connoting that public institutions at large, including the courts, are being overrun by leftist ideologues, and that conservative political leadership may temper these trends. These critiques may well be effective in securing the electoral outcome so desired. The reputational effect on the besieged judge or court in this context is merely a form of collateral damage.

This long-standing association of activism with leftist outcomes may lead to further side effects. These include generating a possible misapprehension – at least in the mind of a lay audience – that any judicial outcome that favours a particular progressive cause is, by definition, illegitimate. Attempts to moderate this scenario have been undertaken by some journalists and legal practitioners in the United States, who argue that 'conservative' activism is also prevalent – but these attempts are yet to gain traction.[49] There is no evidence of any similar project being undertaken in Australia; the widely held preference amongst practitioners here (if not journalists) is to avoid the appellation altogether, rather than to encourage its application across *both* ends of the political spectrum.

---

[49] See Mark Tushnet, *A Court Divided: The Rehnquist Court and the Future of Constitutional Law* (WW Norton & Company, 2005) 338.

Although the possibly deleterious effects of the activism debate on the public perception of the courts is a matter of serious concern, the foregoing should not be read as making the argument that politicians and commentators should be circumscribed on a wholesale basis in their criticism of the courts. Nevertheless, there is a difference between criticising decisions of the courts on the basis of specific shortcomings in written reasons for judgment and making an *ad hominem* attack on a judge or judges. Further, there is a crucial difference between expressing doubt about a particular judicial methodology (or lack of it) and adopting the ill-defined and politically loaded language of activism. This is all the more precarious in a jurisdiction where public awareness of the courts' role is underwhelming. (Recent research, for instance, suggests a significant lack of public awareness of High Court cases, judicial identities, even judges' method of appointment).[50] There is a real question, then, about whether the activist framework clouds what is already a relatively narrow public base of knowledge on how judges work.

Should there be a desire to protect public confidence in the courts in light of the activism debate, then there are two possible methods to overcome the present confusion: to embark on a project of 'settling' a definition across academia and the commentariat, or to move beyond the terminology altogether in public discourse. Given the profusion of meanings and the lack of any progress in isolating a commonly held view of activism over the last three decades, it seems prudent to embark on the latter project instead.

IV Encouraging Abstinence: Informed Public Criticism of the Courts without the Activism Terminology

The project of championing informed criticism of the courts, while at the same time discouraging analysis through the activist lens, is an ambitious task. It is, first and foremost, a task to be undertaken by the legal community as a whole. It is not, however, necessarily a task to be undertaken primarily by individual judges. Past experience has shown that judges, when delivering orations on the topic, are merely reported on as delivering a 'shot across the bow' within a pre-existing activist debate, therefore inadvertently perpetuating the term by denying its

---

[50] See Ingrid Nielsen and Russel Smyth, 'What the Australian Public Knows about the High Court' (2019) 47 *Federal Law Review* 31.

application.[51] The burden of responsibility, therefore, needs to extend beyond the actual recipients of the activist designation.

To this end, a heavy responsibility would lie with academic lawyers in the project of moving beyond the activist language. As the primary providers of legal education in Australia, and in their public roles as interpreters of the courts' work, legal scholars would perhaps need to address any lingering disinclination to engage with the terminology. Instead, if and when opportunities arise to challenge the use of the term in media reportage in the scholar's respective field of expertise, those opportunities would need to be acted upon. Should a scholar be challenged by a commentator who supports the use of the terminology, it seems judicious for the scholar *not* to quibble or insist on a delineation of an agreed definition (lest the commentator view this as obfuscation), but rather, to simply request that the commentator rephrase the question. Subtle as the difference is between the two approaches, the benign justification for requesting a rephrase cannot be seen as obfuscation: all the scholar is attempting to do is to avoid debating at cross-purposes with the commentator. The onus remains on the commentator, unimpeded, to then select a mode of discussion beyond the activism rubric. Similarly, legal educationalists who insist on teaching via the bifurcated 'activism versus legalism' approach may, at the very least, wish to explain that activism is no term of art and that it does not rest upon solid philosophical foundations. It may even be useful to discuss the political use of the term so as to give students an understanding of why the label persists. If the activist term cannot be avoided altogether in legal education, perhaps confusion may be minimised by using it only as a prelude to substantive, practice-specific discussion.

Countering public discussions of activism is no easy task either, but the various peak bodies in the legal community and court administrations may also have an expanded role in this context. The Judicial Conference of Australia, the Law Council of Australia, the various bar associations and state law institutes, continue to issue press releases, articles and social media posts to attempt to correct misinformation and to defend the judiciary from attacks such as those from the

---

[51] To give an example, Justice Kirby's 2004 and Justice Heydon's 2003 publications in this regard are seen as putting the case 'for' and 'against' activism respectively, even though Kirby in fact argued *against* the applicability of the label of activism to common law development: see Kirby, (n 41), and Heydon, 'Judicial Activism and the Death of the Rule of Law' (n 20).

ministers in 2017.[52] Of course, the peak bodies' role is not to directly apprehend accusations of activism, but it is possible that they may have a part to play in discouraging its use if they are able to make direct contact with those media outlets and their employees who continue to use the terminology. The court administrations (as distinct from judges) also produce summary statements of contentious decisions to accompany lengthy written reasons, partly in the hope that media reportage might adopt some of their phrasing rather than hackneyed clichés. This practice dates back to the mid-1990s, when various Australian courts began to employ public information officers or media officers in light of the increased invigilation of the bench by politicians and commentators alike, and given that in some quarters, the traditional 'defender' of the courts, the attorney-general, had stepped back from public intervention.[53]

Strengthening relationships between the courts and newsrooms (and, through the news reporters, the producers of editorial and opinion content) is of crucial importance in any project to temper the activism critique. The broadcast media has already been harnessed by the High Court to transmit material that clarifies and delineates the judicial role for a public audience: Chief Justice Mason consented to an unprecedented television interview on the eve of his retirement; later, Chief Justice Brennan authorised a behind-the-scenes documentary on how the Court functioned.[54] A more recent example illustrates how court administrations may engage more directly with media organisations to explain the *effects* of reportage on the public perception of the courts. The Victorian Supreme Court, through its new podcast 'Gertie's Law', has strengthened the links between the Court and its reporters. It recently released to the public two episodes of candid discussion between judges and journalists on topics relating to criminal trials and journalistic impressions of

---

[52] The Victorian Court of Appeal also handed down judgment on the contempt matter in scathing terms: see n 8.

[53] See generally Jane Johnson, *A History of Public Information Officers in Australian Courts: 25 Years of Assisting Public Perceptions and Understanding the Administration of Justice 1993–2018* (Report, April 2019).

[54] 'Chief Justice Comments on Fundamental Issues Facing Judiciary', *Four Corners*, (Australian Broadcasting Corporation, 3 April 1995) in Geoffrey Lindell (ed), *The Mason Papers: Selected Articles and Speeches* (Federation Press, 2007) 398, 399; *The Highest Court* (Film Art Doco, 1998). A more recent, brief informative video is also available on the High Court website: 'High Court of Australia Documentary', *High Court of Australia* (Web Page, 2010) <www.hcourt.gov.au/about/high-court-documentary>.

courtroom process.[55] Cultivating an open dialogue with court reporters, who usually have a detailed understanding of judicial independence, may have a run-on effect in the newsroom. It is not usually court reporters, but opinion content-makers, that use the activist terminology. A greater scrutiny of the latter's work might follow if the court-specialist news journalists are able to articulate to their colleagues why there are better alternatives than activism through which to critique the courts.

Online media outlets might also be encouraged to provide embedded links to judgments, or court-issued summaries of judgments, in their opinion content. This would enable readers to 'click through' to actual primary sources if they wish and to form a view independently of a commentator's particular 'take' on a judge or decision. The Australasian Legal Information Institute, an online free-access legal database and judgment repository, has embarked on a Twitter campaign to encourage media outlets to 'link through' to full text of judgments for this very reason.[56]

Finally, there is a question of how court administrations and peak bodies might directly engage with the public, without the involvement of external media channels as intermediary. While the courts are understandably hesitant to use social media for anything other than the publicising of judgments, there may still be a role for online platforms to assist in tempering discussions of activism. A development in the United Kingdom may end up a useful exemplar in this respect: a joint undertaking between the Judiciary Office and King's College London has recently produced a free, online course entitled 'The Modern Judiciary'. It explores the everyday working lives of judges and the impact judges have on the public through lectures, interviews with judges, and a forum for subscribers to discuss topical matters.[57] Should activism arise in an online forum, the convenors of the course might be anticipated to have the opportunity to directly address it.

---

[55] *Gertie's Law* (Supreme Court of Victoria, March 2019). See especially 'Reporting the Court: Part 1', *Gertie's Law* (Supreme Court of Victoria, 26 August 2019) and 'Reporting the Court: Part 2', *Gertie's Law* (Supreme Court of Victoria, 30 August 2019).

[56] Australasian Legal Information Institute's ('AustLII') Twitter handle is @austlii.

[57] Judicial Office and Kings College London, 'The Modern Judiciary: Who They Are, What They Do and Why It Matters', *FutureLearn* (Web Page) <www.futurelearn.com/courses/the-modern-judiciary>. Note in Australia that the University of New South Wales' 'The Judiciary Project' website also includes various links to informative judicial resources: 'The Judiciary Resources', *Gilbert + Tobin Centre of Public Law* (Web Page) <www.gtcentre.unsw.edu.au/resources/judiciary>.

Each of these approaches alone will not likely lead to the eradication of the language of activism. Until the politics of the culture wars are exhausted, it is likely that critiques of the courts on these terms will continue in some form or another. However, if consistent, concerted efforts are made across the legal community at large, those efforts might be expected to mitigate the derogatory aspects of the activist critique as it plays out in public discourse.

This chapter has attempted to briefly provide a survey of the uses of 'judicial activism' in the current Australian context, to explain why the terminology has gained currency as a lens through which to examine judicial behaviour; to explain the term's shortcomings; and to provide some tentative suggestions for moving beyond the language of activism in public discourse. The language of activism still has great political force in Australia, evidenced not only by the minister's comments in 2017 but also by the Victorian Court of Appeal's reaction to them. With careful work to sidestep the terminology – even to subject it to ridicule – it may be the case that 'activism' actually becomes the tired and demotic slogan that Justice Heydon assumes it already is. Whether this outcome is ultimately achieved will rest not only on the actions of the politicians and commentators that continue to breathe life into the phrase, but also those in the legal community who choose to challenge the assumptions that underlie it.

PART III

The Judiciary as a Collective

8

Judicial Collegiality

SARAH MURRAY[*]

I Introduction

On taking appointment as a judge, a person is largely cut off from the camaraderie of the Bar, where most judges will have spent a long time. It is not always possible for judges to mix with barristers as much as they formerly did. That is not to say that judges do not get on with other judges. Some even enjoy each other's company. But for the most part, judges call it "collegiality", which implies that it is not as much fun as a barrister's life.[1]

Judicial collegiality, while often presupposed, is a confounding concept. This is partly because it can be used in different senses, and partly because it is not something that judges frequently reflect on publicly,[2] or that others can readily consider in their place.[3] One notable exception is Justice Susan Kiefel who, prior to her elevation to Chief Justice of the High Court of Australia, articulated that:

> It is not possible to discern whether collegiality was something to which judges in earlier times aspired. But it most certainly is today. Civility and courtesy among judges are essential to the discussions that necessarily

---

[*] I would like to thank Professor Gabrielle Appleby and Professor Andrew Lynch for their helpful comments on an earlier draft of this chapter as well as those of Dr Tamara Tulich. Any errors remain my own.
[1] Susan Kiefel, 'On Being a Judge' (Public Lecture, The Chinese University of Hong Kong, 15 January 2013) 1.
[2] Ceremonial judicial sittings are an exception in which it can often be raised: Of many examples, see Transcript of Proceedings, *Welcome to the Honourable Justice Edelman* (Supreme Court of Western Australia, Martin CJ and Edelman J, 25 July 2011) 20; 'In re Retirement of Justice Leander J Shaw, Jr' (Transcript, wfsu Public Media, 21 December 2012) 2, 6; Transcript of Proceedings, *Ceremonial: Retirement of French CJ* [2016] HCATrans 293.
[3] Harry T Edwards, 'The Effects of Collegiality on Judicial Decision Making' (2003) 151 *University of Pennsylvania Law Review* 1639, 1643 ('Effects of Collegiality'); Lewis A Kornhauser and Lawrence G Sager, 'The One and the Many: Adjudication in Collegial Courts' (1993) 8(1) *California Law Review* 1, 2.

take place between judicial colleagues. These values enable a joint judgment to be achieved.[4]

And yet, as Justice Kiefel here recognises, collegiality is far more than whether judges write separately or together, an issue that is the subject of considerable judicial commentary.[5] It is also not as simple as whether judges are friends or tee off together,[6] or how a court is composed.[7] Judicial collegiality, while influenced by and influencing such things, can shape the court ecosystem in a multitude of ways and contribute markedly to the *process* of judging.

This chapter posits that judicial collegiality shapes the quality of the deliberative process on an appellate court. Following a proviso on the focus of the chapter in part I, part II explores the bounds of collegiality, its common usages and inevitable variability. Part III delves into the institutional influences that can shape or impede judicial collegiality in a multimember body as well as collegiality's effect on the curial institution. Finally, part IV looks at the emergence of judicial collegiality as a judicial value. When facilitated and operating at its best, judicial collegiality can enhance the experience of being a judge, strengthen the process of judicial decision-making and, as a consequence, elevate the performance, and even the legitimacy, of the court itself.

II Collegiality – A Proviso

I am particularly conscious of the difficulties of writing about judicial collegiality as an outsider. For this reason, this chapter takes as its prime

---

[4] Susan Kiefel, 'The Individual Judge' (2014) 88 *Australian Law Journal* 554, 556.
[5] See, for instance, Richard A Posner, *The Federal Courts: Crisis and Reform* (Harvard University Press, 1985) 236–43; Patricia M Wald, 'Calendars, Collegiality, and Other Intangibles on the Courts of Appeals' in Cynthia Harrison and Russell R Wheeler (eds), *The Federal Appellate Judiciary in the 21st Century* (Federal Judicial Center, 1989) 171, 179; Ruth Bader Ginsburg, 'Remarks on Writing Separately' (1990) 65 *Washington Law Review* 133; Alan Paterson, *Final Judgment: The Last Law Lords and the Supreme Court* (Hart Publishing, 2013) 99–110; Stephen Gageler, 'Why Write Judgments?' (2014) 36 *Sydney Law Review* 189; Kiefel (n 4); PA Keane, 'The Idea of the Professional Judge: The Challenges of Communication' (Speech, Judicial Conference of Australia Colloquium, 11 October 2014); Susan Kiefel, 'Judicial Methods in the 21st Century' (Speech, Banco Court, 16 March 2017) 7–11. See also Andrew Lynch's chapter, 'Judicial Style and Institutional Norms' in this collection.
[6] Edwards (n 3) 1666.
[7] Cf Dimitri Landa and Jeffrey R Lax, 'Legal Doctrine on Collegial Courts' (2009) 71(3) *The Journal of Politics* 946, where 'collegial' is used as a synonym for a 'multimember' court.

focus judicial voices and scholarship.[8] One of the shortcomings of this approach is that it is inevitably not comprehensive. Much of the judicial experience is not publicly reflected upon in published works or addresses. Further, judicial works that touch on collegiality are not reflective of all judicial views or experiences. As a consequence, this chapter can only hope to scratch the surface of judicial collegiality and its significance to the life of a court.

The focus of the chapter also tends toward superior courts where collegiality is the subject of greater commentary, being part of the quotidian operation of a multimember body sitting and hearing matters jointly and sometimes en banc. As Fricke observes: 'Consultation is close to the heart of an appellate court's work. In a court which consists of trial judges, each judge can go about his or her work independently of colleagues. But appeals, like orchestral performances, call for concerted work'.[9]

This concentration is not, however, intended to diminish the role of collegiality in other judicial quarters, most particularly in lower courts where judges or magistrates often sit alone but still draw on the input of others on the bench to navigate their very demanding roles.[10]

III The Meaning of Judicial Collegiality

In September 2018 the International Criminal Court ('ICC') sent its judges on a retreat at which judicial collegiality was to be addressed.[11] The former ICC president had identified collegiality as indispensable to the court's functioning and the provision of 'high quality justice'.[12] In reflecting on the professional development opportunities of the retreat, the sitting ICC president, Judge Chile Eboe-Osuji, spoke of the advantages of a court characterised by an: 'open, respectful, dignified and inclusive approach to institutional decision-making ... marked by the highest

---

[8] Harry T Edwards, 'Collegiality and Decision-Making on the DC Circuit' (1998) 84 *Virginia Law Review* 1335, 1366.
[9] Graham Fricke, 'A Decade in the Life of the High Court: 1930-1940' (2006) 9 *Canberra Law Review* 1, 8.
[10] Kathy Mack, Anne Wallace and Sharyn Roach Anleu, *Judicial Workload: Time, Tasks and Work Organisation* (Australasian Institute of Judicial Administration, 2013) 30.
[11] International Criminal Court, 'ICC Judges Hold Retreat Focusing on Collegiality and Various Aspects of Judicial Proceedings' (Press Release, 28 September 2018) ('ICC Judges Hold Retreat').
[12] Silvia Fernández de Gurmendi, 'Judges: Selection, Competence, Collegiality' (2018) 112 *American Journal of International Law* 163, 166.

degree of dignity and respect for one another, encouraging judges to share their diverse expertise, experience and professional backgrounds'.[13]

Such descriptions highlight one of the key difficulties with the concept of collegiality. It might be easy to spot but it is so multi-layered that it becomes hard to define or quantify.[14] In a 2013 survey of Australian judges and magistrates only 7 percent and 8 percent, respectively, considered collegiality 'essential'.[15] However, what is not clear is what those surveyed meant by the term. One United States judge described how, in preparing for an address on judicial collegiality, each judge he conversed with saw the concept quite differently.[16] As Judge Chile Eboe-Osuji's conception highlights, collegiality is too multi-layered to be seen as a synonym for friendship.[17] It is frequently described in terms of cooperation, 'collaboration', or teamwork.[18] Or to include trusting relationships which encourage a willingness to share ideas, expertise and experiences.[19] Take, for example, Judge Deanell Tacha's explanation that 'Collegial judges in conference are not advocates of a position but students of an issue – comparing, contrasting, and weighing each other's viewpoints and rationales'.[20]

Or Lord Robert Reed who states that 'It is a curious team because the value of the team depends on everybody using their own individual intelligence and their own experience and so forth and bringing all that to the party, but our working method is very collaborative'.[21]

Interestingly, one of the reasons that a conception of collegiality is hard to pin down is that judges describe it as highly contextual: something uniquely shaped by the particular court, its practices, its size, the judges who comprise it and even the proximity of each judge's chambers

---

[13] 'ICC Judges Hold Retreat' (n 11).
[14] And not unlike the 'I know it when I see it' characterisation made famous in *Jacobellis v Ohio*, 378 US 184, 197 (1964). See, for instance, Frank B Cross and Emerson H Tiller, 'Understanding Collegiality on the Court' (2008) 10(2) *University of Pennsylvania Journal of Constitutional Law* 257.
[15] Mack, Wallace and Roach Anleu (n 10) 27.
[16] Donald E Ziegler, 'Collegiality and the District Courts' (1991) 75(1) *Judicature* 24.
[17] Paterson (n 5) 143, 157–58; Edwards (n 3) 1644–45; Justice Deanell Reece Tacha, 'The "C" Word: On Collegiality' (1995) 56 *Ohio State Law Journal* 585, 587.
[18] Kornhauser and Sager, n 3, 4–5; Helen Collier, 'Collegiality Among Judges: No More High Noons' (1992) 31 *Judges Journal* 4, 5–6; Kiefel (n 4) 560; Paterson, (n 5) 143–44.
[19] Collier (n 18) 6.
[20] Tacha (n 17) 587.
[21] Quoted in Paterson (n 5) 141.

to each other.[22] As Justice Albie Sachs, a former judge of the Constitutional Court of South Africa, recounted, a 'collegial court...has its own vitality, its own dynamic, its own culture'.[23] The departure of a judicial colleague or the arrival of a new member can alter this group 'culture,' just as it alters a court's jurisprudence.[24] While some of this is visible, much of it is not. As Lynch explains:

> Sometimes these developments are clearly signalled – explicitly or implicitly – in a court's decisions. Often they, or at least their catalysts, are opaque. Essentially, and despite the fact that they conduct public hearings and provide reasons which are far more detailed than those supplied by their political counterparts, there is a great deal that we still do not understand about how, behind the veil of the law, multimember courts really work.[25]

What comes across clearly in judicial writing is that collegiality does not mean that judges have to routinely agree. The complexity of cases coming before superior courts would make habitual consonance surprising.[26] Chief Justice Kiefel and Justice Susan Crennan have both separately affirmed this with the axiom 'collegiality is not compromise'.[27] For the chief justice, the richness of judicial relationships is shown in the ability of judges to disagree with each other and talk it out and in so doing enrich the process of decision-making.[28] As Justice Albie Sachs describes:

> The collegiality expresses itself through conflict, through challenge, otherwise it's bland. At the one level it's simply disputation, argument, to get to the right answer. Often you would argue for a position around the table

---

[22] Paterson (n 5) 147; Collins Seitz, 'Collegiality and the Court of Appeals: What Is Important to the Court as an Institution Is the Quality of the Working Relationship among Its Members' (1001) 75 *Judicature* 26; Sir Anthony Mason, 'Reflections on the High Court: Its Judges and Judgments' (2013) 37 *Australian Bar Review* 102, 112; Tacha (n 17) 592; Wald (n 5) 171.
[23] Albie Sachs, *The Strange Alchemy of Life and Law* (Oxford University Press, 2009) 270.
[24] Andrew Lynch, 'Review Essay: Courts and Teamwork: What It Means for Judicial Diversity' (2015) 38 *University of New South Wales Law Journal* 1421.
[25] Ibid.
[26] Frank H Easterbrook, 'Ways of Criticizing the Court' (1982) 95(4) *Harvard Law Review* 802, 805.
[27] Kiefel, (n 4) 560; Transcript of Proceedings, *Ceremonial: Farewell to Crennan J – Sydney* [2014] HCATrans 258; Edwards 'Collegiality and Decision-Making' (n 8) 1361.
[28] Kiefel (n 4) 560; Phillip J Cooper, *Battles on the Bench: Conflict inside the Supreme Court* (University Press of Kansas, 1995) 5.

quite sharply, quite forcefully, but to test it, and you would listen to the others. At times the interchange could be harsh. I can remember at least four occasions when people left the meeting-room crying. Each one was different.[29]

Often, collegiality is described as a 'cohesion' that can withstand and transcend cultural, political and social difference.[30] Collegiality can ensure that the varied skills, backgrounds and experiences of the bench can benefit the court and its decisions as a whole.[31] It can flourish amidst diverse views and dissenting voices.[32] Indeed Justice Claire L'Heureux-Dubé from the Canadian Supreme Court has asserted that:

> At the institutional level, dissenting opinions tend to foster collegial relations among judges, even while they allow them to be true to themselves. First, judges who have a different and minority perspective on certain questions are not obliged to confront their colleagues at every turn, in the hope of having at least a few of their views incorporated into the majority decision. Instead, they may choose to communicate their opinion directly to the legal community and to the public, rather than seeing it nipped in the bud. Secondly, the majority is not continually obliged to attempt to arrive at a compromise that may accommodate as many views as possible at the expense of the clear and coherent enunciation of principles.[33]

---

[29] Albie Sachs, 'Albie Sachs Interview: Constitutional Court Oral History Project' (Interview Records, University of the Witwatersrand, Johannesburg, 2011-2012) 66 <www.historicalpapers.wits.ac.za/inventories/inv_pdfo/AG3368/AG3368-S77-001-jpeg.pdf>.

[30] Stephen Wasby, 'Communication in the Ninth Circuit: A Concern for Collegiality' 187 *University of Puget Sound Law Review* 73, 76; Donald R Songer et al., *Law, Ideology and Collegiality – Judicial Behaviour in the Supreme Court of Canada* (McGill-Queen's University Press, 2012) 5, 14; Tacha (n 17) 587; Edwards (n 3) 1645ff; Sachs (n 29) 66; Corinne Purtill, 'Ruth Bader Ginsburg's Advice for Success in Marriage, the Supreme Court, and Everything in Between', *Quartz* (online, 15 February 2017) <https://qz.com/910784/ruth-bader-ginsburgs-advice-for-success-in-marriage-the-supreme-court-and-everything-in-between/>.

[31] Frank M Coffin, 'The Anatomy of Collegiality' (Seminar, Federal Judicial Center, 1 May 1985) 5; Edwards (n 3) 1649, 1666ff, 1685; Frank B Cross, 'Collegial Ideology in the Courts' (2009) 103 *Northwestern University Law Review* 1399, 1425.

[32] Edwards (n 3) 1645 (saying otherwise collegiality morphs into 'homogeneity or conformity'); Francis P O'Connor, 'The Art of Collegiality: Creating Consensus and Coping with Dissent' (1998) 83 *Massachusetts Law Review* 93; Bernice B Donald, 'The Intrajudicial Factor in Judicial Independence: Reflections on Collegiality and Dissent in Multi-Member Courts' (2017) 47 *University of Memphis Law Review* 1123, 1144.

[33] Claire L'Heureux-Dubé, 'The Dissenting Opinion: The Voice of the Future?' (2000) 38 *Osgoode Hall Law Journal* 495, 513–14.

Much judicial scholarship describes members of a court as having a shared mission or 'shared authority'[34] in which their roles are interlaced and interdependent. A risk with regarding collegiality as wrapped up in a united judicial 'mission' of sorts is to suggest that a bench is always going to be of one mind on this front. As Sir Anthony Mason has contended: 'The High Court is not a monolithic institution. It is at any time a group of seven justices who are obliged to hear and determine, according to their individual judgment, particular cases. The justices may have conflicting views on the role of the Court'.[35]

In often reflecting on collegiality and what it has meant to his work,[36] Judge Edwards describes it as the 'common interest' 'in getting the law right' through 'a *process* that helps to create the conditions for *principled* agreement, by allowing all points of view to be aired and considered'.[37] Paterson, in his significant work on the UK House of Lords, and now Supreme Court, criticises Judge Edwards's conception as too idealised or niche.[38] This disagreement really turns – as is often the case – on what is meant by 'collegiality' and whether it is being applied in a more limited, judgment permutational sense. In the end, both Judge Edwards and Paterson agree that the strength of relationships across the bench can lubricate difficult conversations between judges and make sure that such conversations occur in the first place.

In essence, collegiality is usefully understood as a key force shaping the deliberative judicial process. Rather than being the outcome of, or the motivation for, their endeavour, collegiality is best conceived of as the 'working spirit'[39] through which judges embark upon the practice of judging and interact with each other.

The High Court of Australia has not always been characterised by such a spirit.[40] Justice Michael Kirby recounts how Justice Hayden Starke's

---

[34] Edwards (n 3) 1683; Cross and Tiller (n 14) 257; Bora Laskin, 'The Role and Functions of Final Appellate Courts: The Supreme Court of Canada' (1975) 53 *Canadian Bar Review* 469, 469.
[35] Sir Anthony Mason, 'Foreword' in Haig Patapan, *Judging Democracy: The New Politics of the High Court of Australia* (Cambridge University Press, 2000) viii–ix.
[36] Edwards (n 3) fn 6; Edwards 'Collegiality and Decision-Making' (n 8); Harry T Edwards, 'The Judicial Function and the Elusive Goal of Principled Decisionmaking' (1991) *Wisconsin Law Review* 837, 853, 858.
[37] Edwards (n 3) 1645 (emphasis in original).
[38] Paterson (n 5) 142–43. See also discussion of 'warm and fuzzy' conceptions in Cross and Tiller (n 14) 271.
[39] Cooper (n 28) 142.
[40] Michael Kirby, 'Judicial Stress and Judicial Bullying' (2014) 14(1) *QUT Law Review* 1, 7.

behaviour 'affected the collegiate operations of the High Court', including by snubbing Justices Herbert Evatt and Edward McTiernan.[41] It was also said that Justice Starke would not allow another judge to view his judgment before its handing down.[42] For Justice Kirby such practices were likely to have 'stress[ed]' the other judges and to 'have diminished the possibility even of the minimum internal co-operation necessary for the operation of an appellate court'.[43] A lack of collegiality does not mean that a court necessarily grinds to a halt.[44] One upshot of a discordant bench *could* be that dissenting and separate concurring opinions become more likely[45] – but akin to Tolstoy's depiction: 'each unhappy family is unhappy in its own way'.[46] However, again, just because there is a spell of dissenting judgments does not mean that collegiality on a court is deficient. The Mason era of the Australian High Court saw considerable levels of disagreement but a strong collegial bench operating nevertheless.[47]

Justice Kiefel, prior to her elevation to chief justice, surmised that collegiality, while desirable 'in the workplace of judges as it is elsewhere', is not imperative when '[c]ourts can no doubt function with some judges who are not collegiate' (although this might be taken as suggesting that this ability to still 'function' relates to cases where the paucity of collegiality is confined to only 'some judges' on the court).[48] For Chief Judge Aloyisus Higginbotham from the United States Court of Appeal, collegiality certainly aids optimal functioning and is 'the critical difference between a superb, productive court and a barely functioning one ...

---

[41] Ibid. See also Sir Anthony Mason, 'The High Court of Australia: A Personal Impression of Its First 100 Years' (2003) 27 *Melbourne University Law Review* 864, 874.
[42] Mason (n 41) 874; Kirby (n 40) 7.
[43] Kirby (n 40) 7-8.
[44] Kiefel (n 1) 5. But cf the comment of Justice Ruth Bader Ginsburg that, '[c]ollegiality is crucial to the success of our mission ... We could not do the job the Constitution assigns to us if we didn't – to use one of Justice Scalia's favorite expressions – "get over it"': Purtill (n 30).
[45] Edwards (n 3) 1645. Certainly the High Court under the leadership of Chief Justice Latham presents a clear example of this; see Fiona Wheeler, 'The Latham Court: Law, War and Politics' in Rosalind Dixon and George Williams (eds), *The High Court, the Constitution and Australian Politics* (Cambridge University Press, 2015) 159.
[46] Leo Tolstoy, *Anna Karenina* (Wordsworth Classics, 1995) 1.
[47] Sir Gerard Brennan, 'A Tribute to the Hon, Sir Anthony Mason AC KBE' (Speech, The Mason Court and Beyond Conference, 8 September 1995); Paul Kildea and George Williams, 'The Mason Court' in Dixon and Williams (n 45) 244.
[48] Kiefel (n 1) 5.

a strong sense of collegiality allows a group of competent judges to perform far beyond all reasonable expectations'.[49]

To understand the distinctiveness of judicial collegiality one only needs to put the spotlight on a court at a particular point in time. The idiosyncrasy of each court, combined with the lack of clarity as to judicial collegiality's meaning, can complicate its 'utility' as a concept.[50] When employed less abstractly, judicial collegiality can shed light on the shrouded nature of the judicial role and what makes for a conducive curial environment in which judicial collaboration and reflection can flourish. While it may infuse judicial outcomes, judicial collegiality moulds the nature and quality of judicial interaction. As the next part explores, collegiality is shaped as much by the personalities on the bench as it is by the style of court leadership and institutional practice. Its contribution to the nature of deliberations is therefore central to better understanding the process of judging.

IV Institutional Perspectives on Collegiality

> Some individuals are naturally inclined to consult with others and work collegially. However, collegiality cannot depend on individual temperaments and personalities. Collegiality is vital for the success of the Court and must therefore be promoted institutionally through proactive efforts ...[51]

For some, collegiality is so idiosyncratic that it can only develop organically rather than by design.[52] While this is true to some extent, institutional practices can shape or influence collegiality and allow it to thrive or deteriorate. Judge Edwards identifies collegiality as a key force '"institutionalizing" judges into [a] shared judicial mission', being a 'collection of structures, procedures, rules and customs'.[53] These do not operate unidirectionally. Collegiality between judges can influence institutional mores which can then also stimulate collegiality in turn.[54]

---

[49] A Leon Higginbotham, 'Collegiality and the Courts: Introduction' (1991) 75(1) *Judicature* 24. See also Judge Richard A. Posner, *How Judges Think* (Harvard University Press, 2008) 29.
[50] Paterson (n 5) 143.
[51] Fernández de Gurmendi (n 12).
[52] Tacha (n 17) 592.
[53] Edwards (n 3) 1664. See also Forrest Maltzman, James F. Spriggs II and Paul J Wahlbeck, *Crafting Law on the Supreme Court: The Collegial Game* (Cambridge University Press, 2000).
[54] Edwards (n 3) 1664. See also Donald (n 32) 1126; Arthur Dyevre, 'Unifying the Field of Comparative Judicial Politics: Towards a General Theory of Judicial Behaviour' (2010) 2 (2) *European Political Science Review* 297, 302–4.

Institutional forces can be both internal and external. Internal influences relate to a court's inner workings[55] including prosaic realities, such as caseloads and resourcing,[56] and court practices such as judicial retreats[57] and acting judicial appointments.[58] In some jurisdictions there are rules requiring conferences to follow the hearing and dictating the order in which judges' views are canvassed.[59] Chief Justice Kiefel has indicated that, on the Australian High Court, case conferences are held prior to, and following, the hearing of cases.[60] The Supreme Judicial Court of Massachusetts subscribed to a practice whereby all judges had to be party to any conversation prior to a case being heard.[61] Such practices provide judges with the opportunity to exchange ideas and work through disagreements as a group. Judgment writing practices can also play a role.[62] For instance, the High Court currently has a policy that a judge must include any members of the court into a joint opinion who express such a wish.[63] These institutional tendencies contribute to the collegiality quotient of a court and can also develop relationships which enliven and entrench such practices.

But judicial personality is also central,[64] and 'individuals are influenced, at least to some degree, by those with whom they are sitting'.[65] Judicial behaviour can aid or thwart collegiality, and relationships on the

---

[55] Dyevre (n 54).
[56] Kiefel (n 4) 554.
[57] Randall Shephard, 'The Special Professional' (2002) 35 *Indiana Law Review* 381, 387.
[58] Edwards (n 3) 1664.
[59] Lord Neuberger, 'Sausages and the Judicial Process: The Limits of Transparency' (Speech, Annual Conference of the Supreme Court of New South Wales, 1 August 2014) [14]; Edwards (n 3) 1665.
[60] 'Judicial Methods' (n 5) 2–3 in which Chief Justice Kiefel notes that usually judges only meet once after a case has been heard by virtue of the fact that once judges start penning judgments 'views tend to become entrenched'.
[61] O'Connor (n 32) 94.
[62] Reginald S Sheehan, Rebecca D Gill and Kirk A Randazzo, *Judicialization of Politics: The Interplay of Institutional Structure, Legal Doctrine, and Politics on the High Court of Australia* (Carolina Academic Press, 2012) 122.
[63] Kiefel (n 3) 557. See also discussion of this 'requirement' in: Lynch, 'Collective Decision-Making' (n 5).
[64] Mason (n 22) 112; Maltzman et al. (n 53) 99, where the authors write of the 'collegial game' in which 'justices choose how vigorously to pursue their policy preferences within the strategic constraints imposed by their colleagues'.
[65] Andrew Lynch, 'Judicial Dissent and the Politics of the High Court' in Rosalind Dixon and George Williams (eds), *The High Court, the Constitution and Australian Politics* (Cambridge University Press, 2015) 56, 66, fn 44.

bench can be sources of conflict and even harassment or bullying. Justice Oliver Wendell Holmes is said to have compared the United States Supreme Court to 'nine scorpions in a bottle'.[66] Nastiness on the Australian High Court was particularly pronounced during Chief Justice Gavan Duffy's leadership in the 1930s, and most plainly between Justice Starke and Justice Evatt (which purportedly saw Justice Starke smoke his cigar in such a way as to annoy Justice Evatt with his smoke plumes and saw the latter try to convince his associate to make Justice Starke's cabin bed uncomfortable by 'sprinkl[ing]' it with 'breadcrumbs').[67] Conflict can also be sourced from differences in legal positions adopted in a particular case. For instance, Lord James Atkin was said to have been treated with distinct coldness by the rest of the Lords following his strident dissent in *Liversidge v Anderson* relating to the scrutiny of executive action.[68]

The personality of the chief justice, their leadership style and the court practices they adopt can be crucial.[69] These attributes can significantly influence the cultivation of collegiality on the bench and the response to any lapses of it.[70] Justice Kirby has noted chief justices have innumerable expectations placed upon them and 'collegiate decision-making and the sharing of responsibility of court governance' can lessen the leadership burden.[71] Indeed, flatter leadership styles, which prioritise collegiality in administering a court's agenda, may improve the functioning of a court in place of more 'towering' leadership styles which seek to dictate or control.[72] Judicial relationships can also affect the approach taken to

---

[66] Cross and Tiller (n 14) 259, citing Judge Richard A. Posner, 'A Tribute to Justice William J. Brennan Jr' (1990) 104 *Harvard Law Review* 1, 13–14. Although the Supreme Court is also known for the practice of judges all shaking hands before hearings or court case meetings: Cooper (n 28) 1 citing Willard L King, *Melville Weston Fuller* (Macmillan, 1950) 134; 'The Court and Its Traditions', *Supreme Court of the United States* (Web Page) <www.supremecourt.gov/about/traditions.aspx>.

[67] Fricke (n 8) 2–3.

[68] [1942] AC 206; Justice Michael Kirby, 'Judicial Stress' (1995) 13 *Australian Bar Review* 101, 112. And see Chief Justice Susan Kiefel, 'Judicial Courage and the Decorum of Dissent' (Lecture, Selden Society Lecture, 28 November 2017).

[69] Fricke (n 8) 11–12.

[70] Kathy Mack and Sharyn Roach Anleu, 'The Administrative Authority of Chief Judicial Officers in Australia' (2004) 8(1) *Newcastle Law Review* 1, 8; David K Malcolm, 'The Role of the Chief Justice' (2008) 12 *Southern Cross University Law Review* 149.

[71] Kirby (n 68) 112–13. In support of this, the Judicial College of Victoria now runs training for judges on 'Collegial Leadership': Judicial College of Victoria, *2015/2016 Annual Report* (Report, 2016) 10.

[72] Rosalind Dixon, 'Towering v Collegial Judges', *IACL-AIDC Blog* (Blog Post, 6 March 2019) <https://blog-iacl-aidc.org/towering-judges/2019/3/6/towering-v-collegial-judges>; Rosalind

leading a multimember court. Cowen has described the tension between Chief Justice Samuel Griffith and Justice Isaac Isaacs on the Australian High Court which spilled over and beyond their differences 'in style, in outlook and in legal philosophy' to result in a 'profound temperamental incompatibility', and even 'public rebuke' from the chief justice.[73] Similarly, Sir Anthony Mason has noted:

> The replacement of Menzies by Lionel Murphy [on the High Court] created a tension that did not previously exist, particularly between Barwick and Murphy. At the same time it affected the relationship between Barwick and the other members of the court because Menzies, who had been a valuable link, was no longer there.[74]

Judicial behaviour, court practice and leadership are also influenced by institutional expectations and forces,[75] often sourced externally from the wider socio-legal-political environment. These may include the relationship between the judiciary and between the legislative and executive arms of government, the culture brought from the bar[76] or entrenched principles such as judicial independence.[77] Judges swearing to serve independently and impartially may see their vows as potentially threatened by collegial practices.[78] For others, the duties to the institution also play a powerful role. As Justice Patrick Keane explains:

> ... in our enthusiasm to maintain our independence, including our independence from each other, we lose sight of these institutional connections without which we could not even begin to face the challenges of doing justice...the institutional ethos which enlivens that institution is a practical expression of the best of us. We cannot hope to be wiser or better than the institution of which we are a part.[79]

Dixon, 'Towering v Collegial Judges' in Rehan Aberatyne and Iddo Porat (eds), *Towering Judges* (forthcoming) also noting that other judges can play a 'leading' role even if not formally assigned as such; See also R Dale Lefever, 'The Integration of Judicial Independence and Judicial Administration: The Role of Collegiality in Court Governance' (2009) 24(2) *The Court Manager* 5, 10.

[73] Zelman Cowen, *Isaac Isaacs* (Oxford University Press, 1967), 118–20.
[74] Mason (n 22) 112. See also Jan Crawford Greenburg, *Supreme Conflict: The Inside Story of the Struggle for Control of the United States Supreme Court* (Penguin Press, 2007).
[75] Edwards (n 3) 1663; Laskin (n 34) 476.
[76] Murray Gleeson, *The Rule of Law and the Constitution* (ABC Books, 2000) 89–90.
[77] Dyevre (n 54) 304.
[78] Posner (n 5) 229; Frank B Cross, 'Collegial Ideology in the Courts' (2009) 103(3) *Northwestern University Law Review* 1399; Lynch (n 5); Tacha (n 17) 586.
[79] Keane (n 5) 20.

These principles and expectations can influence judge–judge relations and aspects of court practice. Take for example, the High Court's approach to judgment writing.[80] Chief Justice Kiefel, prior to her elevation, commented that '[i]n a practical sense, our system of justice could not tolerate each judge writing independently in every case'.[81] The dictates of judicial independence would be compromised by equating collegiality with inhibiting separate opinions.[82] Chief Justice Kiefel disputes, however, that judicial independence is mutually exclusive of conferencing or joint opinion writing:

> Agreeing with another's judgment is as much an act of independence as is the writing of one's own judgment. It may involve greater discipline. While joint judgments are not always possible, for the most part reasonable attempts should be made to reduce the number of judgments in any matter. It is the institutional responsibility of the members of the court to do so, in the pursuit of clarity, certainty and timeliness.[83]

Justice Ruth Bader Ginsburg has written in similar terms while acknowledging the tension in stating that: 'Judges on appellate tribunals ... live daily with the competing claims or demands of collegiality and individuality. It is up to each judge to keep those claims in fair balance'.[84]

Former High Court Justice Dyson Heydon has been the most forthright about the risks inherent with collegiality – the 'high price ... paid for agreeable personal relationships and internal harmony'[85] and 'susceptibility to pressure from other judges when writing jointly'.[86] Other judges have seen Justice Heydon as having overstated the risks.[87] Once again it

---

[80] Lynch (n 5).
[81] Kiefel (n 4) 556.
[82] L'Heureux-Dubé (n 33) 513; Cf practices of unanimity: Sophie Turenne, 'Institutional Constraints and Collegiality at the Court of Justice of the European Union: A Sense of Belonging?' (2017) 24(4) *Maastricht Journal of European and Comparative Law* 565, 579; See also Fernández de Gurmendi (n 12).
[83] Kiefel (n 4) 560.
[84] Ginsburg (n 5) 150.
[85] Dyson Heydon, 'Threats to Judicial Independence: The Enemy Within' (2013) 129 *Law Quarterly Review* 205, 213.
[86] Ibid. 216; Scott R Meinke and Kevin M Scott, 'Collegial Influence and Judicial Voting Change: The Effect of Membership Change on US Supreme Court Justices' (2007) 41(4) *Law and Society Review* 909.
[87] Mason, 'Reflections on the High Court' (n 22) 11 ('noting I agree to some extent that the risks identified by the author do exist, they are not, in my view, as great as he suggests'); Peter Heerey, 'The Judicial Herd: Seduced by Suave Glittering Phrases?'(2013) 87 *Australian Law Journal* 460, 461; Gageler (n 5) 192, 197.

becomes a case of being clear about what collegiality is and what it is not. There is also a sense that life on an appellate court, while responding to an array of institutional expectations, is not as individualistically focused as life at the bar. This means that court culture, leadership and the composition of a bench become very influential on how the institution operates and how judge–judge relations play out.

By conceiving of collegiality as a dynamic force influenced by both internal and external workings, collegiality's variability between, and even within, jurisdictions makes some sense. It also explains why court design, court practices, court leadership and institutional pressures can have a real impact on the degree to which a court is able to function collegially. In turn, collegiality can influence court processes, the style of leadership adopted and the nature of deliberation and judgment writing practice.

V Judicial Collegiality: The Rise of a Judicial Value?

Judges consistently espouse the benefits of collegiality in such a way that suggests its emergence as a budding judicial value. Conceiving of judicial collegiality as a value points to its marked impact on the lived experience of judging, the process of judicial decision-making and, in turn, its contribution to the optimal functioning of the court as an institution.

A 'value' is used here to denote something of importance that 'inform[s]'[88] the enterprise of judging. It is not always as simple as this suggests. Values may conflict or need to be reconciled (or raise questions of *for* whom and *by* whom they are defined and derived) but they still allow us to better understand the judging enterprise.[89] To conceive of collegiality as a judicial value is not to align it with a constitutional value,[90] such as judicial independence. It can, however, amount to a *process* value which can operate alongside other broadly similar judicial

---

[88] Justice Allsop's treatment of values in the public law domain is useful here as he acknowledges the inevitable overlap between values and the need for some to fall away at times but with all serving the 'functions of government': James Allsop, 'Values in Public Law' (2017) 91 *Australian Law Journal* 118, 121.

[89] See, for instance, Richard Devlin and Adam Dodek, 'Regulating Judges: Challenges, Controversies and Choices' in Richard Devlin and Adam Dodek (eds), *Regulating Judges: Beyond Independence and Accountability* (Edward Elgar, 2016) 9.

[90] See Dixon's discussion of 'constitutional values' in the Australian context: Rosalind Dixon, 'Functionalism and Australian Constitutional Values' in Rosalind Dixon (ed), *Australian Constitutional Values* (Bloomsbury, 2018) 3ff.

values outlined by Devlin and Dodek including 'representativeness', 'efficiency' or 'transparency'.[91] Values can be classified as having instrumental or intrinsic significance but such attempts can be of questionable and overlapping utility.[92] In this chapter, collegiality as a judicial value is discussed at both an institutional and individual level.

In an institutional sense, judges contend that collegiality enables better quality court decisions.[93] In facilitating an environment where judges with different backgrounds and perspectives tease out thorny issues and debate legal principles, superior court judgments are likely to emerge with greater clarity and efficiency and less chance of error.[94] As Justice Keane has expressed:

> It has been my experience that there are real advantages to judicial cooperation in terms of doing my job as an individual judge. I find the insights of colleagues very valuable. There are often angles to the case or details of the evidence which I have missed ... I do not think that there is any harm in being open to this kind of assistance...there is something distinctly quixotic in the notion that one should make a deliberate effort to avoid assistance from people who are quite likely to be the best lawyers to have considered the problem at hand'.[95]

To the extent that judicial collegiality improves the quality of the deliberative process, better and clearer decisions are likely to result, which in turn can benefit the rule of law. Vital to this is a vibrant collegial practice among judges ensuring enhanced consideration and debate:

> When a court is bereft of collegiality, judges become distrustful of one another's motivations; they are less receptive to ideas about pending cases and to comments on circulating opinions; and they stubbornly cling to their first impressions of an issue, often readily dismissing suggestions that would produce a stronger opinion or a more correct result ... In the end, these tendencies do damage to the rule of law. They make the law weaker and less nuanced.[96]

---

[91] Devlin and Dodek (n 89) 9ff.
[92] As to the need to break down rigid instrumental/intrinsic distinctions, see the work of Dewey: John Dewey, *Democracy and Education* (Sheba Blake Publishing, 2015) 737–41; John Dewey, *The Quest for Certainty: A Study of the Relation of Knowledge and Action* (George Allen & Unwin, 1929) 266.
[93] Cross (n 78) 1399, 1418; Keane (n 5) 20; Tacha (n 17) 592; Wald (n 5) 182.
[94] Gageler (n 5) 197; Heerey (n 87) 461; Neuberger (n 59) [26]; Edwards (n 3) 1685.
[95] Keane (n 5) 19.
[96] Edwards (n 3) 1649.

Similarly, the reputation and the legitimacy of a court is shaped by the quality of its decisions and how it is perceived by those outside it.[97] A respectful and collegial atmosphere (along with the avoidance of spite, which begins at this point to intersect with 'civility' within the profession more generally)[98] – even if not often observed up close by those outside – can create a culture in which there is greater confidence and trust[99] in the institution. Judicial collegiality is more likely to heighten the receptiveness of other members of the court to new ideas.[100] If judges disagree, collegiality may mean that this is done respectfully, avoiding 'the parade of horrible, the slippery slope, the barbed jab'[101] thus preserving the court's outward facing image at the same time as improving the quality and solicitousness of ongoing judicial engagement and debate.[102]

Collegiality as a judicial value also comes into focus at the level of the individual judge. Personally, collegiality can ensure that there is a fair sharing of the caseload and that the working environment is such that judges want to remain on the bench and make the sacrifices that such appointments can require.[103] As one Australian judge commented in a 2012 survey: 'The judges I presently work with are a great bunch of men

---

[97] Brian Galligan, *The Politics of the High Court: A Study of the Judicial Branch of Government in Australia* (University of Queensland Press, 1987) 257; O'Connor (n 32) 95.

[98] Kiefel (n 4) 556, '[c]ivility and courtesy among judges are essential to the discussions that necessarily take place between judicial colleagues'. More generally, see JJ Spigelman, 'Tolerance, Inclusion and Cohesion' (2006) 27 *Australian Bar Review* 133, 139; Suzanne Le Mire and Rosemary Owens, 'A Propitious Moment? Workplace Bullying and Regulation of the Legal Profession' (2014) 37(3) *University of New South Wales Law Journal* 1030; Alice Woolley, 'Does Civility Matter?' (2008) 46 *Osgoode Hall Law Journal* 175; Cheryl B Preston and Hilary Lawrence, 'Incentivizing Lawyers to Play Nice: A National Survey of Civility Standards and Options for Enforcement' (2015) 48(3) *University of Michigan Journal of Law Reform* 701.

[99] Kirby (n 40) 9; High Court of Australia, 'Ceremonial – Retirement of French CJ' (n 2).

[100] I thank Prof Andrew Lynch for his helpful insights on this point. For a recent discussion of the importance of 'constructive' criticism of courts more generally, see the recent response to attacks on court timeliness: Tom Bathurst, 'Who Should Judge the Judges, and How Should They Be Judged' (Speech, 2019 Opening of Law Term Address, 30 January 2019) 20, [63].

[101] Wald (n 5) 182. See also in relation to incivility between judges and between appellate and intermediate courts: Keith Mason, 'Throwing Stones: A Cost/Benefit Analysis of Judges Being Offensive to Each Other' (2008) 82 *Australian Law Journal* 260.

[102] Kiefel (n 68) 10 (referring to Justice Scalia's reference to a point made by the majority as 'applesauce'); Posner (n 5) 232–33; Neuberger (n 59) [30]; Shephard (n 57) 386, 389–90; High Court of Australia, 'Ceremonial – Retirement of French CJ' (n 2); Cooper (n 28) 4.

[103] Ziegler (n 16) 26; Edwards 'Judicial Function' (n 36) 858.

and women but this changes: if you do not get on with your fellow judges the workplace can be very unhappy'.[104]

In a similar vein, United States Judge Frank Coffin has confided in the 'joy' collegiality can bring:

> What I have not said is that life on a collegial court where judiciality is widely shared takes on a joyous quality. Even though judges may disagree on basic issues, they still relish the company of their colleagues and look forward to sitting on another case with them. In short, positive collegiality is a source of much of the joy and fun in being an appellate judge.[105]

Indeed, Judge Story wrote of the United States Supreme Court under Chief Justice John Marshall, 'we are all united as one, with a mutual esteem, which makes even the labors of jurisprudence light'.[106] And to his wife, he penned: 'Our intercourse is perfectly familiar and unconstrained, and our social hours, when undisturbed by the labors of law, are passed in gay and frank conversation, which at once enlivens and instructs'.[107]

Collegiality can also help ease the loneliness and isolation that can plague the life of a judge.[108] Former Chief Justice Bora Laskin from the Supreme Court of Canada wrote:

> The judge of a final appellate court like the Supreme Court of Canada who looks over his shoulder for any comfort will find no one there, unless it be his law clerk who, in my experience, cannot always be relied on to be comforting. There is something of the loneliness of the long distance runner in every judge of a final appellate court ...[109]

The National Judicial College of Australia's judicial mentoring framework, for example, is designed to enhance judicial well-being and promote 'collegiality' among judges.[110] For judges, heightened collegiality on

---

[104] Mack, Wallace and Roach Anleu (n 10) 27.
[105] Coffin (n 31) 9.
[106] Adolph Moses, 'The Friendship between Marshall and Story' (1901) 35 *American Law Review* 321, 324. Similarly, Smith wrote of the Court at the time 'the camaraderie and affection among the justices was as strong as ever': Jean Edward Smith, *John Marshall: Definer of a Nation* (Henry Holt & Co, 1996) 493.
[107] Moses (n 106) 325.
[108] Kirby (n 68) 105; Diane P Wood, 'Justice Harry A Blackmun and the Responsibility of Judging' (1998) 26 *Hastings Constitutional Law Quarterly* 11, 18; Harry A Blackmun, (1974) 1 *Ohio Northern Law Review* 401, 404.
[109] Laskin (n 34) 469.
[110] National Judicial College of Australia, Submission No 113 to Australian Law Reform Commission, *Review of the Family Law System* (14 June 2018) 14.

superior courts is likely to make judges more willing to consult with each other and feel more supported as a result.[111] Such interactions are likely to, in turn, contribute to a court's collegiality quotient.

As Appleby and Le Mire explain, consultations between judges can be particularly useful when ethical issues arise.[112] They do, however, note that heightening judicial diversity as well as the number of judges can become an obstacle to 'social collegiality' among judges.[113] Indeed, Justice Ginsburg in reflecting on the possible, but ultimately non-eventuating, appointment of Justice Florence Ellinwood Allen to the United States Supreme Court in 1949, noted the other judges' concern that it 'Would make it difficult for [the other Justices] to meet informally with robes, and perhaps shoes, off, shirt collars unbuttoned and discuss their problems and come to decisions'.[114]

This raises the degree to which, some 70 years on, judicial collegiality and diversity or 'representativeness' coalesce or jar as judicial values? Diverse views can strengthen the decision-making process by allowing a broader range of perspectives and issues to be canvassed.[115] While much of this process remains hidden from view, and warrants further consideration in the multimember context, there is evidence to suggest that a court rich in diverse experiences and backgrounds 'may yield qualitatively different decision-making processes'.[116] However, there is still much wrapped-up complexity in judicial diversity, in its many forms, and collegiality.[117] For instance, Judge Edwards has reflected on his

---

[111] Gabrielle Appleby and Suzanne Le Mire, 'Ethical Infrastructure for a Modern Judiciary' (2019) 47(3) *Federal Law Review* 335, 338.
[112] Ibid.
[113] Ibid. 340.
[114] Ruth Bader Ginsburg, *My Own Words* (Simon & Schuster, 2016) 75 (citing India Edwards).
[115] Susan B Haire, Laura P Moyer and Shawn Treier, 'Diversity, Deliberation, and Judicial Opinion Writing' (2013) 1(2) *Journal of Law and Courts* 303, 304–5; Benjamin Alarie and Andrew Green, 'Should They All Just Get Along? Judicial Ideology, Collegiality, and Appointments to the Supreme Court of Canada' (2008) 58 *University of New Brunswick Law Journal* 73, 87; Lynch (n 24).
[116] Haire, Moyer and Treier (n 115) 320. See also Edwards (n 3) 1668–70.
[117] For scholarship on a gendered reading of collegiality and female judges see further: Kcasey McLoughlin, '"Collegiality Is Not Compromise": Farewell Justice Crennan, the Consensus Woman' (2016) 42(2) *Australian Feminist Law Journal* 241; Heather Elliott, 'The Difference Women Judges Make: Stare Decisis, Norms of Collegiality and "Feminine Jurisprudence": A Research Proposal' (2001) 16 *Wisconsin Women's Law Journal* 41. See also, as to the multiple influences on judging of which gender may be one: Erika Rackley, *Women, Judging and the Judiciary: From Difference to Diversity* (Taylor & Francis, 2012) ch 5.

experience on the United States Court of Appeals for the District of Columbia Circuit and noted that judicial diversity tended to enrich the judicial process at least when collegiality was functioning well.[118] There is cause to further explore the inter-relationship between these aspects and the degree to which, as judicial values, they can reinforce each other and in what settings this is likely to occur.

Looking at the emergence of judicial collegiality as a value sheds light on the complexity of collegiality as a concept and the extent to which it informs both the institutional and individual judicial experience. The full realisation of the judicial role requires an appreciation of judicial collegiality as a valuable force shaping the behind-the-scenes process of the bench and the experiences of those who undertake them. The interrelationship between collegiality and other judicial values is an area in which further research is warranted to better understand judicial behaviour and the multiple forces operating upon it.

VI Conclusion

Judicial collegiality has the potential to be so multifaceted and idiosyncratic that it becomes difficult to definitively grasp or aspire to. But, its inimitability becomes in some ways its strength. While it may vary quite fundamentally between courts, and even different compositions of the same court, it can allow a multimember court to undertake its role more honestly, more cohesively and more bravely.

Collegiality's emergence as a judicial value recognises its marked contribution to the quality of the deliberative process both at the institutional and individual level. Judicial collegiality, as judicial teamwork at its very best, can be institution-enhancing. Its optimization, while still needing to be better understood on diverse benches, is strongly influenced by institutional and personal dynamics, including judicial leadership. But, if nurtured and facilitated, it has the potential to enhance the enterprise of judging and the operation of courts as institutions.

---

[118] Edwards (n 3) 1668.

9

Individual Judicial Style and Institutional Norms

ANDREW LYNCH[*]

I Introduction

To talk of 'judicial style' is to situate the speaker immediately within the context of the common law tradition of judicial individuality, as distinct from the formal collective practice of judgment under civil law systems. While courts that do not permit the publication of separate reasons, whether concurring or dissenting, may still conceivably reveal some particular form or mode of expressing their decision, it is questionable whether this rises to the heights of what may be called 'style'. As any observable features of the decisions of such a court are unarguably *institutional* in character, to regard them as displaying a style (as opposed, perhaps, to a 'practice' or 'tradition') appears a misnomer – or at least to miss the point. For to look to style is to search for something, if not unique, then distinctive and personal.

So much emerges very clearly from the literature on judicial style considered in this chapter, which places Australian attention to this topic alongside the views of English and American judges, as well as other authors. Unsurprisingly, there is a bias in this literature to the work of judges serving on multi-member senior appellate courts, particularly courts of last resort, and unless specifically noted otherwise, this is also the focus of discussion in this chapter. Across these judicial reflections there is a great deal of consistency on the diverse audiences for whom judges may be writing and how these may influence stylistic choices. Although several discrete taxonomies of style are noted, the essential division that emerges is one between an authoritative or magisterial tone on one hand and exploratory or conversational on the other.

---

[*] I am grateful for the research assistance of Zoe Graus in the preparation of this paper. I also appreciate the feedback of academic and judicial participants at the 'Uncloaking the Judiciary' Workshop held by the Gilbert + Tobin Centre of Public Law, UNSW in July 2018, and especially my co-editor Gabrielle Appleby and Heather Roberts for their additional comments.

But the scope for a discernible judicial style goes far beyond a simple contrast between courts in the English common law tradition and those where any such potential is absent, or severely limited.[1] The latter may effectively be set aside, for as Professor Pasquale Pasquino has said of them, 'egocentrism can play a role, but apparently only in the course of secret deliberation; it remains unknown outside the court'.[2]

Among those courts where individual voices are able to be projected beyond the inner sanctum of the judges' chambers and conference room, the opportunity to exercise and display judicial style may still be markedly distinct. Specific institutional norms will admit of differing forms of individual expression. This is so in two particular senses. First, the way in which judges express their opinions will be shaped by the legal culture of their jurisdiction, the history of the institution on which they serve, its place in the court hierarchy and standing in the polity generally, as well as the implicit and unacknowledged behavioural norms of the current bench, operating as a collegial group, of which the judge is a member. This complex interplay of factors certainly guides, if not constrains, the ways in which an individual judge explains her decisions to external audiences through the publication of reasons. The centrality of these factors as underlying any discussion of judicial style is inescapable. In this chapter, emphasising judicial reflections as a source, I examine central themes as to what constitutes 'good' judicial style and why this is worth judicial effort to hone, despite its elusive qualities.

Additionally, I am interested in a second, more specific, form of institutional norm that affects the capacity for individual expression – and so the discernment by audiences of individual judicial styles. This is the readily observable, even articulated, practices by which a court communicates its decisions and the extent to which these accommodate the development of individual reputation. Strong prioritisation of the court

---

[1] Essentially, this refers to the courts of the civil law jurisdictions of Europe [for a recent and comparative account, see Katalin Kelemen, *Judicial Dissent in European Constitutional Courts* (Routledge, 2018)], but also international courts and tribunals that may deliver only a single unanimous judgment. There is a strong correlation between this jurisdictional divide and that between career/recognition judiciaries (see Nuno Garoupa and Tom Ginsburg, 'Hybrid Judicial Career Structures: Reputation versus Legal Tradition' (2011) 3(2) *Journal of Legal Analysis* 411), with the latter possibly an alternative vehicle for discussion of judicial style.

[2] Pasquale Pasquino, 'E pluribus unum: Disclosed and Undisclosed Votes' in *Constitutional/Supreme Courts*' in Jon Elster, *Secrecy and Publicity in Votes and Debates* (Cambridge University Press, 2015) 206.

speaking with an institutional voice will directly affect style, being less conducive to the use of a personal or exploratory tone than an approach which, to some degree, acknowledges the judicial author's identity. It is widely recognised that differences in style and tone have consequences for the accessibility of the court's reasons beyond a fairly narrow professional audience, and arguably their persuasive force more generally. Following a thematic discussion of matters pertaining to judicial style, including the inevitable issue of time as a constraint, the chapter examines the High Court of Australia's present institutional practices of joint judgment delivery. It contrasts these to the different ways that the final courts of the United Kingdom and the United States accommodate individual voice.

II The Twenty-First Century Judge as a Writer

It seems trite to say that judges are, by profession, writers. As one Australian jurist memorably remarked, '[j]udgment writing is the theme that plays through our judicial lives'.[3] But only in comparatively modern times has the preparation of written reasons for judgment been ubiquitous to the judicial function. Professor William D Popkin has explained the practice of writing judgments as emerging in both England and the United States in response to concerns over the chequered arrangements for reporting court decisions.[4] It is not surprising that accompanying the moves to produce more accurate and authoritative reports in both England and the United States was the judicial adoption of a dedicated practice of writing judgments for publication. Judges did not, of course, begin as writers, but from the mid-nineteenth century it is true to say that writing had become integral to their work.

It is worth being explicit about the authorly aspect of the judicial role because this tends to be subsumed by our appreciation of judges' primary purpose as decision-makers. The judge's written reasons are the means of explaining her decision. Although they are both necessary[5] and will be

---

[3] John Doyle, 'Judgment Writing: Are There Needs for Change?' (1999) 73 *Australian Law Journal* 737.
[4] William D Popkin, *Evolution of the Judicial Opinion: Institutional and Individual Styles* (New York University Press, 2007) 17-19; 82-84.; See also Patricia M Wald, 'The Rhetoric of Results and the Results of Rhetoric: Judicial Writings' (1995) 62(4) *University of Chicago Law Review* 1371, 1371 fn 1.
[5] See, in Australia: *Pettit v Dunkley* [1971] 1 NSWLR 376; *Wainohu v New South Wales* (2011) 243 CLR 181.

immediately examined by multiple audiences for the sufficiency of their discussion and persuasive application of relevant legal sources, it is, typically, the decision contained in the Court's order that is of paramount importance. The judge is there to decide; and fundamentally what is assessed by various audiences is the judge's *reasoning* as revealed by the written judgment, rather than the judgment as a piece of writing per se. But obviously, there is a limit to any strict demarcation of the reasoning and the expression of it.[6] The importance of both may be inferred from the statement of former Australian High Court Justice Michael Kirby that it is 'principally through the pages of written judgments that ... quality may be assessed'.[7] Yet we might also accept that a sound judgment is no more vulnerable to being overturned, whether on appeal or by the same court at a later date, simply because it is a prosaic text.

If it is clear that judges are writers, then it is equally apparent that they are writers of a very particular kind. In his argument that judicial opinions constitute a distinctive genre of writing, Professor Robert A Ferguson emphasised the need for them to 'match experience and form in ways that a citizenry can recognize and accept'.[8] At the same time he pointed to an important duality in the way judicial opinions are both 'a uniquely personal literary product and – from one written opinion to the next – a powerful and continuous publication in American political life'.[9] With rather less earnestness, an American jurist once remarked that 'the place of judicial opinions is rather low in the literary pantheon; as an art form they probably rank slightly above a political speech and just below a sermon'.[10]

Judicial speeches regularly indicate that judgment writing is something about which judges reflect seriously, including law's relationship to literature as conventionally understood.[11] Some may even admit to 'a

---

[6] 'Form is not something added to substance as a mere protuberant adornment. The two are fused into a unity': Benjamin Cardozo, 'Law and Literature' [1925] *Yale Review* 472, 473.
[7] Michael Kirby, 'On the Writing of Judgments' (1990) 64 *Australian Law Journal* 691, 693.
[8] Robert A Ferguson, 'The Judicial Opinion as Literary Genre' (1990) 2 *Yale Journal of Law and the Humanities* 201, 202.
[9] Ibid.
[10] Richard W Wallach, 'Let's Have a Little Humor' [1984] *New York Law Journal* 2.
[11] See Michael Kirby 'Literature in Australian Judicial Reasoning' (2001) 75 *Australian Law Journal* 602; Keith Mason, *Lawyers Then and Now: An Australian Miscellany* (Federation Press, 2012) 187–203. Law and literature is obviously also a field of extensive scholarly endeavour and although I draw upon several key contributions throughout this paper, my main focus is upon the way judges themselves reflect upon their writing and any value they ascribe to stylistic considerations.

certain pride and pleasure' in the expression of their judgment.[12] But judges are not prone to identifying themselves as engaged in the composition of work in a literary form. No doubt this is due at least in part to the difference between the daily experience of a judge's working life and an appreciation of professional writing as a creative career, if not an artistic calling. Judges who have an academic background – such as America's Felix Frankfurter, England's Lady Brenda Hale, and Australia's Dyson Heydon – may conceivably have a distinct perspective in their appreciation for the craft of writing, but even then, the reality of judicial life is that judges write under significant practical constraints that are very particular to their situation. Almost 30 years ago, Justice Kirby said extra-curially: 'The time for reflection, for careful planning, thoughtful research and for polishing prose, *is* strictly limited. And diminishing. It is in this world of unprecedented stress and pressure that most judges, today, complete their judgments'.[13]

So far as a 'diminishing' capacity to write judgments, by 2012, then Justice Susan Kiefel of the High Court of Australia had declared: 'Generally speaking, it is not possible for appellate judges to write a judgment in a timely way on every case that they hear'.[14] This was a stark advance on familiar calls for fewer separate concurrences and more joint judgments as simply desirable on the grounds of clarity and certainty. Whether a commitment to writing individual opinions is in fact no longer feasible in the High Court of Australia – and the significance of this view for judicial independence and the quality of decision-making – became a matter on which members of the Court publicly exchanged competing perspectives.[15] In the year before his retirement from the court, Justice Heydon only delivered separate opinions.[16] Although Justice Stephen Gageler insisted that each member of a final appellate

---

[12] Doyle (n 3).
[13] Kirby, 'On the Writing of Judgments' (n 7) 691. For an American perspective, detailing the rise of unpublished opinions, see Wald (n 4) 1373–5.
[14] Susan Kiefel, 'Reasons for Judgment: Objects and Observations' (Speech, Sir Harry Gibbs Law Dinner, 18 May 2012) 3.
[15] See Andrew Lynch, 'Keep Your Distance: Independence, Individualism and Decision-Making on Multi-Member Courts' in Rebecca Ananian-Welsh and Jonathan Crowe (eds), *Judicial Independence in Australia: Contemporary Challenges, Future Directions* (The Federation Press, 2016) 156.
[16] Andrew Lynch and George Williams, 'The High Court on Constitutional Law: The 2012 Statistics' (2013) 36(2) *University of New South Wales Law Journal* 514, 522, 525–6.

court have sufficient time to consider each case independently of his or her colleagues, including the time to write separate reasons (which may be abandoned should the judge later decide to join with others who have reasoned to the same conclusion), he did concede that the workload in intermediate appellate courts was different and inevitably limited 'the time each member can realistically spend independently reasoning to a conclusion'.[17] The same view has been proffered in the United States by an intermediate court judge.[18]

Two consequences flow from the claim that, at least at the intermediate appellate court level, the modern judiciary works under time constraints that would have been unthinkable to their predecessors. The first is simply to accept that the capacity of judges to hone their opinions as pieces of written composition, including through reflection and revision, is increasingly sacrificed on the altar of expediency. Chief Justice Doyle, for one, was prepared to be pragmatic, telling his judicial audience that 'we should not concern ourselves too much' with reaching 'the lofty standards of a Dixon, a Mason, or a Brennan ... We have to be realistic about what we can achieve'.[19] For him that meant 'more economical and simpler judgments, keeping more to the essential point at issue'.[20] As discussed later, the adoption of such an approach is, of course, a 'style' of judging in its own right – and one that may have a great deal to commend it. But the suggestion of the need for a workmanlike approach to the craft of judicial exposition of reasons contains the hint of regrettable compromise.

The second consequence of a time-poor modern judiciary is that the solution to be found is through appellate judges being more consciously open to collaboration and the delivery of joint opinions.[21] In the United States Supreme Court, this is, of course, the long-held norm of expressing consensus, although it has frayed in recent decades.[22] While Australia's judicial tradition has reflected the historical individuality of the English

---

[17] Stephen Gageler, 'Why Write Judgments?' (2014) 36 *Sydney Law Review* 189, 201.
[18] Diane P Wood, 'When to Hold, When to Fold, and When to Reshuffle: The Art of Decision-Making on a Multi-Member Court' (2012) 100 *California Law Review* 1445, 1448.
[19] Doyle (n 3) 737.
[20] Ibid. 739.
[21] Ibid. 738.
[22] M Todd Henderson, 'From Seriatim to Consensus and Back Again: A Theory of Dissent' [2007] *The Supreme Court Review* 283, 292–94.

bench,[23] the benefits of joint judgments have not gone unacknowledged.[24] This is a theme that the current chief justice has repeatedly emphasised since 2012 and is a strong feature of the court she now heads.[25] Her view, in step with judicial contemporaries elsewhere,[26] is that individualism should be tempered by 'the institutional responsibility of the members of a court ... in the pursuit of clarity, certainty and timeliness' to reduce the number of separate opinions.[27]

The ramifications for judicial style in the production of joint judgments is discussed later in this chapter. At this stage, the point is merely to recognise the particular milieu in which judges exist as writers – they write for a purpose, one that they appreciate, whether through increased workload or contemporary sensibility, as highly time sensitive. The consequence is either that they may find themselves adopting an individual style of expression that is stripped back and essentialist or that they will join more readily with others to produce a single set of reasons. Any discussion of judicial opinions as a literary genre needs to recognise these seemingly inescapable aspects of twenty-first century judging.

Brief mention of two other elements that impact upon the modern judge as a writer is necessary – one specific to judicial work, the other now simply universal. The first is the role that associates or clerks may play in the composition of judicial opinions. Accounts vary quite significantly as

---

[23] See Matthew Groves and Russell Smyth, 'A Century of Judicial Style: Changing Patterns in Judgment Writing on the High Court 1903–2001' (2004) 32 *Federal Law Review* 255.

[24] See, for example, Sir Anthony Mason, 'The Centenary of the High Court of Australia' (2003) 5(3) *Constitutional Law & Policy Review* 41, 42.

[25] Susan Kiefel, 'On Being a Judge' (Public Lecture, Chinese University of Hong Kong, 15 January 2013); Susan Kiefel, 'The Individual Judge' (2014) 88 *Australian Law Journal* 554; Susan Kiefel, 'Judicial Methods in the 21st Century' (Speech, Banco Court, 16 March 2017). As to the rates of joint judgment delivery on the High Court under Kiefel CJ see Andrew Lynch and George Williams, 'The High Court on Constitutional Law: The 2017 Statistics' (2018) 41(4) *University of New South Wales Law Journal* 1134; Andrew Lynch and George Williams, 'The High Court on Constitutional Law: The 2018 Statistics' (2019) 42(4) *University of New South Wales Law Journal* 1443 and A Lynch, 'The High Court on Constitutional Law – the 2019 Statistics' (2020) 43(4) *University of New South Wales Law Journal* 1226.

[26] Lord Neuberger, 'No Judgment: No Justice' (Lecture, Annual BAILII Lecture, 20 November 2012).

[27] Kiefel, 'The Individual Judge' (n 25) 560. Interestingly, it can be said that the seriatim practice, at least on occasion, can ensure a speedier outcome than the effort required to forge consensus around a joint judgment; see, for example, Coper's reflections on the seven opinions issued by the High Court of Australia in the iconic *Tasmanian Dams* case: Michael Coper, *Encounters with the Australian Constitution* (CCH, 1988) 38–9.

to the contribution made by associates in different courts.[28] Certainly in Australia, the tendency is for judges to reject that their associates have much, if any, role in judgment writing.[29] But this is much more commonly accepted in the United States.[30] It is an open question whether any delegation of composition to associates risks losing the value to judicial reasoning that is gained by the judge in the act of writing her reasons. In the United States Supreme Court, where the work of up to four clerks for each Justice includes drafting, the level of assistance may dull judicial motivation for consensus.[31] Although Professor Laura Krugman Ray has bemoaned the modern reliance on clerks in the Supreme Court as promoting 'a generic judicial voice ... erasing the stamp of judicial personality' from opinions, she concedes that contemporary judges have nevertheless found ways to personalise their opinions.[32]

Second, Justice Ruth Bader Ginsburg acknowledged that greater prolixity and fragmentation in the opinions of the United States Supreme Court owes much to today's 'more efficient means to retrieve and process words'.[33] Former Australian Chief Justice Sir Harry Gibbs also memorably warned of the 'dangers in preparing a judgment by calling up slabs of ill-digested material' from a computer (which he rather charmingly referred to in 1993 as 'that device').[34] This must be a chief factor in the great expansion of the average length of judgments over recent decades.[35]

---

[28] For a comparative study of two final courts, see Katharine Young, 'Open Chambers: High Court Associates and Supreme Court Clerks Compared' (2007) 31 *Melbourne University Law Review* 646; for an account of the evolving role of judicial assistants in the United Kingdom Supreme Court, see Alan Paterson, *Final Judgment: The Last Law Lords and the Supreme Court* (Hart Publishing, 2013) 248–57.

[29] JD Heydon, 'Threats to Judicial Independence: The Enemy Within' (2013) 129 *Law Quarterly Review* 205, 221; PA Keane, 'The Idea of the Professional Judge: The Challenges of Communication' (Speech, Judicial Conference of Australia Colloquium, 11 October 2014) 4–5.

[30] A longstanding critic in this regard is Judge Posner, a Circuit Judge of the United States Court of Appeals for the Seventh Circuit, see Richard A Posner, *Reflections on Judging* (Harvard University Press, 2013) 238–45.

[31] Ruth Bader Ginsburg, 'Remarks on Writing Separately' (1990) 65 *Washington Law Review* 133, 148.

[32] Laura Krugman Ray, 'Judicial Personality: Rhetoric and Emotion in Supreme Court Opinions' (2002) 59 *Washington and Lee Law Review* 193, 223.

[33] Bader Ginsburg (n 31) 149.

[34] Sir Harry Gibbs 'Judgment Writing' (1993) 67 *Australian Law Journal* 494, 495. See also, Justice Bryan Beaumont, 'Contemporary Judgment Writing: The Problem Restated' (1999) 73 *Australian Law Journal* 743, 747.

[35] Groves and Smyth, (n 23).

Beyond the issue of information overload and length, does it otherwise matter, as a more universal question about the judicial function, *how* the judge writes her decision?

High Court Justice Sir Frank Kitto certainly thought so. In his much-cited paper 'Why Write Judgments?' he sought forgiveness for 'indulging a personal hate against the judgment that purports to be written but in fact is a transcription of an oration delivered to a stenographer or a dictaphone'.[36] While the passage of time must soon eliminate the dictaphone machine itself, modern voice recognition computer software facilitates the same method. For a reason that bears repeating in full, Justice Kitto strongly advocated writing by hand:

> Intensity is indeed the thing; and only in the throes of putting ideas down on paper, altering what has been written, altering it a dozen times if need be, putting it away until the mind has recovered its freshness, even tearing it up and starting again, can most of us hope to get, in a difficult case, the fruits of the requisite intensity of penetrating thought, the best we can do in the direction of profundity.[37]

Although there are occasional hints that even some recently retired judges have limited computer-literacy,[38] it may be assumed that most are as comfortable and proficient using a word processor as they are a pen and paper, and this number will only continue to increase. The distinction between methods that Justice Kitto drew when railing against dictation does not seem as analogous to the refinement of an opinion using a computer – indeed the ease with which an author can edit and revise using a computer may well be greater than when writing by hand. Conversely, the capacity to achieve greater length by word processing may count against it. As Lord Macmillan explained, to 'write out a judgment with one's own hand promotes conciseness by the automatic operation of the economy of labour'.[39]

Regardless of means, the notable thing that Justice Kitto described is the 'requisite intensity' that accompanies the *process* of writing. Justice Heydon emphasised the importance of writing to the judicial function

---

[36] Sir Frank Kitto, 'Why Write Judgments?' (1992) 66 Australian Law Journal 787, 795. See also Justice Michelle Gordon, 'Applying Reason to Reasons: Start, Middle and the End' (Speech, AGS Administrative Law Forum, 11 November 2016) 2.

[37] Kitto (n 36) 796.

[38] Renai LeMay, 'Dyson Heydon Doesn't Have a PC, Does Not Know How to Email', *Delimiter* (online, 31 August 2015) <https://delimiter.com.au/2015/08/31/dyson-heydon-doesnt-have-a-pc-does-not-know-how-to-email>.

[39] Lord Macmillan, 'The Writing of Judgments' (1948) 26 *Canadian Bar Review* 491, 492.

when he said that 'attempts to state ideas in particular sets of words can alter the ideas as the words change'.[40] As Judge Posner says, 'the process of writing, which means searching for words, for sentences, in which to express meaning, is a process of discovery rather than just of expressing preformed ideas' that may reveal analytical gaps and suggest new ideas.[41] Judge Patricia Wald put it directly when she said that process 'puts the writer on the line' – her use of the universal noun, rather than simply 'judge', pointing to this shared experience across all writing.[42]

The value of writing a judgment may be true even for the basic parts of an opinion that many assume may have been laid down by associates or harvested from legal databases, as Justice Michelle Gordon highlighted when she revealed:

> I type my own judgments. I read and type out each of the relevant statutory provisions. I do not cut and paste them. Why? Because I find that the process of writing reinforces in my mind what statutory provision (or provisions) I am dealing with, and helps me become familiar with its text and where it sits in the framework of the statute.[43]

There is remarkable consistency in these and other judicial reflections, strongly suggesting that while modern court practices may impose greater pressures upon the judge, the appreciation of what makes for good writing has remained constant. But more than that, the pursuit of good writing is justified by its benefit to better judging.

Having now considered the context in which the twenty-first century jurist functions as a writer, what does good judicial writing look like and to what extent is it helpful to approach this as a question of 'judicial style'?

III Substance, Form and Style

Consistent with the idea of the judicial opinion as a literary genre, there are requirements upon the author that are invariably observed and that readers expect from a judgment – an account of the facts, including history of the litigation if on appeal, identification and discussion of relevant statutory provisions and case law, application of the facts to the law as so outlined before a statement in conclusion as to outcome.[44]

---

[40] Heydon (n 29) 221.
[41] Posner (n 30) 240.
[42] Wald (n 4) 1375.
[43] Gordon (n 36) 5.
[44] For a succinct description of these fundamental elements of legal reasons, see ibid.

Law students are inculcated in this practice from the very commencement of their studies and it is sustained by the case law method: 'Since judges in their writings also rely heavily on the forms, substance, and expression of previous courtroom opinions, we should expect generic recognitions to play a special role in their efforts'.[45]

Within the requirements of the genre, it is possible to discuss the style of judgments by reference to matters of form that may be essentially standard to the collective practices and traditions of a court's individual members. These are capable of evolution. In the early 1990s, both Sir Harry Gibbs and Justice Kirby discussed the then quite recent embrace by the Australian judiciary of headings and subheadings in written opinions, as well as the decline in Latin usage and move to gender neutral language.[46] In all three respects, the judgments of today may be contrasted with those of preceding generations.[47] However, even on such matters, there may be disagreement and individual judges may not adhere to the prevailing institutional style. For example, American practices of footnoting were described admiringly by Justice Kirby as 'a way of making a telling point strictly peripheral to the issues at hand',[48] while Sir Harry Gibbs eschewed their use for such purposes, accepting them only for legal citation.[49] Judge Richard Posner of the United States Court of Appeals for the Seventh Circuit rejected them utterly, saying the 'absence of these "scholarly" appendages marks an opinion as informal, even conversational; no one speaks in footnotes and headings'.[50] Elsewhere, he has pointed to these features as indicia of legal formalism 'to make the outcome seem to follow ineluctably from prior authoritative pronouncements with no addition from the writer'.[51] But on the whole, different judges will employ the standard features of contemporary opinions to greater or lesser extent.

---

[45] Ferguson (n 8) 202.

[46] Gibbs (n 34) 501; Kirby, 'On the Writing of Judgments' (n 7) 701–4.

[47] As just one example, Keith Mason has pointed out that Dixon J's judgment in *Bardolph v New South Wales* (1934) 52 CLR 455 contains 'a paragraph that spanned five pages of the *Commonwealth Law Reports*': Keith Mason, *Old Law, New Law: A Second Australian Miscellany* (Federation Press, 2014) 96.

[48] Kirby (n 7) 703.

[49] Gibbs (n 34) 500.

[50] Richard A Posner, 'Judges' Writing Styles (And Do They Matter?)' (1995) 62 *University of Chicago Law Review* 1421, 1427. Justice Stephen Breyer of the United States Supreme Court shares Posner's aversion to footnotes: Popkin (n 4) 176.

[51] Posner, *Reflections on Judging* (n 30) 252.

Ultimately, however, style is much more than form alone.[52] It is inclusive of, but also something more than, those qualities of a judgment on which there is apparently universal consensus, such as 'clarity'; no one would suggest a judgment might usefully be otherwise. Sir Harry Gibbs explained style as raising considerations more particular to the individual author and beyond the universal when he said:

> The principal qualities that give a judgment style are clarity and accuracy of expression, coherence and rationality of thought and reasoning, and the rejection of surplusage. Within those parameters there is scope for much variety, for the style of a judge is characteristic of his or her personality, and experience shows that the judicial personality is infinitely variable.[53]

The role of personality is not merely an incident of the fact that opinions are written by different judges. Given the general observance of standards of form and shared aspirations to the 'judicial trinity' of 'brevity, simplicity and clarity',[54] what personality may be said to bring to judicial style is the quality that Justice Benjamin Cardozo called 'persuasive force'.[55] In his significant examination of the topic, Judge Posner took pains to delineate between the narrow sense of 'rhetoric', with its focus on persuasion, and 'style' as a broader concept capturing distinct aspects of expression that go beyond an intention to induce agreement with or acceptance of the outcome.[56] Similarly, Lord Macmillan viewed the clarity and 'convincingness' of a judgment as essential requirements before the 'embellishments' of 'style, elegance and happy phrasing'.[57] But it is near impossible to make such a distinction in practice since the opinion understood as a whole must be imbued with the intention to convince or persuade.[58] All its elements surely come together for that purpose.[59]

---

[52] Griffin B Bell, 'Style in Judicial Writing' (1981) 1(2) *Journal of the National Association of Administrative Law Judiciary* 26, 29: 'Form holds and preserves substance, and for that reason judges must pay close attention to form. Yet, mere form is not sufficient'.
[53] Gibbs (n 34) 502.
[54] Kirby, 'On the Writing of Judgments' (n 7) 704.
[55] Cardozo (n 6) 492.
[56] Posner, 'Judges' Writing Styles (And Do They Matter?)' (n 50) 1422. See also, Richard Posner, *Law and Literature: A Misunderstood Relation* (Harvard University Press, 1988) 270–2.
[57] Macmillan (n 39) 491.
[58] 'The main object of a judgment is to convince the reader that the judge's findings and reasoning are sound and have led to the correct result and the judgment should be subservient to that purpose': Gibbs (n 34) 499.
[59] Cardozo (n 6) 503.

Posner proceeded to offer three further definitions of style as:

- all that exists beyond that which may be simply paraphrased;
- a 'literary' quality that enables an opinion to become or to be made meaningful to an audience different from the one for which it was written;
- individual signature or 'voice'.[60]

Far from these meanings being mutually exclusive, they may be expected to coincide often. Popkin adopts a definition of style that explicitly combines the first two of Posner's approaches to refer to 'whatever in the judicial opinion seeks to persuade beyond the paraphrasable content of the decision', which he then analyses by use of the concepts of 'voice and tone' (to which I return below).[61] While the objective identification of a core of 'paraphrasable content' may be contentious in some cases, the idea of style as those qualities of a judgment beyond its essential finding as any other author might express it, and instead something particular to the individual who actually wrote it, is probably as close as we can get to defining this elusive notion.

Style need not be flashy or flamboyant. Sir Harry Gibbs defended the commencing of a judgment in a 'commonplace' or 'prosaic' way as having no less deliberate style than one of Lord Denning's most famous judgments beginning: 'It happened on April 19, 1964. It was bluebell time in Kent'.[62] Indeed, what constitutes judicial style may be scarcely perceptible. Although Justice Cardozo enthused that for 'quotable good things, for pregnant aphorisms, for touchstones of ready application, the opinions of the English judges are a mine of instruction and a treasury of joy', this was hardly to exhaust the topic.[63] For 'more important than mere felicities of turn or phrase', are the 'architectonics of opinions ... [the] groupings of fact and argument and illustration so as to produce a cumulative and mass effect'.[64]

---

[60] Posner (n 50) 1422–6.
[61] Popkin (n 4) 143.
[62] Gibbs (n 34) 499 cf Kirby 'On the Writing of Judgments' (n 7) 701. Lord Denning was writing in *Hinz v Berry* [1970] 2 QB 40.
[63] Cardozo (n 6) 498.
[64] Ibid. 503.

A Considerations of Context and Audience

The institutional context in which the judgment is being written and its various intended audiences overlay those general conditions, including pressures of time, that were earlier discussed as affecting judges as writers.

Institutional context operates in two distinct senses. The first is the level of the court on which the judge sits and what this may require when writing opinions. In 2015, Justice Margaret Beazley, then president of the New South Wales Court of Appeal, contrasted the High Court's emerging tendency as she saw it to deliver 'minimalist, largely propositional style of reasons, often with a plurality judgment' with intermediate appellate court reasons that 'have remained more discursive and detailed, particularly, but not only, where social issues are raised'.[65] Justice Beazley described cases on topics as various and challenging as recognition of same-sex marriage, homosexual advance as relevant to a defence of provocation, legal status of a person after sex change, and calculation of damages for breach of contract. In each, a long and searching decision by an intermediate appellate court was answered by 'crisp statements of the law with only short exploratory reasons' from the High Court.[66] Justice Beazley considered a number of possible explanations for the difference, including the fact that intermediate courts have among their audience the justices of the High Court to whom a decision may be appealed. But additionally, she remarked on the following distinctions as explaining such divergent style:

> intermediate appellate courts do not have the same constitutional function as the High Court, and there remains debate as to their declaratory role in the development of the law. Further, appeals in intermediate courts are by way of rehearing, which is likely to require a fuller consideration of factual as well as legal issues ... Finally, intermediate appellate courts are bound to apply the common law of Australia, which necessitates the consideration of judgments of other intermediate courts on the issue in question ...[67]

The second contextual matter concerns the practice of the particular court by which a majority expresses itself. Multi-member courts typically

---

[65] Margaret J Beazley, 'Judgment Writing in Final and Intermediate Courts of Appeal: "A Dalliance on a Curiosity"' (2015) 27(9) *Judicial Officers Bulletin* 79.
[66] Ibid. 81.
[67] Ibid. 82. See further, Ruth McColl, 'The Art of Judging' (2008) 12 *Southern Cross University Law Review* 43, 47–50.

conference after a hearing to exchange views as to the resolution of a matter and, traditionally in some courts or as a result of more recent innovation in others, determine which judge will take the job of drafting an opinion for the majority. In the United States Supreme Court, this opinion will ultimately be identified as written by Justice X 'for the Court'; the United Kingdom Supreme Court, an institution just a decade old, identifies the 'leading judgment' written by one of the bench which is placed first in the order of published opinions regardless of the author's seniority (a more logical way to approach the case and particularly kind to the reader). In Australia, the High Court uses no formal classification of majority opinions, even when these are, as is increasingly the case, joint and the writing of these is discussed and facilitated by post-hearing conferences.[68]

It is clear that the judge who knows that she is writing for a majority that emerged, however loosely, at a post-hearing conference must draft the opinion with a very distinct purpose in mind. Given that the author will often be aware of those who agree with her essential position on how the case is to be resolved (what we may liken to Posner's 'paraphrasable content'), choices as to the way in which that is best expressed will inevitably be decided in favour of keeping that support, not repelling it. This consideration may even extend beyond the immediate controversy, to an ambition to build support for a position in future, related matters. The need to secure agreement can have what Cardozo identified as an inhibiting effect, leaving the judge 'fearful of the vivid word, the heightened phrase'[69] so far as flourishes of individual style are concerned. Accordingly, sometimes the judge's 'best lines are often left on the cutting room floor'.[70] When the judgment is a means of communicating the views of not just the author but also others, this understandably blunts the distinctiveness of individual style.[71] Chief Justice Kiefel has spoken plainly of the necessity of that sacrifice:

---

[68] For two contrasting yet both extremely detailed accounts of the decision-making process see Kiefel, 'Judicial Methods in the 21st Century' (n 25) and Heydon, (n 29).

[69] Cardozo (n 6) 504. The dangers may be more mundane – Justice Blackmun informed Justice O'Connor that he would not join an opinion in which the word 'parameter' appeared: Jan Crawford Greenberg, *Supreme Conflict: The Inside Story of the Struggle for Control of the United States Supreme Court* (Penguin Press, 2007) 68.

[70] Wald (n 4) 1377.

[71] A recent study has attempted to overcome the anonymity of the author of 140 joint opinions in the High Court of Australia by a linguistic profiling exercise which is premised on the belief that individual stylistic identifiers are sufficiently discernible in

> There is a method to writing first drafts. They need to be succinct. A long judgment which says more than is necessary is less likely to attract agreement. Neither will a judgment written in the idiosyncratic style of the author, or in florid language from the classics or nineteenth century literature. It is better to resist the temptation to quote extensively from literature unless the aim is to not have others join in.[72]

By contrast, the judge who is indifferent to such support, even when concurring with the majority, will write opinions free of any such considerations. That is most obviously the case with the judge who is in dissent – especially in intermediate appellate courts where dissent is inevitably solitary. Even when there are others in dissent in a final court, the impetus for a joint statement of reasons is presumably different, if not lessened. The judge is always at liberty to write for an intended audience, but when the judge knows the opinion will be a minority one, then that choice is largely made as a consequence. Accordingly, in sole-authored concurrences and dissents, greater authorial control will enable a clearer observation of individual style, freed of any ambition to forge consensus with others. It is no coincidence that dissents tend to be celebrated as a sub-genre of judicial writing over majority opinions regardless of their later influence or vindication.[73]

Many ruminations on the art of judgment writing reflect on the various audiences for whom opinions are written.[74] These obviously include the parties in the case, the legal profession, and other courts – either those that will need to follow the decision or those higher courts that may possibly hear the matter on appeal. Beyond these self-evident categories, 'there is no unanimity of opinion as to who that audience should be'.[75] In some cases, the judgment may attempt to send a message to those in the political branches of government. Possibly the academy, including those studying the law, are in mind to some degree. But

---

such opinions: Andisheh Partovi et al., 'Addressing "Loss of Identity" in the Joint Judgment: Searching for "The Individual Judge" in the Joint Judgments of the Mason Court' (2017) 40(2) *University of New South Wales Law Journal* 670.

[72] Kiefel 'Judicial Methods in the 21st Century' (n 25) 5.

[73] See, for example, Andrew Lynch, *Great Australian Dissents* (Cambridge University Press, 2016); and Mark Tushnet, *I Dissent: Great Opposing Opinions in Landmark Supreme Court Cases* (Beacon Press, 2008).

[74] For judicial discussion, see Beazley (n 65); Kirby, 'On the Writing of Judgments' (n 7) 692–96. For academic treatment, see Laurence Baum, *Judges and Their Audiences: A Perspective on Judicial Behaviour* (Princeton University Press, 2006); Vicki Waye 'Who Are Judges Writing For?' (2009) 34 *University of Western Australia Law Review* 276.

[75] Kirby 'On the Writing of Judgments' (n 7) 708.

ultimately, there is the larger audience of the community the court serves. It may be anticipated that very few members of the public will seek out and read court judgments; but as the means by which the court's work is presented to the community, the media (generally with the assistance of academic interpretation) is also an important audience.

Sir Harry Gibbs said that a discussion about audience 'seems to me pointless when it deals in generalities ... [a] judgment is a public document available for all to read'.[76] He did though admit that sometimes a judge might have a particular audience in mind such as another court or the legislature. Gibbs was not disposed to write for a non-legal audience, insisting that 'the judge should not write down to their level'.[77] This appears to confirm the sense that generally Australian judges have *not* written for the community at large – as is evidenced by their long, complex style of judgments with elaborate reasoning and detailed discussion of academic sources or previous decisions.[78] Yet many of the changes to judgment writing that were discussed above – the use of headings, the avoidance of Latin – presumably indicate efforts to make judicial opinions more accessible to laypersons.

Posner approaches audience as the key to his dichotomy of pure and impure judicial style and the choices that judges make in writing for either. Judges who are writing for other judges and the parties' lawyers, and for whom everyone else is simply 'an (authorized) eavesdropper', will respond to that audience's 'settled expectations concerning the appropriate diction and decorum of a judicial opinion'.[79] By contrast, 'impure judicial stylists' are described as those writing in a conversational tone and expressing themselves candidly, keeping quotations, cliché and unnecessary details to a minimum.[80] Posner acknowledges that the dichotomy is artificial and in practice most judges sit somewhere in the middle of what is in fact a spectrum. This may well reflect the great difficulty of attempting to write with such diverse audiences in mind – as America's Justice Anthony Kennedy once admitted, 'I've never quite had a precise grasp of whom you're writing for'.[81]

---

[76] Gibbs (n 34) 495.
[77] Ibid. 495.
[78] Waye (n 74) 277. Arguably, the modern use by courts of media officers enables an act of translation of judicial opinions that may be said to lessen any obligation on the judiciary to draft the opinions themselves to be generally accessible.
[79] Posner (n 50) 1431.
[80] Ibid. 1430.
[81] Quoted in Krugman Ray (n 32) 224.

IV Taxonomies of Judicial Style

A strong element in the literature on judicial style is the attempt to create or apply categories based on sketchy pen portraits of different personalities as revealed in judicial opinions. This trend was begun with Justice Cardozo's half-serious effort in 1925 that remains oft-quoted today:

> There is the type magisterial or imperative; the type laconic or sententious; the type conversational or homely; the type refined or artificial, smelling of the lamp, verging at times upon preciosity or euphuism; the type demonstrative or persuasive; and finally the type tonsorial or agglutinative, so called from the shears and the pastepot which are its implements and emblem.[82]

Sir Harry Gibbs was prepared to identify several High Court judges against parts of this taxonomy. While the judgments of Australia's first chief justice, Sir Samuel Griffith, were seen by Gibbs as generally 'magisterial or imperative', those of many, including Chief Justice Dixon, were classified as 'demonstrative or persuasive'.[83]

Other schemata are possible. Justice Kirby cited and applied Lord Justice Templeman's opinion that judges could be divided into 'the philosophers, the scientists and the advocates'.[84] Interestingly, he opined that Chief Justice Dixon was 'probably our greatest "scientist"'.[85]

By far the most convincing examination of individual judicial personality and style is Krugman Ray's lengthy treatment of President Roosevelt's four most significant United States Supreme Court appointees, Justices Black, Frankfurter, Douglas and Jackson – respectively, the homely conversationalist writing for the people, the academic elitist, the 'rugged individualist' and the 'pragmatic man of letters'.[86] Rather than establishing categories in the abstract, Krugman Ray drew these profiles out from a close analysis of the four individuals' judgments, understood by reference to their professional biographies. It is relevant that the emergence of such four distinct voices on the Court came at a time when its established norm of consensus judicial decision-making was rapidly disintegrating under Chief Justices Stone and Viner. This was due not

---

[82] Cardozo (n 6) 493.
[83] Gibbs (n 34) 498.
[84] Templeman LJ quoted in Kirby, 'On the Writing of Judgments' (n 7) 696.
[85] Ibid.
[86] Krugman Ray (n 32).

only to differences of personal style and institutional processes of questionable value, but in fact an ideological battle over the role and direction of the Court itself.[87]

The more helpful contributions on the topic of judicial style are those that shun attempts to create a taxonomy of judicial personality that can tend to stereotype (or even caricature),[88] while also offering a more generalised mode of analysis than that of Krugman Ray with its strong biographical basis. To return to Ferguson's analysis of judgments as a literary genre, he corrals amorphous notions of manner and expression into four distinct framing devices: the monologic voice, the interrogative mode, the declarative tone and (emerging as a product of those three) the rhetoric of inevitability. At their essence is the idea of authorial control over the way the reasons for decision are presented as neutral, compelled, raising 'complexities only to dismiss them in a decisive act of judgment', and dependent on a 'directed or selective sense of history' in the use made of precedent.[89] Ferguson presents these qualities as typical without condemnation but is keen to highlight their connection to more abstract debates around legal formalism, historicism and intentionalism. Certainly, the notions of audience and tone that are in focus are the same that Posner uses to explain the dominance of the 'pure' judicial style and the 'exaggerated formalism' of reasoning that results.[90]

By contrast, Popkin presents us with contrasting styles, which judges may reflect to greater or lesser degree, rather than an illumination of the overarching qualities of the judicial opinion as a literary genre. Accordingly, his work provides the flexibility of application that is found in attempts to identify distinct judicial 'types', while avoiding their rigidity and apparent reliance on persona. Popkin considers style as

---

[87] Noah Feldman, *Scorpions: The Battles and Triumphs of FDR's Great Supreme Court Justices* (Twelve Books, 2010). While Krugman Ray's discussion shows the interconnected quality of these issues and their reflection in style, it is important to distinguish other exercises in the categorisation of judicial 'types' that emphasise role conception but are not especially directed to style, for instance, Sunstein's four judicial 'personae' – heroes, soldiers, minimalists and mutes – which is essentially a different approach to judicial theories of constitutional interpretation: Cass R Sunstein, 'Constitutional Personae' (2013) 8 *The Supreme Court Review* 433.
[88] Kirby 'On the Writing of Judgments' (n 7) 696.
[89] Ferguson (n 8) 210, 215.
[90] Posner (n 30) 237.

consisting of 'voice and tone': 'Voice refers to the author's relationship to the source of law; tone refers to the author's relationship to the audience'.[91]

In explaining 'voice' as ways in which the judge may relate to a source of law, Popkin identifies the technical/professional voice of the legal expert; the grandeur of the magisterial voice in which, as Cardozo put it, 'the movement from premise to conclusion ... is more impersonal than the working of the individual mind' but the 'inevitable progress of an inexorable force'[92] (perhaps, for example, an appeal to natural law or ideals of justice or fairness); and the personal voice which looks to community values, with which the judge proclaims identification.[93] He then turns to the tone with which the judge chooses to communicate with the audience:

> Tone can be either authoritative or exploratory. An authoritative tone speaks down to the audience. The technical/professional and magisterial voices are always authoritative in modern judicial usage – with the judge transmitting law to the reader from a vantage point between the source of law and the audience. By contrast, an exploratory tone draws the reader into a participatory community with the judge, wondering aloud about how to deal with the complexities of the case ... an exploratory tone reveals the multiple perspectives occurring to an individual judge thinking about a case.[94]

The exploratory tone rejects the papering over of difference and presence of indeterminate rules or legal materials that may point in multiple directions that is the hallmark of the calmly authoritative judgment with its 'rhetoric of inevitability'. Further, it acknowledges a diversity of perspectives and experiences as concerns those legal materials and may accommodate, even directly adopt, these in the judge's reasoning. One may analyse judicial tone in this sense through the questions suggested by James Boyd-White:

> What kind of person is speaking here, and to what kind of person does he or she speak? What kind of response does this text invite, or permit? What place is there for me, and for others, in the universe defined by this discourse, in the community created by this text? What world does it assume, what world does it create?[95]

---

[91] Popkin (n 4) 143.
[92] Cardozo (n 6) 493.
[93] Popkin (n 4) 143–7.
[94] Ibid. 147–8.
[95] James Boyd White, *Heracles' Bow: Essays on Rhetoric and Poetics of the Law* (University of Wisconsin Press, 1985) 46.

Just how voice and tone combine to determine judicial style may be reasonably fluid in some cases – notably magisterial/authoritative or personal/exploratory – but the natural limit on combinations that is acknowledged by Popkin does suggest that there may be an awkwardness in his approach. Ultimately, voice seems so determinative of tone that it is unclear just how much is gained by their distinct consideration.

Popkin, using Posner as a substantial case study, makes a direct pitch for the personal voice and exploratory tone in modern judging, if not on all occasions then at least in hard cases. He does so after saying that this is all that 'is left after Legal Realism has called into question an authoritative judicial tone'.[96] Similarly, we might see the major contribution of the global Feminist Judgments writing project, inaugurated by Rosemary Hunter, Claire McGlynn and Erika Rackley,[97] as providing a substantial and multi-jurisdictional resource that evidences the availability and legitimacy of a different perspective within the relevant norms of judicial decision-making.[98] In so doing, that project has punctured the formalist tradition upon which the authoritative presentation of legal decisions may be said to depend.

Yet, the authoritative tone is sustained by the resilience of the technical/professional voice. Certainly, this remains true in the Australian legal setting. But that is not to deny the appeal of the exploratory style. As discussed earlier, when contrasting the form of judgments delivered by Australian intermediate appellate courts to the 'propositional' approach she identified in recent High Court decisions, Justice Beazley emphasised the value of 'presenting a case in its context – factual, legal and, in some circumstances, social and political – so that the basis of the reasoning and therefore the outcome is transparent'.[99] This goes to the central issue of persuasion as an objective of the modern judge when writing – the purpose is not merely to explain one's reasons but surely to do so in order to convince the reader that these are correct.[100] In cases featuring contemporary social challenges, sufficient persuasive force may not be provided by resort to the authoritative tone but instead only by frank

---

[96] Popkin (n 4) 153.
[97] Rosemary Hunter, Clare McGlynn and Erika Rackley (eds), *Feminist Judgments – From Theory to Practice* (Hart Publishing, 2010).
[98] See also Gabrielle Appleby and Rosalind Dixon (eds), *The Critical Judgments Project: Re-reading Monis v The Queen* (The Federation Press, 2016).
[99] Beazley (n 65) 82.
[100] Posner (n 56) 272.

acknowledgment of the complexity of the issue and the presence of competing views upon it.[101]

V The Institution and Individual Style

One might readily accept the benefits of the personal/exploratory style over a more formal, technical, or 'pure', style but still see the challenge that lies in its realisation on a multi-member court. Specifically, it is not straightforward to see how those benefits can be captured on a court which has an institutional norm or significant practice of joint judgments in pursuit of the goals of clarity and timeliness. So, for example, in 2012, Lord Neuberger advocated a writing style that 'must speak as clearly as possible to the public', yet also expressed strong reservations about judicial individuality – including the frequency of dissenting judgments.[102] But if, as suggested at the start of this chapter, style is a concept that is significantly about the distinctive or memorable expression of reasons, then suppression of the individual voice does not necessarily further the goal to render judgments more accessible and effective in communicating the work of courts to the public.

This seems particularly true in respect of the High Court of Australia given not just its growing tendency to deliver joint judgments, but the lengths to which it goes to subsume the individual judge within a collective, if not a strictly institutional, voice. As noted earlier, an aversion to the tradition of seriatim opinions has been ascendant in the High Court of Australia over the last 20 years. The arguments in favour of joint judgments are well known and appreciable, and in some cases there will be much to be gained by the effort required to achieve them. But as Sir Anthony Mason has said, the Court's record over much of its first century was 'one of strong individualism'.[103] An acceptance of that tradition as consistent with the greater persuasive potential of an exploratory judicial style may enrich, even challenge, the tenor of the contemporary discussion about how the Court should decide cases.

What is especially striking about the current practice of the High Court is that the identity of the author of the majority opinion is not revealed to the reader. This is in contrast to the different ways in which

---

[101] See Boyd-White (n 95) 135.
[102] Neuberger (n 26).
[103] Sir Anthony Mason, 'Reflections on the High Court: Its judges and judgments' (2013) 37 *Australian Bar Review* 102, 117.

the author of the opinion 'for the court' in the Supreme Court of the United States and the 'leading judgment' in the Supreme Court of the United Kingdom is made plain. A joint opinion for the majority in the High Court simply lists at its head (in order of seniority) all those who agree with it. But Chief Justice Kiefel has candidly admitted on several occasions that 'it is more often the case that there is only one author'.[104] The identity of that person is wholly obscured by the practice of 'joining in' which '*requires* the author of a judgment to join in any judge who circulates a concurrence with the judgment'.[105] The effect is:

> to render the author largely anonymous. Some might argue that a reader should know who the author is, although it is difficult to see what the benefit of that knowledge could be. On occasions a justice might wish the practice was otherwise, when it is felt that he or she has written a particularly good judgment, but it is always understood that if the practice were not followed justices would be encouraged to write separately more often, which is what the practice seeks to avoid.[106]

Other current members of the High Court have affirmed the stance of the Chief Justice – with one explicitly linking a predisposition to join in judgment with a notion of the judge as a 'professional'.[107] Justice Virginia Bell was frank when she said that 'if the price ... is the loss of the individual judge's "voice", I suspect that few outside the Academy would count that a bad thing'.[108]

But the anonymity of author that follows from the practice of compulsory 'joining in' any member who expresses agreement with an opinion is about more than judicial ego. The author of the opinion is unknown to the audience and although Chief Justice Kiefel said that 'it is difficult to see what the benefit of that knowledge could be', the practices of other final courts and views expressed by figures as diverse as Thomas Jefferson and Dyson Heydon suggest that individual accountability across the bench is enhanced when authorship is identified.[109] But additionally, the practice also carries significant implications for judicial style in the way the Court explains its decisions.

---

[104] Kiefel 'Judicial Methods in the 21st Century' (n 25) 6. See also, Kiefel 'Reasons for Judgment: Objects and Observations' (n 14) 4.
[105] Kiefel 'The Individual Judge' (n 25) 557 (emphasis added).
[106] Kiefel 'Judicial Methods in the 21st Century' (n 25) 7.
[107] Virginia Bell, 'Examining the Judge' (Speech, Launch of Issue 40(2) UNSW Law Journal, 29 May 2017); Keane (n 29).
[108] Bell (n 107) 2.
[109] Kiefel 'Judicial Methods in the 21st Century' (n 25) 7.

When the Court's practice is formally to obscure the identity of the author of a joint opinion, then that presumably exerts a particularly pronounced influence on the tone of the opinion itself, stifling anything that smacks of a personal flavour, such as doubt, exploration and choice, in favour of an authoritative style that accords with the focus on the institutional or collective voice. Whether this is the result of changes requested by those who indicate an intention to join an individual's draft opinion or whether it is consciously or otherwise adopted by the author when initially drafting that opinion is impossible to say, and not really to the point. An opinion that will appear under the names of all those who join it must presumably read as if *any* of them had written it – as opposed to simply an opinion written by a named colleague and with which they happen to signal agreement and adoption, as in the final courts of both the United States and the United Kingdom. We might consider Justice Beazley's assessment of High Court joint judgments as confirming the relatively succinct and self-assured nature of opinions that are produced pursuant to this practice.

Coinciding with the rise of joint majority opinions in the High Court, the institution has developed a tradition of a 'welcome judgment' which is a distinctly converse practice. In a case soon after their appointment, new justices on the Court write a sole-authored opinion with which the rest of the majority separately deliver bare concurrences.[110] In this way, a new justice is 'introduced' to the public as a member of the Court, notably by providing the opportunity to express her individual voice. It is evident that this opportunity is engineered, and indeed constrained; the practice requires an opinion with which others may simply agree, perhaps making it more akin to a disaggregated joint opinion than the typical practices of either of the two foreign Supreme Courts mentioned above. But at least the identity of the author is not masked, and how she approaches the task of explaining the reasons for the decision is fully attributable to that individual.

Inevitably, a judge writing for the majority, under whatever institutional practice pertains, will be seeking to gather adherents to the opinion rather than to delve into idiosyncrasy. It is not suggested that the High Court practice of 'joining in' is alone in this respect. But it does place a particularly low value on individual identity and reputation.

---

[110] Although on occasion, some concurring opinions have broken out of step and offered more, including distinct views on the question at hand. See Lynch and Williams (n 25) 'The High Court on Constitutional Law: The 2017 Statistics', 1143.

While that may, as Chief Justice Kiefel says, avoid the proliferation of separate concurrences, it seems reasonable to assume that it has, more so than joint judgments in which individual authorship is attributed, an effect upon the way such opinions are written. And that effect must, presumably, be to entrench the pure or formalist style over the impure or personal in Australia's highest court.

VI   Conclusion

There are many dimensions to the topic of judicial style, what influences it, how it may be observed, and what impact it has. This chapter has sought to highlight the connections between Australian judicial reflection on style and some of the classic and contemporary considerations given in the United States and United Kingdom. But it has also sought to consider how style as a predominantly individualistic phenomenon of voice and tone is supported or constrained, not just by institutional context but institutional *priorities* – specifically toward joint expressions of reasons. This is especially so when majority reasons not only have to reflect a consensus, but deny the role of the individual author assigned to give expression to that consensus.

For all that has been written about judicial style, a gap that remains is to more fully explore the achievement of institutional efficiency and timely dispensing of justice without sacrificing the optimal conditions for the production of accessible and engaging judicial reasons.

10

Values and Judicial Difference in the High Court

RACHEL CAHILL-O'CALLAGHAN*

I Introduction

The right to deliver a dissenting opinion is a feature of the final courts of appeal in many common law jurisdictions. It is staunchly protected, and consistently justified, by the judiciary and legal academy.[1] Indeed, Professor Andrew Lynch highlights the routine maintenance of an odd number of judges on multi-member courts as evidence that disagreement may be a positive objective of the law.[2] A published dissent is a public manifestation of this disagreement. There is increasing recognition in both the academic and judicial community that dissent in the highest courts is not simply a reflection of disagreement on the legal issues. It is also a reflection of the individuals making the decision. Although all judges are bound by the constraints of the judicial office, a published dissent is not typically constrained by the necessities of compromise. As such, the dissenting judgment is a reflection of the individual behind the decision.[3] The recognition of the importance of the individual judge

---

* This research was supported by a research visit fellowship (UNSW) and a research leave fellowship (Cardiff University). I would like to thank the editors and the members of the workshop for their feedback and support.
[1] Andrew Lynch, 'Dissent: The Rewards and Risks of Judicial Disagreement in the High Court' (2003) 27(3) *Melbourne University Law Review* 724; Lord Kerr, 'Dissenting Judgments: Self Indulgence or Self Sacrifice?' (Birkenhead Lecture, Gray's Inn, 8 October 2012); Lord Neuberger, 'Some Thoughts on Judicial Reasoning across Jurisdictions' (Mitchell Lecture, Edinburgh, 11 November 2016); Michael D Kirby 'Judicial Dissent: Common Law and Civil Law Traditions' (2013) 123 *Law Quarterly Review* 379; Sarah A Binder and Forrest Maltzman, *Advice and Dissent: The Struggle to Shape the Federal Judiciary* (Brookings Institution Press, 2009); Edward M Gaffney, 'The Importance of Dissent and the Imperative of Judicial Civility' (1993) 28 *Valparaiso University Law Review* 583.
[2] Andrew Lynch, 'Judicial Diversity: Is Disagreement a Positive Object in Law?' (2012) *University of New South Wales Law Research Series* 41.
[3] Kevin M Stack, 'The Practice of Dissent in the Supreme Court.' (1995) 105 *Yale Law Journal* 2235. The individual is not only reflected in dissenting judgments. A sole-authored

in decision-making underpinned the disquiet expressed by Chief Justice Barwick back in 1977 in the *Second Territory Senators' Case*:

> It may be granted that a change in the personal composition of the Court is not itself any reason to entertain the question whether the decision of a Court differently composed is erroneous. But, on the other hand, the fact that there has been a change in the personal composition of the Court since an earlier decision was given can be no reason, in my opinion, why any Justice should refrain from expressing what he is convinced is the right conclusion in the matter before the Court.[4]

In that case, the change in the composition of the bench, and each individual Justice's faithfulness to precedent and the consistency it provides, resulted in a decision which upheld the validity of legislation which the majority recognised as unconstitutional.[5] In his dissenting judgment Chief Justice Barwick highlighted the importance of the individual judge's approach to the law on the final decision. The role of the individual on a judicial panel was at the centre of a later dissenting opinion of Justice Kirby in the 1999 decision of *Re Wakim; Ex parte McNally* ('*Re Wakim*'), in which he wrote

> This Court's decision in *Gould v Brown* was published in February 1998 ... The unanimous decision of the judges of the Federal Court of Australia, upholding the validity of the legislation, was not disturbed. Yet within a matter of months fresh challenges to the constitutionality of the legislation were commenced. Within less than a year this Court was hearing again arguments, most of which had been advanced unsuccessfully in *Gould*.
>
> What has changed? The Australian Constitution stands unaltered, resistant to formal change. No relevant change has been proposed to it. ... Only the membership of the Court has changed in the intervening

---

concurrence supporting a majority decision may also provide insight into the individual judge.

[4] *Queensland v Commonwealth* (1977) 139 CLR 585 ('*Second Territory Senator's Case*') was decided by Barwick CJ, Mason, Jacobs, Murphy, Gibbs, Stephen and Aitken JJ. The legal question centred on the validity of the *Northern Territory Representation Act 1922* (Cth), and *Australian Capital Territory Representation (House of Representatives) Act 1973* (Cth) which had been decided earlier in *Western Australia v Commonwealth* (1975) 134 CLR 201 ('*First Territory Senators' Case*'), decided by Barwick CJ, Barwick CJ, Mason, Jacobs, Murphy, Gibbs, Stephen and McTiernan JJ. In the intervening period, McTiernan J retired from the bench to be replaced by Aitken J. The decision in Western Australia closely divided the bench with the majority McTiernan, Mason, Jacobs and Murphy JJ holding that the legislation complied with the *Constitution*.

[5] *Queensland v Commonwealth* (1977) 139 CLR 585.

year. ... It is an old and wise maxim of the law, which courts usually strive to observe, 'to keep the scale of justice steady, and not liable to waver with every new judge's opinion.' On the face of things there could hardly be a plainer violation of that maxim.[6]

Kirby J was the sole dissent in the decision in *Re Wakim*, which found the statutory foundation of jurisdictional cross-vesting invalid. The 'change' he was referring to was the retirement of Brennan CJ and Toohey J, who had been joined by Gaudron, McHugh, Gummow JJ in *Gould v Brown*. The decision less than two years earlier had upheld the validity of the same statutory foundation of the *Corporations Act 1989* (Cth) and the *Jurisdiction of Courts (Cross-Vesting) Act 1987* (Cth). *Gould v Brown* divided the six member court evenly with the decision of Brennan CJ, Toohey and Kirby JJ prevailing.[7] In his strongly worded dissenting judgment in *Re Wakim*, Kirby J shifted the frame from the legal context to the individuals making the decision, attributing the different outcome to individual choice rather than legal change. In doing so, Kirby J highlights the importance of the individual in a multi-member court and how individual judicial difference can influence the final outcome. It is through the publication of dissent that this individual difference is revealed.

Many of the justifications of dissent relate to the perception of the democratic legitimacy of the judiciary. Indeed, John Alder would suggest that dissent is essential to 'offset the democratic deficit in the common law'.[8] A democracy, Adler argues, does not embody an internally consistent set of values; rather it embodies disparate and often competing values and a 'democratic' judiciary should reflect these incommensurable values. Thus, the publication of a dissenting judgment is an overt reflection of these competing social values. While Lynch notes that judicial officers do not represent constituencies of values, this chapter will demonstrate the diversity of competing values which are at the heart of judicial disagreement and individual decision-making.

This chapter draws on a value framework developed in psychology which locates highly conserved human values in 10 overarching

---

[6] *Re Wakim; Ex parte McNally* (1999) 198 CLR 511, 596–7 [178]–[179].
[7] For further discussion on cross-vesting and the substantive decisions see Henry Burmester, 'Cross-Vesting: Why Not and What Next?' (1999) 22 *Australian Institute of Administrative Law Forum* 27.
[8] John Alder, 'Dissents in Courts of Last Resort: Tragic Choices?' (2000) 20 *Oxford Journal of Legal Studies* 221, 223.

motivations.[9] In reaching a decision, an individual will prioritise one or more values above others. The value framework was used to create a coding scheme for content analysis of judgments which relates legal concepts with value positions.[10] This system of value identification was applied to cases which divide judicial opinion in the High Court of Australia. It is in the reasoning of such cases that we are privy to the complexity of the decision-making processes and the multiple factors that influence the individual decision, and ultimately the final outcome. It is in judgments of these cases that values are identified.[11]

The analysis of the values expressed in judgments of cases which divide judicial opinion recognises the complexity of the decision-making process and reframes the judicial decision from a decision on the disposition of a case, to one which requires the nuanced balancing of alternative values. In doing so, the chapter highlights the importance of individual justices and their value priorities on the outcome of uncertain decisions. The chapter is set out in four parts. Part I presents the method of identification and quantification of values in High Court judgments drawing on a single case study. Parts II and III explore the consistency of judicial value expression in related cases, and demonstrates the impact of individual value choice on outcomes in multi-member courts. Part IV examines value expression in a single constitutional case, *Rowe v Electoral Commission*[12], which highlights the complex nature of the High Court decision-making process and the many factors that play a role. In conclusion, the chapter draws on the preceding analysis to present an argument for value diversity on the High Court bench.

II Identifying Values in High Court Judgments

The terms 'values' and 'value judgments' are used in legal literature to cover a variety of concepts including interests, likes, preferences, duties, wants, goals, needs, moral obligations and other kinds of selective

---

[9] Shalom H Schwartz, 'Universals in the Content and Structure of Values: Theoretical Advances and Empirical Tests in 20 Countries' (1992) 25 *Advances in Experimental Social Psychology* 1.

[10] This method of content analysis was validated in a small experimental study which related legal decisions with reasoning and psychometric assessment of values. See Rachel J Cahill-O'Callaghan, 'The Influence of Personal Values on Legal Judgments' (2013) 40(4) *Journal of Law and Society* 596.

[11] Ibid.

[12] (2010) 243 CLR 1 ('*Rowe*').

orientations.[13] This chapter draws on a narrow definition of values, which places values within a psychological framework of decision-making, which identifies values as: *'enduring beliefs that a specific mode of conduct or end-state of existence is personally or socially preferable to an opposite or converse mode of conduct or end-state of existence'*.[14]

In this context, values act as guides for the evaluation of the social world and influence decisions and behaviour. An individual appraises objects, actions and situations in relation to their values, but does so with very little cognitive effort and therefore values may serve as an implicit influence on decision-making.[15] Studies in the UK Supreme Court have highlighted the association between values and decisions in cases which divide judicial opinion, Dworkin's 'hard cases', where the outcome is 'not clearly dictated by statute or precedent'.[16]

A   Identification of Hard Cases

This chapter examines the values expressed in 'hard' cases decided in the High Court.[17] These cases were selected using the following criteria. First, although there is no recognised definition of the legal uncertainty hard cases represent, the close division of a court on the disposition of the case may be considered an indication of the strength of legal argument supporting opposing outcomes and thus indicate a high level of legal uncertainty which facilitates such a close division. The influence of the individual decision-maker in a multi-member court is most profound in those cases which result in a close call, the cases in which a single

---

[13] Milton Rokeach, *Understanding Human Values: Individual and Societal* (Free Press, 1979).
[14] Milton Rokeach, *The Nature of Human Values* (Free Press, 1973) 5.
[15] Norman T Feather, 'Values, Valences and Choice: The Influence of Values on the Perceived Attractiveness and Choice Alternatives' (1995) 68(6) *Journal of Personality and Social Psychology* 1135; Anat Bardi and Shalom H Schwartz, 'Values and Behaviour: Strength and Structure of Relations' (2003) 29(10) *Personality and Social Psychology Bulletin* 1207.
[16] Ronald Dworkin, 'Hard Cases' (1975) 88 *Harvard Law Review* 1057, 1057; Cahill-O'Callaghan (n 10); Rachel J Cahill-O'Callaghan, 'Winner of the SLS Annual Conference Best Paper Prize 2014: Reframing the Judicial Diversity Debate' (2015) 35(1) *Legal Studies* 1; Jack Meakin, 'Questionable Neutrality: Personal Values in Judicial Adjudication' in Alberto Febbrajo (ed), *Law, Legal Culture and Society: Mirrored Identities of the Legal Order* (Routledge, 2019) 121.
[17] Dworkin (n 16) 1057.

justice divides the majority and minority and divide the court 3:2 or 4:3. To identify a subset of these cases, a narrow time frame was selected and a database of cases which divided judicial opinion between 2008 and 2013 was created.[18] Within this time frame, 23 cases closely divided judicial opinion.

Second, the size of the judicial panel may also be evidence of the difficulty of the decision. A full court is convened to determine constitutional cases and cases where the Court is invited to depart from previous decisions or those that involve a principle of law which is of major public importance.[19] Within the dataset selected for this chapter, seven close call cases were determined by a full court. Finally, in reaching a decision to publish an individual judgment in a case, the strength of the individual justice's motivation to express her or his view must overcome pressures of time, collegiality and workload. This suggests that cases in which the majority of Justices published a judgment reflect a significant strength of opinion on the legal issues and perhaps evidence of the degree of difficulty the Justice faced in reaching a decision. Based on this, a case was only selected if it elicited five or more separate judgments.

These selection criteria identified four 'hard' cases, *HML v The Queen* (*'HML'*), *Rowe v Electoral Commissioner* (*'Rowe'*), *BBH v The Queen* (*'BBH'*) and *Lee v New South Wales Crime Commission* (*'Lee'*).[20]

B Identifying Values in Legal Judgments

To identify values in legal judgments of the High Court, this chapter employs a content analysis method based on a coding framework grounded in the Schwartz model of values which has been used to

---

[18] This time period represents the end of the Gleeson Court and start of the French Court. The database was created from data provided by Professor Andrew Lynch (UNSW).

[19] 'Operation of the High Court', *High Court of Australia* (Web Page, 2010) <www.hcourt.gov.au/about/operation-of-the-high-court>.

[20] *HML v The Queen* (2008) 235 CLR 334 (*'HML'*); *Rowe v Electoral Commissioner* (2010) 243 CLR 1 (*'Rowe'*); *BBH v The Queen* (2012) 245 CLR 499 (*'BBH'*); *Lee v New South Wales Crime Commission* (2013) 251 CLR 196 (*'Lee'*). It is interesting the selection process identified two related cases, the decision of *HML* was reviewed in *BBH*. For completion, a fifth case *X7 v Australian Crime Commission* (2013) 248 CLR 92 (*'X7'*) was included as it was fundamental to the reasoning and division in *Lee*. This case closely divided a panel of five justices. Three judgments were delivered, two joint judgments and one individual judgment.

identify values expressed in UK Supreme Court judgments.[21] This model presents all stable values within 10 overarching motivations.[22] The motivations are driven by three requirements: first, the needs of individuals as biological organisms; second, the requirements of coordinated social interaction; and finally, the requirements for the smooth functioning and survival of groups.[23] The 10 motivational goals, which encompass universal values, are *self-direction, stimulation, hedonism, achievement, power, security, conformity, tradition, benevolence* and *universalism*. Of these, six values (*self-direction, power, security, conformity, tradition and universalism*) are more commonly affirmed in legal judgments.[24] Drawing on text from judgments of 'hard' cases, the balance of this section will set out in brief the method of content value analysis demonstrating how value motivations are evidenced in High Court judgments.[25]

Universalism is the broadest value in the model with the motivational goal of understanding, appreciation, tolerance and protection of the

---

[21] This model of values and the psychometric instrument on which the model has been based has been used in a wide range of studies including studies of personality, behaviour and decision-making: Gregory R Maio and James M Olson, 'Values as Truisms: Evidence and Implications' (1998) 74(2) *Journal of Personality and Social Psychology* 294; Mark M Bernard, Gregory R Maio and James M Olson, 'The Vulnerability of Values to Attack: Inoculation of Values and Value-Relevant Attitudes' (2003) 29(2) *Personality and Social Psychology Bulletin* 63; Gregory R Maio et al., 'Changing, Priming, and Acting on Values: Effects via Motivational Relations in a Circular Model' (2009) 97(4) *Journal of Personality and Social Psychology* 699; Wolfgang Bilsky and Shalom H Schwartz, 'Values and Personality' (1994) 8(3) *European Journal of Personality* 163; SH Schwartz; Lilach Sagiv and Klaus Boehnke, 'Worries and Values' (2000) 68(2) *Journal of Personality* 309; Sonia Roccas et al., 'The Big Five Personality Factors and Personal Values' (2002) 28(6) *Personality and Social Psychology Bulletin* 789; Shalom H Schwartz, *Beyond Individualism/Collectivism: New Cultural Dimensions of Values* (Sage Publications, 1994); Lilach Sagiv and Shalom H Schwartz, 'Cultural Values in Organisations: Insights for Europe' (2007) 1 *European Journal of International Management* 176; Anat Bardi and Shalom H Schwartz, 'Relations among Sociopolitical Values in Eastern Europe: Effects of the Communist Experience?' (1996) *Political Psychology* 525; Shalom H Schwartz and Anat Bardi, 'Influences of Adaptation to Communist Rule on Value Priorities in Eastern Europe' (1997) 18 *Political Psychology* 385.
[22] Schwartz analysed a total 25,863 value questionnaires completed by students and teachers in 20 countries. See Schwartz 'Universals in the Content and Structure of Values' (n 9) 1; Shalom H Schwartz 'Are There Universal Aspects in the Structure and Content of Human Values?' (1994) 50 *Journal of Social Issues* 19.
[23] Schwartz 'Universals in the Content and Structure of Values' (n 9) 21.
[24] Rachel J Cahill-O'Callaghan 'Reframing the Judicial Diversity Debate: Personal Values and Tacit Diversity' (2015) 35(1) *Legal Studies* 1.
[25] More detailed discussion of the method is available in Rachel Cahill-O'Callaghan, *Values in the Supreme Court: Decisions, Division and Diversity* (Hart Publishing, 2020).

welfare of all people and nature. This motivational goal includes values such as equality, wisdom, social justice and protecting the vulnerable.[26] An individual who prioritises universalism above other values will place the needs of society as a whole above those of the individual.[27] Expressions of the value within legal judgments includes the affirmation of equality, for example: 'There was a distinct element of inequality in permitting the Victorian evidence to be led by the prosecution but precluding HML from establishing the current status of the accusations'.[28]

And fairness: 'To exclude such evidence as irrelevant would occasion unfairness by requiring each complainant to give an incomplete account of her evidence'.[29]

Universalism is opposed to *power*, a value with a defining goal of control or dominance over resources and people. *Power* was frequently espoused in judgments, most often as the power of the court to achieve just outcomes. The importance of the power of the court was recognised by French CJ in *Lee* when he wrote:

> In my opinion, however, those considerations did not deprive the Court of Appeal of power to make the orders it did in this case. In so saying, I observe that the grounds for appeal for which special leave was granted do not raise any question whether the Court of Appeal's discretion miscarried when it made the orders it did. The question is one of power.[30]

This theme was also affirmed by French CJ in a joint judgment with Crennan J in *X7 v Australian Crime Commission* ('*X7*'): 'The courts have long had inherent powers to ensure the court processes are not abused'.[31]

Tradition is also commonly espoused in legal judgments and was evident in the judgments of the High Court. Tradition has the motivational goal of respect, commitment and acceptance of the customs and place cultural

---

[26] *Universalism* is contrasted with *benevolence* which focuses on the individual rather than society as a whole: Schwartz (n 9).

[27] It is recognised in a legal context, that the court has a duty since the ratification of the European Convention of Human Rights to protect minorities against the morality of the majority. This is reflected in this *universalism* with the protection of the welfare of all people, equality and protection of the vulnerable. The needs of society do not reflect the needs of the majority rather the needs of every member of society rather than advocating personal interest.

[28] *HML* (2008) 235 CLR 334, 374–5 (Kirby J).

[29] Ibid. 480 (Crennan J).

[30] (2013) 251 CLR 196, 230.

[31] (2013) 248 CLR 92, 116 (French CJ and Crennan J).

customs and ideals above personal interests. This includes the prioritisation of legal conventions. For example:

> That rationale not only has deep historical roots; it serves important contemporary ends. It respects the distinct contemporary functions, enhances the distinct contemporary processes, and fulfils the shared contemporary expectations of the legislative and judicial branches of government.[32]

Conformity is closely related to *tradition*; both require the subordination of the individual for socially imposed expectations. Conformity values derive from the requirement to avoid disruption to smooth group functioning. Within a legal context it is affirmed through preventing uncertainty in the law and requiring adherence to the rules. For example Heydon J in *Rowe* when discussing an individual's duty to enrol on the electoral register stated: 'They have not taken the steps to enable them to vote which were not only available to them, but required by them by s 101. They are simple steps. It would have been very easy to take them. There was ample time to take them'.[33]

Both tradition and conformity are encompassed within the broader dimension of conservation which emphasises order, preservation of the past and resistance to change. The other value in this dimension is *security* which affirms national and family security. The opposite dimension to conservation is openness to change which emphasises independence of thought and action and a readiness to change. It includes *self-direction* and *stimulation*. Although *stimulation* is not identified in legal judgments, self-direction, which has the motivational objective of independent thought and action, is evident through the affirmation of individual autonomy, including a Justice's decision to disagree. For example; '[b]ecause it is one upon which I depart from the conclusion of Hayne J, I will explain how it arises; why I disagree; and why the consequence is not ultimately determinative of the disposition'.[34]

An individual can affirm all values; however in reaching a decision between competing values, it is how opposing values are prioritised which is psychologically significant.[35] In reaching a decision between competing values, the decision-maker will prioritise one value or set of values above

---

[32] *Lee* (2013) 251 CLR 196, 309–10 (Gageler and Keane JJ).
[33] (2010) 243 CLR 1, 95 (Heydon J).
[34] *HML* (2008) 235 CLR 334, 372 (Gleeson CJ).
[35] Shalom H Schwartz, 'Value Priorities and Behaviour: Applying a Theory of Integrated Value Systems' in Clive Seligman, James M Olsen and Mark P Zanna (eds), *The Psychology of Values: The Ontario Symposium* (Lawrence Erlbaum Associates, 1995) vol 8.

another. Although values may underpin a variety of judicial decisions, the expression of values and balancing of value positions in legal judgments is evident in hard cases where there is uncertainty about the outcome.[36]

This uncertainty was recognised by the Justices in the cases analysed. For example, Hayne J discussed the inherent uncertainty in the law governing the test to be applied when determining whether evidence of other sexual misconduct should be introduced into a child abuse case in *HML*: 'The nature and extent of the uncertainty can be indicated by comparing the decision of the full court of the Supreme Court of Australia in Neiterink with the decision in the Court of Appeal of Victoria in R v Vonarx'.[37]

Legal uncertainty presents the judge with a choice, one which requires a nuanced balancing and prioritising of sets of competing values, and in making that choice, the prioritisation of values is evident in the judgments. This can occur at an innate level of decision-making. The response may be affirmed or rejected by more conscious processes not least of which may be the conscious evaluation by the decision-maker of particular value positions. There is evidence of this balancing in the judgments of the High Court for example:

> However, with respect to these three groups of adult citizens there will be disenfranchisement, and arguments that these groups are but limited or exceptional cases are no answer unless the consideration upon which the Commonwealth relies supplies substantial reason in the sense used in the reasons by the two majority judgments in *Roach*.[38]

In this extract from the joint judgment of Gummow and Bell JJ, the Justices acknowledge the impact on minority populations in society which is encompassed within *universalism* but suggest that this impact is legitimate if it has foundation in precedent therefore elevating legal tradition and the precedent encompassed in *tradition* above *universalism*.

III Consistent Value Priorities and Division in Related Cases: Analysis of *HML v The Queen* and *BBH v the Queen*

This part turns to consider two related cases to explore the consistency of expression of judicial values. Within the selected cases from the data set

---

[36] Cahill-O'Callaghan (n 25).
[37] Hayne J discussing the inherent uncertainty in the law governing the test to be applied when determining whether evidence of other sexual misconduct should be introduced into a child abuse case: *HML* (2008) 235 CLR 334, 396.
[38] *Rowe* (2010) 243 CLR 1, 57–8 (Gummow and Bell JJ).

were two cases which centred on the use of 'relationship evidence', that is, evidence of an incident(s) not of the charged offences but of other related offences, in child sexual assault cases. In *HML*, the High Court heard three appeals from the South Australia Supreme Court in which the admissibility of relationship evidence and the judicial direction related to that evidence was challenged.[39] In dismissing the appeals, all of the Justices agreed that uncharged acts of sexual misconduct are likely to be relevant to the facts at issue in a child sexual assault case, but three of them (Gummow, Kirby and Hayne JJ) argued that the evidence should be subject to the *Pfennig* standard which requires that evidence is only admitted if 'there is no reasonable view of the evidence consistent with the accused innocence'.[40] In contrast, the majority (Gleeson CJ, Heydon, Crennan and Kiefel JJ) held that the *Pfennig* test did not apply to relationship evidence in this case, with Crennan and Kiefel JJ arguing that the test did not apply to any relationship evidence. Each justice delivered an individual judgment.[41] As anticipated, the division in the court was reflected in the values espoused in the judgments.

The entire judgment ran to 517 paragraphs and contained 104 value coded statements. The majority affirmed values encompassed in four different categories, *tradition, conformity, self-direction* and *universalism*. Of these, the dominant value was *universalism* which includes affirmation of protection of the vulnerable and fairness:

> The question is extremely difficult because to be raised against the argument supporting their view are numerous arguments bearing on its unfairness to the witness, and on the social interest in convicting those guilty of crimes against small children which are both grave and difficult to prove.[42]

Indeed, fairness to the complainant was central to the decision: 'To exclude such evidence as irrelevant would occasion unfairness by requiring each complainant to give an incomplete account of her evidence'.[43]

Like Crennan and Heydon JJ, Kirby J, who supported the minority position, identified the importance of fairness: 'Fairness suggests that

---

[39] David Hammer, 'Admissibility and Use of Relationship Evidence in *HML v The Queen*: One Step Forward, Two Steps Back' (2008) 32 *Criminal Law Journal* 351.
[40] *Pfennig v The Queen* (1995) 182 CLR 461. For further discussion see CFH Tapper, 'Dissimilar Views of Similar Facts' (1995) 111 *Law Quarterly Review* 381.
[41] Gummow J delivered a short judgment which only ran to four paragraphs.
[42] *HML* (2008) 235 CLR 334, 450 (Heydon J).
[43] Ibid. 480 (Crennan J).

HML should have been afforded the chance to attempt (so far as he could) to deal with such potentially prejudicial, and effectively unanswerable, evidence and statements'.[44]

Kirby J also affirmed the importance of protecting the vulnerable and in doing so affirmed values encompassed within *universalism*:

> The law has an important obligation to protect truthful complaints about sexual abuse ... This observation has particular force where the abuse has allegedly been suffered by children as a result of the conduct of family members who owe the child special duties of trust and protection.[45]

But the values encompassed within *universalism* were not dominant in the judgments of the minority. In contrast to the majority, the dominant value expressed was *conformity* and certainty in the law. For example, Gummow J wrote:

> So much has been written about the foregoing questions in earlier decisions of this Court, and now in these proceedings, that I hesitate to add to the elaboration lest what I write ends up contributing to the uncertainties. ... Such directions or warnings must be framed so as to be understood by a jury of ordinary Australian citizens who do not have the luxury of hours (still less months) of cogitation. Therefore, this is a case where, if at all possible, this Court should make a particular effort to speak with a clear voice.[46]

When the expression of values was quantified, the differences in value expression associated with the decision reached were evident. The following is a graphic representation of the value expression in the judgments supporting the majority and minority position (Figure 10.1).

The quantitative value analysis highlights the differential pattern of values expressed in the majority and minority judgments. Although the pattern of some values including *tradition* and *self-direction* are similar, the data suggests in this case those supporting the majority position prioritise *universalism* when opposed to *conformity*. In contrast, the judgments supporting the minority position, although recognising and affirming the importance of values encompassed within *universalism*, prioritise *conformity*. Other more subtle differences were identified. Nine percent of the values expressed in the minority judgments affirmed *power*, a value that was not expressed in the majority judgments. The

---

[44] Ibid. 374 (Kirby J).
[45] Ibid. 367 (Kirby J).
[46] Ibid. 363 (Gummow J).

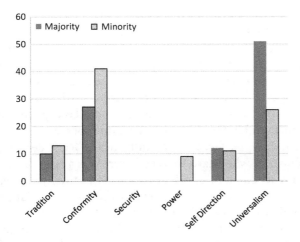

Figure 10.1 Value analysis of *HML v The Queen*. The horizontal axis presents the value motivations expressed in the case. On the vertical axis, the values are expressed as a percentage of the total of number of value statements in the judgments supporting each position and thus the data is controlled for the number and length of judgments.

affirmation of *power* in the minority judgments centred on the *power* of the court to grant leave. For example:

> It is only in an exceptional case that this Court will give special leave to appeal from a decision of a Court of Criminal Appeal affirming a conviction when the point the applicant seeks to raise was not taken either at trial or in the Court of Criminal Appeal.[47]

The quantitative analysis provides insight into the balancing of values in decisions which divide judicial opinion and the complexity of factors that influence judicial decision-making. Two justices were notable in their value expression: Heydon and Kirby JJ. Although the dominant values expressed in Heydon J's judgment supporting the majority position were in *universalism* (52%) with a focus on transparency, there was also a high level of coding within *conformity* (41%). Kirby J, supporting the minority position, also had unusual value coding with equal coding in both *universalism* (34%) and *conformity* (31%). Based on value analysis alone, both of these Justices who aligned to opposing positions in this case could have aligned with either position.

---

[47] Ibid. 408 (Hayne J).

Studies of judicial decision-making have highlighted the many factors that influence the final outcome.[48] Indeed, the influence of values on decision-making is not without external and internal constraint. Values are subject to 'trade-off', where a decision-maker will reach a decision which is in conflict with his or her personal values but achieves an alternative agenda.[49] In the context of judicial decisions, a value-based decision may be traded for legal consistency, collegiality, consensus, future support in another decision or other perceived benefits. Yet, despite the numerous factors that influence a legal decision, for the majority of justices who heard this case, there was a relationship between the decision reached and the values expressed in their judgments.

Six years later, the court again tackled the issue of relationship evidence in another child sexual assault case in *BBH*.[50] Five of the Justices who sat on the bench in *HML* also decided *BBH*: Gummow, Hayne, Heydon, Kiefel, and Crennan JJ. They were joined by French CJ and Bell J. The majority (Heydon, Crennan, Kiefel and Bell JJ) dismissed the appeal and held that relationship evidence, as evidence of propensity to commit such offences, was relevant and admissible. Once again, Hayne J, with whom Gummow J agreed, argued that the evidence should be subjected to the high standard of admission set out in *Pfennig*. Chief Justice French joined the minority arguing that the evidence was irrelevant and thus inadmissible. Although there was less value expression[51] than *HML*, several values were espoused in the judgments including *conformity* and *universalism* and there was a relationship between the values expressed and the decision reached. As in *HML*, *universalism* was the dominant value of those supporting the majority and *conformity* was dominant of those in the minority (Figure 10.2). Indeed, individual justices affirmed the values they prioritised in *HML*. In the majority, Kiefel and Crennan JJ espoused *universalism*.[52] In the minority, the dominant value in the judgment of Hayne J was *conformity*. As with *HML*,

---

[48] See, for instance, Penny Darbyshire, *Sitting in Judgment: The Working Lives of Judges* (Bloomsbury Publishing, 2011); Alan Paterson, *Final Judgment: The Last Law Lords and the Supreme Court* (Bloomsbury Publishing, 2013).
[49] Jonathon Baron and Mark Spranca, 'Protected Values' (1997) 70(1) *Organisational Behaviour and Human Decision Processes* 1.
[50] *BBH* (2012) 245 CLR 499.
[51] There is an association between length of judgments and value expression. *BBH* was shorter than *HML* and only ran to 204 paragraphs. Gummow J's judgment only ran to three paragraphs.
[52] In a joint judgment: *BBH* (2012) 245 CLR 499, 536–50.

VALUES AND JUDICIAL DIFFERENCE IN THE HIGH COURT 247

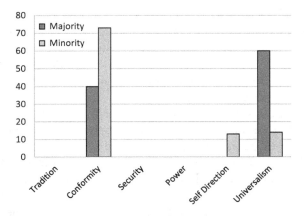

Figure 10.2 Value analysis of *BBH v The Queen*. The horizontal axis presents the value motivations expressed in the case. On the vertical axis, the values are expressed as a percentage of the total of number of value statements in the judgments supporting each position and thus the data is controlled for the number and length of judgments.

Heydon J again espoused both *universalism* and *conformity* at almost equal frequency. The consistency in the differential pattern of value expression between the majority and minority highlights the relationship between values and decision-making in the High Court. The analysis also highlights consistency in decision-making and value affirmation of individual Justices. In the context of this area of law, in reaching a decision between *universalism* and *conformity*, Kiefel and Crennan JJ affirmed *universalism*. In contrast, Hayne J affirmed *conformity*. The value analysis of his judgments suggests that Heydon J could affirm either value.

HML and *BBH* centre on the emotive issue of evidence in child sexual assault cases. In such cases, it is not difficult to contemplate a role for values in the decision-making process. But the expression of values in legal judgments is not limited to cases with such emotive facts. Two other cases were identified though the study selection criteria and a differential pattern of value expression between the majority and minority judgments were identified in both.

IV Values and the Influence of the Individual Justices: Analysis of *Lee v New South Wales Crime Commission* and *X7 v Australian Crime Commission*

The introduction of this chapter highlighted two seminal cases, which closely divided judicial opinion, and in which the identity of the judge was a facet of the judicial reasoning. This was also evident in the two cases considered in this part: *X7* and *Lee*.[53] In *Lee*, Hayne J, in the minority, stated: 'All that has changed between the decision in *X7* and the decision in this case is the composition of the Bench. A change in composition of the Bench is not and never has been, reason enough to overrule a previous decision of this Court'.[54]

Lee was heard less than five months after the decision in *X7*[55] which established that an individual could be summoned to answer questions about the subject matter of a charged offence. The decision in *Lee* saw this precedent overturned. The court divided four to three on the application of the 'principle of legality': a rule of statutory interpretation which requires Parliament to use clear statutory language if it intends to restrict fundamental rights or depart from general principles of law.[56] *Lee* centred on the *Criminal Assets Recovery Act 1990* (NSW) which authorises the Crime Commission to examine a person about her or his affairs before the Supreme Court.[57] In this case, an application was refused on the basis that the evidence may interfere with the ongoing criminal trial. The question before the High Court was whether the Act authorised compulsory examination, where the examination would deal with matters which were subject to pending criminal proceedings, and whether this compulsory examination interfered with an individual's right to remain silent. Whilst all the Justices agreed that the right to remain silent was an important element of the criminal justice system, they reached different positions on the application of the principle of legality in this context. The majority of French CJ, Crennan, Gageler and Keane JJ held that the legislative intent of the Act was sufficiently clear and the requirement that the examination occurred before a court protected the individual from prejudice in the pending proceedings.[58]

---

[53] Respectively, (2013) 248 CLR 92 and (2013) 251 CLR 196.
[54] (2013) 251 CLR 196, 233. *Lee* departed from the precedent set in *X7* (2013) 248 CLR 92 in which Hayne J was in the majority.
[55] *X7* (2013) 248 CLR 92.
[56] *Lee* (2013) 251 CLR 196.
[57] For detailed analysis of the legal foundation of the case see Bruce Chen, 'The Principle of Legality: Protecting Statutory Rights from Statutory Infringement?' (2019) 41(1) *Sydney Law Review* 73.
[58] Of note it was held in *X7* that the *Australian Crime Commission Act 2002* (Cth) did not demonstrate a sufficiently clear intention to restrict an accused person's right to silence. The case was heard by five justices (Hayne, Kiefel and Bell JJ) in the majority, French CJ and Crennan J in dissent.

The minority, Hayne, Kiefel and Bell JJ, held that the language of the Act was not sufficiently clear to permit such a significant departure from the fundamental principles of criminal justice and the examination in the context of ongoing criminal proceedings posed a real risk to the administration of justice. Once again, there was a differential pattern of value expression associated with the disposition of the case. In this case, the majority affirmed values encompassed within *universalism, tradition* and *power*, the most frequently espoused was *power* which included the power of the court as reflected in the following quotation from the judgment of French CJ:

> As was pointed out by Basten JA in the Court of Appeal, an examination under s 31D attracts the powers of the Supreme Court under the Uniform Civil Procedure Rules and its inherent power to supervise and control its own processes and to ensure that they are not abused. Those powers also include the power to take appropriate action to prevent injustice.[59]

In contrast, although the minority affirmed *power*, the dominant values were encompassed within *universalism*, including fairness, justice and the protection of the vulnerable:

> It is to be assumed that the Court or its officer would act to prevent oppression of the person examined and would act to prevent misuse or abuse of the process of examination, whether by limiting or precluding publication of what transpires at the examination, or otherwise. But if the trial of the person being examined is pending, the Court (or the officer of the Court) cannot know, and cannot predict, what might harm the defence of that person at trial.[60]

Indeed, it is the balance between these two values which is central to the decision (Figure 10.3).

The decision in *Lee* overruled an earlier decision in *X7* in which the majority held that the *Australian Crime Commission Act 2002* (Cth) did not demonstrate a sufficiently clear intention to restrict an accused person's right to silence, the position adopted by the minority in *Lee*. It is the difference in outcome between *X7* and *Lee* which prompted Hayne J to highlight the importance of panel composition and the individuals who hear the case. *X7* was heard by a panel of five justices, all of whom later decided *Lee*.[61] Unlike the decision in *Lee*, in *X7* Hayne J was in the

---

[59] *Lee* (2013) 251 CLR 196, 223.
[60] Ibid. 236 (Hayne J).
[61] *Lee* was decided by two additional Justices, Gageler and Hayne JJ joined the five Justices who decided *X7*.

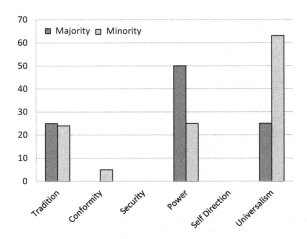

Figure 10.3 Value analysis of *Lee v New South Wales Crime Commission*. The horizontal axis presents the value motivations expressed in the case. On the vertical axis, the values are expressed as a percentage of the total of number of value statements in the judgments supporting each position and thus the data is controlled for the number and length of judgments.

majority with Kiefel and Bell JJ, and it was French CJ and Crennan J who were in the minority. The majority (Hayne, Bell and Kiefel JJ) held that 'requiring the accused to answer questions about the subject matter of a pending charge prejudices the accused in his or her defence of the pending charge (whatever answer is given)'.[62]

The minority in *X7* (French CJ and Crennan J) supported the opposite position which was the position affirmed by the majority in the later case of *Lee*. Although there was a wider range of values expressed in *X7*, the values which were expressed in the judgments reflected those expressed in the judgments of *Lee*. Hayne J, in the majority with Kiefel and Bell JJ, affirmed *universalism* when opposed to *power* (Figure 10.4). Chief Justice French and Crennan J, who were in the minority in X7 and majority in *Lee*, adopted the opposite position and affirmed *power* when opposed to *universalism*.

The Justices were consistent in their positions on the legal questions in both cases and this was reflected in the consistent expression and

---

[62] *X7* (2013) 248 CLR 92, 127 (Hayne and Bell JJ).

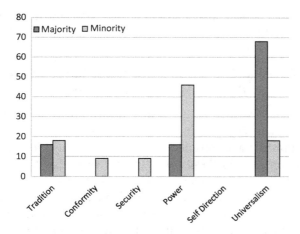

Figure 10.4 Value analysis of *X7 v Australian Crime Commission*. The horizontal axis presents the value motivations expressed in the case. On the vertical axis, the values are expressed as a percentage of the total of number of value statements in the judgments supporting each position and thus the data is controlled for the number and length of judgments.

affirmation of their value positions in their judgments. When *universalism* is in opposition to *power*, Hayne, Bell and Kiefel JJ prioritised *universalism* and French CJ and Crennan J prioritised *power*. The analysis on values moves the focus away from the outcome of the decision to the individual decision-makers and the values they affirm. The Justices who heard both cases were consistent in their value priorities. The decision in both cases placed two values, *universalism* and *power*, in opposition. The addition of two different Justices who affirmed *power* to the court in *Lee* tipped the balance and the final outcome of the case. Barmes and Malleson made a strong argument for the study of the superior courts at a group level rather than as individuals and the analysis of values facilitates this.[63] It offers an opportunity to reflect both on the individuals who make the decisions and the impact of these individuals on a panel and the final outcome.

The analysis of these cases also assists us to identify a degree of consistency in the values affirmed by particular justices. But values are only one factor in the complex decision-making process in the High

---

[63] Lizzie Barmes and Kate Malleson, 'Lifting the Judicial Identity Blackout' (2018) 38 *Oxford Journal of Legal Studies* 357.

Court and this individual consistency was not evident in the constitutional case analysed: *Rowe*.[64]

V Value Expression in the Constitutional Case
Rowe v Electoral Commissioner

Lynch has highlighted a tendency for constitutional cases to give rise to greater division on the bench relative to the Court's total caseload. The constitutional case considered in this part, *Rowe*, certainly divided judicial opinion. It is in these constitutional cases that the approach to judicial function is most evident. Discussions of judicial activism and its opposite, self-restraint, are often focused on matters of constitutional interpretation.[65] Indeed, this case was identified by James Allan as an example of activism which he defined as where judges employ interpretive techniques to significantly inflate their own discretionary powers at the point of application of the Constitution.[66] *Rowe* centred on how legislation introduced in 2006, which removed the seven-day grace period for enrolment onto the electoral register after an election was called, impacted the constitutional demand that representatives should be 'chosen by the people'.[67] The majority of French CJ, Gummow, Bell and Crennan JJ held that the provisions of the Act contravened the constitutional requirements. Justices Hayne, Heydon and Kiefel reached the opposite decision. Central to the decision was the opposition between two values: *tradition* and *universalism* (Figure 10.5). Those in the majority prioritised *universalism* and *self-direction* when opposed to *tradition* and *conformity*. In contrast, the minority prioritised *tradition* and *conformity*.

Values encompassed within the motivation of *tradition* in this context included the affirmation of the separation of powers, restraint and

---

[64] *Rowe* (2010) 243 CLR 1.
[65] Robert French, 'Judicial Activists Mythical Monsters?' (Speech, Constitutional Law Conference, 2018); Archibald Cox, 'The Role of the Supreme Court: Judicial Activism or Self-Restrain' (1987) 47 *Maryland Law Review* 118; Justice Dyson Heydon, 'Judicial Activism and the Death of the Rule of Law' (2003) 47 *Quadrant* 9.
[66] Anne Twomey (2012) 'Rowe v Electoral Commissioner – Evolution or Creationism?' (2012) 31 *University of Queensland Law Journal* 181; James Allan 'The Three 'Rs' of Recent Australian Judicial Activism: Roach, Rowe and (O)'riginalism' (2012) 36 *Melbourne University Law Review* 743.
[67] *Electoral Referendum Amendment (Electoral Integrity and Other Measures) Act 2006* (Cth). Sections 7 and 24 of the *Constitution* require that both Houses of Commonwealth Parliament are 'chosen by the people'.

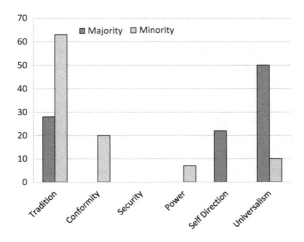

Figure 10.5 Value analysis of *Rowe v Electoral Commissioner*. The horizontal axis presents the value motivations expressed in the case. On the vertical axis, the values are expressed as a percentage of the total of number of value statements in the judgments supporting each position and thus the data is controlled for the number and length of judgments.

respect for parliamentary sovereignty. In contrast, *universalism* recognises the limits on this power for the benefit of society. The following paragraph from French CJ highlights these value oppositions:

> If a law subject to constitutional challenge is a law within the legislative competency of the Parliament that enacts it, the question whether it is a good law or a bad law is a matter of Parliament and, ultimately, the people to whom the members of Parliament are accountable. But where the Constitution limits the legislative power of a Parliament in any respect and where a question of the validity of a law is raised and has to be answered in order to determine a matter before the Court, then the Court must decide whether constitutional limits have been exceeded.[68]

Other facets of *universalism* were also expressed including protection of the vulnerable: 'So much can be accepted but the effect of the earlier cut-off upon people living in remote areas and itinerant and homeless people is to be considered as one of the practical consequences of the impugned provisions'.[69]

---

[68] *Rowe* (2010) 243 CLR 1, 14, 22.
[69] Ibid. 14 (French CJ).

Once again, *universalism* was a dominant value, and in this case was the value most frequently affirmed by French CJ, Gummow, Bell and Crennan JJ.

The minority also recognised the importance of protection of the vulnerable but distinguished its importance in this case, so did not prioritise it:

> History teaches that, in some countries, registration and voting systems have been devised and administered in ways that have systematically disadvantaged particular groups in the society. But the plaintiffs' complaint in the present case was not of that kind.[70]

Instead, the minority prioritised the importance of parliamentary sovereignty, a value encompassed within *tradition*:

> It would be wrong to take steps towards effectively entrenching it by requiring that legislation concerning elections ensure the maximum exercise of the franchise. It would be inconsistent with the intention expressed in the Constitution: that Parliament be free to legislate in this area from time to time.[71]

Conformity was also affirmed by the minority, which included the individual's responsibility to conform to obligations:

> It is they who disqualify, disenfranchise, exclude or disentitle themselves, not the legislature. The conduct of all these categories of people who fail to enrol, or, being enrolled, fail to vote, does not prevent the legislature being described as 'chosen by the people'.[72]

In addition to highlighting the value differentiation between the majority and minority positions, the case also highlights the multifaceted and complex nature of decision-making in the High Court, of which values are only one element. The decision in this case opposed values encompassed within *universalism* and conservation (*tradition and conformity*). Some Justices reached decisions which aligned with their value priorities in the other cases analysed. For example, Bell J affirmed *universalism*. It is notable, however, in this constitutional case that Kiefel J, who consistently affirmed values within *universalism* in the previous cases, affirmed values encompassed within conservatism. The value analysis of this case highlights the humanity of the decision-maker, the complexity of the decision, and the nuanced interaction between value prioritisation, the

---

[70] Ibid. 75 (Hayne J).
[71] Ibid. 131 (Kiefel J).
[72] Ibid. 96 (Heydon J).

legal context, and the individual approach to the judicial role which influences the final decision.

VI Value Diversity, Dissent and the Individual

Judicial dissent in a multi-member court is traditionally conceptualised as disagreement on legal issues. This chapter suggests that division also reflects value diversity and differences in value priorities. Drawing on content analysis techniques developed in the analysis of judgments of the UK Supreme Court, this chapter demonstrates that judgments supporting opposing outcomes in 'hard' cases, which divide judicial opinion in the High Court of Australia, reflect different patterns of value expression and prioritisation. This differential pattern of value expression was evident in a range of cases in a variety of areas of law. Even within this limited dataset, the judgments provided evidence of value diversity and affirmation of different value priorities. Adler suggests that the democratic legitimacy of the final courts of appeal is founded on a judiciary which reflects the incommensurable values of society and the value analysis provides evidence of these incommensurable values at the heart of dissent in the High Court.

The value analysis also provides an insight into the individuals on the High Court bench, their differences in value expression, and affirmation, and the influence individual value prioritisation may have on the final outcome. The expression of values is not without constraint, and this study highlights the influence of other factors, not least the legal issues at the centre of the case, on value expression. But even within this small study, there was consistency in the pattern of value expression by some judges. Research on the UK Supreme Court suggests that agreement in cases which divide judicial opinion is evidence of shared value priorities.[73] In the context of the High Court, Lynch and Williams have identified coalitions that arise in constitutional cases.[74] The value analysis in this chapter suggests that these coalitions may be associated with value agreement in cases which divide judicial opinion. Barmes and Malleson argue that the identity of the individual Justice should be

---

[73] Cahill-O'Callaghan, 'Winner of the SLS Annual Conference Best Paper Prize 2014: Reframing the Judicial Diversity Debate' (n 16).
[74] Andrew Lynch and George Williams, 'The High Court on Constitutional Law: The 2016 and French Court Statistics' (2017) 40(4) *University of New South Wales Law Journal* 1468.

understood within the collective and the analysis of values provides an insight into the individual in a multi-member court.[75] This study identified individuals on the judicial panel with different patterns of value expression and highlighted the influence of individual priorities on the final outcome. Indeed, in cases where a decision by a single Justice divides the court, individual value priorities may have a significant influence on the final outcome.

The presence of judges on a judicial panel who express opposing values and the publication of the dissent associated with this value diversity is an important aspect of transparency and legitimacy. It also serves as evidence of 'effective' decision-making. In 2003, Sunstein highlighted the importance of dissent in decision-making, arguing that conformity, unchecked by dissent, can produce harmful outcomes.[76] Drawing on a range of psychological studies Sunstein argued that 'effective' dissent holds a mirror to the majority, encourages debate, refines decisions, stimulates innovation and reduces bias in panel decision-making.[77] Indeed, Sunstein argued that dissent was of fundamental importance in judicial panels.[78] Value analysis of the judgments highlights the diversity of values affirmed by members the bench, but it does not demonstrate judges adopting polarised binary value positions, rather it presents the decision as a nuanced balancing of opposing values in which the outcome reflects the prioritisation of one or more values above others. Value diversity on the bench provides judges with the opportunity to reflect on their opposing positions and thus may play an important function in refining decision-making in the High Court. The study suggests that a diversity of perspectives and value priorities should be encouraged on the High Court bench, as important evidence of judicial difference but also to promote disagreement. It is disagreement, Sunstein suggests that disrupts conformity, and encourages discussion and debate, which should surely be at the heart of decision-making on the High Court.

---

[75] Barmes and Malleson (n 63).
[76] Cass R Sunstein, *Why Societies Need Dissent?* (Harvard University Press, 2003).
[77] Charles A O'Reilly, Kathryn Y Williams and Sigal Barsade 'Group Demography and Innovation: Does Diversity Help?' in Deborah H Gruenfeld (ed), *Research on Managing Groups and Teams* (JAI Press, 1998); Stefan Schulz-Hardt et al., 'Group Decision Making in Hidden Profile Situations: Dissent as a Facilitator for Decision Quality' (2006) 91(6) *Journal of Personality and Social Psychology* 1080; Charlan J Nemeth et al., 'Improving Decision Making by Means of Dissent' (2001) 31(1) *Journal of Applied Social Psychology* 48.
[78] Sunstein (n 76).

PART IV

Perceptions

11

Judges and the Media

MATTHEW GROVES

I Introduction

Constitutional law theory posits that the separation of each arm of government in liberal modern democracies is essential to the effective operation of different sources of powers. Courts require more than separation from other arms of government. They also require independence, so the exercise of judicial power can remain free of improper external influence. A different influence, which lies outside the boundaries of constitutional law, is the fourth estate – the media.[1] The media is vital to publicising the work of the courts, so much so that Jeremy Bentham famously proclaimed that 'Publicity is the very soul of justice'.[2] But publicity is not always favourable. For that reason, the relationship between courts and the media has long been uneasy. It can also be damaging. Media coverage of the courts and judges that is inaccurate or unfair can damage public confidence in the courts, more so when it takes the form of personal criticism of judges.[3] The potential impact of the media upon courts and judges is compounded by the one-sided nature of their relationship. The constitutional position of judges means they cannot easily return fire without imperiling their own neutrality. Judges who engage with the media risk comprising their independence and neutrality. In this sense, the fourth estate is not unlike the different arms of government. Courts and judges require the presence of the media, but also safe distance from the media, in order to function effectively. This chapter examines why that distance is necessary and does so with reference from the common law world, with particular

---

[1] The media was described as the 'fourth estate' by the US Supreme Court in *Richmond Newspapers Incorporated v Virginia* 448 US 555 (1980).
[2] Jeremy Bentham, *The Works of Jeremy Bentham* – John Bowring (ed) (Simpkin, Marshall, 1843) 316.
[3] See recounts of such attacks in AWB Bradley, 'Judicial Independence Under Attack' [2003] *Public Law* 397.

attention to Australia as the jurisdictional focus of this book, though the argument of the chapter is that these issues arise in all common law jurisdictions.

II The Kilmuir Rules and Their Decline

Many commentators who lament public attacks on judges forget that these have a long history. At the start of the twentieth century, for example, an English judge was criticised by a journalist as 'an impudent little man in horsehair, a microcosm of deceit and empty-headedness'. The journalist was held to have scandalised the court and fined the large sum of £100.[4] Such outrageous insults of judges may have been relatively rare across the common law world, but they did occur. Formal judicial responses to the media were infrequent during much of the early twentieth century. Courts kept their distance from the media; judges remained deliberately silent, even when faced with strong or unfair criticism.

That judicial attitude was encapsulated within the Commonwealth by the influential statement of Lord Kilmuir in 1955, when he refused an invitation from the BBC to participate in a series of radio broadcasts about significant English judges. The broadcasts were intended to educate the public about English legal history, but Lord Kilmuir recoiled at the prospect. He feared that any public comment by a senior judge, even for benign educational purposes, could only damage the courts. Lord Kilmuir thought the 'overriding consideration' for judges was to ensure they were 'insulated from the controversies of the day'.[5] Judges must understand 'that as a general rule it is undesirable for members of the judiciary to broadcast on the wireless or to appear on television'.[6] Lord Kilmuir did not suggest judges could or should never speak in public outside their official role. He instead strongly discouraged the practice because

> So long as a Judge keeps silent his reputation for wisdom and impartiality remains unassailable: but every utterance which he makes in public, except in the course of his official duties, must necessarily bring him within the focus of criticism.[7]

---

[4] *R v Gray (Howard Alexander)* [1900] 2 QB 36.
[5] Lord Kilmuir's letter is reproduced in AWB Bradley, 'Judges and the Media: The Kilmuir Rules' [1986] *Public Law* 384.
[6] Ibid., 385.
[7] Ibid. In the U.S. at that time, a narrower convention precluded judges speaking about pending cases: Frances Zemans, 'The Accountable Judge: Guardian of Judicial Independence' (1999) 72 *Southern California Law Review* 625, 636.

The Kilmuir rules were never formal or binding,[8] but they guided judicial conduct within Britain and most Commonwealth nations. Their effect was explained in pragmatic terms in 1972, when the Lord Chief Justice suggested that the 'best judge is the man who is least known to the readers of the *Daily Mail*'.[9] The rare instances when the rules were enforced provide an incomplete picture of their impact.[10] The rules also appear to have helped to foster a convention that politicians would mirror judicial reticence by declining to make public criticism of judges.[11]

The precise demise of Kilmuir rules is unclear but appears to have occurred during the 1990s. The rules were too informal to require formal repeal, but their cessation was confirmed in England and Wales in 2000, when the Lord Chief Justice issued a document entitled 'Media Guidance for the Judiciary'.[12] The document did not mention the Kilmuir rules, let alone explain their demise.[13] It provided judges and tribunal members with guidance on why and how they might deal with the media. In this time, courts and judges elsewhere recognised that many changes to media coverage and social expectations had overtaken the Kilmuir rules.[14] This shift was also reflected in the development of judicial codes

---

[8] Although some modern judges seem to regard the rules has having been binding. See, for instance, Lord Hodge, 'Upholding the Rule of Law: How We Preserve Judicial Independence in the United Kingdom' (Speech, Lincoln's Inn Denning Society, 7 November 2016) [33], <www.supremecourt.uk/docs/speech-161107.pdf>.

[9] Lord Pannick QC, 'An Amazing Amount Has Changed Over a Lifetime of Covering the Law' *The Times*, 7 February 2019, 53. Pannick attributed the statement to Lord Chief Justice Widgery in 1972, but it was also attributed to Lord Justice MacKinnon many years earlier.

[10] Instances where the rules were invoked against English judges, usually in the form of private admonishments by more senior judges, are recounted in Diana Woodhouse, *The Office of the Lord Chancellor* (Hart Publishing, 2001) 34.

[11] Sir Louis Blom Cooper suggested the Kilmuir rules were accompanied by a further convention, that judges were not publicly criticised by politicians, journalists or members of the public: Louis Blom Cooper, 'The Judiciary in an Era of Law Reform' (1966) 37 *Political Quarterly* 378.

[12] The current version, issued by the Courts and Tribunals Service in 2018, is available at <www.judiciary.gov.uk/announcements/new-media-guidance-issued-by-hm-courts-and-tribunals-service/> The key current policy on judicial dealings with the media, a pamphlet of hints, is not publicly available.

[13] A leading UK barrister attributed this to the appointment of Lord Mackay of Clashfern as Lord Chancellor in 1987, who was said to have decided the judiciary should adopt a 'more mature approach to the media': Lord Pannick QC, 'An Amazing Amount Has Changed Over a Lifetime of Covering the Law' *The Times*, 7 February 2019, 53.

[14] GL Davies in 'Judicial Reticence' (1998) 8 *Journal of Judicial Administration* 88.

of conduct, which provided guidance on when and why judges might deal with the media to disseminate information about the courts.[15] Those codes provided subtle imprimatur for judges to engage, perhaps sparingly, with the media.[16]

III The Decline of the First Law Officers as Judicial Defenders

As the Kilmuir rules declined, another constitutional norm also changed and greatly affected the inclination of judges to engage with the media. That was the increased reticence of first law officers, such as attorneys-general and the Lord Chancellor, to defend the judiciary. This change was explained by Australian Attorney-General Daryl Williams on two key grounds.[17] One was that the convention requiring the attorney to defend the courts and judges was not in fact supported by clear, established practice.[18] Williams also argued that the status of Australian attorneys-general, as elected politicians and members of cabinet, meant their office had 'become more exclusively political'.[19] The argument was effectively one that Australian attorneys-general had rightly chosen to side with closer political friends rather than more distant judicial relatives.[20] Many judges and legal commentators bristled at these claims but none doubted that Australian attorneys-general essentially abandoned their role as defender of the judiciary.[21]

The more complex British arrangements are difficult to summarise or compare to the Australian ones, though changes to the role of the Lord

---

[15] See, for instance, Canadian Judicial Council, *Ethical Principles for Judges* (1998) 11, which explained that the public might not always get a balanced view of the value of judicial independence, so judges should take advantages of 'appropriate opportunities' to better inform the public.

[16] An important predecessor to judicial codes of conduct were influential books by judges about judicial ethics and related issues. See, for instance, JO Wilson *A Book for Judges* (Canadian Judicial Council, 1980) and JB Thomas, *Judicial Ethics in Australia* (Butterworths, 1988).

[17] Daryl Williams, 'The Role of the Attorney-General' (2002) 13 *Public Law Review* 252.

[18] Ibid., 254–58. Analysis of political practice supported that claim: Paul Donegan, 'The Role of the Commonwealth Attorney-General in Appointing Judges to the High Court of Australia' (2003) 29 *Melbourne Journal of Politics* 40.

[19] Williams (n 17), 254.

[20] See further discussion of the context of the remarks in Enid Campbell and Matthew Groves, 'Attacks on Judges Under Parliamentary Privilege: A Sorry Australia Episode' [2002] *Public Law* 626.

[21] See, for instance, Ruth McColl, 'Reflections on the Role of the Attorney-General' (2002) 14 *Public Law Review* 20.

Chancellor provide a useful parallel. That office has also long been a strange blend of political, executive and other roles.[22] The Lord Chancellor was traditionally seen by many judges as their 'friend at court' in cabinet and responsible for 'defending and preserving the independence of the judiciary'.[23] The role was changed significantly by the *Constitutional Reform Act 2005* (UK), which affirmed that all ministers were responsible for maintaining 'the continued independence of the judiciary',[24] but made the Lord Chief Justice the head of the British judiciary and assigned that office with the responsibility 'to have regard to that independence'.[25] An important practical component of these changes was the appointment of non-lawyers as Lord Chancellor, one of whom was described by Sir Stephen Sedley as 'a political enforcer'. The consequence, Sedley explained, was that 'the rule of law was from now on, like everything else, going to be negotiable'.[26] That caution appears prescient in light of recent proposals that the Lord Chancellor take a more active and politically hued focus on functions, such as judicial appointments and carriage of legislation to reform the role of the courts.[27]

IV Changing Perceptions of Judges and Changing Cases before the Courts

The changing role of first law officers in defending the judiciary does not answer a key question: Why have judges come under renewed scrutiny and criticism from the media in recent decades? One reason is changing perception of judges. An English judge (writing extra-judicially) explained that transformation as follows:

> ... the High Court judge was, in the late 1980s, typically portrayed in some parts of the media as a 'portsoaked reactionary, still secretly resentful of the abolition of the birch and hostile to liberal influences of any

---

[22] Graham Gee, Robert Hazell, Kate Malleson and Patrick O'Brien, *The Politics of Judicial Independence in the UK's Changing Constitution* (Cambridge University Press, 2015) 32.
[23] Quotes taken respectively from Lord Hailsham, 'The Office of the Lord Chancellor and the Separation of Powers' (1989) 8 *Civil Justice Quarterly* 308, 314, 311.
[24] *Constitutional Reform Act 2005* (UK) s 3(1).
[25] *Constitutional Reform Act 2005* (UK) s 3(6).
[26] Sir Stephen Sedley, 'Beware Kite-Flyers' (2013) 35 *London Review of Books* 13. See also Patrick O'Brien, '"Enemies of the People": Judges, the Media and the Mythic Lord Chancellor' [2017] *Public Law (Special Issue)* 135, 136.
[27] Richard Ekins, *Protecting the Constitution – How and Why Parliament Should Limit Judicial Power* (Policy Exchange, 28 December 2019).

kind.' The same judge is now, in the same parts of the media, 'an unashamedly progressive member of the chattering classes, spiritually if not actually resident in Islington or Hampstead, out of touch with "ordinary people", and diligently engaged in frustrating the intention of Parliament with politically correct notions of human rights.[28]

The authors who recounted this speech noted that changing perceptions of judges have been mirrored by changes in the issues that come before the courts. In his personal account of the *Miller* case,[29] Lord Sales similarly suggested that the decline of political ideals such as ministerial responsibility meant the role of the courts as guardian of constitutional fundamentals had 'become more pronounced in the past 50 years, as non-legal forms of political custom and morality which previously filled that function broke down'.[30] The key factor in these changes in the UK is the advent of cases involving the *Human Rights Act 1998* (UK), which requires 'judgments of a more 'evaluative' kind, prompting complaints that judges are striking down policies of the democratically elected'.[31] Lord Dyson has noted human rights claims involve issues that members of the public 'can understand and upon which they have opinions which they express freely'.[32] The same is surely true in all other common law jurisdictions.[33] Another relevant issue is the growing public concern about the environment, which has seen more public interest groups seek relief in the courts in order to restrain high profile development or business decisions made by governments. Such cases, one of which is explained below, inevitably attract media criticism.

The sum total of such changes led the Chief Justice of Canada to suggest that her colleagues might think 'this is not the world we judges

---

[28] Shimon Shetreet and Sophie Turenne, *Judges on Trial: The Independence and Accountability of the English Judiciary* (2nd ed, Cambridge University Press, 2013). The quoted marks indicate the parts those authors draw from a speech of Sir Mark Potter J, the details of which are not provided.

[29] *R (on the application of Miller) v Secretary of State for Exiting the European Union* [2018] AC 68.

[30] Sir Philip Sales, 'Legalism in Constitutional Law: Judging in a Democracy' [2018] Public Law 687, 705. See also Gee, Hazell, Malleson and O'Brien (n 22).

[31] Sales (n 30), 705.

[32] Lord Dyson, 'Criticising Judges: Fair Game of or Off-Limits?" (3rd Annual Bailii Lecture, 27 November 2014) 18–19 <www.bailii.org/bailii/lecture/03.pdf>.

[33] While Australia remains an outlier because it lacks a bill of rights, it experiences similar issues in its unique tribunal system that allows administrative bodies to remake government decisions in areas such as migration, town planning and occupational licensing of professionals. These tribunals are generally required to reach the 'correct or preferable' decision on the facts of a case, and their decisions regularly attract media controversy.

thought we knew, comfortable and secure. What, we are driven to ask, is happening?'.[34] The simple answer is that this confluence of issues created a perfect storm for the judiciary. Politicians, the media and the public became more inclined to criticise judges,[35] just as the courts become more involved in contentious issues. It arguably also follows that the strident media commentary made about high profile cases such as *Miller* are simply examples of the wider populism of recent times.[36] Judges are caught in this crossfire.

V What Is a Judge to Do?

The growing willingness of politicians, journalists and members of the public to voice criticisms of the judiciary and the simultaneous decline of the Kilmuir rules led judges into new terrain. These shifts in convention theoretically leave judges with discretion to determine when and why they might speak publicly,[37] and the right to remain silent. That discretion flows from the individual freedom and independence of each judge, but Enid Campbell cautioned that one enduring limitation remains – the unique constitutional role that judges occupy. The exercise of judicial power can affect any citizen, or all of society, and the other arms of government. The wide reach of judicial power is an important reason why judges must be, and appear to be, impartial. That impartiality promotes public confidence in the courts, by ensuring that judges are not associated in a personal sense with the disputes they may be required to determine. On this view, the freedom of judges to speak, whether to respond to public criticisms or to air their views in public on almost any other matter is necessarily restrained.[38] Campbell saw this restraint as one consequence of the acceptance of judicial appointment.[39] She also drew a clear distinction between matters of political and other possible

---

[34] Beverley McLachlin, 'The Role of Judges in Commonwealth Society' (1994) 110 *Law Quarterly Review* 260, 261.
[35] See, for instance, MD Kirby, 'Attacks on Judges: A Universal Phenomenon' (1998) 72 *Australian Law Journal* 599.
[36] Alison Young, 'Populism and the UK Constitution' (2018) 71 *Current Legal Problems* 17.
[37] JB Thomas, *Judicial Ethics in Australia* (3rd ed, Lexis Nexis, 2009) 129. In theory, this discretion was always available but what arguably changed with the decline of the Kilmuir rules was the changing perception among judges about when and why they could speak in public.
[38] Enid Campbell, 'Judges' Freedom of Speech' (2002) 76 *Australian Law Journal* 499.
[39] See also United Kingdom Judges Council, *Guide to Judicial Conduct* (2020) 7.

controversy, which judges should studiously avoid, and matters related to the legal system and judiciary which were generally appropriate subjects for judges to speak about. In other words, judges can "talk shop" in public but should be cautious on other issues. The implication is that judges who choose to speak publicly outside a narrow range of issues become fair game for the media.

Lines are never easy to draw in the law and usually blur as they come into closer view. A useful example is the regular public discussion by judges of judicial appointments. This issue clearly falls within the topics identified by Campbell as relevant to the effective operation of the legal system and its judiciary, but it can easily stray into controversial territory even if judicial statements remain general in character. Lady Hale made a pointed entry into this debate in a decision about the effect of prenuptial agreements, which typically have a much greater impact upon women than men. Lady Hale mused that some might think the question was 'ill-suited to decision by a court consisting of eight men and one woman'.[40] Lord Sumption took direct issue with that assertion in a subsequent speech examining the British and European systems for judicial appointment.[41] He identified several reasons, albeit unconvincing, why far fewer women and members of minority groups were offered or accepted judicial appointments. Lady Hale politely skewered those claims in a later paper.[42] Calls for greater diversity in judicial appointments are, like similar calls made in any other area, likely to create controversy and attract media attention and criticism. Yet few would argue that public discussion and polite disagreement between judges about such an issue is not valuable. That value is not likely to depend on whether individual judicial entries into that debate attract media attention.

Outside the relatively narrow matters of 'court business', the decline of the Kilmuir rules and the willingness of first law officers to speak in defence of judges leave judges with an apparently wide freedom to speak as they wish. Justice Beatson has suggested this seeming freedom now available to judges has led them into 'a sort of Garden of Eden' with

---

[40] *Radmacher (formerly Granatino) v Granatino* [2011] 1 AC 534, 577 [137].

[41] Lord Sumption, 'Home Truths about Judicial Diversity' (Bar Council Law Reform Lecture, 15 November 2012) 19, <www.supremecourt.uk/docs/speech-121115-lord-sumption.pdf>.

[42] Lady Hale, 'Appointments to the Supreme Court' in Graham Gee and Erika Rackley (eds), *Debating Judicial Appointments in an Age of Diversity* (Routledge, 2017) 302.

many temptations.[43] Too much choice is apt to create confusion. The Chief Justice of New South Wales has suggested judges now sit in 'a catch-22'. He also confessed uncertainty whether maintaining silence would assist judges, but also whether 'talking to the media from time to time has improved the situation either'.[44] That uncertainty is consistent with a recent empirical study of Australian judges, who were found to generally favour providing greater information to prevent and correct misleading media coverage of the courts.[45] At the same time, however, most judges appeared to believe that information should not be provided by individual judges.

The Australian solution has been threefold. One part has been to engage the media in a range of ways, such as employing specialist media officers, issuing press releases when reasons for high profile cases are delivered, stream or televise a selection of hearings and conduct regular public tours of courts. The other important change is the inclusion of guidance in judicial codes of conduct, which explain why and how judges should deal with the media. Particular attention is given to commentary that judges might feel is 'unfair, inaccurate or ill-informed.' Judicial guidelines suggest that any response in these cases should be made by the head of the relevant court.[46] There are many advantages to this institutional approach. It provides institutional support for the relevant judge. The head of the relevant court can act as a circuit breaker of sorts, to pause and seek advice including whether any response should be made, or whether any response should come from court officials or the head judge. Such institutional practices suggest an understanding on the part of courts and judges that a level of direct engagement with the media is necessary, desirable and ultimately a matter for the court. A third part of the judicial response, which also has an institutional dimension, is the work of the Judicial Conference of Australia. The activities of that body include the regular issue of press releases that seek to correct or clarify unfair or inaccurate criticisms or courts and judges. The wide

---

[43] Sir Jack Beatson, 'The New Model Judiciary and the Other Two Branches of the State' [2015] *Judicial Review* 63, 65.
[44] TF Bathurst, 'Opening Address' (Speech given to the Community Awareness of the Judiciary Program, Sydney, Australia, 30 October 2014) 3 <www.supremecourt.justice.nsw.gov.au/Documents/bathurst_20141030.pdf>.
[45] Kathy Mack, Sharyn Roach Anleu and Jordan Tutton, 'The Judiciary and the Public: Judicial Perceptions' (2018) 39 *Adelaide Law Review* 1.
[46] Australian Institute of Judicial Administration, *Guide to Judicial Conduct* (3rd ed, 2017) 5.7.2.

membership of that body means it is well placed to speak about issues affecting many courts, or the judiciary as a whole, thus providing a response on behalf of the wider judiciary where a single court or Chief Justice may feel unable to do so.

Common law courts have largely not adopted some of the more radical solutions initiated elsewhere. A notable one is the 'press judge' system used by Dutch courts.[47] A press judge is essentially the point of contact between the media and a court. As the name suggests, this point of contact is a sitting judge. In theory, this role lies with the head of each relevant court, but it is usually delegated to a nominated judge. More recently, the role of press judges has evolved toward a national approach, so that judges with expertise in particular areas such as criminal or family law can speak on behalf of all judges of those areas. Press judges receive media training and are assisted by specialist media officers. The often demanding nature of the task means judges typically occupy the role only for a few years. That turnover does, however, disperse judicial awareness about dealing with the media.

The Dutch scheme has been instrumental to courts providing greater accommodations for the media, such as providing dedicated facilities for reporters. The work of press officers has also stimulated wider changes, including the development of guidelines for the broadcast of some hearings, regular meetings between court officials and the media, including a large conference between members of the judiciary and the media. The only substantial English language analysis of this system was ambivalent.[48] The author, Lieve Gies, accepted that press judges had greatly increased and improved judicial communications with the media and provided a useful means to manage difficult instances of media coverage about judges (such as plainly wrong news stories, or ones that made inappropriate personal criticisms of judges). But Gies also argued that press judges constituted a preemptive ploy by the Dutch judiciary, using the fig leaf of apparent openness to disguise judicial control of dealings with the media.

---

[47] Netherlands Council for the Judiciary, *The Judiciary and the Media in the Netherlands* <www.rechtspraak.nl/SiteCollectionDocuments/The-Judiciary-and-the-Media-in-the-Netherlands.pdf>.

[48] Lieve Gies, 'The Empire Strikes Back: Press Judges and Communication Advisers in Dutch Courts' (2005) 32 *Journal of Law and Society* 450. This study preceded the wider use of national press judges.

VI Three Examples of Judges in the Media

The principles governing judicial dealings with the media provide little real guidance on how those dealings can unfold and what dangers they can present to judges and courts. This section discusses three recent examples in which judges have somehow been the subject of media commentary. The commentary in two of these cases took the form of spleenful media criticism of judges and their decisions. Both cases illustrate that judges can be subject to hostile, even abusive, media treatment that seems little more than personal disagreement with those decisions. The first example is quite different. It involves a judge who was not subject to any personal criticism but instead felt compelled to answer perceived criticisms of his court. That well-intentioned judge suffered serious consequences after speaking with the media. These different examples suggest that judicial silence may be the best, or least unsatisfactory, response.

The judge in this first example was a magistrate who presided in rural New South Wales. Many of his cases were ones of domestic violence that involved Aboriginal defendants and victims. A national newspaper published a story about such cases that was informed by complaints from the Aboriginal Legal Services (ALS), about 'errant, idiosyncratic and overly harsh' sentences imposed by unnamed judges that 'cannot be justified under state sentencing law'.[49] The story was heavy on rhetoric but light on detail. The magistrate wrote to the newspaper, complaining how the story simplified complex social problems of rural areas.[50] The letter was not published but the journalist who wrote the story contacted the magistrate. During friendly discussions, the journalist complained about the difficulty in gaining information from the court. The magistrate attributed this to instructions that judges not have direct personal contact with journalists. As the two become more familiar, the magistrate became more frank. He complained about the 'campaign' of the ALS and its many dubious tactics. Those remarks were selectively quoted in two subsequent articles, which said the ALS had 'declared war' on the magistrates of New South Wales.[51]

---

[49] Natasha Robinson, 'Courts "harsher" on Aboriginal Driving Offences' *The Australian*, 19 October 2012, 29.
[50] *Gaudie v Local Court of New South Wales* [2013] NSWSC 1425, [43].
[51] Natasha Robinson, 'Kids Prefer Jail to Abuse at Home, Says Magistrate' *The Australian*, 8 January 2013, 1; Natasha Robinson, 'Magistrate Attacks ALS over Rash of Not Guilty Pleas' *The Australian*, 18 January 2013, 25.

When the ALS later represented an Aboriginal defendant facing charges involving the issues the magistrate was quoted on, it sought his recusal for apprehended bias. The claim succeeded because the Supreme Court accepted that the magistrate had become 'a strong public advocate in the media, commenting on a wide range of issues extending beyond the published articles'.[52] The Supreme Court held that no apprehension of bias would have arisen if the magistrate had confined himself to the general comments about domestic violence, as such remarks were often made during sentencing and included in judicial bench books.[53] The Court suggested the magistrate should have cast aside his understandable displeasure at the initial story and adhered to official guidelines for judges aggrieved at inaccurate media accounts of their work.[54]

The second example is of the more common variety. A judge did his job. He delivered a carefully reasoned decision and was vilified in the media for doing so. The case was *Gloucester Resources Ltd v Minister for Planning (Gloucester Resources)*,[55] decided by the Chief Justice of the New South Wales Land and Environment Court (LEC) in early 2019. Preston CJ upheld an official refusal of approval to develop a large coal mine in rural Australia, holding that the proposal sought to establish a coal mine 'in the wrong place at the wrong time'.[56] This conclusion took account of many factors, including the impact of the mine on traditional owners of the land, its potential contribution to both the local economy and to global warming, and issues of public interest as required by the governing statute and relevant precedent. Preston CJ's lengthy analysis of these issues led him to the unremarkable point that the impact major resource developments may have on the environment and global warming was a relevant issue to consider in assessments of public interest criterion. On any measure, the more than 200-page decision was a careful analysis of those matters; but subsequent media attention focused almost entirely on the weight Preston CJ gave to the contribution the mine would make to global warming.

That focus ignored important aspects of the case. One was that, unlike many landmark environmental cases, the challenge was brought by a

---

[52] *Gaudie v Local Court of New South Wales* [2013] NSWSC 1425, [211].
[53] Ibid., [182]-[183].
[54] Ibid., [178], [211].
[55] [2019] NSWLEC 7.
[56] [2019] NSWLEC 7, [662].

developer rather than an environmental protection group.[57] The case could, and arguably should, have therefore been characterised as one pursued by corporate rather than environmental zealots. A separate but logically related point was that the development application was initially refused by a government agency, which somehow was also spared negative publicity. The fact that Preston CJ had simply upheld that refusal was lost in the media glare. The subsequent decision of the company to not appeal the decision also received little attention, particularly from those media outlets that had vigorously attacked Preston CJ and his decision.[58]

A key attack on Preston CJ was that he had fired the latest salvo of 'green lawfare'.[59] The terminology of lawfare began as a criticism of those who used domestic legal remedies, such as human rights claims, against governments and their armed forces. This lawfare is argued to constitute a tactical means of impeding military action, by choking military forces with litigation. Similar criticisms have been made in Australia, particularly by politicians and conservative commentators about legal proceedings by environmental bodies,[60] even though empirical analysis has shown the claims are baseless.[61] Preston CJ was said in one report to have 'contaminated' the legal system with his allegiance to such dangerous rhetoric, which that particular commentator equated with the dictatorial rule of Hugo Chavez in Venezuela.[62] Another report hinted that the judge was biased because he had worked in an environmental body more than 30 years earlier and failed to mention this.[63]

As the final example is the best trodden, it is the one I will deal with most briefly. This is the decision of the English Divisional Court in the *Miller* case,[64] in which a three-member court held that legislation was

---

[57] A public interest environmental group joined the action but only months after its commencement: *Gloucester Resources* [2019] NSWLEC 7, [23]-[24].
[58] Peter Hannam, 'Decision to Block Coal Mine Will Stand' *Sydney Morning Herald*, 8 May 2019 12.
[59] See, for instance, Jack Houghton, 'Eco Lawfare' *Daily Telegraph*, 12 February 2019 1. An editorial used the same language: Editorial, 'Green Lawfare Decision Will Deter Global Capital' *The Australian*, 11 February 2019 11.
[60] See, for instance, George Brandis, '"Green Lawfare" and Standing: The View from Within Government' (2017) 90 *Australian Institute of Administrative Law Forum* 12.
[61] Chris McGrath, 'Myths Drive Australian Government Attack on Standing and Environmental "Lawfare"' (2016) 33 *Environment and Planning Law Journal* 3.
[62] Nick Cater, 'Greens Take Their Cues from Chavez's Calamitous Follies' *The Australian*, 1 April 2019, 12.
[63] Jack Houghton, 'Mine Judge's Green Links' *Daily Telegraph*, 12 February 2019, 4.
[64] *R (on the application of Miller) v Secretary of State for Exiting the European Union* [2017] 1 All ER 158.

required to authorise notice of the intention of the UK to leave the EU. Although that case was later upheld by the Supreme Court, particular media outrage was directed to this lower court decision. Two major English papers attacked the judges in front page stories. One used a large headline to declare the judges, whose photos were reproduced, 'Enemies of the People'.[65] That story complained that one judge was 'an openly gay ex-Olympic fencer', another had founded a European law group, while the third had billed taxpayers 'millions' as a barrister. In a story titled 'The Judges versus the people', the other described the decision as 'the day democracy died'.[66] The tone of this and other tabloid media coverage was vituperative and amplified in the eyes of many when a senior government minister described the decision as 'an attempt to frustrate the will of the British people and it is unacceptable'.[67] Many judges and lawyers thought that the response of the Lord Chancellor was slow, tepid and unhelpful.

When one of the judges, Sir Philip Sales (now Lord Sales of the Supreme Court) recounted his perspective, he preferred to 'pass over the decidedly inadequate' responses of the Lord Chancellor and Secretary of State for the Home Department and voice concern for the 'judicial system as a whole'.[68] Sales explained that he 'felt unusually exposed when moving around London on foot and public transport' but that a real sense of threat at a personal level arose when members of the police anti-terrorism unit visited his home to conduct a security assessment.[69] He also thought that matters appeared to cool when the case moved to the Supreme Court because the 11 members of that court 'offered a more diffuse target. The press caravan had moved on'.[70] One of the Supreme Court judges to whom the caravan had progressed was Lady Hale, who noted that the press coverage became a little less personalised though it listed the supposed European sympathies of several judges. She also suggested the newspaper that labelled lower courts judges as enemies was 'very clever' when it similarly labelled the dissenting members of the Supreme Court as 'champions of the people'.[71]

---

[65] *Daily Mail*, 4 November 2016.
[66] *Daily Telegraph*, 4 November 2016.
[67] Hon Savid Javid MP, *Question Time*, BBC 1, 3 November 2016.
[68] Sir Philip Sales, 'Legalism in Constitutional Law: Judging in a Democracy' [2018] *Public Law* 687, 688.
[69] Ibid., 689.
[70] Ibid.
[71] Lady Hale, 'Moral Courage in the Law' (The Worcester Lecture 2019, 21 February 2019) 5. Available at <www.supremecourt.uk/docs/speech-190221.pdf>.

An obvious lesson from these examples may be that those judges who seek out the media, such as the magistrate, expose themselves to great risk. That is because interviews are the natural terrain of journalists. When judges step onto that terrain, they cannot control what happens. The selected way in which the magistrate was quoted is also hardly a ground for criticism. After all, judges readily consent to law reports of their decisions that are headed by a summary headnote. The media is surely entitled to devise its own equivalent for its different readers. Was the studied silence of Preston CJ more appropriate? It allowed the press attention to fade away, but the hysterical and wrongful criticisms of the judge might linger in the minds of the public. Sir Philip Sales was publicly silent about his experience for many months and even then he spoke about the media rather than to it. These last two incidents reveal a single common truth. A response from the judge, his colleagues or the relevant court would only have amplified and extended the bitter media comment. Turning the other cheek seems the least damaging of all possible responses.

VII Judges Criticising Courts and Other Judges in the Media

The principles and examples discussed so far involve commentary and criticisms of judges that originate from the media itself. Judges and courts are rarely criticised by their own, but there are occasional exceptions. When those criticisms are ventilated in the media, they can be very damaging to the standing and morale of the judiciary. Such criticisms have a greater impact because the remarks of judges are associated with the prestige of their office, plus the further assumption in the public mind that a judge may speak with 'inside knowledge'. This section examines a case where criticisms were made by a retired judge. Retired judges occupy a curious position. They are largely free from the professional restraints of judicial office, yet in the eyes of the public they may carry the same prestige and authority as sitting judges.[72] The nebulous position of

---

[72] A danger anticipated in the Australasian Institute of Judicial Administration, *Guide to Judicial Conduct* (3rd ed, 2017) 5.12. Most codes of judicial conduct do not provide seek to regulate or guide former judges in any detailed manner. See Gabrielle Appleby and Alysia Blackham, 'The Growing Imperative to Reform Ethical Regulation of Former Judges' (2018) 67 *International and Comparative Law Quarterly* 505. The current Canadian guidelines do not regulate former judges, but draft revisions to them now include such regulation after a political scandal in which the government of the day sought legal advice from more than one former Justice of the Supreme Court of Canada:

retired judges enables them to speak on behalf of courts with a directness their former colleagues typically cannot use.[73] This possibility can valuably inform public discussion of the judiciary and provide occasional support for judges besieged by the media. One judge noted the two-edged nature of that sword when he conceded that 'if serving judicial officers on occasions appreciate retired judges coming to our defence, we can hardly complain if we are also kicked by retired judges'.[74] However, this possibility sits uneasily with the *Bologna Milano Global Code of Judicial Ethics 2015*.[75] Clause 9.6.1 of that code states judges should not 'act in such a way as to create the impression that he or she is speaking with judicial authority.' It is this very authority sitting judges hope retired colleagues can marshal when defending the judiciary.

A vigorous kicking was recently delivered by Dyson Heydon QC, who had been a member of the High Court of Australia and before that was a member of the New South Wales Court of Appeal. Heydon was no stranger to media attention, having courted public controversy on previous occasions. The most notorious was a speech given not long before his appointment to the High Court, where he decried judicial activism.[76] Heydon has repeatedly catalogued the limitations of the methods of other judges,[77] but this speech gained enormous media attention because it was characterised as an informal application for appointment to the High Court. That media attention was ironic given that the paper lamented

see further [Canada] Office of the Conflicts of Interest and Ethics Commissioner, *Trudeau II Report* (2019); Canadian Judicial Council, *Draft Ethical Principles for Judges* (2019) 5.E.1-5.E.5, <https://cjc-ccm.ca/sites/default/files/documents/2019/EPJ%20-%20PDJ%202019-11-20.pdf>.

[73] This is especially so for judges at the point of retirement, who carry the knowledge and current authority of judicial office but may feel less constrained by their impending retirement. An astonishing example occurred in Australia when a Queensland Supreme Court Justice about to retire made an extraordinary attack on his Chief Justice. See Rebecca Ananian-Walsh, Gabrielle Appleby and Andrew Lynch, *The Tim Carmody Affair: Australia's Greatest Judicial Crisis* (New South Publishing, 2016) ch 4.

[74] Peter Applegarth, 'Coverage and Criticism of the Courts' (Paper, Judicial Conference of Australia Colloquium, Darwin, 8 June 2019) 8.

[75] Approved at the International Conference for Judicial Independence, June 2015 <www.icj.org/wp-content/uploads/2016/02/Bologna-and-Milan-Global-Code-of-Judicial-Ethics.pdf>.

[76] Dyson Heydon, 'Judicial Activism and the Death of the Rule of Law' (2003) 23 *Australian Bar Review* 110.

[77] See, for instance, Dyson Heydon, 'Threat to Judicial Independence: The Enemy Within' (2013) 129 *Law Quarterly Review* 205.

(unnamed) ambitious judges who fell prey to the temptation of seeing 'the judicial name in the newspapers'.[78]

After retiring, Heydon delivered a speech with scathing criticism of delay in select Australian courts. It included disturbing examples, such as one decision that was reserved for 700 days. The ad hoc examples Heydon used did not explain why his most withering criticism was directed at the Federal Court of Australia, though his concluding salvo seemed an indictment of Australian courts in general. Heydon complained that slow Australian judges just try to avoid corruption by a torpid shared culture of slackness, languor and drift and he suggested that they must become more diligent in their work.[79] In other words, judges had to do their job properly. The publication of the speech in a national newspaper left no doubt that one of its goals was to attract publicity. And so it did. Much of the subsequent media attention either endorsed Heydon's central criticisms about the extreme delay of some judgements,[80] or sympathised with judges for their heavy workload.[81]

A companion piece of sorts, clearly inspired by Heydon's speech, was published in another national newspaper. That piece was described as part of a 'study' of 69 past and present judges of the Federal Court of Australia, who were listed according to the speed of delivering judgment. The study contained no criteria for the quality of the judgment, such as whether cases were overturned upon appeal, or the complexity of their issues. The study did, however, pass comment on several judges. Several were described as 'efficient' and one said to be 'well regarded, but no Speedy Gonzalez'.[82] One, later elevated to the High Court, was described as a 'dynamo'.[83] Another who had also been elevated to the High Court was said to have 'stunned observers with the speed of his work' upon appointment to the Federal Court, though the article bemoaned the judge as 'notoriously verbose, and nothing has changed since he joined the High Court . . .'.[84]

---

[78] Heydon (n 76), 118.
[79] Dyson Heydon, 'Courts in the Crosshairs' *The Australian*, 29 September 2018 17.
[80] Editorial, 'A Fair Judgment of Slow Judges' *The Australian*, 1 October 2018, 13; Nicola Berkovic, 'Judges Leaving Families Hanging' *The Australian*, 15 November 2018, 3.
[81] Michael Pelly, 'Judges Plead for "Unreasonable" Workloads to End' *Australian Financial Review*, 12 October 2018, 31.
[82] Michael Pelly, 'Heydon Was Right: 12 Months Is Too Long for a Judgment' *Australian Financial Review*, 26 October 2018, 33.
[83] Ibid.
[84] Ibid. The reference to the gender of the judge removed any doubt about his identity and, by a process of elimination, enabled identification of the judge mentioned in the previous sentence.

This news story astutely noted that Heydon had long since retired but 'was still a former judge. The judiciary knew people would listen and quote him back'.[85] That prediction was borne out by a speech by Chief Justice Allsop of the Federal Court, which took strong issue with Heydon's key points, even though neither Heydon nor his speech were mentioned by name. That response instead focused on 'the broad body of generalisations taken from a narrow group of metrics' by Heydon.[86] That response also noted the limited value of statistical analysis of judicial work, obvious flaws in Heydon's comparisons of Australian and English courts, the different forms of accountability for judges and courts, the unique constitutional and social position of judges and why such considerations meant notions of efficiency or productivity could not be easily transposed to courts.[87]

The response of the Chief Justice was arguably more notable for the matters it did not raise, though that reticence was understandable. Judicial productivity as measured by delivering judgments quickly has occupied the Federal Court in a series of appeals against the rulings of a lower court judge. That judge has become renowned for delivering quick oral judgments, particularly in asylum cases, to great public controversy.[88] He has also been overturned on many occasions by the Federal Court, in a series of decisions that have expressed grave concern about the judge's failure to comply with elementary requirement of fairness.[89] In cases involving appeals from a different judge of that lower court, the Federal Court overturned decisions affected by egregious unfairness.[90]

---

[85] Ibid.
[86] James Allsop, 'Courts as (Living) Institutions and Workplaces' (2019) 93 *Australian Law Journal* 375, 375.
[87] Ibid., 378, 382.
[88] See, for instance, Nicola Berkovic, 'Judge has 47 Rulings Reversed in 3 Years' *The Australian* 6 March 2018, 7; Nicola Berkovic, 'Judge Mentored After Rulings Rejected' *The Australian* 3 September 2019, 7; Helen Davidson, 'Snap Judgment: Why Sandy Street's Record on Asylum Cases Stands Out' *Guardian (Australia)* 22 September 2019. Heydon did not mention this issue.
[89] The scale of the problem is deftly hinted at in *CIT17 v Minister for Immigration and Border Protection* (2018) 265 FCR 572, 573. That authorised report, which would have been approved by the presiding judges, includes a lengthy preliminary note listing many of the decisions of the lower court judge reversed on similar grounds. No such list has ever been included in an Australian law report. It is difficult to interpret it as anything other than exasperation on the part of the Federal Court.
[90] *Jorgensen v Fair Work Ombudsman* (2019) 271 FCR 461; *Gambaro v Mobycom Mobile Pty Ltd* (2019) 271 FCR 530. These two cases have now been reported in their authorized report series. The amendments reflect those new references.

The extent to which the Chief Justice could contradict Heydon with specific examples from the Federal Court showing how efficiency (in the form of speed) has caused grave injustice was clearly limited. How could Allsop CJ engage this problem without endangering his ability to resolve that same issue in the future? Other issues limited the ability of the Chief Justice to engage with Heydon's criticisms, particularly in the media. One was the difference in their status. Chief Justice Allsop is a serving judge. Heydon is a retired one and therefore not subject to the professional rules and norms that restrain his judicial critics, such as the rule that judges should not make public statements which are controversial and should adopt a cautious approach in any contribution they make to public discussion of the legal system.[91] Another restraint is the widely observed norm, discouraging superior court judges from engaging in needless or insensitive comments about lower court judges.[92]

The different audience of each paper was also important. Chief Justice Allsop delivered the type of speech a judicial audience would expect. It was thoughtful, learned and moderately expressed. To an outside observer it would have been utterly boring, which is why it attracted no media attention. Heydon's after-dinner speech, by contrast, was filled with cutting jibes and quotes that were sufficiently entertaining to distract readers from its threadbare empirical foundation. Heydon did not simply outgun the Chief Justice with a far more media friendly speech; he seemed to intuitively understand the greater public appeal of a superficial but flashy rhetorical approach.

If Heydon had made his provocative attack on the Federal Court while sitting as a member of the High Court, he might have been required to recuse himself from appeals from the Federal Court.[93] He was therefore able to criticise other judges, using his knowledge and experience as

---

[91] Australasian Institute of Judicial Administration, *Guide to Judicial Conduct* (3rd ed, 2017) 5.7–5.12. The equivalent guidelines for retired judges are far more limited: 7.1–7.6. The British equivalent advises retired judges to 'exercise caution' and be mindful of *all* principles governing serving judges: United Kingdom Judges Council, *Guide to Judicial Conduct* (2020) 4.

[92] Keith Mason, 'Throwing Stones: Cost/Benefit Analysis of Judges Being Offensive to Each Other' (2008) 82 *Australian Law Journal* 260.

[93] Questions of bias in the High Court are in theory a matter for each individual judge, though past practice suggests High Court judges sometimes consult their colleagues. While there is no right of appeal over such decisions, they could be overturned by the Full Court on the grounds of unfairness: Enid Campbell, 'Review of Decisions on a Judge's Qualification to Sit' (1999) 15 *Queensland University of Technology Law Journal* 1, 6–7.

judge, without the consequences that a sitting judicial officer would have to face. This situation arises from the curious position of retired judges. Power without restraint is something judges spend much of their judicial careers seeking to prevent, but it is the very thing they may hold in retirement. Heydon could rightly say that his remarks were in no way intended to provoke subsequent media coverage of the courts, in which judges were compared to cartoon characters, or mocked as verbose, but could someone so experienced in public life really be surprised this happened?

One solution may be greater ethical regulation of former judges. Appleby and Blackham called for that step, arguing that the conduct of former judges can reflect adversely on the judiciary and thus lessen public confidence in the courts.[94] Those authors were mindful of the adverse possible impact of speeches, such as those given by Heydon, but did not suggest that the freedom of former judges to speak publicly should be curtailed. There are good reasons why it should not be. Restrictions could damage public confidence in the judiciary because such rules, even if expressed in a gentle and nonbinding form, could invite the public to wonder why retired judges were muzzled. There are powerful reasons why retired judges should face no such restraints. The freedom to speak with the media, whether directly by giving interviews or indirectly by delivering papers likely to attract media interest, is a personal one for each judge to exercise. It is also a reflection of the independence of every judge. The freedom is arguably increased when judges retire because the concerns arising from judicial life, such as possible recusal, cease. No one would complain if retired judges waxed lyrical about their former work, so why should they not be able to say unfavourable things?

The criticisms made by Heydon must now be viewed in light of the grave complaints and findings of sexual harassment made against him, which are outlined in Chapter 1. The full implications of these shocking events are hard to predict.[95] Prime Minister John Howard, who oversaw Heydon's elevation to the High Court, made clear he 'stood by' that

---

[94] Appleby and Blackham (n 72).
[95] One respected commentator suggested the events 'make the case for a federal judicial commission unanswerable': François Kunc, 'Sexual Harassment and the Judiciary' (2020) 94 *Australian Law Journal* 575, 576. The federal attorney-general has indicated a willingness to consider such a reform: Phillip Coorey, 'High Court Moved on Heydon after Receiving Legal Letter' *Australian Financial Review*, 4 August 2020.

decision because 'Heydon was an excellent Judge of the High Court of Australia'.[96] Such astounding bravado cannot disguise the fact that Heydon's gravitas as a public commentator has evaporated.[97] There are many implications of this tale for the wider topics of judges and the media. It confirms the value of media scrutiny of the courts. The intense media attention has sharpened focus on sexual harassment in Australia's legal profession. No court or judge has questioned the remedial value of that attention, or the pivotal role of journalists in exposing these events. Heydon's response to the claims against him also showed an acute awareness of the impact of appearances in the media. His sole public response was a short statement, issued through his lawyers, which denied the allegations and took issue with the format of the High Court's investigation.[98] Heydon's wise avoidance of the media suggests that his prior cultivation of media attention may have been equally well planned. But what effect does Heydon's decline as a public critic of the courts have on the many criticisms he had made? Their effect cannot be so easily erased from the public mind.

VIII Social Media and the Courts

This chapter has focused on what can be called the 'traditional media' – newspaper, radio and television reports. The challenges presented by digital and social media ('modern media') are so great that they cannot be fully explored, though some key points can be usefully made.[99] One is the entirely different speed of modern media. Opinions can be written and made public in mere seconds. The slower pace of traditional media typically provided many chances for pause, review and reconsideration. Those cautions are absent in modern media. Modern media also removes barriers because it allows direct contact between judges and the public. Perhaps most importantly, judges are direct participants in modern

---

[96] Jacqueline Maley, Rob Harris and Kate McClymont, 'Howard Stands by Heydon as Questions Mount Over Knowledge of Alleged Harassment' *Sydney Morning Herald*, 23 June 2020.

[97] Many years earlier, Heydon himself proclaimed that probity was an 'essential judicial virtue': Heydon (n 76), 118.

[98] That tactic drew a blistering response from one retired conservative politician: Pru Goward, 'Mr Heydon, the High Court's Judgment is a Moral One' *Sydney Morning Herald*, 25 June 2020.

[99] The key issues are explained in Alysia Blackham and George Williams, 'Social Media and Court Communication' [2015] *Public Law* 403.

media. Judges use Facebook, Twitter and Instagram to read and post content, so they participate in modern media in ways they have not in traditional media.[100] An otherwise unremarkable French hearing illustrates the dangers that unprepared judges face. Two French judges who had become distracted and bored began to pass their time by tweeting back and forth. They forgot that their Twitter feeds were public, so what they thought was a private chat was quite the opposite. One messaged the other to ask a 'legal question' which was 'if any exasperated assessor/magistrate strangles his chief justice during a hearing, how much would that be worth'. Another tweet quipped, 'I haven't been listening to anything being said for the past two hours'.[101] The subsequent scandal was a striking lesson in 'going viral'.

A more considered approach to judicial use of social media occurred when the Florida Supreme Court held that a judge who 'friends' people on Facebook does not create a relationship or connection that necessarily impedes the public perception of the judge's neutrality.[102] The Supreme Court held that Facebook friendship between a judge and someone aligned with a case before the judge, did not, of itself warrant disqualification. The Florida decision was notable on several counts. It reflects a growing trend of American superior court decisions which suggest 'it's fine for judges to be on social media, but proceed with caution'.[103] The need for caution was obvious in Florida because the Supreme Court decision effectively overruled contrary advisory opinions issued by the State's Judicial Ethics Advisory Committee.[104] Those opinions were themselves surprising given that Florida's court system encouraged its judges to use social media to engage and inform people and 'increase

---

[100] Such communications are arguably novel in form only, as their substance retains the traditional mode of judges speaking *at* rather than *with* the public: Andrew Henderson, 'The High Court and the Cocktail Party from Hell: Can Social Media Improve Community Engagement with the Courts?' in Tania Sourdin (ed), *The Responsive Judge: International Perspectives* (Springer, 2018).

[101] Karen Eltis, Does Avoiding Judicial Isolation Outweigh the Risks Related to "Professional Death By Facebook"?' (2014) 3 *Laws* 636, 643.

[102] *Law Offices of Herssein & Herssein, PA v United Services Automobile Association* 271 So 3d 889 (2018).

[103] John G Browning, 'Why Can't We Be Friends? Judges' Use of Social Media' (2014) 68 *University of Miami Law Review* 487, 510.

[104] Those opinions are analysed in Carolina Del Campo, 'To Friend or to Unfriend: It's Time to Update the Status on What It Means to Be Facebook Friends' (2019) 32 *St Thomas Law Review* 53.

public trust and confidence in the judiciary....'.[105] The Supreme Court decision was notable for the narrow guidance it provided, namely that Facebook friendship *alone* would not *normally* provide a basis for recusal. That very qualified guidance clearly anticipates lower courts will further explore and refine issues, using the incremental method of the common law.

The superficial distinction between these two decisions is the contrast of a clumsy accident in court and the considered step of a superior to provide guidance to judges on a limited but important issue. Each nonetheless reveals judicial confusion about new forms of media. The French instance highlights the immediate and open nature of social media, which enables it to be seen instantly by others. The Supreme Court of Florida decision reflects an acceptance that social media use by judges is inevitable and requires guidance from superior courts, though the narrow and heavily qualified guidance provided suggests that courts will tread warily. Different courts have provided similar guidance in America,[106] and elsewhere.[107] The digital age and social media are still in their infancy, so the questions of when and how ethical codes and other principles governing modern media will move from adaptations drawn from the traditional media to instruments that are entirely creatures of the age of modern media is not yet clear.

IX Concluding Observations

At first glance, the different tales recounted in this chapter might suggest that the media present nothing but danger for courts and judges. That conclusion ignores several important points. One is that mistakes often provide useful learning experiences, or at least cautionary tales. Judges are no exception and one can fairly assume that the judges whose

---

[105] This quote is taken from the social media home page of Florida's court system, which lists over 100 links to different court social media sites: <www.flcourts.org/Resources-Services/Education-Outreach/Social-Media>.

[106] The US National Centre for State Courts guidance on social media for judges includes court codes, rules, advisory opinion and informative accounts of disciplinary decisions involving judges and social media. See <www.ncsc.org/cje>. The US Federal Courts Service has published an informative social media resource kit, *Developing Guidelines on Use of Social Media by Judicial Employees* <www.uscourts.gov/sites/default/files/social medialayout_0.pdf>.

[107] International examples are collected in the Global Judicial Integrity Network, *Discussion Guide: The Use of Social Media by Judges* (2019) <www.unodc.org/res/ji/import/policy_papers/social_media_discussion_guide/discussion_guide_social_media.pdf>.

experiences were analysed in this chapter learned a salutary lesson. The same is almost certainly true for the colleagues of those judges.[108] The unhappy nature of these judicial experiences invites consideration of the alternatives. Would it be better if judges received filtered (preferential or uncritical) media coverage? Would that enhance confidence in the courts, or strengthen the rule of law? The answer to those questions is obvious when one considers the countries in which independent, critical media coverage of courts and judges does not occur. As recalled of Apartheid South Africa by the eminent Justice Albie Sachs, the rule of law does not prosper in such countries.[109]

---

[108] See, for instance, the speech of the President of the Judicial Conference of Australia, examining the lessons judges could draw from *Gaudie* and other cases: Robert Beech-Jones, 'The Dogs Bark but the Caravan Moves On: Extra Judicial Responses to Criticism' (Speech, South Australian Magistrates Conference, 8 May 2017) <www.jca.asn.au/wp-content/uploads/2017/07/P83_02_02-Extra-Judicial-Responses-to-Criticism-for-publication.pdf>.

[109] *R v Mambolo* 2001 (3) SA 409, [77] (Sachs J).

12

The Good Judge in Australian Popular Television Culture

PENNY CROFTS

I Introduction

Legal themes dominate popular culture,[1] explicitly in the form of syndicated reality courts, true crime, lawyer, police and detective shows and implicitly through the use of legal structures to 'judge' contestants in reality television show competitions.[2] Despite the dominance of legal themes in popular culture, judges do not always make an appearance, and when they do, tend to be secondary and/or caricatures. Despite (or even because of) their relative absence and peripheral nature in popular culture, the portrayal of judges gives insight into broader public assumptions and values about the relationship of judges to the law and justice. This chapter analyses the portrayal of the judiciary through the prism of Australian popular culture and is part of a broader legal cultural studies project examining popular culture for how it reflects and expresses assumptions, values and wishes for and about the legal system.[3]

---

[1] There is a great deal of academic literature analysing the precise definition of 'popular culture'. For the purposes of analysis, this chapter adopts a conventional definition of popular culture as any product that is commercially made for the consumption of ordinary people: Michael Asimov and Shannon Mader, *Law and Popular Culture* (Peter Lang Publishing, 2004); Kimberlianne Podlas, 'The Tales Television Tells: Understanding the Nomos Through Television' (2006) 13 *Texas Wesleyan Law Review* 31; David M Spitz, 'Heroes of Villains? Moral Struggles vs Ethical Dilemmas: An Examination of Dramatic Portrayals of Lawyers and the Legal Profession in Popular Culture' (2000) 24 *Nova Law Review* 725.
[2] Naomi Mezey and Mark Niles, 'Screening the Law: Ideology and Law in American Popular Culture' (2005) 28 *Columbia Journal of Law and the Arts* 91.
[3] Judge Richard A Posner, *Law and Literature: A Misunderstood Relation* (Harvard University Press, 1988); Richard K Sherwin, *When Law Goes Pop: The Vanishing Line between Law and Popular Culture* (University of Chicago Press, 2000); Richard Sherwin, 'Nomos and Cinema' (2001) 48 *University of California Law Review* 1519; Richard K Sherwin, 'Law/Media/Culture: Legal Meaning in the Age of Images' (1999) 43 *New York Law School Law Review* 653.

This chapter analyses two key themes in the *nomos* of the judiciary, that is, the stories of judges in the cultural world. First, the portrayal of judges as marginal or secondary characters. Second, in legally themed entertainment, characters often express a wish for a 'good judge'.[4] This chapter interrogates the concept of the portrayal of a good judge in terms of authority, legitimacy and relationship with law through jurisprudence. How is the concept of the good (and of course the bad) constructed? Is there a necessary relationship between judgment and justice in this normative evaluation of the judge?[5] What does the secondary role of judges in popular culture tell us about the way that they are understood generally by the community?

Part I of the chapter situates this analysis within the context of law and popular culture studies and part two introduces the three television series considered in this chapter and justifies their selection. The next two parts consider the key themes of judges as minor caricatures and the quest for a good judge in popular culture. These themes are then examined in light of the portrayal of the relationship of judges with the truth and law. The penultimate part analyses the flip-side of the 'good' judge – the 'bad' judge. I conclude by considering how the portrayal of judges in popular culture relates to broader public perceptions of law and justice.

II Law and Popular Culture Studies

There is a great deal of academic literature about the intersection of law and popular culture and much of this is focused on American popular culture. There is general consensus among scholars as to the influence of popular culture on modern society. For example, Lawrence Friedman provides an early and influential illustration of the use of popular culture as a source material for the study of law.[6] Friedman asserted that popular legal culture – everything that people know or think they know about law from their consumption of popular culture – was both shaped by law and

---

[4] Ideas about the 'good lawyer' have been explored in surveys and academic research: Spitz (n 1) 737.
[5] Justice is a complex concept. Yet popular culture will often hold out a particular conception of what justice would require and/or involve. Whether or not this justice is delivered is another question.
[6] Lawrence M. Friedman, 'Law, Lawyers, and Popular Culture' (1989) 98 *Yale Law Journal* 1579. See also Cynthia Bond, 'We, the Judges: The Legalized Subject and Narratives of Adjudication in Reality Television' (2012) 81 *University of Missouri at Kansas City Law Review* 1.

had the power to shape law. Popular legal culture could provide insight into how law is regarded by consumers of the legal system.[7]

In the legal field, some scholars have expressed concerns about the misrepresentation of law in popular culture and how this may cultivate inaccurate beliefs.[8] These arguments are particularly salient given the relative absence of first-hand experience of the legal system by the public. The majority of people will never appear before a judge or read primary sources such as statutes or cases – their primary experience of law is through its representation in popular culture.[9] These concerns about misrepresentation are exacerbated by popular portrayals that explicitly blur the line between fiction and reality – with stories that are 'ripped from the headlines',[10] fictionalised re-creation of real events, and syndicated TV judges deciding 'real cases'.[11]

In the American context, Susan Bandes has pointed to substantive ramifications of popular culture in the 'stock images, characters with which we become familiar'.[12] Bandes argues that the populist portrait of the judiciary from legal popular culture not only affects the attitudes and conduct of viewers who eventually participate in the legal system, but also influences the voting choices made by prime-time viewers in judicial elections, a phenomenon which occurs at the state level in the United States. In that particular context, viewers' popular notions about the bench will influence who will become a judge,[13] who stays a judge, and the (permissible) scope of judicial power. Although the public does not choose judges in Australia, Bandes's arguments about the influence of legal popular culture are salient in Australia. She asserts that the judiciary are still aware of public sentiment and popular culture portrayals of

---

[7] Jo Carrillo, 'Links and Choices: Popular Legal Culture in the Work of Lawrence M Friedman' (2007) 17 *Southern California Interdisciplinary Law Journal* 1.

[8] Diana Mutz and Lilach Nir, 'Not Necessarily the News: Does Fictional Television Influence Real-World Policy Preferences?' (2010) 13(2) *Mass Communication and Society* 196, 198. See also, Susan Bandes, 'We Lost It at the Movies: The Rule of Law Goes from Washington to Hollywood and Back Again' (2007) 40 *Loyola Los Angeles Law Review* 621.

[9] Ibid.

[10] The series *Rake*, harvests decided legal cases to form the basis for trials in the show. For example, 'R v Murray', *Rake* (Essential Media and Entertainment, 2010) is based on a German cannibalism case.

[11] For example, the rider for *Judge Judy* is '[t]he people are real, the cases are real, and the rulings are final'.

[12] Bandes (n 8).

[13] Tanuya Lovell Banks, 'Here Comes the Judges: Gender Distortion on TV Reality Court Shows' (2008) 39 *University of Baltimore Law Forum* 38.

judges and this may influence the behaviour of judges, how their opinions are received, assumptions as to the role of judges,[14] and possibly even the content of judicial opinions themselves.[15]

In contrast, other scholars are more sanguine about the intersection of law and popular culture. Scholars note that visual meanings are polysemic and audiences can interpret the same text differently, digesting information in their own ways.[16] This research emphasises viewers' capacity to reappropriate and re-envision television and thus to remake or resist television's core messages of consumerism and social control.[17] Others have also downplayed the influence of popular culture. For example, Stanley Fish has noted that law in television and film are as much about television and film as they are about law.[18] They also have different aims – television court trials are to entertain; real trials are (hopefully) struggling toward justice.[19]

This chapter does not seek to resolve the question of the positive or negative influence of popular culture upon understandings of law and the construction of the law itself. Rather, this chapter draws upon the idea that law is more than just formal institutions and rules but rather includes how people construct and conceive of the law, and the stories that they tell about it.[20] Society's narratives give the law interpretive function and meaning. It is not only productive but necessary to 'attend to the cultural lives of law and the ways law lives in the domains of culture'.[21] These stories are the means by which we legitimise and make sense of law.

---

[14] Richard A Posner, *Overcoming Law* (Harvard University Press, 1995).
[15] Bandes (n 8).
[16] Asimov and Mader (n 1). This is consistent with Fiske's definition of popular culture emphasising popular culture is what people actually do with mass culture, rather than just passive reception: John Fiske, *Understanding Popular Culture* (Routledge, 1989) 25.
[17] Bond (n 6).
[18] Stanley Fish, 'Theory Minimalism' (2000) *San Diego Law Review* 761.
[19] David Ray Papke, 'The American Courtroom trial: Pop Culture, Courthouse Realities, and the Dream World of Justice' (1999) 40 *South Texas Law Review* 919, 931.
[20] Robert M Cover, 'The Supreme Court, 1982 Term: Foreword' (1983) 97 *Harvard Law Review* 4. For examples of academics drawing upon Cover's concept of the *nomos* see Podlas (n 1); Sherwin, 'Nomos and Cinema' (n 3); Bernard Hibbitts, 'Making Sense of Metaphors: Visuality, Aurality and the Reconfiguration of American Legal Discourse' (1994) 16 *Cardozo Law Review* 229.
[21] Austin Sarat and Austin Kearns, 'The cultural lives of law' in Austin Sarat and Austin Kearns (eds), *Law in the Domains of Culture* (The University of Michigan Press, 2000), 5.

III Television Shows Analysed

This chapter focuses primarily on the portrayal of judges in three Australian-made television series – *SeaChange*, *Rake* and *Janet King* ('*JK*'). One reason for limiting this analysis to television shows is that television remains a primary source of contemporary popular legal culture.[22] Another is that although some have argued that there are different types of legal content between film and television,[23] the secondary, minor role of judges is common across both film and television.[24] I have selected these three series on the basis that they are legally themed, the prevalence of the judiciary in plots, the longevity and success of the show, and my ability to access (and willingness to watch) each program. Throughout I make comparisons with international television shows and academic analysis in order to enunciate whether there is a quintessentially Australian popular culture portrayal of judges.

Television shows which place the greatest emphasis on the character of judges are syndicated television court shows or reality court shows, reflected and reinforced by eponymous titles, such as *Judge Mathis* (USA), *Judge Rinder* (UK) and, of course, *Judge Judy* (USA).[25] Reality courts provide the dominant narrative of law on television,[26] and have been subjected to a great deal of academic analysis.[27] While foreign reality court shows are available in Australia, Australia does not have its own reality court show. Although legal themes dominate popular culture, with the exception of reality court judges, it is hard to actually think of many major judicial characters on television or in film. Leaving aside the reality court judges, there are two major exceptions to the peripheral role of judges in popular culture. The first are shows where a judge is charged with an offence, and the show presents the trial of the judge for those offences. I will consider this category of judges as

---

[22] Podlas (n 1).
[23] Mezey and Niles (n 2).
[24] For example, in the classic legal comedy-drama, *The Castle* (1997), while the lawyers are memorable, it is hard to remember any of the judges in the trials.
[25] There are also non-English speaking reality courts such as Das Jugendgericht (The Youth Court) analysed in Leslie Moran, Beverley Skeggs and Ruth Herz, 'Ruth Herz Judge Playing Judge Ruth Herz: Reflections on the performance of judicial authority' [198] (2010) 14 *Law, Text, Culture* 198–219.
[26] Podlas (n 1).
[27] See, for example, Bond (n 6); Steven A Kohm, 'The People's Law versus Judge Judy Justice: Two Models of Law in American Reality-Based Courtroom TV' (2006) 40 *Law and Society Review* 693; Lovell Banks, 'Here Comes the Judges' (n 13).

'villains' toward the end of this chapter, but at this stage will note that these shows are primarily a meditation about the judge as accused and may draw on public expectations of judicial conduct, but are not directed to the judge acting as judge.

The second exception to the judge as minor character are series where the lead character is a judge. The title is often eponymous. International examples include *Judge John Deed*[28] and *Judging Amy*,[29] both of which frequently appear on free-to-air television in Australia. The Australian example is *SeaChange*, which ran from 1998 to 2000 on the Australian Broadcasting Corporation – and which was reprised on commercial television in 2019.[30] It featured Laura Gibson, a high-flying corporate lawyer who undergoes a professional and lifestyle 'sea change' with her children Rupert and Miranda after her husband is arrested for fraud and it transpires that he is having an affair with her sister. Laura leaves her city practice to become the magistrate for the small coastal town of Pearl Bay.[31]

While Laura is the central character in *SeaChange*, judges also appear in the other legally-themed Australian series discussed in this chapter – *Rake* and *JK*.[32] *Rake* (Australian Broadcasting Corporation, 2010–16) is about a brilliant but self-destructive Sydney barrister, Cleaver Greene. *JK* (2014–20) was created as a spin-off from the 2011, less successful, legal drama *Crownies*, concerning the state prosecution service. The later series follows the story of Senior Crown Prosecutor Janet King.

IV The Judge as Caricature in Popular Culture

Despite the dominance of the judiciary in legal theory, and their place at the pinnacle of the legal profession's hierarchy, judges do not regularly appear in legally themed television series. Most police and detective shows culminate with the unveiling of the culprit, leaving an assumption that justice will be done off screen.[33] In many series about lawyers, much of the activity occurs outside the courtroom, with cases settled or

---

[28] (British Broadcasting Corporation, 2001–07) 6 seasons.
[29] (CBS, 1999–2005) 6 seasons.
[30] This chapter confines its discussion to the initial run of the series.
[31] The American show *Judging Amy* (1999–2005) has a similar plot premise.
[32] Both series are available internationally on Netflix and *Rake* was remade for American audiences in 2014, starring Greg Kinnear.
[33] The majority of detective and police shows never reach the courtroom. Exceptions include the original *Law and Order* series and *Broadchurch* (season 2).

resolved outside the court. Law is frequently distanced or decentred from the courtrooms and judiciary.[34] For example, in *JK* and *Rake*, despite the legal theme, the bulk of (legal) action takes place outside of the courtroom. The maximum amount of time spent in the courtroom in *JK* is about four minutes in an hour-long episode. In *Rake*, much of the action takes place outside the courtroom – in his chambers, bedroom or cafes. When there is action in the courtroom, much of the focus is on Greene and other characters. The judge is a foil, a source of reaction to the familiar leads. Similarly, in *SeaChange*, while much of 'Full Fathom Five' is in the courtroom, from then onwards, the bulk of the action is not in court.

When they do appear, judges are 'relatively one-dimensional'[35] and 'rarely a full-bodied character'.[36] Judges take up little screen time and often little is known about their characters. While criminal law provides the primary plot source for legal dramas, white collar crime rarely makes an appearance, and when it does, judges rarely appear.[37] Compared with other legal players such as lawyers, police and detectives, judges are minor characters: 'To put it trivially, the judge in film is a character. To put it less trivially, the judge in film is often a trivial character'.[38]

Rake and *JK* reflect the popular culture focus on crime, revealing an assumption that the time when judges are most needed (but still rarely) is to impose judgment on traditional criminal offences.

There are very common codes for judges that are easily distinguishable to audiences. They usually appear only in the courtroom itself (and sometimes in chambers if they retreat with lawyers) – which is usually traditional in style with wooden paneling, large doors and a hushed atmosphere. The judge sits at a raised bench with a uniformed bailiff in view. Judges are frequently filmed at a low angle, upwardly tilted, replicating their authority. The judge's bench 'stands like an altar at the exact centre-front and rises above, suggesting something higher and truer'.[39] Both *Rake* and *JK* reflect and reinforce these codes. In contrast,

---

[34] Kohm (n 27).
[35] Papke (n 19).
[36] Ibid.
[37] Moohr has noted that lawyers and judges are largely absent from white collar crime films. Geraldine Szott Moohr, 'White Collar Movies and Why They Matter' (2015) 16(2) *Texas Review of Entertainment and Sports Law* 119. Recent series that include white collar crime focus particularly on lawyers for instance, *Suits* and *The Good Fight*.
[38] David Black, 'Narrative Determination and the Figure of the Judge' in MDA Freeman (ed), *Law and Popular Culture* (2005) 677, 679.
[39] Papke (n 19).

in 'Full Fathom Five', *SeaChange* disrupts this *mise-en-scene* as an indicator that Laura's experience and perspective as a new magistrate will be central. The audience sees the ramshackle courthouse and then her chambers from Laura's perspective. The camera adopts Laura's point of view as she enters the courtroom, undermining the usual trope of judge as enigma.

Judges in popular culture tend to be costumed in robes and wigs. They have a limited repertoire of behaviour such as shouting 'order', ruling on objections ('sustained'), telling lawyers to 'approach the bench', usually to chastise them for grandstanding, and banging their gavel (although no gavels are used in the three series under examination, faithfully reflecting their absence from Australian courts). Judges in American popular culture tend to be caricatures. In contrast, in the bulk of episodes of *Rake* and *JK* (leaving aside the villainous Judge Renmark in *JK*), there is such an absence of characterisation of judges that they are not even caricatures. In both series, on the rare occasion on which there is a trial scene, even if judges have a speaking part, such as, 'I'll allow it', this may be off-screen or they may just be a blurred image behind more important characters. The audience is unlikely to know the name of the judge; he or she is referred to as 'Your Honour'. The predominant action of judges on *Rake*, *SeaChange* and *JK* is to call adjournments or recesses.

In light of the relative absence of memorable judges from film and television (with the exception of reality court judges) is there much to be learned from analysis of the representation of judges in popular culture? This chapter will argue that there are important insights to be gained from the portrayal of the 'good judge'. Frequently lawyers and clients in these shows will express a hope for a 'good judge'. Laura Gibson is a high-achieving perfectionist and wants to be a 'good' magistrate. In *JK*, a character comments in 'A Song of Experience', 'we get the right judge and we're sweet'. I will explore the idea of the good (and bad) judge in popular culture through the insights of American Realists. Who or what is portrayed as a good judge in television shows, and what is their relationship to law and authority? And how does the notion of the good judge relate to the secondary role of judges in popular culture?

V Who the Judge Is Matters

The quest for the good judge in popular culture is contrary to Weber's ideal of rational legal power – in which judges are replaceable and interchangeable, one judge among many. According to Weber, citizens obey judges not as an individual, but because of an impersonal legal order. Judges are elevated to that position by the formal rules of the land, and judges are bound by the same rules that legitimise and authorise. The quest for the 'good judge' is more in accordance with American Realists who argued that who the judge is matters. American Realism was a reaction to the 'black letter' approach to law, which advocates a formal, syllogistic application of law to facts, sometimes labeled formalism or a simplified form of positivism. Realists contrasted the traditional mechanical notion of logic epitomised in the syllogism with the pragmatic understanding of logic as the consequence of experience.[40] Realists played down 'law in books' or established rules and instead argued the need to understand law in action, the non-legal factors behind judicial decisions.[41] Realists were sceptical of general rules to provide solutions to particular cases, in other words, the ability of rules to predict what the courts will do. Instead of mechanistic application of law to facts posited by positivists and formalists, realists argued that it was necessary to find instead the 'real' rules behind the rules. Although open-ended, these non-legal factors would include morality, public opinion, judicial prejudice, governmental pressure, and so on. Accordingly, for realists in contrast to theorists such as Weber, who the judge is matters. Judges are human and their political and moral decisions will inevitably influence decisions.

The idea that who the judge is matters is arguably a core theme of popular culture representation of judges.[42] The most common reference in legally-themed shows in America is to the politics of the judge – as Democratic or Republican. Lawyers may seek to ingratiate themselves with the judge with cheap strategies, such as references to the judge's favourite baseball team or making sympathetic political claims. This reflects the implicit idea that a judge will rule in favour of the lawyer who he or she likes, or who most accords with his or her political values. Australian shows do not tend to label judges according to political allegiance. This could be because these allegiances are not so quickly and easily portrayed or alternatively because of the less overtly politicised judicial appointments process.

---

[40] John Dewey, 'Logical Method and Law' (1924) 10 *Cornell Law Quarterly* 17, 21. See also 'the life of the law has not been logic: it has been experience': Oliver Wendell Holmes, *The Common Law* (Little, Brown, 1881) 1.
[41] Oliver Wendell Holmes, 'The Path of the Law' (1887) 10 *Harvard Law Review* 457, 461.
[42] Many legal-themed shows suggest that who the police officer or lawyer is has implications for the likelihood of justice being achieved.

Australian series do, however, portray the threat of politics to judicial independence and impartiality as a plot device. In *SeaChange*, local entrepreneur and mayor Bob Jelly is initially excited by the arrival of the new magistrate, because Jelly has heard 'he' is a 'corporate lawyer' and so may be pro-development. In both *Rake* and *JK*, the attorney-general attempts to influence judicial proceedings, predominantly by pressure on police and the director of public prosecutions (DPP), but also by attempting to 'stack the bench'. In neither series do these political interventions seeking to influence judges directly succeed, and none of the series represent the intervention as being due to the attorney-general's membership of a particular political party – it is simply portrayed as attempted political intervention in the legal sphere. In *JK*, the political pressure appears to have a negative effect, with the chief justice stacking the bench against the DPP. The only judge who speaks relishes allowing the appeal, refuses to allow the DPP to speak, and gives a decision against the DPP within two minutes. This suggests that there is some personal bias or satisfaction by the bench in that case, but it is also made clear to the viewer that the DPP has a very weak case and deserved to lose.

Both *SeaChange* and *JK* raise the spectre of decisions made by judges on the basis of mood: 'The chances of reopening the case depend on whether the judge has had a good night's sleep or not' (*JK*, 'Lurking Doubt'). *SeaChange* portrays Laura doodling in the courtroom after her husband breaches bail conditions and comes to Pearl Bay. Laura does not hear the charges read by the police sergeant. In *JK* the police superintendent Rizzoli tells Janet:

> RIZZOLI : 'Judges get it wrong, it happens all the time.'
> JANET : 'But a judge who is known to be pro-police?'
> RIZZOLI : 'He might have had a fight with his wife, he might have an undiagnosed brain tumour ... The judge is just another variable we deal with every day'. ('Lurking Doubt').

This conversation accepts the insight of American Realism on two levels. First, there is the acceptance that judges may be biased before a case commences, whether in favour of the defence or prosecution. Second, there is the suggestion that a judge may be influenced by externalities that are irrelevant to a case. This reflects the American Legal Realist perspective that justice is 'what the judge ate for breakfast'.[43] The influence of

---

[43] Alex Kozinski, 'What I Ate for Breakfast and Other Mysteries of Judicial Decision Making' (1993) 26 *Loyola of Los Angeles Law Review* 993.

extraneous factors such as time of day and meal breaks was confirmed by a study of parole decisions made by experienced judges.[44] When Janet loses a trial, she wonders if she lost because Judge Renmark did not like her. However, excluding the corrupt Judge Renmark in *JK*, in the majority of television series, American or Australian, a judge's personal feelings are not portrayed as having substantive effects on the outcome of cases.

Both American and Australian series highlight the ongoing relationships between legal actors. This probably reflects the reality of the legal profession and the practical needs of television for ongoing character development. Many of these relationships are between police and prosecutors. In *SeaChange*, Laura's law clerk is engaged to the police prosecutor. *Rake* extends this analysis to relationships between lawyers and the judiciary. For example, in 'R v Dana', the prosecutor Makepeace was previously married to the judge. Makepeace and Greene make arguments in the judge's chambers while he eats lunch. When it appears that Greene is making headway with the judge, Makepeace says 'you're a weak man, Jim'. After she leaves the room, the judge comments to Greene: '18 years I spent married to that cow'. In light of these relationships, it appears that the judge will have sympathy for Greene's defence, but this is not borne out by the results.

One way in which television has explored the significance of the judge as individual is through relative levels of expertise. *SeaChange* explicitly explores the issue of inexperience through a depiction of Laura's first day as magistrate. Laura is portrayed as a perfectionist and is concerned that she does not know the 'etiquette' of judging. In 'Something Rich and Strange', Laura light-heartedly asks, 'how hard can it be?' to be a magistrate in comparison with being a corporate lawyer. However, in 'Full Fathom Five' she states 'I'm about to be sitting behind a bench for the first time and it's a huge responsibility'. We see the courtroom from her perspective and she asks her clerk, 'what am I doing wrong?'. She then practices court etiquette in her chambers in front of a mirror: 'do I look like a magistrate?'. 'A Matter of Taste' begins a month later and Laura has clearly mastered the etiquette of judging. *JK* raises the opposite issue, asking of Judge Renmark, a 'geriatric judge' due to retire: 'Was he just getting lazy and didn't want to write a judgment?'. There is little in

---

[44] Shai Danziger, Jonathan Levav and Liora Avnaim-Pesso, 'Extraneous Factors in Judicial Decisions' (2011) 108(17) *Proceedings of the National Academy of Sciences of the USA* 6889.

jurisprudence that analyses the impact of experience (or lack thereof) on judging.[45]

Although not touched upon directly by the American Realists, a logical extension of their insights is the importance of judicial diversity. In American series, the portrayal of judges in popular culture frequently offers greater diversity than exists in real life. The website TV Tropes notes that judges on television are 'generally filled by stern black women (with hair pulled tightly back) or gruff older white men'.[46] Giving black women relatively minor but authoritative roles can often be a cheap gesture towards addressing gender/racial imbalances on the show. The gender/racial makeup of the judge has relatively limited plot significance except to explore the plight of a judge acting against his or her conscience and/or background. In contrast to American legal television series, Australian television shows tend to portray judges as predominantly old, white males. In fact, the actor portraying Judge Renmark in *JK* also portrays a judge in *Rake* – suggesting that there is a classic image of judges on television. Every so often there will be an old, white, female judge. *JK* presents some of the impact of the dominance of male judges when Judge Renmark treats Janet in a disparaging and sexist way in 'A Song of Experience'. Renmark's comments do not immediately label him as a villain, just a sexist judge.

An episode of *Rake* ('R v Marx') provides a rare meditation on the impact of judicial diversity. In that episode, the government tries to ensure that the charges against a woman for jury tampering to save her daughter from a murder conviction will not succeed. To this end, the attorney-general in collusion with the DPP, ensure that an inexperienced prosecutor is allocated the case and seek to stack the Bench: 'do we have a mother on the bench?'. Judge Mason, a single mother of four, is then allocated to the case. In response, Greene comments: 'they want her [the accused] to walk

---

[45] There is practical recognition of judicial inexperience, with 'Baby Judges School' running in American to make sure that judges know the fundamentals of the job: '"Baby Judge School" Is Underway for New Federal Judicial Appointees', *CBS News* (online, 7 February 2018) <www.cbsnews.com/news/baby-judges-school-is-underway-for-new-federal-judicial-appointees/>. In addition, arguments to lift retirement ages and to allow judges to return to the bench as temporary judges are made on the basis that valuable experience might be lost. Whilst concern with incapacity has become exacerbated with better understanding of aged-related diseases such as dementia. Alysia Blackham, 'Judges and Retirement Ages' (2016) 39 *Melbourne University Law Review* 738.
[46] 'The Judge', *TV Tropes* (web page) <http://tvtropes.org/pmwiki/pmwiki.php/Main/TheJudge>.

free ... she [the judge] will give her a bloody medal'. The assumption by the politicians and lawyers is that the judge will be ruled by personal experience and be biased – she will empathise with the actions of the accused to protect her daughter and acquit her. Greene, representing the accused, who has told him she wants to go to prison to ensure her daughter's case gets more publicity, aims to offend the judge with a rant. Mason recalls Greene to her chambers and chastises him for presenting a negligent defence. Mason seems unaware that she was allocated to the case for political reasons. The case concludes with Mason ruling a mistrial and referring Greene to the Bar Association. Despite the shenanigans outside the courtroom, Mason shows no bias at all, and only a preference that each lawyer acts according to legal and ethical requirements.

There has been a great deal of academic commentary about the distortion of race and gender in legal themed shows.[47] The focus of this analysis is primarily on the portrayal of lawyers but it can be extended to judges. In terms of women, female judges outnumber male judges on reality courts, but female judges, especially black and other nonwhite judges, are still the exception in real courts.[48] Furthermore, even though there may be central female characters who are lawyers or judges – they may not be portrayed in as positive light as their male counterparts.[49] The suggestion is that women can either have a successful career in law or be successful at relationships – they cannot have both. They choose inappropriate lovers, crave motherhood, or have difficulty in balancing work and motherhood. In *SeaChange*, Laura's husband blames the failure of their marriage on her ambition: 'you were busy'. She works long hours as a corporate lawyer: 'I'm their mother in name only'. Miranda agrees when Laura asks her if she is the worst mother she knows and later comments that nothing has changed since she has become a magistrate. Theorists argue that culture is telling liberated women that they are

---

[47] Stacey Caplow, 'Still in the Dark: Disappointing Images of Women Lawyers in the Movies' (1999) 55 *Women's Rights Law Reporter* 69; Lovell Banks (n 13); Tanuya Lovell Banks, 'Judging the Judges: Daytime Television's Integrated Reality Court Bench' in Michael Asimov (ed), *Lawyers in Your Living Room!: Law on Television* (2009) 309; Cynthia Lucia,'Women on Trial: The Female Lawyer in the Hollywood Courtroom' in Martha Albertson Fineman and Martha McCluskey (eds), *Feminism, Media and the Law* (1997); David Ray Papke, 'Cautionary Tales: The Woman as Lawyer in Contemporary Hollywood Cinema' (2003) 25 *University of Arkansas at Little Rock Law Review* 485.
[48] Lovell Banks (n 13).
[49] Ibid.; Caplow (n 47); Lucia (n 47).

destined to be miserable.[50] There is no analogous tension for men between their roles as legal practitioners and their roles as men. In *Rake*, Greene is a shambolic mess, but this is portrayed as a personality flaw rather than due to a failure to balance work and homelife.

Although popular culture devotes time to the idea of characters seeking a 'good judge', the bulk of shows do not confirm the insight of American Realism that the individual judge impacts upon results. In *Rake* and *JK* (and the bulk of American television series), the good judge is in accordance with Weber's ideal – judges are essentially interchangeable with other judges, peripheral characters who apply the law correctly and without bias. There are suggestions that mood, values and personality may impact on judgment, but these are almost never borne out in final judgments in television series. While characters in Australian shows muse on American Realist insights that who the judge is matters, this is not borne out in the bulk of the legal shows. Arguably the portrayal of good judges as essentially interchangeable is a positive reflection of the rationality and fairness of the law.

A   The Relationship of the Judge to Law and Facts: What Am I? A Potted Plant?

Given that judges are predominantly portrayed as being bound by law, popular culture also explores ideas about the implications of this relationship of judges with the law. I will consider first the American Realist arguments about the plasticity of law and facts and whether or not truth can be established in the courtroom, then go on to examine what happens when judges are confronted with laws that are against their conscience.

Judges and the Relationship between Law and Facts

In accordance with their shift away from a priori mechanistic reasoning, American Realists divided themselves into fact and rule sceptics.[51] Fact sceptics such as Jerome Frank emphasised the elusiveness of facts. Frank asserted that witnesses and judges are humanly fallible, thus the discovery of the 'real rules' will not help because the problem of the slipperiness of the facts remains. Legally themed shows rarely reflect

---

[50] Susan Faludi, *Backlash: The Undeclared War Against American Women* (Crown Publishing, 1991).
[51] Jerome Frank, *Law and the Modern Mind* (Bientano, 1930).

Frank's scepticism as to the 'facts'. The audience usually knows or comes to know the facts. Often this is because of out of court antics by other actors who investigate and ensure justice is done. In both *JK* and *Rake*, the main characters are frequently very active in investigating to ensure the 'truth'. The fact that the audience is frequently an omniscient viewer who knows more than the judge can undermine the authority of the judge. However, the judge usually becomes aware of the truth, frequently thanks to the cleverness of other legal actors such as police and lawyers.

Despite some ambivalence about the law, particularly the rules of evidence, most legally themed shows portray truth as obtainable – even if it is not achieved in the courtroom.[52] *JK* portrays several examples of the 'truth' not surfacing in the courtroom. For example, in one case, a solicitor who assaulted a man is found guilty of the offence as she was legally unable to tell the court that he was a pedophile. While this is portrayed as unfair, the solicitor did commit the assault and was correctly found guilty. In *JK*, the court is frequently a site of truth, mainly due to Janet's expert cross-examination of witnesses, rather than by any intervention of the judge. The ongoing mystery of the murder of police officer Steven Blakely is resolved through cross-examination in the courtroom, when in a separate case it becomes apparent that Drew Blakely hated his father. Likewise, *Rake* shows the truth as obtainable, but not necessarily in the courtroom. For example, Greene is told that a client he successfully acquitted for murder 'did do it, you know'. When Greene says, '[w]ell you should have made a better case mate', the police officer responds: 'Couldn't, my hands were tied'. The officer provides sufficient information that both Greene and the audience are persuaded that the accused had committed the murder (R v Lorton). This failure to deliver the truth in court is not due to the judge but the law. In another case, the lawyers and judge collude in chambers to keep evidence out of court that the second unidentified person in a bestiality DVD was the wife of the accused to protect their daughter who is studying law. This shows the theme of a community of legal actors making decisions outside the courtroom together. In these types of legal series, the stars are not the judges but the lawyers. 'Good' judges appear to be those who give the lawyers (the stars) sufficient leeway to succeed.

SeaChange also plays with the courtroom as a reliable site of truth. The community knows the truth, but the magistrate (and frequently the

---

[52] Ibid.

audience) will not until later. The 'truth' is often explained to Laura outside of the courtroom. For example, the law clerk and police constable admit in chambers that 'everyone knows' that Bucket was 'stitched up' and should not have been found guilty of assault. Laura battles against the provision of evidence outside the courtroom saying 'you know damn well I can only decide the case on information I hear out [in the courtroom]', but she is obviously influenced in her decision-making by the background information. This is not portrayed in a negative way, but rather as a 'city lawyer' learning the ways of a small town.

Rule sceptics such as Karl Llewellyn, argued that formal rules were unreliable guides in the prediction of decisions. Llewellyn and Oliphant pointed to the vast panoply of precedent, numerous techniques of interpretation, logical indeterminacy of established rules as giving room to judges to manoeuvre. Judges could pick the outcome that they wanted and use law in a flexible way to achieve that. Accordingly, a judge's prejudices and beliefs would influence which precedents they used and how they applied them. In popular culture, judges are often assisted in this process by lawyers – finding a technique of clever interpretation to enable the judge to achieve a 'just' outcome. This would suggest that judges were only loosely bound by law, and their own personal predilections could triumph.

In *SeaChange* Laura shows a capacity and passion for using her expert knowledge of the law to achieve the best outcome for her corporate client ('A Song of Experience'). She appears to be motivated to win, rather than by a concern for justice or fairness. However, *SeaChange* depicts a growing desire by Laura to deliver just results to the community of which she is now a part. She portrays herself as law bound, and there is argument within the community about the extent to which she would go outside the law: 'I don't think she'd turn you in'. 'Yes she would, she's a judge, it's her job'. Increasingly Laura uses her legal expertise and power creatively. For example, in 'Natural Justice', in the absence of adequate legal representation of Meredith, Laura assists with a series of rhetorical questions that indicate her awareness that the local council was acting corruptly in pursuing Meredith for unpaid fees. As a consequence, the council drops the case and offers to waive the fees against Meredith. Laura performs obedience to the law,[53] but her actions were on the edge of (un)lawfulness. The series does not explore whether or not Laura carried out extra

---

[53] Lawrence Baum, *Judges and Their Audiences: A Perspective on Judicial Behaviour* (Princeton University Press, 2006).

research on the corporation in question because of her personal animus toward Mayor Jelly, but the result is presented as correct and just.

Television series rarely reflect the insights of American Realists about the impossibility of arriving at the truth. These series do however play with the question of whether the courtroom is necessarily a site of truth – or whether truth is achieved outside the courtroom, in the absence of the judge. In terms of arriving at the truth, the role of the judge remains secondary and tends to involve giving the main characters sufficient leeway to find the truth. Television series do portray the flexibility of the law and the ways that it can be used to arrive at particular desired results, but once again these are primarily due to clever lawyer antics, with the judicial role secondary in accepting these arguments. As I argue in the next section, there is, however, a celebration of judges who deliver clever judgments that deliver 'justice'.

Judges and Civil Disobedience in Popular Culture

In *Overcoming Law*,[54] Chief Justice Richard Posner noted that judges are frequently portrayed as mere referees, contributing to a misconception of judging and Posner asking about his judicial role: 'What am I? A potted plant?'.[55] Given the secondary role and limited repertoire of the judiciary in popular culture, are judges portrayed as mere referees or potted plants? That is, do judges have a limited or passive role to play in popular culture? The secondary role of judges is portrayed in both *Rake* and *JK*, with both series more concerned with establishing the brilliance of the main characters than showing interest in the judges before whom they appear. This is particularly the case in jury trials, where lawyers play to the jury and the judge is only able to respond to jury findings. For example, in *Rake* ('R v Chandler'), Greene presents a critique of the rules of bestiality and our hypocritical relationship with animals. In the absence of instructions by the judge that juries must decide according to law, rather than whether a law is right or wrong, the accused is found not guilty, despite clear evidence to the contrary.

Despite their marginal role, judges are portrayed as more than potted plants in popular culture. There is a celebration of the clever judge – who is bound by law but nonetheless delivers a just and satisfying result. This can be done subtly. For example, in *Rake* ('R v Dana'), Greene plays more to the jury than the judge in his arguments that the criminalisation of

---

[54] Posner, *Overcoming Law* (n 14) ch 8.
[55] See also Bandes (n 8).

bigamy is archaic. Greene's arguments go awry when a third wife and family is discovered. Greene claims to the accused that up until that point, 'I had the Judge in my pocket', however it is not established if this claim is true or not. The jury finds the accused guilty, but the Judge then has an opportunity to deal with the arguments of Greene and Makepeace. He provides an example of balancing the arguments, recognising the arguments by Makepeace (his ex-wife) that the accused had deceived three women, and 'worse, he lied to the court', but also merit in Greene's argument that the penalties under the law greatly outweigh the impact of the crime'. The judge then imposes a three-year sentence, with all but the first three months suspended. This result is clever and, after the judge has provided reasons, appears to the audience to be a fair and just result.

SeaChange provides examples of the role of magistrate as being more than a referee, which is consistent with Laura's role as a major character in the series. As Laura increases in confidence, she exercises her power and imagination to impose sanctions that will have positive impacts on the community. For example, she requires Meredith's niece to remain in Pearl Bay after she is found guilty of fraud, a 'punishment' that will provide her with support during her pregnancy. Her knowledge of corporate law is also of increasing assistance in response to the local council's corruption. Laura establishes that she is indeed more than a potted plant and knows the law: 'she's smart, for a magistrate' ('The Official Story').

In American legal shows, on the rare occasions when judges are portrayed as major characters, it is often when they are torn between legal requirements and their personal beliefs.[56] Television tends to focus on the sensational or aberrational and this includes cases which are normatively challenging.[57] Cases challenging judges on a personal level present an exploration of the extent to which judges are bound by law. The issue of judges applying the laws of an unjust regime is a common trope in jurisprudence.[58] Robert Cover has argued that in cases of civil disobedience, judges must choose between different interpretations and

---

[56] The issue of judges being confronted with laws with which they disagree is a common theme in popular culture. The outcome is by no means guaranteed.

[57] Judge Bruce M Selya, 'The Confidence Game: Public Perceptions of the Judiciary' (1996) 30 *New England Law Review* 909.

[58] See, for instance, HLA Hart, 'Positivism and the Separation of Law and Morals' (1958) 71 *Harvard Law Review* 593; Lon Fuller, 'Positivism and a Fidelity to Law: A Reply to Professor Hart' (1958) 71 *Harvard Law Review* 661.

meanings of the law.[59] This is an extension of American Realist insight about judges having leeway in which laws they apply and how they apply them.

Cover notes that one approach is to assert that their hands are bound by the law – even though they may disagree with a law, they are compelled to apply it.[60] This is effectively a formalist approach, applying the law and shutting down alternative interpretations. Judges are effectively claiming that like the legal subject, they too are subject to institutional force and must obey the hierarchy. Fundamental reforms should be left to parliament. This also occurs in real-life cases, where judges may express dissatisfaction with a law but that they are nonetheless bound to rule consistently with that law.[61] This approach is formalist because it avoids substantive questions as to the purpose or justice of the law. In *Rake*, Greene frequently raises questions about the substance of laws, and while judges may accept his arguments as a consideration, they express no emotional difficulties in their application of the law.

Alternatively, Cover argues that judges can exercise judgment and interpret legal provisions in a substantive way in accordance with internal obligations, such as justice, that a culture is assumed to follow. It is not enough that the law orders violence, but that the judge finds the application of the violence to be merited on substantive grounds,[62] an approach celebrated by the American Realists as the Grand Style of judging.[63] In *Rake*, the bigamy case provides an example whereby the judge takes note of Greene's arguments but also notes the harm done by the accused and sentences the accused to prison. The judge outlines the reasons why the imposition of a custodial sentence is merited on substantive grounds.

SeaChange meditates upon the violence of the law and flags the issue of civil disobedience and the possibility of Laura acting in accordance with the Grand Style. Laura is initially uncomfortable with the power of her role as magistrate asking, 'what right do I have to confine a man to a

---

[59] Cover (n 20) 46–8.
[60] Ibid. 54–5.
[61] Crofts summarises judgments in compulsion defences for homicide, where judges frequently articulate dissatisfaction with the law but still rule in accordance with it: Penny Crofts, *Wickedness and Crime: Laws of Homicide and Malice* (Routledge, 2013) ch 5.
[62] Cover (n 20) 58.
[63] It should be noted that positivism also made room for judicial law making when there were hard cases: HLA Hart, *The Concept of Law* (Clarendon Press, 2nd ed, 1994) post scriptum.

small dark room for six months?' Her clerk responds, 'You're the magistrate'. There is an acceptance by the community that this is part of her job, but there are questions of the extent to which she can and should be bound by the law. This is raised particularly in 'The Official Story', when a man comes before court for persistently failing to renew his licence. The entire community (except Laura) is aware that he is a fraudster who has evaded the law for years and has since started a community farm to assist young offenders. In recognition of his community work, Laura reluctantly imposes a $200 fine instead of a custodial sentence. The case raises two issues. First, throughout the series, Laura has to deal with community responses to her judgments. Although Laura 'can't bow to community pressure', this pressure is shown to be very strong. She is praised when she makes the 'right decision' and offered 'lunch on the house' at the town pub. When Laura refuses the offer of a free lunch, she is told that the hotelier, Meredith, overcharged her the week before for convicting another local, and she has felt bad about it since. She is also ignored and treated badly when the community does not agree with a decision that she has made. The series portrays Laura as grappling with the requirements of law and delivering judgments recognised as good and fair by the community. Second, the case of the incognito fraudster raises personal issues for Laura as her husband, Jack, has likewise been charged with fraud. This becomes particularly salient when Jack visits Pearl Bay in breach of his bail conditions. Laura tells Diver Dan in relation to the fraudster: 'I'm here to uphold the law ... you've got to let me do my job'. Diver Dan asks, 'do you really think society will be better off?', to which Laura responds 'I have to think like that, it's my job'. This suggests a positivist approach to law, whereby Laura does not need to consider whether the law is just or good. The town provides an alibi to Jack so that he is not charged with breaching bail conditions, and Diver Dan comments to Laura: 'you wouldn't want to see a good man go to prison, would you?' ('The Official Story'). Laura demonstrates a willingness to suspend the law so that her husband can remain in town for their son's birthday.

Interestingly, popular culture reflects the same ambivalence as jurisprudence towards the issue of obedience. Popular culture is sympathetic to the judge who applies the law, even though he or she disagrees with it. The judge is portrayed as part of a rational legal authority, one judge among many. The law may be painted as restrictive,[64] but nonetheless, it

[64] Nicole Rafter, *Shots in the Mirror: Crime Films and Society* (Oxford University Press, 2006).

is parliament not the courts where substantive law reform is accomplished. The personal costs for the judge in applying or not applying the law are made clear. On the other hand, popular culture also celebrates the activist judge who manages to find an alternative interpretation or overtly breaches the law in order to deliver justice. This celebration of the activist judge in popular culture is not sustained in popular rhetoric about real life judges. *SeaChange* leaves open the question of whether or not Laura would impose a custodial term on the other fraudster. He is arrested and brought before a different court, so the series avoids the issue.

Popular culture reflects the uncertainties and ambivalence of jurisprudence with regard to the relationship of judges to law. There is sympathy expressed for the judge who rules in accordance with the law but against his or her own personal beliefs; and there is a certain amount of celebration of heroic judges who make value judgments. There is also applause for lawyers who assist judges to make judgments using legal technicalities, even though in real life this kind of sophistry is frowned upon. There is also celebration of judges who are bound by law but within these restrictions make judgments that deliver justice and are clever.

VI   The Judge as Villain in Popular Culture

The flipside of the good judge is of course the bad judge – the biased, the vulgar or downright villainous.[65] Bias is gestured toward in popular culture. In *JK*, this takes the form of Judge Renmark making sexist comments and by the chief justice stacking the bench in response to political intervention. Judge Renmark is not motivated by bias but by corruption and in relation to the stacking of the bench, while the judges have personal motives, the results are portrayed as correct. Similarly, in the episode of *Rake* discussed above, although the judge was previously married to the prosecutor, his judgment is shown to be uninfluenced by bias.

In American television, the portrayal of judges charged with criminal offences such as murder and sexual assault, is a common plot point. These stories often explore the unthinkability of judge as villain, and the various obstacles stopping the hero from achieving justice as the judge is protected by the legal hierarchy. While American television

---

[65] Bandes (n 8).

might explore the judge as villain, getting away with substantive criminal offences, Australian television explores the issue of judicial corruption. In *SeaChange*, the former magistrate Harold Fitzwalter had been blackmailed to make judgments in favour of the corrupt Mayor Jelly. Harold is the first defendant before Laura, charged with blowing up the Jelly public toilet and being drunk in a public place. The community appears to accept Harold's corruption – although he has 'done terrible things' he remains a beloved member of the community. There appears to have been nothing they could do in response to the corruption about which everyone knew. Jelly expresses the hope that Laura will be just like Harold. Once Laura becomes aware of the blackmailing of Harold and the potential for corruption, she makes a public announcement that she has a husband in prison on remand before Jelly is able to use this information. She also exercises her imagination in response to the charges against Harold, recording no conviction and requiring only that he repay the council for any damage.

A major plot point in series one of *JK* is Judge Renmark's corruption. The first indicator of this is that Janet loses a case that she believes she should have won. Renmark's findings in the judge-only trial of the child pornographer Moreno are 'perverse'. As a consequence, despite recognition that it is a politically sensitive business to pursue a judge, Janet asks a solicitor to analyse Renmark's judgments. The solicitor tells Janet that when Renmark became a judge his decisions were initially consistent with overall trends, but then his judgments changed, first acquitting everyone and then finding everyone guilty, except Moreno. The series suggests that while Renmark being pro- or anti-prosecution may be understandable, this shifting between acquittals and then convictions for everyone is 'dodgy'. While the acquittals may be explained by laziness, the shift to conviction for everyone suggests that the 'judge is pursuing a personal agenda'. Janet responds: 'that's not an agenda, it's corruption' ('Lurking Doubt'). An unlikely plot point is that only the solicitor realises that the judge has been misusing precedent to 'bend his judgments'. It transpires that senior police officer Rizzoli has discovered the child pornography ring and has been using it to blackmail powerful people to do what he wanted - the police have a 'judge in their pocket' ('Overtime'). Unlike Janet, Rizzoli does not trust the legal system to deliver law and order. Prior to committing suicide, Rizzoli says to Janet: 'I want good people like you to be safe. They do whatever I want. The system works. The state hasn't been this safe in years ... those images gave me a way of controlling things' ('The Greatest Good').

The series ends suggesting that Rizzoli's lack of trust in the system may be correct. The AG celebrates Rizzoli as an excellent police officer, concealing his corruption so that there is no need to reconsider past trials. Likewise, the DPP are bribed in a backroom deal with extra funding to keep the corruption quiet. Although at the conclusion of Series One, 'all the bad guys are dead or in jail' ('The Greatest Good'), questions are raised about the corruption of law and politics, and the capacity for the legal system to deliver justice.

If, as American Realism asserts, who the judge is matters, then the potential for judicial corruption is a logical extension of American Realism. While American series are more likely to explore the judge as criminal, they are reluctant to explore judicial corruption. In contrast, all the Australian series considered in this chapter accept and explore the possibility of judicial corruption, raising questions about the possibilities for justice in a corrupt world. Each series portrays judges using their position of power and their knowledge of law to deliver 'perverse' judgments. Perhaps this difference reflects a more idealistic perception of the legal system in American television than in Australia, that justice will be delivered despite the flaws of the legal system.

VII Conclusion

There are myriad reasons as to why judges tend to play marginal roles in popular culture. Not all these reasons are bad.[66] Perhaps the simplest reason for the secondary role of judges is story structure. Legal cases provide a natural script organisation, with a beginning, middle and end. The beginning introduces the character, the middle provides complications and obstacles for the character/s to deal with, and the end provides a resolution or circumvention of these obstacles. Judges often do not play a part until the end, articulating a resolution. In addition, popular culture raises dilemmas which have no easy solution. Many solutions are posited throughout a story. Judges may provide a result for hard cases, but the show does not necessarily provide a *solution*. As Stephen Gillers has explained: 'A story must have an ending of sorts; a court proceeding must have a judgment. Yet due regard for the ambiguity

---

[66] David Ray Papke, 'From Flat to Round: Changing Portrayals of the Judge in American Popular Culture' (2007) 31 *Journal of Legal Professionals* 127.

and complexity of issues like these makes it imperative that the show not pretend to have solved them in less than an hour'.[67]

This secondary role of judges may not necessarily accord with how judges see themselves, as one part of a resolution, albeit the institutionally sanctioned resolution. However, frequently television series posit alternatives or show how parties cope with the judicial resolution. The judgment is not the only part of the narrative.

The depiction of judges as marginal characters through stereotypes and with simple signifiers is in accordance with Weber's ideal of rational legal power – judges are replaceable and interchangeable, one judge among many. Arguably this is a positive portrayal of judges. Although many characters in popular culture hope for a 'good' judge, in the bulk of shows, the judge as individual does not usually have an impact on the outcome. Popular culture does on occasion portray judges as more than 'potted plants' – particularly in a trope of clever judges, who although bound by law deliver judgments which provide justice beyond what is expected by characters or audience. Popular culture portrays the dilemma faced by judges in applying laws with which they fundamentally disagree thoughtfully and sympathetically, reflecting some of the key themes explored in jurisprudence. Interestingly, Australian popular culture has been more open than its American counterpart to exploring judicial corruption. This is portrayed as a failure by an individual judge, rather than by the legal system itself. It is predominantly in these cases of judicial corruption that the idea of American Realism that who the judge is matters is sadly borne out.

---

[67] Stephen Gillers, 'Taking LA Law More Seriously' (1989) 98 *Yale Law Journal* 1067, 1611.

INDEX

Introductory Note

References such as '178-79' indicate (not necessarily continuous) discussion of a topic across a range of pages. Wherever possible in the case of topics with many references, these have either been divided into subtopics or only the most significant discussions of the topic are listed. Because the entire work is about the 'judiciary', the use of this (and certain other terms which occur constantly throughout the book) as an entry point has been minimised. Information will be found under the corresponding detailed topics.

ability, 28-30, 32, 36-38, 44, 193, 196, 277, 287, 291
Aboriginal peoples, 90, 93, 95-98, 101, 174, 269-70
ABS 92 *see* Australian Bureau of Statistics
abuse, 242, 244, 249
  sexual, 244
accountability, 7, 11, 56, 59, 61-65, 69, 71-72, 118-19, 126-30, 139-40
  Chief Justices, 61-65
  individual, 230
  value of, 62, 64-65
activism, 8, 16-17, 163, 165-86, 252
  appellation, 172-73, 180-81
  characterisations of, 167-69, 171
  conservative, 181
  debate, 163, 167, 180, 182
  informed public criticism of courts without activism terminology, 182-86
  language of, 166, 175, 178, 180-81, 183, 186
  meanings, 166-72
  perceived, 172, 177
  in political discourse, 172-77
  reasons for enduring appeal of term in popular discourse, 172-80
  repercussions for courts, 180-82
  terminology, 166, 172, 176, 182, 185
  use of activist language in legal community, 178-79
activist critiques, 176-77, 186
activist judges, 13, 168-69, 303
  hard-left, 58, 163
activist language, 183
  use in legal community, 178-79
adjournments, 154-55, 157, 159, 162, 290
administrative decisions, 119, 142
administrative powers, 47, 62
affection, 3, 89, 160
affective work, 143-46
age, 96, 100-1, 107, 136, 281
agency, 16, 146, 156
algorithmic risk assessments, 117, 139
algorithms, 125, 128, 130
  opaque machine-learning, 16
allegiances, 271, 291
Allsop, Chief Justice, 121, 276-77
ambiguities, 47, 180, 305
ambivalence, 297, 302-3

INDEX

American Realism, 8, 173, 228, 290–94, 296, 299, 301, 305–6
American television, 294–96, 303, 305
analysis
 bifurcated, 169, 179
 content, 18, 236, 238–39, 255
 critical, 25, 32
 quantitative, 71, 245
 statistical, 15, 123, 135, 276
 value, 245, 247, 251, 254–56
analytics, 137, 139
 predictive, 134, 138
ancestry, 93, 95, 100, 105, 110
anger, 144, 149–58, 160
antagonism, 150, 153, 157
appellate courts, 5, 17, 190–91, 196, 202, 208
 final, 205, 212
 intermediate, 213, 221, 223, 228
appointments, judicial 65 *see* judicial appointments
apprehended bias, 134–35, 270
appropriateness, 3, 8, 164
arbitrariness, 34, 40
artificial intelligence, 20, 122–23
 applications, 16, 117
assault, 297–98
 sexual, 242–43, 246–47, 303
assessment, 34, 53–55, 73, 90, 159–60, 168, 180, 270
 objective, 149, 152
 risk, 124, 129, 138
attributes, 51, 86, 90–91, 98, 110, 112–14, 143, 199
attrition, 85, 111–13
audiences, 209–11, 220–21, 223–24, 226–27, 230, 286, 289–90, 297–98, 300
 judicial, 213, 277
Australia 54 *see Introductory Note*
Australian Bureau of Statistics (ABS), 92, 94–97, 100–6, 108–10
Australian Constitution, 22, 170, 173, 177, 234
authorial control, 223, 226
authoritative tone, 227–28
authority, 33–34, 37–38, 64, 273–74, 284, 289–90, 297

judicial, 154, 156, 161, 274
automated systems, 16, 119, 126, 128–30, 132–34, 136, 138–40
automation, 117–19, 122–23, 129, 138–41
 of decision-making, 122–25
 tools, 118, 124, 129, 132, 141
awareness, 154, 158, 160, 298
 public, 131, 182

backgrounds
 academic, 212
 professional, 93–94, 136, 192
 social, 83, 98–99
bail conditions, 292, 302
balance, 18, 43, 55, 111, 239, 249–51
 fair, 201
 work-life, 112, 296
bamboo ceiling, 84
Bandes, Susan, 285
barristers, 84, 99, 111, 189, 272, 288
Beazley, Justice, 221, 228, 231
behaviour, 36–39, 41, 113, 150, 154, 162, 172, 286, 290
 judicial, 116, 172, 180–81, 186, 198, 207
beliefs, personal, 300, 303
Bell, Justice, 15, 242, 246, 249–54
bias, 16, 87, 89, 134–35, 139–40, 150, 153, 295–96, 303
 absence of, 126, 133
 actual, 134–35
 apprehended, 134–35, 270
 institutional, 57, 131
 unconscious, 89
birth, country of, 93, 100, 106, 136
black armband historians, 174–75
boundaries, 16, 33, 156, 159, 259
Boyd-White, James, 227
branches
 executive, 58–59, 65, 200
 judicial, 6, 51–52, 56, 62, 241
 political, 6, 60, 75, 223
Brennan, Chief Justice, 60, 74–76, 127, 131, 184, 235

Campbell, Enid, 99, 265–66
Canada, 88, 90, 113, 122, 184, 194, 205, 264

INDEX

capacity, 4, 6, 126, 132, 140, 146, 153, 209, 213, 216
Cardozo, Justice Benjamin, 44, 219–20, 222, 225, 227
careers, 83, 85, 88, 91, 99, 111, 115
caricatures, 226, 283–84, 288, 290
caseloads, 198, 204, 252
caution, 10, 263, 280
censuses, 15, 85, 92–94, 97, 100–1, 104–10, 115
  questions, 92–93, 100, 105, 107
challenges, 4, 8, 13, 15, 56, 59, 68, 128–29, 140
chambers, 60, 155, 192, 209, 289–90, 293–95, 297–98
Chief Justices, 13–14, 50–77, 193, 196, 199–200, 213–30, 268, 276–77
  see also individual names
  accountability, 61–65
  and delivery of judgments, 69–72
  and efficiency, 68–72
  independence, 57–61
  and judicial appointments, 73–76
  and judicial discipline, 62–65
  judicial leadership and reflections on office, 4, 52–55
  legitimacy values and relational pressures, 55–76
  and representativeness, 72–76
  retired, 54–55
  role, 5, 52, 55, 76
  and technology, 66–68
  and transparency, 65–68
children, 120, 150, 179, 243–44
  feuding, 31
chilling effect, 113
civil disobedience, 300–1
civility, 161, 189, 204
clarity, 17, 25, 33–34, 45, 197, 203, 212, 219, 229
  pursuit of, 14, 46, 201, 214
clerks, 123, 205, 214–15, 293, 298, 302
clients, 290, 297–98
coalitions, 112, 164, 175–77, 255
codes, 130, 262, 289
  ethical, 281
  judicial, 261, 267
coherence, 22, 40, 45, 219

collective institutions, 5, 11
collective practices, 8, 218
collegial courts, 17, 193, 205–6
collegiality, 7, 13–17, 23, 48, 67, 189–207, 238, 246
  institutional perspectives, 197–202
  meaning, 191–97
  rise of judicial value, 202–7
commentators, 139, 165–68, 171–72, 175–77, 180–86, 271
common law tradition, 13, 208–9
communication, interpersonal, 149, 152
community, 10, 15, 28, 34, 88–90, 224, 227, 297–98, 300–2, 304
  legal, 172, 178–79, 182–83, 186, 194
COMPAS system, 124–25, 129–30, 132
compassion, 148, 150, 155
competing values, 18, 235, 241–42
complaints, 5, 7, 10, 61–64, 69–70, 254, 264, 269
complexity, 56, 58, 63, 72–73, 110–12, 139, 145, 226–27, 229, 236
compliance, 37, 140, 162
composition
  ethnic, 95
  ideal, 91, 95
  of judiciary/courts, 83–84, 89, 95–98, 113, 115, 202, 207, 212, 214–15, 248
conceptual framework, 32, 47
concurrences, 212, 223, 230–32
conduct, judicial, 3, 62, 154, 160, 162, 261, 288
confidence, public, 60, 63, 68, 73, 88–89, 127, 181–82, 259, 265, 278
conflicts, 19, 38–40, 57, 60, 122, 193, 199, 202, 246
  underlying, 32, 34
conformity, 152, 239, 241, 243–47, 252, 254, 256
confusion, 41, 182–83, 267, 281
conscience, 6, 294, 296
consensus, 34, 166, 180, 213–15, 225, 232, 246, 284
consent, 31, 273
conservation, 44, 241, 254
conservatives, social, 173–74

consistency, 124, 133, 208, 217, 236, 242, 246–47, 251–52, 255, 234
constituencies, 181, 235
Constitution, Australian, 22, 170, 173, 177, 234
constitutional cases, 236–38, 252, 254–55
constitutional context, 23–26
constitutional functions, 5, 221
constitutional limits, 22–23, 26, 253
constraints, 24, 26, 87, 139–41, 159–60, 210, 212, 233, 255
  institutional, 159
constructivism, strict, 169
consultations, 191, 206
  public, 92
contempt, 13, 58, 164
content analysis, 18, 236, 238–39, 255
control, 32–33, 128, 146, 149, 151, 154–56, 161, 199, 240, 249
  authorial, 223, 226
  social, 37–38, 286
convention, 18, 60, 241, 261–62, 265
corruption, 132, 140, 275, 300, 303–5
  judicial, 131, 304–6
counsel, 70, 129, 149, 151, 154, 161
country of birth, 93, 100, 105–6, 136
court administrations, 183–85
courtroom, 67–68, 120, 127, 150, 154–59, 161, 288–90, 292–99
  participants, 154, 156, 159
courts 5 *see also Introductory Note*
  collegial, 17, 193, 205–6
  criminal, 121, 127
  final, 18, 205, 210, 212, 223, 230, 233, 255
  hierarchy, 101, 209
  highest, 63, 115, 233
  intermediate, 149, 213, 221, 223, 228
  leadership, 5, 197, 202
  lower, 47, 100, 148, 191, 276, 281
  multi-member, 7, 11–13, 17, 193, 200, 207, 229, 233–37, 255–56
  role, 5, 22, 26, 119
Crennan J, 240, 243, 246–54
crime, 124, 151, 156–58, 243, 283, 289, 300

criminal courts, 121, 127
criminal sentencing, 119, 123–24, 139–41
criticism, public, 59, 61, 127, 135, 178, 182, 261, 265
criticisms, personal, 259, 268–69
cross-examination, 144, 297
cross-institutional dynamics, 65
culture, 4, 17, 136, 193, 200, 204, 286, 295, 301
  popular, 19–20, 283–87, 289–90, 294, 296, 298–99, 302–3, 305–6
  wars, 173–74, 186
custodial sentences, 301–2

decision-makers, 141, 237, 241–42, 246, 251, 254
  quasi-judicial, 116, 142
decision-making, 119, 122, 125–26, 132–37, 139, 237, 246–47, 256
  automation, 122–25
  processes, 116, 118–19, 122, 128, 132–34, 206, 236, 247, 251
decision-support, 122, 125
  systems, 123–24, 133
defendants, 124, 146, 159, 161, 269–70, 304
delay, 69–70, 138, 154, 173, 275
delegation, 132, 154, 159, 215
deliberations/deliberative processes, 13, 17, 144, 190, 195, 197, 202–3, 207
  secret, 209
delivery of judgments, 8, 275–76, 302
  and Chief Justices, 69–72
democracy, 19, 92, 176, 235
democratic legitimacy, 235, 255
descriptors, 166–67, 172, 176, 179–80
Devlin, Richard, 7, 14, 16, 51–52, 56–57, 61, 65, 126, 131
differential pattern of value expression, 244, 247–49, 255
differential treatment, 113, 134
digitisation, 118–22, 128, 131–32, 140
  processes, 120–21
dignity, 66, 76, 154, 192
dilemmas, 64, 305–6
  ethical, 4, 62
disability, 72, 93, 98, 100, 107, 110, 136
  mental, 107

INDEX

disadvantaged groups, 85, 94
disagreement, 20, 23, 25, 52, 195–96, 198, 233, 235, 255–56
discipline, 4, 62, 86, 145, 201
   judicial, 62–65
discovery, 15, 66, 116, 124, 139–40, 217, 296
discretion, 3, 16, 34, 47, 76, 84, 90, 118, 129, 138
   executive, 84, 115
discrimination, 16, 86, 118, 140
   systemic, 76
disenfranchisement, 242, 254
disorder, 161
   social, 45
dispassion, judicial, 16, 144, 158, 162
display rules, 151, 159–61
dispute resolution, 14, 27, 29–33, 39, 222, 305–6
   inter-party, 29, 31
   judicial form, 27–35, 37–40, 42–43, 46–48, 306
   mechanisms, 28, 35–36, 40, 118
   methods, 28–30, 37
   by reference to chance, 29, 32
   by reference to merit, 29–30
   by reference to might, 28–29, 37
   systems, 35–37
   taxonomy of methods, 28–33
   third-party, 29, 31, 38
      merit-based, 31, 33, 45, 48
dissenting judgments/opinions, 18, 194, 196, 223, 229, 235, 255–56
diversity, 15, 72, 84–98, 110–15, 126, 136, 139–41, 206–7, 294
   age, 101–2
   ancestry, 105, 110
   characteristics, 15, 85, 90–94, 101, 112, 115
   composition of Australian judiciary, 98–100
   composition of Australian population, 95–97
   country of birth, 106
   deficit, 15, 83–115, 137
      measuring, 94–111
      redressing, 111–14
   disability, 107
   educational status, 93, 100, 108
   gender, 87, 109–10, 112–13, 115
   justifying, 85–90, 92, 94, 114
   languages spoken, 107
   marital status, 102–3
   national census and diversity characteristics, 92–95
   new national census dataset, 100–11
   of perspectives, 227, 256
   religion, 104–5
   and technology, 136–37
   value, 13, 18, 236, 255–56
   variables, 101, 115
Dixon, Chief Justice, 170–71, 173, 213, 225
Dodek, Adam, 7, 14, 16, 51–52, 56–57, 61, 65, 68, 131
dominant cultural script of judicial dispassion, 162
dominant values, 243–46, 249, 254
duties, 65, 69–70, 76, 89, 200, 236, 241, 260
dynamics
   cross-institutional, 65
   institutional, 17, 23
   relational, 4, 8

echo chamber, 135, 179–80
education, 5, 86, 93, 100, 108, 110, 136
   judicial, 4–5, 61, 66, 85, 111, 114
   legal, 34, 183
effectiveness, 38, 52, 156
efficacy, 24, 34, 37, 39–40, 42, 44, 137, 179
efficiency, 16–17, 48, 56, 69–72, 121–22, 125–26, 137–40, 203, 276–77
   and Chief Justices, 68–72
   and technology, 137–39
e-filing, 15, 120–21
elections, 175, 252, 254, 285
elites, 168, 173, 176
emotion management, 145, 151, 154–56, 158, 162
   strategies, 154–58, 161–62
emotion work, 16, 143–62
   and emotion, 143–47
   interview segments, 148–51
   limits, 151, 158–59
   research design and method, 147

emotions, 16, 20, 149, 151–60, 162
  background, 146, 151, 157–58, 162
  and emotion work, 143–47
  expression of, 156, 160
  judicial, 10, 162
  in judicial work, 151–61
empathy, 148, 150–51, 153, 155–60
enforcement, 27, 37, 162
  mechanisms, 45
engagement, judicial, 5, 13, 18, 47, 204
English judges, 208, 212–13, 220, 260, 263
environment, 24–25, 114–15, 203–4, 264, 270
  judicial, 85, 113
  normative, 154, 160
equality, 73, 85–86, 91, 113, 115, 136, 240
  and technology, 133–36
error, 97, 101, 203
ethical dilemmas, 4, 62
ethical goals, 162
ethics, 87
  judicial, 62, 160, 274
ethnicity, 83, 136
everyday work, 139, 148, 151, 154, 162
evidence, 135, 138, 140, 203, 206, 238–40, 242–44, 246–48, 255–56, 297–98
  documentary, 121, 149
  expert, 132, 140
  relationship, 243, 246
  rules of, 34, 297
executive branch, 58–59, 65, 200
executive discretion, 84, 115
exercise of power, 6, 38, 47, 141, 259, 265
expectations, 3–4, 14, 65, 68, 72, 90, 152, 161, 197, 201
  institutional, 200, 202
  public, 19, 70, 288
experience, 15–16, 86–87, 90, 156–57, 190–94, 203, 205–7, 290–91, 294
  judicial, 99, 191, 207, 281
expert evidence, 132, 140
expert knowledge, 31, 298
expert systems, 123, 128–29

expertise, 140, 183, 192, 268, 293, 298
exploratory tone, 210, 227–28
extra-curial activities, 4, 76

Facebook, 127, 133, 280–81
fair balance, 201
fairness, 31, 34, 227, 240, 243, 249, 276, 296, 298
  procedural, 138
family members, 150, 159, 244
federal level, 6, 8
feeling rules, 155, 159–62
  and display rules, 159–61
  implicit, 160, 162
feelings, 151–62
  personal, 143, 293
female judges/judicial officers, 98, 102–4, 109, 148, 294–95
feminist scholars, 74–76
final courts, 18, 205, 210, 212, 223, 230, 233, 255
final outcomes, 235–36, 246, 251, 255–56
fiscal independence, 57, 131
force, 28, 37, 160, 176, 200, 244
  armed, 271
  persuasive, 210, 219, 228
formal rules, 160, 291, 298
formalism, legal, 218, 226
formalists, 291, 301
forms, judicial, 27–28, 33, 42
frameworks, 4, 51, 53–77, 121, 145, 162, 217
  conceptual, 32, 47
  normative, 6–7, 14, 47, 52, 76, 166
  value, 18, 51–53, 55–56, 235–36
Frank, Jerome, 296–97
fraud, 288, 300, 302
freedom, 86, 125, 174, 265–66, 278
French, Chief Justice, 50, 60, 178, 240, 246, 248–49, 252–54
Friedman, Lawrence, 284
functions, 22, 26, 45–48, 76, 89, 196, 202, 259, 263–64
  constitutional, 5, 221
  judicial, 14, 22, 26–28, 35, 38, 42, 45–46, 48, 210, 216

INDEX

gender, 72, 74, 83, 85, 87–88, 90, 101–2, 105–9, 136–37, 148
   diversity, 87, 112–13, 115
genre, literary, 214, 217, 226
Gibbs, Sir Harry, 218–20
Gibson, Laura (TV character), 288, 290, 292–93, 295, 298, 300–4
Gleeson, Chief Justice, 6, 63, 70, 74, 178, 243
goals, 48, 114–15, 125, 138, 151, 159, 229, 236, 275
   ethical, 162
   motivational, 239–40
good humoured tone, 151, 159
governance, 27, 35–36, 38–39, 42, 45
   conclusions, 43–45
   good, 35, 38, 44
   normative, 38, 41, 48
   social, 12–14, 22, 28, 35–36, 41, 45, 126
   through power, 36–38
   through rules, 38–43
government, 10–11, 35–37, 45, 60, 65, 77–79, 115, 259, 264–65
green lawfare, 271
Greene, Cleaver (TV character), 288–89, 293, 295–97, 299–301
guidance, 70, 91, 261–62, 267, 281
Gummow, Justice, 235, 242–44, 246, 252–54

Hale, Lady, 266, 272
hard cases, identification, 237–38
Hayne, Justice, 241–43, 246–52
head of jurisdiction, 4, 8, 51, 62, 72–73
hearings, 15, 127, 267–68
   online, 122
   public, 193
Heerey, Justice, 116, 135, 142
Heydon, Justice, 11–13, 47–48, 178–79, 201, 212, 216, 241, 243, 245–47, 274–78
hierarchy, 56, 146, 154–55, 161, 301, 303
   court, 101, 209
High Court, 11–13, 47–49, 173–75, 195–200, 221–22, 229–31, 233–56, 274–77
high profile cases, 265, 267
historians, black armband, 174–75

history, 9, 50, 58, 74, 83, 89, 93, 209, 217, 226
   English legal, 260
hubris
   judicial, 168, 171, 175, 181
   political, 180
human nature, 116, 142, 150, 153
human rights, 86, 168, 176, 264, 271
ideals, 127, 227, 241
   political, 264
identities, judicial, 158, 169, 182
illness, 71 *see also* disability
   mental, 114
imagination, 300, 304
impartiality, 6–7, 32, 34, 56–58, 62, 88–89, 125–27, 131–37, 139–41, 160–62
   and technology, 133–36
implied rights jurisprudence, 163, 175, 177
inclusive judiciary, 15, 83–115
independence, 11, 52, 56, 58–59, 61–62, 70–73, 130–32, 140, 200–2, 263
   Chief Justices, 57–61
   fiscal, 57, 131
   institutional, 57, 131–32
   and technology, 130–32
   threats to, 11, 48, 75
   value of, 56–58, 61, 127
Indigeneity, 87, 114
individual responsibilities, 3–4, 6, 12, 15, 254
individualism, 214, 229
individuality, 13, 19, 201
   historical, 213
   judicial, 208, 229
inevitability, 28, 42, 114, 226–27
   rhetoric of, 226–27
information, 92–93, 130–31, 135, 147–48, 152, 267, 269, 297–98, 304
injustice, 44, 46, 88, 153, 249, 277
innovation, 22, 222, 256
   technological, 10, 66
institutional context, 7, 145, 221, 232
institutional dynamics, 17, 23
institutional expectations, 200, 202

INDEX

institutional independence, 57, 131–32
institutional norms, 208–32
institutional practices, 13, 197, 210, 231, 267
institutional requirements, 6, 9, 162
institutional responsibilities, 4, 201, 214
institutional role, 3, 14
institutional values, 4–5, 7, 11, 14–16, 52, 56, 59, 62, 72–77
institutions, 6, 8, 14–15, 36–37, 55, 57, 62–63, 200–2, 207
   collective, 5, 11
   curial, 19, 190
   and individual style, 229–32
   judicial, 6, 13–15, 45, 51, 56, 63, 71–72
   public, 93, 173, 181
instructions, 220, 269, 299
intentions, 166, 219, 231, 249, 254, 264, 272
inter-curial dynamics, 12
interests, 31, 33–37, 76, 89–90, 93, 127, 131, 171, 173–74
   of justice, 44
   potential, 90, 93
   public, 43, 127, 264, 270
   social, 31, 243
interlocutors, 171, 180
intermediate courts, 149, 213, 221, 223, 228
inter-party resolution, 29, 31
   chance-based, 29, 32
   merit-based, 29–30
   might-based, 29–30
interpersonal communication, 149, 152
intersections, 10, 72, 76, 284–86
intervention, 31, 59, 77, 292, 297
interview methodology, 147
interviews, 4, 16, 67–68, 145, 147–50, 156, 162, 273, 278
intra-curial dynamics, 48
isolation, 5, 44, 112, 205

Janet King - JK (TV series), 287–90, 292–97, 299, 303–4
joint judgments/opinions, 69, 190, 198, 201, 212–14, 229–32, 240, 242

journalists 181, 184, 260, 265, 269, 273
   see also media
judges 293 *see also individual judges* and *Introductory Note*
   celebration of, 299, 303
   female, 148, 294–95
   individual, 3–12, 14–19, 71, 130–31, 137–38, 203–4, 229–30, 246–47
   male, 87, 294–95
   portrayal of, 19, 283–84, 287, 303
   retired, 216, 273–74, 278
   secondary role, 284, 299, 305–6
   unelected, 42, 168, 174
   women, 5, 75–76, 113, 148
judgments 69 *see also Introductory Note*
   delivery 8 *see* delivery of judgments
   joint, 69, 190, 198, 201, 212–14, 229–32, 240, 242
   length, 253
   majority, 222–23, 229–31, 242, 244
   minority, 243–45, 247, 254
   written, 169, 211
judicial activism 8 *see* activism
judicial appointments, 64, 84, 86, 99, 177, 198, 263, 265–66
   and Chief Justices, 73–76
judicial authority, 154, 156, 161, 274
judicial behaviour, 116, 172, 180–81, 186, 198, 207
judicial branch, 6, 51–52, 56, 62, 241
judicial codes, 261, 267
judicial collective, 4–5
judicial collegiality 7 *see* collegiality
judicial conduct, 3, 62, 154, 160, 162, 261, 288
Judicial Conference of Australia, 5, 58, 183, 267
judicial corruption, 131, 304–6
judicial decision-making method, 26, 34, 43
judicial discipline, 62–65
judicial dispassion, 16, 144, 158, 162
judicial diversity 13 *see* diversity
judicial education, 4–5, 61, 66, 85, 111, 114
judicial engagement, 5, 13, 18, 47, 204
judicial ethics, 62, 160, 274
judicial experiences, 99, 191, 207, 281

INDEX

judicial form of dispute resolution, 27–35, 37–40, 42–43, 46–48, 306
judicial form of social governance, 35–45
judicial function(s), 14, 22, 26–28, 35, 37, 42, 45–46, 48, 210, 216
  in Australia, 22–48
  revisited, 45–48
judicial hubris, 168, 171, 175, 181
judicial identities, 158, 169, 182
judicial independence 7 see independence
judicial individuality, 208, 229
judicial institution, 6–8, 13–15, 45, 51, 56, 63, 71–72
judicial leadership, 4, 50, 52–55, 207
judicial legitimacy, 52, 55–56, 156
judicial methodology, 166, 180, 182
judicial misconduct, 10, 62
judicial officers, 5, 16–17, 84–86, 89, 98, 100–11, 114–15, 144, 147–48, 154–57, 160–62 see also judges; magistrates
  female, 98, 102, 109
  male, 101, 109
  population of, 113, 147
judicial opinions, 211, 214, 217, 220, 224–26, 236–37, 245, 255
judicial performance, 17, 53, 90, 152, 154, 162
judicial personality, 198, 215, 219, 225–26
judicial power, 8, 22–26, 46, 73, 265, 285
  exercise of, 6, 141, 259, 265
  nature and limits of, 22, 24
judicial practices, 47, 161, 167, 169, 172, 176
judicial process, 6, 66, 68, 128, 132, 195, 207
judicial reasoning, 130, 170, 215, 248
judicial relationships, 4, 193, 199
judicial resolution, 33–35, 38, 42–43, 48, 306
judicial role, 7–12, 15–18, 20, 22, 43–44, 117–19, 132–33, 158–59, 299
  and technology, 142

judicial scholarship, 8–10, 195
judicial selection, 88, 111–12
judicial style 13 see style
judicial systems, 5, 15, 34, 42, 86, 115
judicial transparency, 126, 129, 139
judicial values, 7–8, 55, 57, 61, 117, 119, 125–26, 136–37, 139–42, 202–7
judicial wellbeing, 7, 56, 61, 70, 205
judiciary 205 see also Introductory Note; judges; judicial officers; magistrates
  Australian, 20, 26, 83, 89, 98–100, 107–9, 114–15, 136–37, 165, 171
  diverse, 84, 90, 111, 136
  inclusive, 15, 83–115
juries, 121, 150, 153, 244, 294, 299–300

Kiefel, Chief Justice, 13, 18, 193, 198, 201, 222, 230–32
Kilmuir rules, 260–62, 265–66
Kirby, Justice, 63, 86, 196, 199, 212–25, 234–35, 243–45
knowledge, 86, 130, 132, 164, 182, 230, 277, 300, 305
Kourakis, Chief Justice, 65, 131

labels, 8, 13, 176, 178, 183, 294
language, 30, 32, 83, 86, 93–98, 100, 107, 130, 163, 173
  of activism, 166, 175, 178, 180–81, 183, 186
law clerks 123 see clerks
law officers, 18
  first, 262–63, 266
law-making, 41–42, 45
leadership, 11, 20, 50, 53–56, 59, 75, 112, 200, 202
  court, 5, 197, 202
  judicial, 4, 50, 52–55, 207
  roles, 8, 61
legal community, 172, 178–79, 182–83, 186, 194
legal education, 34, 183
legal educationalists, 179, 183
legal formalism, 218, 226
legal profession, 66, 75, 83, 111, 115, 223, 293

legal realism, 8, 173, 228
legal system, 46, 90, 118, 120, 266, 271, 277, 283, 285, 304–6
legal uncertainty, 237, 242
legalism, 8, 170–71, 173, 178–79, 183
legislation, 170, 234, 252, 254, 263, 271
   overturning, 172
   tax, 141
legislature, 6, 51, 224, 254
legitimacy, 34, 36, 41, 47, 56, 85, 88, 91–92, 173, 176
   democratic, 235, 255
   judicial, 52, 55–56, 156
liberty, 24, 223
   individual, 7, 141
literary genre, 214, 217, 226
literature, 74, 87, 89, 93, 113, 148, 208, 211, 223, 225
   academic, 165, 284
   chilly climate, 113
Llewellyn, Karl, 298
logic, 91, 130, 141, 170, 291, 294, 305

machine learning, 16, 117, 124
Macmillan, Lord, 216, 219
magistrates, 15, 85–86, 98–102, 107–8, 115, 191–92, 269–70, 273, 293, 300–2 *see also* judicial officers
   new, 290, 292
majorities, 13, 221–23, 230–31, 234–35, 238, 243–44, 246–52, 254, 256
   large, 105, 178
majority judgments/opinions, 222–23, 229–31, 242, 244
male judicial officers, 101, 109
marital status, 93, 100, 102–3
Mason, Sir Anthony, 20, 178, 195, 200, 229
meanings, 16–17, 42, 44, 50, 133, 165–68, 171–72, 182, 217, 220
mechanisms, 28, 31–32, 39, 41, 45, 116, 140, 143
media, 13–14, 18–20, 51, 67–69, 128, 165, 180, 224
   attention, 64, 266, 270, 274–75, 277
   changing perceptions of judges and changing cases before courts, 263–65

   coverage, 68, 128, 259, 261, 267–68, 272, 278, 282
   decline of first law officers as judicial defenders, 262–63
   examples of judges in the media, 269–73
   and judges, 259–82
   judges criticising courts/other judges in the media, 273–78
   Kilmuir rules, 260–62, 265–66
   new forms of, 77, 281
   outlets, 184–85, 271
   possible judicial responses, 265–68
   reportage, 165, 168, 173, 180, 183–84
   social, 4, 66–67, 133, 183, 185, 279–81
   traditional, 279–81
merit, 29–34, 45, 73–76, 88, 300
   criteria, 33
   resolution by reference to, 29–30
   third-party, 33, 45
methodology, 20, 98–100, 140, 166–67, 171
   interview, 147
   judicial, 166, 180, 182
metrics, 71–72, 141, 276
might, resolution by reference to, 28–29, 37
ministers, 13, 58–59, 164, 171, 179, 184, 263, 270
   federal, 165, 179
minorities, 75–76, 167, 223, 238, 244, 246–52, 254, 266
minority judgments/positions, 243–45, 247, 254
misconduct, 7
   judicial, 10, 62
   sexual, 242–43
misinformation, 67, 183
morality, 34, 264, 291
motivational goals, 239–40
motivations, 195, 203, 215, 238–39, 252
   overarching, 235, 239
   political, 9
   value, 239, 245, 247, 250–51, 253
multi-member courts, 7, 11–13, 17, 193, 200, 207, 229, 233–37, 255–56

INDEX

national census
   and diversity characteristics, 92–95
   new dataset, 100–11
native title, 163, 173–75, 177
neutrality, 3, 143, 259, 280
New South Wales, 5, 20, 70–71, 221, 238, 247, 267, 270, 274
newspapers, 164, 269, 272, 275, 279
non-legal factors, 33, 291
normative development, 43, 46
normative framework, 6–7, 14, 47, 52, 76, 166
norms, 7, 34, 36, 38, 154, 159–62, 277
   institutional, 208–32
   social, 33, 36, 145–46

oath, 3–4, 6, 89, 160
obedience, 131, 298, 302
obfuscation, 17, 180, 183
objective assessment, 149, 152
obligations, 11, 17, 27, 30, 61, 75–76, 89, 137, 157, 254
   moral, 236
online hearings, 122
open justice, 126–30
opinions, judicial 211 *see* judicial opinions
orations, 178, 182, 216
outcomes, 5, 30, 32–33, 217–19, 235–37, 240, 249–51, 256, 298
   final, 235–36, 246, 251, 255–56
   supporting opposing, 237, 255
outsiders, 120, 190

Parliament, 60, 71, 117, 248, 253–54, 264, 301, 303
parliamentary sovereignty, 253–54
patience, 148, 154, 156
patterns, 41, 107, 128, 134–35, 137, 140
   differential, 244
   of value expression, 255–56
peak bodies, 183–85
perceptions, 4, 18, 67, 74, 148, 153, 158, 235
   changing, 263–64
   public, 19, 136, 165, 182, 184, 280, 284

performance, 7–8, 15, 50–51, 53, 74, 114, 146, 159, 190
   judicial, 17, 53, 90, 152, 154, 162
permissiveness, 173, 177
personal beliefs, 300, 303
personal criticisms, 259, 268–69
personal feelings, 143, 293
personal relationships, 50, 201
personal voice, 227–28
personalities, 50, 197–99, 219, 225, 296
persuasion, 47, 219, 228
persuasive force, 210, 219, 228
pipelines, career, 85, 111, 115
police, 272, 283, 288–89, 292–93, 297–98, 304
political branch, 6, 60, 75, 223
political debate, 77, 180
political interventions/pressures, 56, 292, 303
political strategy, 176–77
politicians, 18, 165, 172, 176, 181–82, 184, 186, 261, 265, 271
politics, 115, 173–74, 186, 291–92, 305
Popkin, William D, 210, 220, 226–28
popular culture, 19–20, 283–87, 289–91, 294, 296, 298–99, 302–3, 305–6
   importance of who the judge is, 290–303
   judge as caricature, 288–90
   judge as villain, 303–5
   judges and civil disobedience, 299–303
   studies, 284–86
positivist approach, 170, 291, 302
Posner, Richard, 217–20, 222, 224, 226, 228, 299
power, 6, 9, 23–24, 36–37, 239–40, 245, 249–51, 253, 298, 300–1
   exercise of, 6, 38, 47, 141, 259, 265
   governance through, 36–38
   judicial, 8, 22–26, 46, 73, 265, 285
   limited, 63, 65
   separation of powers, 23–24, 51, 59, 131, 252
precedent, 41, 170–71, 226, 234, 237, 242, 248, 270, 298, 304
predictability, 11, 14, 34, 39, 43–46

predictions, 39, 124, 276, 298
predictive analytics, 134, 138
prejudices, 133, 150, 153, 248, 291, 298
pressures, 10, 19, 51–52, 57, 71, 84, 201, 212, 217, 221
  political, 56, 292
  relational, 51, 55, 63, 76
Preston, Chief Justice, 270–73
principles, 23, 40, 43, 59, 72, 86, 91, 126–28, 131, 171
  fundamental, 118, 249
  general, 41, 248
priorities, value, 236, 242–47, 251, 254–56
prioritisation, 4, 8, 18, 56, 138, 209, 236, 241, 254–56
  of universalism, 240, 244, 251–52
  of values, 74, 242, 254
prison, 295, 301–2, 304
productivity, 70, 113, 196, 276
professional background, 93–94, 136, 192
propositional style, 48, 221
prosecutors, 146, 159, 293–94, 303
protection, 6, 14, 22, 24, 53, 168, 239, 243, 249, 253–54
psychology, 18, 53, 235
public awareness, 131, 182
public confidence, 60, 63, 68, 73, 88–89, 127, 181–82, 259, 265, 278
public criticism, 59, 61, 127, 135, 178, 182, 261, 265
public discourse/discussion, 59, 90, 164, 166, 178, 182, 186, 266, 274, 277
public expectations, 19, 70, 288
public institutions, 93, 173, 181
public interest, 43, 127, 264, 270
public law, 20–21, 170
public perceptions, 19, 136, 165, 182, 184, 280, 284
public roles, 43, 118, 183
public scrutiny, 4, 165
public statements, 65, 277
public trust, 91, 132, 280
publicity, 259, 271, 275, 295

qualifications, 84, 108–9, 140, 180
quality, 85–86, 88, 97, 133, 136–37, 203–4, 207, 211–12, 219–20, 226

quantitative analysis, 71, 245
quasi-judicial decision-makers, 116, 142
Queensland, 55, 60, 67, 121, 168, 177
questions, census, 92–93, 100, 105, 107

race, 72, 85–90, 93, 136–37, 295
Rake, 287–90, 292–97, 299, 301, 303
rational legal power, 290, 306
rationality, 31, 153, 219, 296
readiness to change, 44, 241
real time transcripts, 120, 138
realism, 8, 173, 228, 290–94, 296, 299, 301, 305–6
reality court shows, 283, 287, 290, 295
reasoning, 89–91, 140, 144, 170–71, 211, 213, 219, 224, 226, 228
  judicial, 130, 170, 215, 248
recusal, 270, 278, 281
referees, 30, 299–300
reflexivity, 148, 151–54, 157, 162
reform, 26, 41, 47, 65, 68–69, 84–85, 112, 263, 301, 303
relational pressures, 51, 55–76
relationship evidence, 243, 246
relationships, 14, 33, 40–41, 51, 76–77, 198–200, 246–47, 259, 293, 295–96
  judicial, 4, 193, 199
  personal, 50, 201
religion, 83, 86, 93–95, 100, 104–5, 111
Renmark, Judge (TV character), 290, 293–94, 303–4
reportage, 19, 176, 184
representativeness, 7, 17, 52, 56–57, 101, 136, 203
  and Chief Justices, 72–76
  value, 74–76
reputation, 35–36, 59, 63, 77, 172, 204, 209, 231, 260
resolution 12 *see* dispute resolution
resources, 38, 147, 156, 158, 162, 240
  positive, 16, 151, 162
responses, 12–13, 19, 52, 57–59, 61–62, 67–71, 152–53, 267–68, 272–73, 303–4
  public, 59, 61

responsibilities, 20, 38, 44, 51, 63–65, 68, 70–72, 74, 92
  individual, 3–4, 6, 12, 15, 254
  institutional, 4, 201, 214
results-oriented decisions, 167–68, 173, 180–81
retired Chief Justices, 54–55
retirement, 3, 11, 48, 75, 113, 184, 212, 235, 278
rhetoric, 219, 269, 271, 303
  of inevitability, 226–27
rights, 22, 24, 30, 36, 58, 86, 125, 131, 171, 177
  human, 86, 168, 176, 264, 271
  individual, 119, 142
risks, 20, 28, 67, 77, 113, 124–25, 136, 195, 201
  assessments, 124, 129, 138
    algorithmic, 117, 139
roles, 4–7, 14, 23–25, 41–42, 48–49, 53–58, 117, 150–51, 262–64, 268
  of chief justice, 52, 55, 76
  of courts, 5, 22, 26, 119
  institutional, 3, 14
  judicial, 7–12, 15–18, 20, 22, 43–44, 117–19, 132–33, 158–59, 299
  public, 43, 118, 183
  secondary, 19, 290, 299
  social, 27, 44
rule of law, 74, 181, 203, 263, 282
rules
  of evidence, 34, 297
  formal, 160, 291, 298
  governance through, 38–43

Sachs, Justice, 17, 193, 282
Sales, Lord, 264, 272–73
sanctions, 19, 47, 300
scholars, 17, 52, 118, 124, 167, 183, 284–86
scholarship, 8–9, 16, 53, 110, 191, 194
scrutiny, public, 4, 165
SeaChange, 287–90, 292–93, 295, 298, 303–4
secondary role, 19, 290, 299
security, 161, 239, 241
  assessment, 272
  national, 116

selection, 88, 112, 267, 284
  judicial, 88, 111–12
  processes, 85, 112
self-direction, 239, 241, 243–44, 252
self-restraint, 166, 169–70, 252
sentences, 124, 132–33, 175, 217, 269, 300–1
  custodial, 301–2
sentencing, 58, 68, 127, 129, 139, 159, 164, 270
  criminal, 119, 123–24, 139–41
separation of powers, 6, 12–13, 24, 46, 51, 59, 130, 252
sex, 86, 89, 93, 100–3 *see also* gender
  ratios, 109–10, 113
sexual assault/misconduct, 242–43, 246–47, 303
sexuality, 114, 136
silence, 74, 177, 181, 249, 267, 269, 273
site of truth, 297, 299
skills, 29–30, 153, 194
social backgrounds, 83, 98–99
social conservatives, 173–74
social control, 37–38, 286
social disorder, 45
social governance, 12–14, 22, 28, 126
  judicial form, 35–45
social media, 4, 66–67, 133, 183, 185, 279–81
social norms, 33, 36, 145–46
social order, 37–38, 46
social roles, 27, 44
social values, 41–42, 45, 235
solicitors, 99, 111–12, 297, 304
sources, 6, 58, 74, 77, 97, 109, 199, 205, 209, 227
South Africa, 17, 106, 193, 282
South Australia, 54–55, 64, 131, 243
sovereignty, parliamentary, 253–54
speeches, 4, 11, 48, 55, 65, 70–71, 121, 264, 266, 274–78
stability, 26, 35, 43–44, 60, 177, 181
standards, 4, 62, 155, 213, 219
statements, public, 65, 277
statistical analyses, 15, 123, 135, 276
statistics, 69, 74, 92, 98, 135
step-by-step programming, 123
stereotypes, 19, 87, 89, 226, 306

INDEX

strategies, 15–16, 60, 111–14, 145, 147, 150–51, 155–59, 161–62
style, 13, 17–18, 197, 200, 208–32
   context and audience, 221–24
   individual, 214, 222–23
   institution and individual style, 229–32
   judges as writers, 210–17
   personal, 226, 229
   propositional, 48, 221
   substance
      form and style, 217–24
   taxonomies, 225–29
substantive criteria, 28
Sunstein, CR, 256
support, 4–5, 61–62, 65, 70–71, 126, 132–33, 175, 222–23
Supreme Courts, 31, 64, 67–68, 127–28, 172–73, 176, 248–49, 270, 272, 280
   UK, 222, 237, 239, 255
   United States, 199, 205–6, 213–15, 222, 225
   Victoria, 13, 16, 58, 184
sympathy, 150–51, 153, 156–59, 293, 303

taxonomies, 165, 208
   dispute resolution methods, 28–33
   judicial style, 225–29
teamwork, 192, 207
techniques, 117, 123–24, 298
technology, 10, 15, 61, 92
   and Chief Justices, 66–68
   and diversity/representation, 136–37
   and efficiency, 137–39
   and foundational judicial values, 125–39
   impact, 15, 133
   and impartiality/equality before the law, 133–36
   and independence, 130–32
   and judicial role, 142
   and open justice, 126–30
   spectrum of technologies used by courts, 119–25
   tools, 117–18, 139, 141
   use, 15, 66, 116, 118

television, 260, 283–306
   American, 294–96, 303, 305
   shows, 287–88
temptations, 223, 267, 275
tenure, 54, 56, 61, 73–74, 113
terminology, 165, 171–73, 178, 182–84, 186, 271
   activism, 166, 172, 176, 182, 185
terrorism offences, 58, 164, 177
third-party resolution, 29, 31, 38
   merit-based, 31, 33, 45, 48
   by reference to chance, 29, 32
threats, 11, 48–49, 52, 66, 75, 176, 272, 292
timeliness, 137, 201, 214, 229
title, native, 163, 173–75, 177
tone, 151, 161, 210, 220–31, 272
   authoritative, 227–28
   good humoured, 151, 159
tools, 14, 17, 23, 85, 117–18, 124–25, 128–29, 132, 139–41
   automated, 132, 138
   automation, 118, 124, 129, 132, 141
Torres Strait Islanders, 90, 93–98, 101
touchstones, 47, 76, 91, 94, 220
trade secrets, 118, 129, 140
traditional media, 279–81
traditions, 59, 208, 213, 218, 229, 239–44, 249, 252–54
transcripts, 149, 152
   real time, 120, 138
transparency, 17, 52, 56–57, 59, 62, 65–66, 68, 126–30, 139, 141
   and Chief Justices, 65–68
   lack of, 129, 139–40
trivialisation, 66–67
trust, 88, 115, 127, 163, 204, 244, 304–5
   public, 91, 132, 281
truth, 273, 284, 296–99
   site of, 297, 299
turnover, 113, 268
Twitter, 67, 127–28, 185, 280

uncertainty, 42, 46–48, 91, 237, 242, 244, 267, 303
under-represented groups, 75, 85
unelected judges, 42, 168, 174
unfairness, 240, 243, 276

INDEX

United Kingdom, 18, 112, 117, 185, 210, 230–32, 263–64, 272, 287
   Supreme Court, 222, 237, 239, 255
United States, 53, 67, 90, 117, 169, 172, 181, 210–32
   Court of Appeal, 196, 207, 218
   Supreme Court, 199, 205–6, 213–15, 222, 225
universalism, 239–40, 242–47, 249–54
   prioritisation, 240, 244, 251–52
use of technology, 15, 66, 116, 119
utility, 71, 77, 85, 88, 91, 136, 166, 197, 203

value analysis, 245, 247, 251, 254–56
value diversity, 13, 18, 236, 255–56
value expression, 18, 236, 242, 244–46, 252–55
   differential pattern of, 247–49, 255
   patterns, 255–56
value framework, 18, 51–53, 55–56, 235–36
value motivations, 239, 245, 247, 250–51, 253
value priorities, 236, 242–47, 251, 254–56
values, 7, 17–18, 52, 55–58, 65–70, 72–74, 235–46, 249–56
   of accountability, 62, 64–65
   competing, 18, 235, 241–42
   consistent value priorities and division in related cases, 242–47
   diversity
      dissent and individual, 255–56
      dominant, 243–46, 249, 254
      identification in High Court judgments, 236–42
   and influence of individual judges, 247–52
   institutional, 4–5, 7, 11, 14–16, 52, 56, 59, 62, 72–77
   judicial, 7–8, 55, 57, 61, 117, 119, 125–26, 136–37, 139–42, 202–7
   and judicial difference, 233–56
   opposing, 241, 256
   prioritisation of, 74, 242, 254
   social, 41–42, 45, 235
   value expression in *Rowe v Electoral Commissioner*, 252–55
victims, 144, 149–51, 155–59, 269
Victoria, 5, 59, 61, 68, 127–28, 164, 166, 171, 177, 179
   Supreme Court, 13, 16, 58, 184
video-links, 120–22, 138, 140
violence, 37, 124, 301
   domestic, 269–70
vitality, 17, 39, 41, 45, 193
vulnerable witnesses, 120, 138

Warren, Chief Justice, 13, 58–59, 61, 67, 75, 128
wellbeing, 10, 137
   judicial, 7, 56, 61, 70, 205
Williams, Daryl, 255, 262
witness box, 149, 151, 158
witnesses, 138, 149, 151, 155, 158, 161, 243, 296–97
   vulnerable, 120, 138
women, 75, 87–91, 109, 111, 113, 115, 148, 266, 294–95, 300
   judges, 5, 75–76, 113, 148
workloads, 66, 71, 112, 213–14, 238, 275, 296
workplaces, 70, 111–12, 148, 196, 205